$6.50

This text is based upon the lecture notes developed by the author while teaching a course at the University of California described as "Neliac, a dialect of Algol." This course was taught twice, in each case to a group which was extremely heterogeneous, including both experienced programmers and others who were completely unfamiliar in computers. Further, the interest of the students varied widely from individual to individual, including business, engineering, mathematics, and real-time control. In an effort to interest and challenge all groups simultaneously, a basic self-compiler (covered in chapters 5 through 10), served as neutral material from which the novices in various fields could develop proficiency in both the language and in the type of thinking required in handling compilers, while at the same time it provided the devotees with the necessary background from which they themselves soon started suggesting efficient routines and improved techniques in the writing of compilers. Consequently, this book is therefore designed to teach the student how to write to computers in the Neliac language and then to teach him how to teach the computer how to read Neliac, if it does not already know.

MACHINE-INDEPENDENT COMPUTER PROGRAMMING

MACHINE-INDEPENDENT COMPUTER PROGRAMMING

Maurice H. Halstead, Ph.D.

SPARTAN BOOKS   WASHINGTON, D. C.

Dedicated to the memory of
Roger Remple
"From zero to infinity"

PREFACE

This text is based upon the lecture notes developed by the author while teaching an evening course, described as "Neliac, a Dialect of Algol," for the University of California Extension. This course was taught twice, in each case to a group which was extremely heterogeneous, including both experienced programmers and others who were completely unfamiliar with computers. Further, the interests of the students varied widely from individual to individual, including business, engineering, mathematics, and real-time control.

In an effort to interest and challenge all groups simultaneously, a basic self-compiler written for the purpose was used as the principal example. This compiler, which is covered in Chapters 5 through 10, served as neutral material from which the novices in various fields could develop proficiency in both the language and in the type of thinking required in handling computers, while at the same time it provided the devotees with the necessary background from which they themselves soon started suggesting more efficient routines and improved techniques in the writing of compilers. The many contributions of these students are gratefully acknowledged.

From the foregoing it may be seen that this book is designed to teach the student how to "write to" computers in the Neliac lan-

viii

guage, and then to teach him how to "teach" a computer to read Neliac if it does not already know.

Returning to the preparation of the text, it would not be proper to confuse the latter with the development of the concepts it describes. These concepts result from the work of many pioneers in the computer field, as well as others such as Charleton Laird, whose penetrating work *The Miracle of Language* is not concerned with computers at all. The basic concepts involved were crystalized primarily at the Navy Electronics Laboratory, where Roger Remple, Lt. Kleber Masterson, Lt. Comdr. Robert McArthur, Dr. Robert Goss, Lt. John White, Ens. Arthur Lemay, Sidney and Catherine Porter, Robert Johnson, Charles Tappella, Herman Englander, Joel Donnelly and James Warrington each have made contributions to one or more of the family of Neliac compilers. The work of automatic-programming experts at other installations, including Prof. Richard Thatcher, Wesley Landon and Dr. W. H. Wattenburg, has also been of great value, while the advice and inspiration of Prof. Harry Huskey has been basic to the entire development.

Special thanks are due to Joel Donnelly, Lt. White, Ens. Lemay, and Sidney and Catherine Porter, and to the Technical Director of the U. S. Navy Electronics Laboratory for permission to cite those works given in the appendices.

Finally, the author wishes to apologize for whatever deficiencies exist in the presentation, asking indulgence on the grounds that the field of automatic machine-independent programming is still quite new.

San Diego, Calif.
February, 1962

Maurice H. Halstead

CONTENTS

FOREWORD

More than a century ago Ada Augusta, Countess of Lovelace and only daughter of Lord Byron, writing about Charles Babbage's "Analytical Engine," said that it might develop three sets of results simultaneously—symbolic results, numerical results, and algebraic results in literal notation. In 1842 Mr. F. L. Menbrea, in an article translated by the Countess of Lovelace, stated that the (punched) cards (which controlled the calculation) were merely a translation of algebraic formulae, or, to express it better, another form of analytic notation.

Menabrea in the same article goes on to say: "When once the engine [calculator] shall have been constructed, the difficulty [of doing calculations] will be reduced to the making out of cards; but as these are merely the translation of algebraic formula, it will, by means of some simple notation, be easy to consign the execution of them to a workman. Thus the whole intellectual labour will be limited to the preparation of formulae, which must be adapted for calculation by the engine."

Babbage failed to complete his Analytical Engine, and it was little over a decade ago that we had our first card-controlled calculators. It has been less than a decade since stored program computers have been available commercially. Furthermore, it is only with the development of stored program computers that the processes described above have come to pass.

This book is the story of such a process. These "simple notations" were "adapted for calculations by the engine" on a computer which was very appropriately called "The Countess."

The aim in developing a language for specifying computational processes or algorithms has been not so much to consign the execution of them to a workman as it has been to make the use of automatic computers more easily accessible to scientists and engineers without an elaborate training program. Thus the use of languages such as that described in this book makes it possible for people to do large-scale problems on such computers after only hours of training instead of months or years.

Neliac (*Navy Electronics Laboratory International Algol Compilers*) was developed concurrently with the development of the algorithmic language Algol 58. As the Neliac language took shape it became necessary to develop its structure in advance of the completion of Algol 58, since a translator must take definitive action for anything that can be said in the algorithmic language. The motivation for these decisions differed from those in the development of Algol. There a general and complete language was required suitable for all scientific and engineering calculation. In the development of Neliac, a specific data-processing problem was of primary importance. Thus arithmetic (in the original Neliac) was fixed-point; only one-dimensional arrays had to be considered; it was of utmost importance to pack information into computer words (part-word operations); and while functions were not critical, closed subroutines were. With Neliac, experience has shown that what has been lost in generality has been more than regained in terms of compiling speed and controlled efficiency of object programs (for example, in the control of indexing operations).

Without doubt the most significant feature of Neliac is that the translator is written in its own language. This means that the card listing of the system is its own description and, consequently can never be out of date. This also means that it is possible to modify the compiler for some particular purpose; there have been more than a dozen operational versions of Neliac in use at the University of California.

Thus, Neliac is a dialect of the Algol family and represents the result of a set of decisions motivated by the desire for a system most efficient in a data-processing application.

University of California   HARRY D. HUSKEY
Berkeley, Calif.
August, 1961

MACHINE-INDEPENDENT COMPUTER PROGRAMMING

CHAPTER 1

INTRODUCTION TO MACHINE-INDEPENDENT PROGRAMMING

Algol, or more specifically Neliac, can be considered as a language by means of which a person can write instructions to a high-speed electronic digital computer. These instructions can tell the computer how to solve a problem in mathematics or engineering, how to prepare payroll checks, or how to control the equipment attached to the computer in cases of real-time automation.

Although the language does not provide any of the thinking which a person must do in deciding how to handle the mathematical or engineering problem, the payroll, or the automation, it does provide a direct and comparatively easy means for instructing the computer once that thinking has been done.

A complete set of instructions for the solution of a specific problem is known as a *program*. When a program is typed on the proper equipment,[1] a typewritten copy (or *hard copy*) as well as a punched paper tape, punched cards, or magnetic tape are produced. The tape or card copy is fed to the computer, and the hard copy retained for reference.

[1] Friden Corporation Flexowriter with Neliac keyboard, or Remington Rand Corporation Synchro-Tape typewriter with Neliac keyboard.

Programs are written using a basic set of letters, numbers, arithmetic operators and punctuation marks. This set, consisting of 88 symbols, is shown in Table I.1.

TABLE I

THE NELIAC CHARACTER SET

1 2 3 4 5 6 7 8 9 0

a b c d e f g h i j k l m n o p q r s t u v w x y z

A B C D E F G H I J K L M N O P Q R S T U V W X Y Z

, ; : .

( ) [ ] { }

× − + / → ↑ |

= ≠ < > ≤ ≥

∪ ∩ ₈

Although the uses of the characters of Table I are described in detail later in the book, it might be well to note here the names of the last 23 of them:

,	Comma	↑	Exponent sign, or Up arrow
;	Semicolon	|	Absolute sign
:	Colon	=	Equal
.	Period	≠	Not equal
( )	Left and right parenthesis	<	Less than
[]	Left and right brackets	>	Greater than
{}	Left and right braces	≤	Less than or equal to
+	Plus	≥	Greater than or equal to
−	Minus	∩	And
×	Multiply	∪	Or
/	Divide	₈	Octal sign, or sub-eight
→	Arrow, or Right arrow		

---

[2] Univac M-460, Univac M-490, CDC 1604, Burroughs 220, IBM 704, IBM 709, IBM 7090, and indirectly the Philco CXPQ, Packard Bell 250, IBM 1401, and CDC 160A.

When the program has been written, the tape or card copy can then be fed into any computer for which a Neliac compiler has been written.[2]

The compiler is itself a computer program, which gives the computer the instructions it must have in order to convert any program from the Neliac language into the numerical language of the individual computer.

The use of the language can be classified into three distinct phases, each requiring a different level of familiarity on the part of the user. The first, and definitely the easiest, is the use of the language to read computer programs that have been written to accomplish specific tasks. By careful reading it is possible to determine whether or not a completed program is adequate for the problem involved; whether or not it follows some predetermined policy; and the extent to which it can be combined with other programs in the solution of problems in a more comprehensive area. The acquisition of a reading knowledge of the language seldom requires more than an hour or two, and can be obtained entirely from a thorough study of Chapter 2.

The second phase in the use of the language consists of writing computer programs for the solution of specific problems by the computer. For those already accustomed to writing any type of instructions in a terse, complete and unambiguous fashion, the ability to write in the language seldom takes more than a few hours to acquire. The development of fluency and confidence, however, usually requires a few weeks of actual use. Although all of the necessary basic knowledge can be found in Chapters 2 and 3, a greater depth of understanding—with a resultant improvement of expression and increased efficiency in programming—will be gained from even a superficial study of the material following Chapter 3.

The third use of the language is in the preparation of compilers and other automatic programming techniques for computers. Methods and procedures in this area are among the most complex in the field of computer programming, and make up the remainder of this text. However, a compiler is itself nothing more than an explicit set of instructions whereby a computer is taught how to supply the proper machine language coding to implement the source language statements. It follows that the study of the way in which a compiler is written must also produce, as a by-product, at least an introduction to machine coding as well.

Historically, the programming of all stored program electronic digital computers has followed a course which began with what is called *machine-language coding*, whereby each individual instruction was originally written by the programmer in the numerical language of the specific computer for which the program was intended. Since a given computer has scores of different instructions in its repertoire, each of which may be modified in many ways, and since each of these machine-language instructions accomplishes only a minute fraction of the total problem, the task of programming a computer in machine language is not only extremely complex but inordinately tedious as well. From receipt of a fairly large problem to final checkout of the program, a professional programmer can write only four or five machine-language instructions per hour. For extremely large programs, involving the coordinated work of many programmers, this figure may drop as low as 0.25 machine-language instructions per man-hour.[3]

The first important improvement in programming occurred with the advent of *assemblers*, which allowed the programmer to refer to computer functions or to memory storage addresses symbolically, with letters instead of numbers. The assemblers speeded the work considerably but still required that each machine-language instruction in the program be individually written. As a result, a person wishing to solve a problem by means of a computer still had to devote a great deal of time in learning to use the assembly language of the individual computer, then had to prepare his program on an instruction-by-instruction basis.

Many of the limitations of assemblers were overcome by the next development, that of *compilers*. Compilers of various types have been written, all of which are intended to allow the computer user

---

[3] For an itemized accounting, see H.D. Bennington, "Production of Large Computer Programs," in *Proceedings of the Symposium on Advanced Programming Methods for Digital Computers,* Office of Naval Research Report ACR-15, 1956, pages 15-27.

to express his problem in a language more nearly approaching his own. In general, early compilers were restricted to use on a given machine, or series of machines, and to the expression of problems of a given class. These early compilers have led, in natural steps, to the present *self-compilers*. Self-compilers, having languages of sufficient versatility to handle problems in any field, are now reaching the stage in which problems can be stated in a language that is fast and powerful, yet sufficiently easy to acquire—so that the accountant, scientist, or engineer can, if necessary, write his own computer programs.

Of even greater potential significance than the development of self-compilers is the fact that computer users in Europe and the United States have realized the need for the adoption of a single language for the publication of computer procedures in the field of mathematics. This language, first known as the *International Algebraic Language* or IAL is now called *Algol,* or the Algorithmic Language. Algol, which may be thought of as a "pure" language, has been implemented for actual computer use in a number of "dialects,"[4] all of which are nearly but not precisely, identical in the source language which they accept. Neliac (from *Navy Electronics Laboratory International Algol Compilers*) is one of the early implementations, its compiling history dating back to February, 1959.

---

[4] In addition to Neliac, these include the following translators or compilers: DASK ALGOL, the Danish Algol compiler in use at Regnecentralen, Copenhagen; MAD, the University of Michigan Algorithm Decoder; ALGO, the Bendix Corporation Algol compiler; BALGOL, the Burroughs Corporation 220 Algol compiler; JOVIAL, the Systems Development Corporation self-compiler (for Jules [Schwartz] Own Version of IAL); and ВХОДНОЙ ЯЗЫК (Hardware Language) of the Academy of Science of the U.S.S.R., described by Ershov *et al.* of Novosibirsk.

CHAPTER 2

HOW TO READ NELIAC OR ALGOL

The words FOR, IF, IF NOT, GO TO, DO, and COMMENTS have precise and specific meanings in Neliac, and can be used only in their restricted sense. All other words or phrases are used at the discretion of the programmer, to mean whatever he defines them to mean. In pure Algol the list of precise or restricted words is considerably longer. In both dialect and pure language, however, all unrestricted words must be treated either as nouns or as verbs. The nouns may be thought of as variables, while the verbs are procedures, or the names of procedures.

The program itself is always divided into two parts. The first part is the *dimensioning statement*, often called the *noun list*, which enumerates the words or phrases to be used as nouns, tells whether or not they initially have known numerical values, and gives information about the lengths and forms of any arrays or lists. The dimensioning statement or noun list ends with the first semicolon. The noun list is followed by the *body* of the program, the basic directives to the computer. These directives are given in the form of specific logical procedures to be followed, known as *algorithms*. Since the body of the program is nothing more than a statement of the logic to be followed, it is often referred to as the *program logic.* By means of the program logic the programmer sets forth the individual steps that he wants the computer to follow in solving his problem. He directs it to perform arithmetic operations with the numerical values of the nouns he has listed, or with numerical constants he inserts. Often he requires the computer to repeat a given set of operations many times, making specified changes each time. He may also direct the computer to follow different branches of his program at different times, selecting its *decision* or course of computation on the basis of a comparison of the numerical values of two or more of the nouns.

Let us examine the simple example below, whereby the computer is instructed to compute the average cost of a number of separate items. The problem will be treated first in its most simple and straightforward form, then examples will be given to show the use of more powerful techniques applied to the same problem.

EXAMPLE 1.
NR OF APPLES = 50,
NR OF ORANGES = 100,
NR OF LEMONS = 75,
NR OF FRUIT,
COST PER APPLE = 10,
COST PER ORANGE = 15,
COST PER LEMON = 8,
COST OF APPLES,
COST OF ORANGES,
COST OF LEMONS,
COST OF ALL FRUIT,
AVERAGE FRUIT COST;

FIND AVERAGE FRUIT COST:
  FIND COST OF EACH:
    NR OF APPLES × COST PER APPLE → COST OF APPLES,
    NR OF ORANGES × COST PER ORANGE → COST OF
      ORANGES,
    NR OF LEMONS × COST PER LEMON → COST OF
      LEMONS,

```
        GO TO FIND TOTAL COST.
     FIND TOTAL COST:
        COST OF APPLES + COST OF ORANGES + COST OF
            LEMONS → COST OF ALL FRUIT,
        GO TO SUM NR OF FRUIT.
     SUM NR OF FRUIT:
        NR OF APPLES + NR OF ORANGES + NR OF
            LEMONS → NR OF FRUIT,
        GO TO FIND AVERAGE COST.
     FIND AVERAGE COST:
        COST OF ALL FRUIT / NR OF FRUIT → AVERAGE
            FRUIT COST,
        GO TO EXIT.
     EXIT: . .
```

This example shows several features of the language. First, the writer has used twelve nouns or noun phrases in his program, to the first three of which he has assigned initial numerical values. The fourth noun phrase, NR OF FRUIT, has no assigned value. Therefore it must be such that the program is expected to compute one. It should be noted in this connection that even the specified initial values may be changed by the program itself, whenever the program is written to accomplish this purpose.

After finishing the noun list as signified by the first (and in this example the only) semicolon, the writer has used six verbs or verb phrases which he has defined. These are:

1. FIND AVERAGE FRUIT COST:
2. FIND COST OF EACH:
3. FIND TOTAL COST:
4. SUM NR OF FRUIT:
5. FIND AVERAGE COST:
6. EXIT:

The definition of each verb or verb phrase is given immediately following the colon. For the first verb, which serves as the title or name of the entire program, the definition consists merely of the name of the next verb. Each of the following verb definitions spells out the precise procedure which the writer wanted the computer to follow, ending with an instruction showing which part of the program to do next. The definition of the sixth verb is seen to be only a double period (. .), the special notation used to denote the end of a program.

While all of the words and phrases in the preceding example are written out quite fully, larger problems are usually expressed with less verbosity. For instance, in the preceding example, if the phrase GO TO FIND TOTAL COST had been omitted, no operation would have been lost, since the next verb encountered would, in any event, have been FIND TOTAL COST.

Further shortening of the written instructions is often accomplished by the use of lists and subscripts. Looking back at the noun list or dimensioning statement of Example 1, it can be seen that of the twelve nouns used, four refer to the number of items, four to the total cost of classes of fruit, three to the cost of individual items, and one to the final answer desired.

If instead of listing separately each of the nouns that refer to *number* all four of them were combined, then instead of the four noun phrases NR OF APPLES, NR OF ORANGES, NR OF LEMONS and NR OF FRUIT, we could have used only the single noun, NR. Since four separate items must still be referred to by the noun NR, it follows that NR must be a list, with provision for four entries. Individual items within any list may be referred to by subscripting.

The concept of subscripting, as used both in the language and in mathematics and engineering is quite straightforward. Suppose, for example, that there is a list of names of employees, and that this list is called the EMP list. If the eighth name in the list were Jones, C.C., then it could be referred to as the Jones entry, or more generally, as EMP_8. Rather than writing the subscript (in this case the eight) as a small character below the line as in mathematics, however, a special symbology will be used—solely as a concession to the typewriter. This symbology consists merely of putting brackets around the subscript, so that EMP$_8$ becomes EMP[8] instead.

By using subscripting in Example 1, then NR[0] could be used to mean NR OF APPLES, NR[1] could stand for NR OF ORANGES, NR[2] could stand for NR OF LEMONS, and NR[3] could represent NR OF FRUIT. Items referring to COST, and to TOTAL COST, could be grouped similarly. The way in which such listings actually operate is shown diagrammatically in Figure 1.

FIGURE 1. SCHEMATIC DIAGRAM OF MEMORY ALLOCATION FOR SUB-SCRIPTED LISTS.

Noun	Computer Storage	Description
NR[0]	50	NR OF APPLES
NR[1]	100	NR OF ORANGES
NR[2]	75	NR OF LEMONS
NR[3]		NR OF FRUIT
COST[0]	10	COST PER APPLE
COST[1]	15	COST PER ORANGE
COST[2]	8	COST PER LEMON
TOTAL COST[0]		COST OF APPLES
TOTAL COST [1]		COST OF ORANGES
TOTAL COST[2]		COST OF LEMONS
TOTAL COST[3]		COST OF ALL FRUIT
AVERAGE COST		THE ANSWER

Using this subscript notation, Example 1 could readily be written as in Example 2, where the entry inside the parentheses, ( ), in the dimensioning statement or noun list shows the maximum number of entries in the list, and the number inside the brackets, [ ], in the body of the program shows which individual item is being specified.

EXAMPLE 2.
    NR(4) = 50, 100, 75, ,
    COST(3) = 10, 15, 8,
    TOTAL COST(4),
    AVERAGE COST;

FIND AVERAGE FRUIT COST:
FIND COST OF EACH:
    NR[0] × COST[0] → TOTAL COST[0],
    NR[1] × COST[1] → TOTAL COST[1],
    NR[2] × COST[2] → TOTAL COST[2],
    FIND TOTAL COST:
        TOTAL COST[0] + TOTAL COST[1] + TOTAL
            COST[2] → TOTAL COST[3],
    FIND NR OF FRUIT:
        NR[0] + NR[1] +NR[2] → NR[3],
    FIND AVERAGE COST:
        TOTAL COST[3]/ NR[3] → AVERAGE COST,
    EXIT: . .

In Example 2 it should be noted that indexing (or the counting of items in a list) begins not at one but at zero, and that (as in Example 2) initial values of nouns may be entered in the dimensioning statement. Where an initial value is not needed, no numerical entry is made. For example, in the last item in the list, NR, which was reserved for the total count of all items, no entry was made. Actually, the last comma could also have been omitted, since the (4) would have provided for the required number of locations.

The subscripting used in Example 2 is a rather powerful device when more fully exploited. Consider how the process defined as FIND COST OF EACH could have been further simplified by a generalized use of subscripting, by noting Example 3.

EXAMPLE 3.
FIND COST OF EACH:
   $0 \rightarrow$ I,
  COUNT COST:
  NR[I] $\times$ COST[I] $\rightarrow$ TOTAL COST [I],
  IF I $=$ 2: FIND TOTAL COST.
  IF NOT, I $+$ 1 $\rightarrow$ I, GO TO COUNT COST.

While in this particular case the number of words required is approximately the same as in Example 2, the technique of Example 3 would not be any longer, even though there had been hundreds of different kinds of fruit to be handled. The index I would merely have been increased by one at a time until it reached the total number, and the required multiplication would have been performed in each case.

In Example 3 one can see the use of the comparison, or *If Statement*. In the comparison, any equality, or even the inequalities: not equal, $\neq$; less than, $<$; greater than, $>$; less than or equal to, $\leq$; and greater than or equal to $\geq$, can be expressed—provided only that the comparison is followed by a colon. If the expression is true the computer executes the instructions found between the colon and the first semicolon or period. If the expression is not true, the computer executes instead those instructions found between the first and second semicolons or periods. After executing either alternative the program continues.

In Example 3, the initial value of I has been set to zero. After performing the first multiplication and storage operation, the index I will of course still be zero, and not yet 2. Consequently, the process will take the false, or *If Not* alternative. This will increase I by one and return the process to the point defined as COUNT COST. Going through the process with I equal to 1, it repeats, raises I to 2, and repeats again. This time, however, since the comparative is finally satisfied, it must take the first (or true) alternative. It will therefore go on to the part of the program defined as FIND TOTAL COST.

While the comparison statement is used very frequently in writing programs, and can be said to give the computer whatever ability it may have to "make decisions," the particular case shown in Example 3 is more often written as a loop, using the *For Statement*. Such a treatment is shown in the following example.

EXAMPLE 4.
FIND COST OF EACH:
    FOR I $= 0(1)2$ { NR[I] $\times$ COST[I] $\rightarrow$ TOTAL COST[I],},
    GO TO FIND TOTAL COST.

Here the *For Statement* might be read as: For I initially equal to zero, and then increasing by steps of one until it equals 2, repeat the process which is enclosed by the braces.

With this notation, the previous examples might be rewritten as follows:

EXAMPLE 5.
NR(4) $=$ 50, 100, 75,
C(3) $=$ 10, 15, 8,
T(4),
A;
FIND AVERAGE:
    For I $= 0(1)2$ { NR[I] $\times$ C[I] $\rightarrow$ T[I],},
    T[0] $+$ T[1] $+$ T[2] $\rightarrow$ T[3],
    NR[0] $+$ NR[1] $+$ NR[2] $\rightarrow$ NR[3],
    T[3] / NR[3] $\rightarrow$ A..

With only a little more sophistication the same process could be expressed even more tersely if the programmer were so inclined, as demonstrated by the following example:

EXAMPLE 6.
NR(4) $=$ 50, 100, 75,
C(3) $=$ 10, 15, 8,

```
T, A;
FIND AVERAGE:
   0 → NR[3] → T,
   For I = 0(1)2 { T + ( NR[I] × C[I] ) → T,
      NR[3] + NR[I] → NR[3],},
   T / NR[3] → A..
```

The first point to notice is that the last comma in the dimensioning of initial values of the noun list NR has been dropped. It was actually unnecessary, since the figure 4 in the parentheses following NR specifies the length of that list; after the first three constants have been entered the list will in any case be completed with blanks or zeros. This new use of parentheses is merely that of algebraic grouping, and makes certain that the noun T is not added to the noun NR before the latter is multiplied by the noun C.

The process of adding partial sums has been accomplished inside the *For Statement*, or *Loop*. Notice that before starting the loop, the words NR[3] and T were cleared by putting a zero into both of them, thereby erasing any prior computation which they might have contained.

Another concept frequently encountered is the special treatment of a part of a program whereby it can be used more than once by being called upon, or entered from different parts of the main program. Such a special part is called a *subroutine*, and it can be illustrated in the following way. Suppose, for instance, that in the problem of the previous examples it were actually required not only to find the average value but also to adjust that average by changing the mixture. Suppose that a mixture of fruit for which the average price would lie between 10 and 13 cents was required, and that this mixture was to be found by increasing the number of either the most expensive or the least expensive type.

In this case it would be preferable to treat the routine FIND AVERAGE as a subroutine, making use of it in a routine which might be called ADJUST MIXTURE. The computer program required might be written as in the following example.

EXAMPLE 7.

ADJUST MIXTURE:
  FIND AVERAGE,
  If A < 10: INCREASE AVERAGE.
  If not, TEST UPPER LIMIT.
  INCREASE AVERAGE:
    NR[1] + 1 → NR[1], Go to ADJUST MIXTURE.
  TEST UPPER LIMIT:
    If A < 13: EXIT.
    If not, NR[2] + 1 → NR[2], Go to ADJUST MIXTURE.
  EXIT: ..

In Example 7, the subroutine FIND AVERAGE will first determine the average cost, A, on the basis of the initial values of the parameters. Then this average will be tested, and if it is found to be less than the desired 10 cents, the first adjustment will be made. One additional orange, having a value of 15 cents, will be added to the current number of oranges (originally 100) in the mixture, and a new average will be computed. On the other hand, if the average is not less than 10 cents the writer has directed that the process determine whether or not it is less than 13 cents. If it is, the computation terminates by stopping at the double period. If it is not, one more of the least expensive items — the lemons — must be added to the value of NR[2], before a new average is computed.

Example 7 could be simplified by using a more powerful comparison statement, the *Between Limits* comparison. In this case the *Less Than* symbol is used twice, e.g., If 10 < A < 13: . The statement is true only if the value of A is greater than 10 and less than 13. The preceding example can then perform the same function more efficiently if it is rewritten in the following style:

EXAMPLE 8.

ADJUST MIXTURE:
  FIND AVERAGE,
  If 10 < A < 13: Go to EXIT. If not, ;

> If A < 10: NR[1] + 1 → NR[1];
> If not, NR[2] + 1 → NR[2];
> Go to ADJUST MIXTURE.
> EXIT: ..

In order that the routine above can make use of the routine FIND AVERAGE each time that it needs it, and find its way back to the main program after it has used it, FIND AVERAGE must be defined not as a routine entry point as it was in earlier examples, but as a subroutine. This is done by enclosing the entire routine inside a pair of braces immediately following its name, at the time that it is being defined. This is illustrated in the following, in which the entire program is rewritten.

EXAMPLE 9.
NR(4) = 50, 100, 75,
C(3) = 10, 15, 8,
T, A;
ADJUST MIXTURE:
    FIND AVERAGE,
    If 10 < A < 13: EXIT. If not, ;
    If A < 10: NR[1] + 1 → NR[1];
If not, NR[2] + 1 → NR[2];
Go to ADJUST MIXTURE.
FIND AVERAGE:
    { 0 → NR[3] → T,
    For I = 0(1)2 { T + (NR[I] × C[I] → T,
        NR[3] + NR[I] → NR[3],},
    T / NR[3] → A,},
    EXIT: ..

In reading a program such as the example above, it is easier if one remembers that braces are always used in pairs, whether in loop control or in limiting subroutines. Therefore one may examine a program by considering either the *innermost* or the *outermost* sets of braces as units.

In scientific notation, very large or very small numbers are customarily expressed as the significant part of the number multiplied by a positive or negative power of 10. This is done in the *Noun List Statement* as illustrated in the next example.

EXAMPLE 10.

PI = 3.1416 × 0,
Million = 1.0 × 6,
Millionth = 1.0 × − 6;

As can be seen, instead of representing one million as 1.0×10^6 in accordance with scientific notation, or even as 1.0 × 10 ↑ 6 as in the normal exponentiation introduced later, the 10 itself is implied and only its exponent given. The number following the multiplication sign is therefore the power of 10 being specified. This feature will be found only in noun lists, and never in the program logic itself.

Returning to the example of the apples and oranges, if it had been necessary to express the figures as decimal fractions of a dollar and to include greater precision, one might have written the noun list of Example 9 in the following way:

EXAMPLE 11.

NR (4) = 5 × 1, 1 × 2, 7.5 × 2, 0 × 0,
C(3) = 1 × 1, 1.5 × 1, 8 × 0,
T = 0 × 0,
A = 0 × 0;

It should be noted that when the greater accuracy available with the *Floating Point* notation is used, it is necessary to specify it, even when initial values of zero are intended.

Although the preceding examples have been written to illustrate most of the basic techniques which will be encountered, there are still several additional items that should be recognized. These are the notations used to specify mathematical function of exponentiation, partial word operations, the octal number system, and the computer rather than the compiler language. These four topics will be explained in order.

The symbol ↑ is used to denote raising to a power, or exponentiation. With earlier-model keyboards lacking this symbol a crude substitution was required, whereby the division sign / and the underline ___ were combined with a backspace to give the symbol ∠. The preferred and the earlier forms are both shown in the next example.

EXAMPLE 12.

A × 10 ↑ 2, or A × 10 ∠ 2,
B × 2 ↑ 3, or B × 2 ∠ 3.

The first line in the example above might be read "A multiplied by 10 squared," while the second line reads "B times 2 cubed." Multiplying and dividing by powers of 10 in decimal computers, and by powers of 2 in binary computers, is frequently resorted to merely to shift the decimal or binary point; in fact, 2 or 10 is often the only base for which exponentiation has been implemented in a given compiler.

In order to take full advantage of the word size of a given computer, it is often desirable to hold two or more small numbers in a single *Word*, or memory cell. This can be done by keeping track of the binary digits [5] involved, and using the available notation. For instance, since none of the *Cost Per Unit* entries in Examples 1 through 9 were larger than 15, it would have been possible to hold all three of them in a single word or computer memory cell. They could have been shown in the noun list or dimensioning statement as such in the following way:

EXAMPLE 13.

UNIT COST: { COST PER APPLE(0→5),
          COST PER ORANGE (6→11), COST PER LEMON (12→17),},

In some data-handling situations the named partial words in a single whole word may be arranged to overlap if required.

The dimensioning of partial words in the noun list should not

---

[5] For the purposes of this book, it is not at all necessary to use or to understand binary arithmetic except where needed to understand programs written by someone who does. If the need arises, the reader is referred to Chapter 5.

be confused with indirect addressing, which looks very similar but is actually quite different. In indirect addressing, a noun may be used whose address within the machine language program will also be used by that program. Although the case would not come up in this particular way, suppose for example that the address or location of the noun UNIT COST in the example above was needed not only by the machine-language program but within the program logic as well. In that event, the noun list would have contained an entry similar to the following:

EXAMPLE 14.
ADDRESS OF UNIT COST = {UNIT COST},
or
UNIT COST LOCATION = { UNIT COST },

Returning to the use of partial words, it should be noted that even when the programmer has not specified a partial word in his noun list, he may nevertheless refer to a part of any whole named noun in his program logic, in the following way:

EXAMPLE 15.
CODE(0→10) → FORM(15 →25), LIST A[I](3 → 7) → B,
C(15→20) + D(25→30) → C(0 →6),

The first line would indicate that bits 0 through 10 of the word CODE are to be transferred to bit positions 15 through 25 in the noun *Form,* and that the I*th* entry in the array named A will supply the values in bit positions 3 through 7 to the whole word B, where they will be *right-justified* — that is, they will occupy the least significant positions, or bits 0 through 4. While in the case of B, in which the whole word was entered, any previous value in the word would have been destroyed. Such would not be true in the case of FORM, since a particular part of the word was specified. In that case, all bit positions not specified in the transfer remain unaltered.

[6] While it is not essential to the use of the language, a knowledge of the binary and octal number systems is quite helpful in the preparation of compiler systems. An explanation will be found in Chapter 5.

In neither case, of course, is any change made to the contents of the nouns CODE or LIST A.

Line 2 of Example 15 shows a case in which two partial words are added and the sum stored in a third. In this case the programmer has allowed one more bit position to hold his answer than he had in either addend, thus preventing possible overflow.

Another symbol, used occasionally by those familiar with the various number systems, is the octal sign, $_8$, which has one direct and one indirect meaning. The direct meaning, of course, is that which signifies that the integer preceding it is in the octal number system instead of the decimal number system.[6]

Here again, because the octal symbol was not available on earlier keyboards, a combination of the right arrow, a backspace, and a left bracket was used to form a substitute, [→. Unlike the substitutions discussed previously, however, the substitute octal symbol was used in a different position from the preferred symbol. Whereas the true octal symbol is used as a subscript following a number, the earlier substitution preceded the number.

The indirect meaning inherent in the octal symbol indicates a lapse from normal compiler language to the direct machine language of a particular computer. This is called *crutch notation,* a term expressing the fact that the use of any machine language in a program renders it machine-dependent and therefore inoperative on any other computer. There are circumstances under which crutch coding can be desirable, however; those familiar with the machine-language repertoire of a given computer use it occasionally. Originally a perpendicular sign made up from an absolute sign, a backspace, and a underline, | , which preceded the numerical computer instruction, crutch notation was later combined with octal notation so that now it consists merely of the symbol $_8$ separating the functional portion from the address portion of the machine-language command. Crutch coding will be found principally in the input-output area, since many Neliac compilers are deficient in that department.

Two additional symbols, used only in comparative statements, are the Boolean *and* and *or,* shown as ∩ for *and* and ∪ for *or.* The earlier symbols $\otimes$ and $\oplus$ had the same meanings. They can be quite powerful in expressing conditional alternatives, such as those in the next example.

EXAMPLE 16.

If A = B $\cap$ C < D: *or*   If A = B $\otimes$ C < D:
If A $\leq$ B $\cup$ C $\neq$ D: *or*   If A $\leq$ B $\oplus$ C $\neq$ D:

The first line is merely the equivalent of "If A is equal to B and C is less than D," while the second line is the statement "If A is either less than or equal to B, or if C is not equal to D, the true branch of the alternative is to be followed."

Comments that are not to form a part of the program itself, so far as instructions to the computer are concerned, may still be desired to increase clarity or to remind the writer of an important point. Such comments may be inserted at any point whatsoever, provided that they begin with a left parenthesis followed by the word COMMENT and a colon. A comment terminates upon reaching the first right parenthesis.

Publication Algol

Algol is a basic language of which Neliac is a dialect. Originally published in December, 1958,[7] by an international committee of mathematical computation experts as an attempt to specify a common language for scientific computation, it was revised in February, 1960.[8] Algol 60, as it is presently called, has three distinct forms:

Form 1: The reference language.

Form 2: The publication language.

Form 3: The hardware language.

---

[7] See A. J. Perlis and K. Samuelson, "Preliminary Report, International Algebraic Language," in *Communications of the Association for Computing Machinery*, Vol. 1, No. 12, Dec. 1958.

[8] See P. Naur (Ed.), "Report on the Algorithmic Language ALGOL 60," in *Communications of the Association for Computing Machinery*, Vol. 3, No. 5, May, 1960.

Forms 1 and 2 are strictly specified, while Form 3 allows the latitude deemed necessary for the implementation of compilers or translators for actual computers. It is in the sense of Form 3, or the *Hardware Language* that the Neliac family of compilers is considered to be a member of the Algol family of languages.

By virtue of its acceptance as the predominant language for the publication of scientific programs, Algol has become extremely important in this field. Since February, 1960, the *Communications of the Association for Computing Machinery* has devoted a portion of each issue to the publication of frequently needed computational procedures and their subsequent certification in Publication Algol.

In order to publish a Neliac program in this format, certain symbols must be replaced by English-language words in boldface type, and the Neliac right arrow → must be replaced by the Publication Algol 60 equivalent of a left arrow, the colon-equal symbol, :=. Further, names used in the noun list must be specified as **integer, real,** or **array** in boldface type. The following example will illustrate what is meant.

EXAMPLE 17. The program of Richard Kenyon for the calculation of binomial coefficients.[9]

Comments

> This procedure computes binomial coefficients $C_m^n = n!/m! (n - m)!$ by the recursion formula $C_{i+1}^n = (n - 1)C_i^n/(i + 1)$ starting from $C_0^n = 1$:

integer procedure	C(m,n) ;
integer	m, n ;
begin	**integer** i, a, b ;
	a := 1 ;
	if 2 × m > n **then** b := n − n **else**
	b := m ;
	for i := 0 **step** 1 **until** b **do**

---

[9] Reproduced directly from *Communications of the Association for Computing Machinery*, Vol. 3, No. 10, October, 1960.

$$\textbf{begin } a := (n - i) \times a \div (i + 1) \textbf{ end}$$
$$C := a$$

end   binomial coefficients

EXAMPLE 18. Neliac version of the Algol Publication Language program of the preceding example.

(Comments: This procedure computes binomial coefficients $C[m] \uparrow n$ = n factorial/m factorial $\{n - m\}$ factorial by the recursion formula: $C[i + 1] \uparrow n = \{n - 1\}C[i] \uparrow n /\{i + 1\}$, starting from $C[0] \uparrow n = 1$. Note that $\uparrow$ means superscript, not exponent.)

a, b, C;

FIND BINOMIAL COEFFICIENT C:
{ 1 → a,
    If 2 × m > n: n − m → b; if not, m → b;
    For i = 0(1)b Do {(n − i) × a/(i+1) → a},
    a → C }..

It can be seen from the two examples above that the grouping symbols of Neliac were replaced by the words **begin** and **end,** that the colon used in the comparison became the boldfaced word **then,** that the words *if not* were replaced by the word **else,** that in the loop the left parenthesis was replaced by the word **step,** and that the right parenthesis became the boldfaced word **until.**

While the differences are minor and almost obvious, perhaps it would be well to illustrate more specifically by examining Example 9 as recast into Publication Algol 60 in the following example.

EXAMPLE 19.
INTEGER ARRAY NR[0:3], C[0:3]
INTEGER I, T, A
BEGIN
Adjust mixture: NR[0] := 50
                  NR[1] := 100
                  NR[2] := 75
                  C[0]   := 10
                  C[1]   := 15

```
                        C[2]   := 8
Find average:    NR[3] := T := 0
                 FOR I := 0 STEP 1 UNTIL 2 DO
                 BEGIN T := T + ( NR[I] × C[I] )
                       NR[3] := NR[3] + NR[I]   END
                 IF 10 < A AND IF A < 13 THEN GO TO Exit
                 IF A < 10 THEN NR[1] := NR[1] + 1 ELSE
                       NR[2] := NR[2] + 1
                 GO TO Find Average
        Exit: END Adjust mixture
```

CHAPTER 3

HOW TO WRITE IN THE LANGUAGE

The ability to read the language with understanding, as acquired in Chapter 2, implies the corresponding ability to write it intelligently. However, a number of rules were observed in the writing of the examples which may not have been apparent to the reader. These were rules of grammer and syntax, which tend to be both trivial and important—trivial because they are concerned solely with detail, important because unless they are followed a program cannot be translated into computer language by a compiler.

Let us first examine those rules which apply specifically to the noun list or dimensioning statement. All nouns that are to be used in a program must begin with a letter of the alphabet, must contain only letters, spaces, and numbers, and must be uniquely determined within the first 15 characters. Capital and lower-case letters are interchangeable and may therefore be used at the discretion of the writer.

The six single letters I, J, K, L, M, and N, when standing alone, are always used as indices, tallies or counters, and are not included in the noun list. They may, however, be used in arithmetic provided they are treated as integers.

When combining a number of smaller programs to operate as one larger program, it might sometimes happen that the same noun or verb had been used to mean different things in different programs. If so the last definition written will be the only one used by any of the programs unless remedial action is taken. The action required is to place an absolute sign | after the first letter of all of the nouns and verbs which the writer wishes to restrict to *local* significance. This device is used to reduce compilation time (especially in large programs where the number of names is great) even when ambiguity is not expected. On earlier keyboards, this localization was produced by underlining the first letter of a local name. For nouns, the absolute sign should be used only in the noun list or dimensioning statement. For verbs or verb phrases— the entry points—it should be used only at the point at which the verb is being defined. Inserting the absolute sign after the first letter of a word elsewhere will do no harm but requires unnecessary typing and additional time for compilation.

The use of punctuation in transferring the flow of computation from one point in a program to another follows simple rules of syntax, but these must be observed rigorously. Whenever a name is preceded by any nonarithmetic operator and followed by a period, the program flow will jump to the point where the routine bearing that name has been defined, and it will not return. If the name involved has been defined as a subroutine, an error will result. On the other hand, if instead of a period the name had been followed by a comma, the flow would have made only a temporary jump to a subroutine. It would return to the next statement following the comma after executing the instructions in the subroutine. Here again, if the name involved had been defined as a straight routine entry point instead of as a subroutine, an error would have resulted.

The relationship is shown diagrammatically in Figure 2, where the letter X is used to represent a straight entry point, and Y to represent a subroutine.

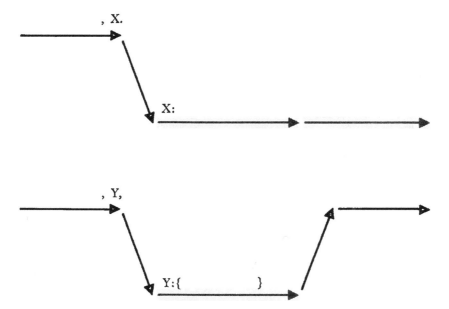

FIGURE 2. USE OF PUNCTUATION IN TRANSFERRING FLOW OF COMPU-
TATION FROM ONE POINT TO ANOTHER IN A PROGRAM.

Considerably more variability is allowable in the body of the
basic program than has been illustrated by the examples in Chapter 2. This occurs primarily in the loop control or *For Statement*;
in the subscripting of nouns, or even of verbs; and in comparative or
If Statements.

In the *For Statements*, the following forms are all useful.

EXAMPLE 20.
```
FOR I  = 0(1)17 {        },
FOR J  = 16(−1)0 {       },
FOR K = 0(3)15 {         },
FOR L = START(1)END{ },
FOR M= 0(1)END + 1{  },
FOR N = N(1)100 {        },
FOR NOUN = 0(1)3{        },
```

Care must be taken to assure that the end point of the loop will be reached precisely by a given number of increments added to the starting value. This is a restriction that has been removed from most but not all Neliac compilers. It should also be kept in mind that upon completion of the last iteration of a loop, the index may have been reset to zero. However, whenever the process jumps out of the loop before completion, the index value existing at that time is preserved and is therefore available for use. This can be illustrated as follows:

EXAMPLE 21.

For i = 1(1)10 { A[i] → B[i],
    If i = 7: Go to EXIT. If not, ;},
EXIT: ..

While no problem would ever be written as in Example 21, it illustrates the case in which the program would inevitably go to the routine entry EXIT with the value of *i* still set at 7, never finishing the eighth, ninth, or tenth iterations. The use of negative increments, with the larger limit leading and the lower limit following, often results in more efficient computer programs.

The subscripting of nouns is normally done by any one of the six index letters I, J, K, L, M or N; or by an actual decimal integer. These can be combined if care is taken to place the index first and the decimal number second, as shown. It is also permissible to use another noun as an index, although this capability is not always implemented in a given compiler.

EXAMPLE 22.

LIST[I] → LIST [I + 3],
WORD [j − 2] → WORD[0],

While the use of a negative increment which is larger than the value of the index used in subscripting is not obviously illogical, it should be avoided, since its functions can be found only by examining an individual compiler.

The concept of a switch can be realized merely by applying subscripting to verbs, provided that they have been written with that objective in mind. The following example demonstrates the principle involved.

EXAMPLE 23.

If A = B: go to ENTRY[I].
If not, go to ENTRY[J].
ENTRY:
    go to ENTRY 0.
    go to ENTRY 1.
    go to ENTRY 2.

In the example above, it is assumed that ENTRY 0, ENTRY 1, and ENTRY 2 are each defined somewhere else in the program.

It is of considerable value to note that if a subscript is used alone, and is not associated with a name at all, it will refer directly to the corresponding absolute address in the memory of the computer itself. This feature proves quite valuable in the writing of compilers themselves, although it is seldom used otherwise. It is shown in the next example.

EXAMPLE 24.

[10] → CLOCK,

or,

    10 → J, [J] → CLOCK,

In both these cases the contents of memory cell 10 of the computer would be entered into the noun CLOCK.

Comparatives or *If Statements,* which form the basis for branching or decision selection, may be extended indefinitely on the left side of the conditional symbol but must consist of only a single term, unqualified by any binary digit references, on the right of that symbol. The following examples will serve to illustrate some of the legal forms:

EXAMPLE 25.

If A = B:
If A + 10 < B:
If A / 3 + 7 $\neq$ B:

If A[I + 3] + C' ≤ B[J]:
If A(0→7) + B(9→16) ≤ B:
If A < B < C:
If A < B ∩ C = D ∩ E > F:
If A > B ∪ C = D ∪ A = D:

With most compilers it is not legal to mix Boolean *Ands* with *Ors,* although this restriction should eventually be overcome.

It is possible, and often quite convenient, to combine the results of a calculation with a comparison, as in the next example.

EXAMPLE 26.

If A + B + C → D < E:

or

If X × (Y + Z) → U = V:

The use of punctuation in comparison statements is extremely important. The entire process is perhaps best visualized diagrammatically, as in Figure 3, where the four possible cases of an unnested comparison are shown. The usual case is given first, showing that if the group of instructions to be followed when the comparative is true, as well as the group to be executed if it is false, ends with semicolons, the process continues with the next statement no matter which alternative was followed. This includes the case in which either alternative included a call upon a subroutine. If the last instruction in either alternative had itself been a subroutine call, such as ,Y, in Figure 2, the semicolon would have replaced the comma in addition to signaling the end of the alternative, giving ,Y; as the form.

On the other hand, whenever an alternative contains a straight transfer to another routine, such as ,X. in Figure 2, it will terminate that alternative, and the flow will not return to the continuation point.

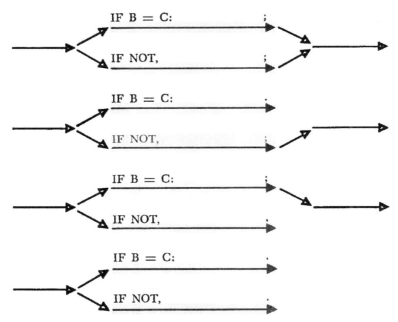

FIGURE 3. USE OF PUNCTUATION IN COMPARISON STATEMENTS.

At this point it should be noted that the punctuation used in the comparison statement is unique. As a result, the words IF and IF NOT are redundant, and they may be omitted at the discretion of the writer. The same rule applies to the other restricted words, DO, GO TO, and FOR, provided that they are being used in the Neliac dialect and not in Publication Algol. Their use should be encouraged, however, since they add a great deal to the clarity of a program.

Another item left to the discretion of the user is spacing. Spaces outside of noun or verb phrases are ignored by the compiler, and may be used by the writer or the typist in such a way as to show more clearly the organization of the program logic. The only exception occurs with respect to the restricted, redundant words discussed in the previous paragraph. These must be preceded and followed by at least one space. This results from the fact that they are unneeded by the compiler, and filtered out during loading. In order to prevent filtering of the letter combinations when they occur within another word, as the *for* in the word *form*, the convention has been established that they must stand alone.

Conditional statements may be nested inside other conditional statements, provided that the user is quite meticulous in following the rule that *an inner conditional statement must be complete within a single alternative of an outer conditional statement.* A study of the following example should be sufficient on this point.

EXAMPLE 27.

```
IF A = B:   IF B = C: C → D;
            IF NOT, E → D;    ;
IF NOT,     IF G = H: 3 → D, 7 → E;
            IF NOT, go to EXIT.    ;
9 → F,
```

In this example, a 9 will be inserted into F regardless of whether or not A = B, unless the program finds that both of the comparisons, A = B and G = H are false, and therefore jumps to EXIT. It is worth noting that the second semicolon in Example 27 terminates the nested comparison B = C, while the third semicolon terminates the true alternative of the outer comparison, A = B. Both are needed. In the last line, the period after Exit terminates the false alternative of the nested comparison G = H, and the semicolon terminates the false phase of the outer comparison, A = B.

Functional notation is of value not only for the simple functions such as sines and cosines, but also for more complex items in which a considerable number of parameters serve as inputs or outputs. The notation employed is the form F(a, b, c; x, y, z,) where any name not otherwise used can be substituted for F. The letters preceding the semicolon represent nouns in the program whose current values must be used in computing the function, while those following the semicolon represent nouns whose values are to be computed by the evaluation of the function.

The definition or writing of a function, on the other hand, is quite similar to the writing of a subroutine. The form for definition of a function is:

$$F(u, v; w) :\{ \qquad \},$$

where the input and output parameters, u, v, and w are local names used only within the function itself. Correspondence between the nouns in the program which serve as input parameters when the function is specified and the local names used within the function itself is obtained purely on the basis of the order in which they appear. Output parameters behave in the same way. While there is no maximum, a function must have at least one input parameter. Since output parameters may not be required, the semicolon is only used in case they are.

Input-Output

The pure Algol language does not contain any specifications regarding methods to be used in transmitting information into a computer via tape or cards, or from a computer to printers, tapes or cards. Consequently the methods originally used with the Neliac system depended upon the use of subroutines, such as the one in Example 39, or the actual borrowing of the input-output packages of other systems. While it is probable that this solution will continue to be the most satisfactory, a machine-independent technique has been devised and implemented on a few of the Neliac compilers.

This technique makes use of the *Less Than* and *Greater Than* symbols to serve an additional duty as quotation marks. The following three basic forms of symbology then result:

$$
\begin{array}{llll}
\text{Form 1.} & , A \{ B & << C >> & \} \\
\text{Form 2.} & , A \{ B & < C > & \} \\
\text{Form 3.} & , A \{ B & > C < & \} \\
\end{array}
$$

Form 1 is used to specify the output of headings, Form 2 to specify the output of numerical data, and Form 3 to call for the reading of data into the computer. In each case the letter A may be replaced by any appropriate comment, such as *Print Heading,*

Print Data, or *Read Data.* It may also be omitted entirely. In all three cases the letter B refers to the name of any particular peripheral equipment. Machine independence is achieved by virtue of the fact that if the entry at B is either omitted or calls for equipment not available at a given installation, the equipment of choice of that installation will be automatically selected. For instance, if a program called for output on an *On-Line* Flexowriter by specifying Form 1 as:

, Print Headings { Flex << LIST >> },

but if no Flexowriter was available, the compiler would generate the machine-language instructions needed to write on, say, a high-speed printer, whenever that program was compiled.

In Form 1, the material between the double quotes will be printed by the program. Any symbols may be included, with the exception of the absolute sign, the exponent sign, and, of course, the greater-than sign.

Absolute signs are used to denote relative spacing, while the exponent sign merely counts as 10 absolute signs. The method followed by the compiler in interpreting spacing orders is as follows: All nonspacing symbols between the quotes are counted and subtracted from the available line length. The remainder is then divided by the number of absolute signs to give the number of spaces corresponding to one sign. In the event that this quotient is less than one, signs are discarded one at a time, starting from the right. This latter feature makes it possible for the user to force an absolute value of one if he so desires.

In Form 2, the letter C represents the name or names of nouns or noun lists whose numerical values are to be printed. Similarly, the letter C in Form 3 represents the noun into which the data being entered is to be stored.

Since it is necessary to print answers in many different ways, usually in tabular form, any compiler should provide some method whereby the user can specify the general features of the output format he desires. In Neliac this is achieved by referring back to the form used in the noun list. For example, if an answer is to be be printed in scientific notation, then when the word Answer was entered in the noun list it would have been so specified, as:

$$\text{Answer} = 0 \times 0;$$

whereupon the statement:

$$, \text{Print Result } \{ \quad < \text{Answer} > \}$$

would produce a number in the form

$$+.1234567890 \times 10 \uparrow +2.$$

Another form often required is that in which an answer is desired in standard decimal notation, even though the problem is to be solved within the computer in the more accurate scientific notation. The method by means of which this objective is indicated is to show the following form in the noun list:

$$\text{Answer} = 00.000 \times 0;$$

whereupon the statement

$$, \text{Print Results } \{ \quad < \text{Answer} > \quad \},$$

would print the number in the form

$$+12.345$$

without rounding.

While there are a total of seven possible forms available, the two illustrated above are sufficient for most work. A discussion of the other alternatives will be found in Chapter 10.

Program Testing or Debugging

Most Neliac compilers include sufficient program testing features to provide that errors in syntax or the violation of grammatical rules will be detected upon compilation. Error print-outs include the noting of attempts to use either nouns or verbs without defining them, or to define them more than once; attempts to use subroutines as direct entry points and vice versa; and typing errors that resulted in variant spellings for the same word. In addition, the use of operators in illegal combinations is noted, as well as the use of any unmatched parentheses or other grouping symbol.

While a study of the material covered in this and the earlier chapters should suffice to avoid most mistakes, anyone who wishes to obtain a thorough mastery would do well to continue with the following chapters, thus acquiring an insight into the *why* as well as the *how* of the Neliac language. With the advent of self-compilers it is indeed true that no manual can answer all possible questions. A compiler itself, however, is at once a complete and unambiguous description of the process of compilation, and perhaps would make the best manual.

Errors in semantics, or the meaning of the words, cannot be discovered by the compiler. All that has been achieved at present is the ability to print lists of names encountered, specifying whether they were used as nouns or verbs, and giving their locations after compilation. The most important element in expediting the discovery of logical errors in programs appears to involve the writing style used in the program itself. The greater the attention given to selection of meaningful names for nouns and verbs, and the fewer the obscure abbreviations used, the faster are logical errors detected and corrected.

CHAPTER 4

BASIC CONCEPTS
OF SELF-COMPILERS

Having seen in earlier chapters that all of the various types of statements in the Neliac language must be converted from that language into the machine language of an individual computer by a specific Neliac compiler, it is now time to examine the methods of accomplishing this conversion. Perhaps the most significant feature of all Neliac compilers—apart from the fact that they accept the same input language—is that they themselves were originally written in the Neliac language, and subsequently compiled. We must exclude from this statement 20 per cent of the first compiler, which was written in computer language, then rewritten in Neliac, and compiled by the basic handwritten version.

Once the basic portion had been compiled, all subsequent portions were written in Neliac, compiled, and added to the original. At this point the entire compiler was recompiled, so that it always appears in its own language. Neliac-C, the first of the series, is a compiler of Computer C, the Remington Rand Univac M-460, or Countess.

Using Neliac-C both as a model and also to perform the compilation in the Countess, a second compiler, called Neliac-C→1604, was written and compiled. Neliac-C→1604 was written in such a way that it would operate in the Countess and accept programs in the Neliac language, but translate them into the machine language of the Control Data Corporation 1604 computer. Then another compiler, still patterned after Neliac-C was written in the Neliac language. It was compiled by Neliac-C→1604, and became Neliac-1604, a compiler which was completely independent of the original Neliac-C. Neliac-1604 operates in the CDC 1604 to produce programs in 1604 machine language from programs written in the Neliac language.[10]

The process was then repeated for the Burroughs 220, the IBM 704, and the IBM 709. Since the 704 and 709 are so nearly alike, only one intermediate compiler was required for both. The result of these operations was the production of the compilers Neliac-C→B and Neliac-C→704/709 to produce Burroughs and IBM machine language with the Countess. These compilers were then used to produce Neliac-B, Neliac-704 and Neliac-709 for the computers in which they operate.

At this point the process branched, and Neliac-709 was used to prepare compilers for Sylvania and IBM computers not in the original list.

With this brief introduction, and remembering that the specific words of Algol, such as DO, GO TO, and IF are actually redundant in Neliac, we may proceed to a discussion of the two distinct levels of multilinguality achieved in the language. The first level is that of human languages. Any language that can be expressed with the Latin alphabet may be used, since the symbols for punctuation, grouping, and mathematics are themselves already universal.

The next four examples will demonstrate this property of multilinguality by showing a crude program for the calculation of the speed of sound in sea water as it might be written in each of four languages. Although greatly simplified for purpose of demonstration purposes, the program is nevertheless completely operable. The objective of the program is to calculate sound speed at as

---

[10] For a technical account of this operation, see Kleber S. Masterson, Jr., "Compilation for Two Computers with Neliac," *Communications of the Association for Computing Machinery*, Vol. 3, No. 11, Nov., 1960.

many as one hundred points from data on temperature, depth, and salinity. It involves a table of 300 values used for determining the sound-speed correction due to temperatures, and a table of 20 values for salinity correction, neither of which table is given. This same program is presented first in English, then in German and Danish, and finally in the more verbose Hawaiian language. All of these programs, while yielding different input tapes or cards, produce the same identical machine language program when compiled for the same computer.

EXAMPLE 28.

Nr of points,
Sound Speed (100),
Temperature (100),
Salinity (100),
Depth (100),
Temp corr,
Sal corr,
Depth corr,
Temp corr table (300),
Sal corr table (20),
Sal table base = 20,
Standard speed = 1446,
Depth corr const = 210;
Compute speed at all points:
   I = 1(1)Nr of points
     { Temperature[i] → j,
      Temp corr table[j] → Temp corr,
      Salinity[i] − Sal table base → k,
      Sal corr table [k] → Sal corr,
      Depth[i]/Depth corr constant → Depth corr,
      Standard speed + Temp corr + Sal Corr +
      Depth corr → Sound speed[i]}..

The same program, as it might have been written in German, would appear as follows:

EXAMPLE 29.

Nr Punkten,
Schallgeschwindigkeit (100),
Temperatur (100),
Salzigkeit (100),
Tiefe (100),
T Berichtigung,
S Berichtigung,
Tiefe Bericht,
T Bericht Tafel (300),
S Bericht ·Tafel (20),
S B Tafel Einheit = 20,
Normalgeschwindigkeit = 1446,
Tiefe B Konst = 210;
Rechnen Geschwindigkeit allen Punkten:
   i = 1(1)Nr Punkten
     { Temperatur[i] → j,
       T Bericht Tafel[j] → T Berichtigung,
       Salzigkeit[i] − S B Tafel Einheit → k,
       S Bericht Tafel[k] → S Berichtigung,
       Tiefe[i]/Tiefe B Konst → Tiefe Bericht,
       Normalgeschwindigkeit + T berichtigung +
       S Berichtigung + Tiefe Bericht →
       Schallgeschwindigkeit[i]}..

The same program, as it might be written in Danish, would appear in the following example.

EXAMPLE 30.·

Nr af punkter,
Lydhurtighed (100),
Temperatur (100),
Salt (100),
Dyb (100),
T Tillag,
S Tillag,

D Tillag,
T Tillagstavle (300),
S Tillagstavle (20),
S Tavle begyndese = 20,
Normalhurtighed = 1446,
Dybde tillags vardi = 210;
Regn hurtighed alle punkter:
   I = 1(1)Nr af punkter
     { Temperatur[i] → j,
       T Tillagstavle[j] → T Tillag,
       Salt[i] — S Tavle begyndese → k,
       S Tillagstavle[k] → S Tillag,
       Dyb[i]/Dybde tillags vardi → D Tillag,
       Normalhurtighed + T Tillag + S Tillag +
       D Tillag → Lydhurtighed[i]}..

Merely as a further illustration that the language chosen need not even be scientific, the same program (with some difficulty in the choice of equivalent terms, and with suitable apologies) has been written in Hawaiian in the next example.

EXAMPLE 31.

Helu a kumumanao,
Kani holomama (100),
Wela ame ke anu (100),
Miko nui (100),
Hohonu (100),
Hoopololei wela ame ke anu,
Hoopololei miko nui,
Hoopololei hohonu,
Hoopololei papa wela ame ke anu (300),
Hoopololei papa miko nui, (20),
Papa miko nui mole = 20,
Hae holomama = 1446,
Kupaa hohonu hoopololei = 210;
Helu holomama apau kumumanao:

I = 1(1)Helu a' kumumanao
{ Wela ame ke anu[i] → j,
  Hoopololei papa wela ame ke anu[j] →
    Hoopololei wela ame ke anu,
  Miko nui[i] — Papa miko nui mole → k,
  Hoopololei papa miko nui[k] →
    Hoopololei miko nui,
  Hohonu[i]/Kupaa hohonu hoopololei →
    Hoopololei hohonu,
  Hae holomama + Hoopololei wela ame ke anu +
    Hoopololei miko nui + Hoopololei hohonu →
  Kani holomama[i]}
Pau: ..

The second level of multilinguality, on the other hand, obviously lies in the area of the numerical languages of the individual types of computers. This can be illustrated by taking any one or all of the four preceding examples and compiling for each of several computers. The next four examples show the results of compiling for the Remington Rand Univac M-460, the Burroughs 220, the CDC 1604, and the IBM 704. For the Burroughs computer the machine-language program will be given in its decimal form (since that computer is a decimal type machine) while the other three will be shown in the octal representation of the internal binary code. In general, storage cells whose initial values are zero are not given.

EXAMPLE 32. Machine-language program resulting from the compilation of any of the four preceding examples for the Univac M-460 Countess.

Address	FF	jkb	yyyyy	Address	FF	jkb	yyyyy
10100	00	000	00000	11440	14	030	10722
11424	00	000	00024	11441	11	031	10555
11425	00	000	02646	11442	03	000	00036
11426	00	000	00322	11443	23	030	11426

11427	12	100	00001	11444	14	030	10723
11430	12	231	10245	11445	10	030	10723
11431	10	032	10724	11446	26	030	10722
11432	14	030	10721	11447	26	030	10721
11433	10	031	10411	11450	26	030	11425
11434	27	030	11424	11451	14	031	10101
11435	07	000	00036	11452	71	130	10100
11436	12	370	00000	11453	61	000	11430
11437	10	033	11400	11454	61	400	10000

The next example was also obtained by compiling any of the multilingual programs for computing sound speed, in this case using Neliac-B, operating in the Burroughs 220 computer. The lack of a sufficiently large number of index registers as part of the equipment of this computer can be seen to require a considerably longer program in this particular case. To a certain extent this disadvantage might have been reduced by writing the original program with this in mind.

EXAMPLE 33. Machine-language program resulting from the compilation of any of the four preceding multilingual programs on the Burroughs 220.

Address	+	cccc	ff	aaaa	Address	+	cccc	ff	aaaa
0001	8	0000	30	0729	0745	8	0000	13	0726
0726	0	0000	00	0020	0746	8	0000	40	0765
0727	0	0000	00	1446	0747	8	0000	42	0765
0728	0	0000	00	0210	0748	9	0000	10	0706
0729	8	0000	10	0772	0749	8	0000	40	0404
0730	8	0000	13	0772	0750	8	0000	42	0763
0731	8	0000	40	0763	0751	9	0000	10	0303
0732	8	0001	10	0772	0752	0	0001	48	0010

0733	8	0000	12	0763		0753	8	0000	15	0728
0734	8	0000	40	0763		0754	8	0000	40	0405
0735	8	0000	18	0002		0755	8	0000	10	0727
0736	8	0000	34	0762		0756	8	0000	12	0403
0737	8	0000	42	0763		0757	8	0000	12	0404
0738	9	0000	10	0103		0758	8	0000	12	0405
0739	8	0000	40	0764		0759	8	0000	42	0763
0740	8	0000	42	0764		0760	9	0000	40	0003
0741	9	0000	10	0406		0761	8	0000	30	0732
0742	8	0000	40	0403		0762	8	0000	30	0000
0743	8	0000	42	0763		0772	0	0000	00	0001
0744	9	0000	10	0203						

The next example shows the machine-language program resulting when one of the preceding Neliac programs was compiled on the Control Data Corporation 1604 computer with Neliac-1604. On this computer, each computer word contains two instructions, or one word of data. It should not be considered to be a "two-address" machine, however, for that terminology has already been pre-empted to describe a computer in which one operation, such as addition, may call upon data at two locations.

EXAMPLE 34. Machine language for the CDC 1604 produced by compiling any of the multilingual examples cited with Neliac-1604.

Address	fff	yyyyy	fff	yyyyy	Address	fff	yyyyy	fff	yyyyy
40000	750	41340	500	00000	41351	532	41333	122	40625
41325	000	00000	000	00024	41352	200	40622	121	40312
41326	000	00000	000	02646	41353	150	41325	200	41334
41327	000	00000	000	00322	41354	533	41334	123	41301
41340	571	41332	572	41333	41355	200	40623	121	40456
41341	573	41334	574	41335	41356	030	00057	270	41327

41342	575 41336	576 41337	41357	200 40624	120 41326

41342	575 41336	576 41337	41357	200 40624	120 41326
41343	120 41364	750 41345	41360	140 40622	140 40623
41344	120 41332	140 41364	41361	140 40624	201 40002
41345	200 41332	531 41332	41362	750 41344	500 00000
41346	150 40001	500 00000	41363	760 40000	500 00000
41347	220 41350	222 41363	41364	000 00000	000 00001
41350	121 40146	200 41333			

The last example in this series shows the machine language which was produced by compiling the same programs, this time with Neliac-C→704. In this case the number of program steps represents a certain amount of inefficiency in the intermediate compiler. While intermediate compilers (which operate in one computer to prepare machine instructions for a different computer) are not inherently less efficient, the fact that most of them are only used during a transition period generally precludes their further development with resulting increases in efficiency. Intermediate compilers which are intended for general use, such as those that compile programs for a small computer on a large computer, generally warrant and receive attention to improvement of efficiency of the output programs.

EXAMPLE 35. Machine-language program for the IBM-704 computer which resulted from the compilation of any of the preceding multilingual examples by Neliac-C→704.

00000	0	20000	0	01340	01355	0	60100	0	00515
00011	0	00000	0	00322	01356	0	50000	1	00662
00012	0	00000	0	02646	01357	0	76500	0	00043
00013	0	00000	0	00024	01360	0	22100	0	00011
01340	0	53400	1	00010	01361	−0	75400	0	00000
01341	1	00001	1	01342	01362	0	76300	0	00043
01342	0	50000	1	01172	01363	0	60100	0	00514

01343	0	76700	0	00022	01364	0	50000	0	00012
01344	−0	73000	2	00022	01365	0	40000	0	00516
01345	0	50000	2	00513	01366	0	40000	0	00515
01346	0	60100	0	00516	01367	0	40000	0	00514
01347	0	50000	1	01026	01370	0	60100	1	01336
01350	0	40200	0	00013	01371	1	00001	1	01372
01351	0	76700	0	00022	01372	−3	00144	1	01342
01352	0	60100	0	00003	01373	1	77777	1	01374
01353	−0	53400	4	00003	01374	0	00000	0	00000
01354	0	50000	4	00037					

Any attempt to compare the relative efficiencies of either the various machines or of the compilers used in the preceding four examples would prove futile. This is primarily due to the fact that the compilers used represented widely varying stages of development, so that another test made even a few months later might yield quite different results. Let us see why this is so.

The total function of any compiler can be stated simply as the translation of a statement of the method whereby a problem is to be solved from the language in which the statement is expressed into the numerical language of the required computer.

This total function can be accomplished in an ever-increasing number of ways. Even so, it is generally true that a distinct number of major steps must be accomplished, and that these major steps can be classified in roughly the same ways no matter how the particular compiler operates. The compiler to be discussed in the next few chapters will be divided into six major components.

First, a *Load Program* is required which will accept the numerical code punched by a card or paper tape punching keyboard and convert this code to another numerical code in which each character is uniquely represented by a single two-digit number. Since upper- and lower-case shifts are punched as separate frames by a typewriter, this decoding process is not a direct transliteration. Chapter 5 will discuss load programs in detail.

Second, the string of symbols decoded by the load program must be separated into two parts—the noun list or dimensioning statement and the body or program logic. The second major function of the compiler therefore consists of the examination of the noun list, the allocation of computer memory or storage cells to the various nouns and noun arrays, the interpretation and storage of numerical constants, and the formation and storage of masks which may be required to deal with any part words that have been dimensioned.

The group of routines required to satisfy these requirements make up the program called *Process the Noun List,* which is treated in detail in Chapter 6.

The third important function required is that of examining and interpreting the body of the program—the statement of the algorithms or procedures by means of which the program is expected to solve the given problem. In Neliac compilers this process is based upon the examination of combinations of two operators, such as punctuation or arithmetic symbols, and the intervening operand as a single unit. By processing in this pattern of Current Operator-Operand-Next Operator units, some amount of dependence upon context is introduced, from which certain advantages in the efficiency of the compiled machine-language program is thought to result. The group of programs that perform this basic processing will be discussed in detail in Chapter 7.

The insertion of actual machine-language instructions into the final program is accomplished by a set of many *generators,* which are called upon by the basic processing routines as their need is determined by the Current Operator-Operand-Next Operator combinations. While the functions of the generators themselves are not machine-dependent, their internal operations are quite dependent upon the computer for which the compiler is being implemented. The most frequently used generators will be studied and their implementation discussed in Chapter 8.

Two additional functions of a compiler, though not required by the definition, are nevertheless of real importance. These are the implementation of those capabilities required if the compiler is to be used as a system, compiling many programs together, and those capabilities needed to assist the programmer in detecting and correcting errors in his programs. These two items will be discussed briefly in Chapter 9, along with the details of the process whereby a compiler is itself compiled.

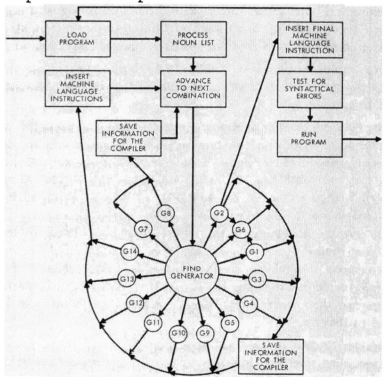

FIGURE 4. GENERALIZED COMPILER FLOW DIAGRAM.

In order to understand the relationship of the material in each of the next five chapters, it is recommended that Figure 4 be studied carefully. It shows a generalized flow diagram of a compiler, from which the major operations and the order in which they occur can be determined. For instance, the fact that some of the generators do not actually generate machine-language instructions, but only find and store information that will be needed at later stages of compilation, should be apparent from an examination of the role of generators 7 and 8, as shown in the smaller circles.

CHAPTER 5

LOAD PROGRAMS

In the initial typing of any Neliac program, the depression of each key results in the punching of a set of holes corresponding to a given number on either a paper tape, a card, or both. On a six-channel paper tape, for example, each line of holes across the tape, called a frame, has space for three different holes on either side of a row of smaller guideline or sprocket holes along the center.

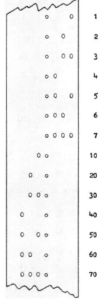

FIGURE 5. METHOD OF ASSIGNING NUMERICAL VALUES TO PUNCHES IN PAPER TAPE.

The method of assigning numerical values to these holes follows the scheme shown in Figure 5, in which the direction of tape movement is assumed to be toward the top.

To be precise, these tape holes, of course, are merely holes, not numbers, and are converted into electrical impulses by electro-mechanical feelers or by photoelectric readers. These pulses — still not numbers — are then fed directly by the reader into the computer, or perhaps stored first as magnetic charges on a magnetic tape. Once inside the computer they are transformed into positive or negative electrical or magnetic charges. Although these charges, like the tape holes, are not actually "numbers," it is much easier for people if they think of them as numbers.

In doing so, it is customary to let a single light represent each possible bit of information in a given computer word or memory cell. If, for instance, a given computer has a *word length* of 30 bits, then it can be represented by 30 lights. The value of the cell then depends upon which lights are lit, just as in Figure 5 the numerical value on the tape depends upon which holes have been punched — or, rather, upon which spaces have been punched and which have not.

The lights themselves have been numbered, and each numbered light has been assigned a numerical value. Beginning with the least significant, or zero*th*, light, to which is ascribed the value 1, each succeeding light is given a value twice as large. Since light No. 0 has a value of 1, light No. 1 has a value of 2, and light No. 2 has a value of 4. By combining these binary digits, called *bits*, any numerical value can be represented. The numerical value represented by a row of lights can be converted to the decimal number system by adding the appropriate power of two for each light which is lit.[11] The conversion can be illustrated with the 30-bit binary number in the next example, in which the least significant bit is on the right.

---

[11] The zero*th* power of any number is 1, while the first power is the number itself. This explains why a numbering system starting at zero instead of at 1 is so widely used throughout the computer field.

EXAMPLE 36.

001   010   011   100   101   110   111   000   001   010

By using Table II, it can be shown that this binary number represents the decimal number 175, 304, 202.

The numbering system used on the punched tape of Figure 5 still is not completely explained, however, until another system has also been examined. This is the system based neither upon 10 nor 2, but upon 8, and called the *octal number system*. In this system each three binary digits are taken as a unit, to become one octal digit. Since with three lights only the numbers from 0 through 7 can be represented, there are no 8's nor 9's, and the number that follows 7 is 10. In the octal number system the binary number of Example 36 can be shown to be 1234567012, or, in Neliac 1 234 567 012$_8$.

The following table, which gives the numerical value assigned to the first 30 binary digits, is of value whenever conversions are required. It can readily be extended if required.

TABLE II

NUMERICAL VALUE OF EACH BINARY IN A 30-BIT COMPUTER WORD

Bit (or N)	Decimal Value (or $2 \uparrow N$)	Octal Value (or $(2 \uparrow N)_8$)
0	1	1
1	2	2
2	4	4
3	8	10
4	16	20
5	32	40
6	64	100
7	128	200
8	256	400
9	512	1 000

10	1 024	2 000
11	2 048	4 000
12	4 096	10 000
13	8 192	20 000
14	16 384	40 000
15	32 768	100 000
16	65 536	200 000
17	131 072	400 000
18	262 144	1 000 000
19	524 288	2 000 000
20	1 048 576	4 000 000
21	2 097 152	10 000 000
22	4 194 304	20 000 000
23	8 388 608	40 000 000
24	16 777 216	100 000 000
25	33 554 432	200 000 000
26	67 108 864	400 000 000
27	134 217 728	1 000 000 000
28	268 435 456	2 000 000 000
29	536 870 912	4 000 000 000

Primarily due to the way the original teletypes were built a generation ago, the actual numerical values of the tape holes punched by a Neliac keyboard are as shown in Table III.

TABLE III

DECIMAL AND OCTAL EQUIVALENTS OF TAPE HOLES PUNCHED BY THE
FOUR ROWS OF KEYS ON THE NELIAC KEYBOARD

Dec	Upper	Lower	Oct
42	+	1	52
60	−	2	74
56	=	3	70
52	[	4	64
50	]	5	62
54	∨	6	66
58	/	7	72
48	×	8	60
27	(	9	33
31	)	0	37
62	←	8	76
61	∩	U	75
37	CR	CR	45
29	Q	q	35
25	W	w	31
16	E	e	20
10	R	r	12
01	T	t	01
21	Y	y	25
28	U	u	34
12	I	i	14
03	O	o	03
45	P	p	55
46	~	~	56
47	LC	LC	57
24	A	a	30
20	S	s	24
18	D	d	22
22	F	f	26
11	G	g	13
05	H	h	05
26	J	j	32
30	K	k	36
09	L	l	11
36	:	;	44
40	≠	−	50
39	UC	UC	47
17	Z	z	21
23	X	x	27
14	C	c	16
15	V	v	17
19	B	b	23
06	N	n	06
07	M	m	07
38	∧	∨	46
34	↑	•	42
49	BS	BS	61

04 SPACE BAR 04

Stop Code = 35 = 43_8; Color shift = 02.

This code, while adequate for entering the computer, must be organized quite differently before it can be operated upon by a compiler. For example, both a left and a right brace are indicated by a 56, the difference being only in whether an upper-case code, a 47, or a lower-case code, a 57, has most recently appeared. A primary function of the load program, therefore, is to convert from the code of Table III to the internal code of Table IV, which is given below. At this point it is interesting to note that despite the fact that the organization of the internal compiler code is of basic importance in determining the number of decisions required (and thereby the efficiency of a large number of routines in the com- ·piler) no systematic study of the proper organization of such a table has yet been undertaken.

TABLE IV

THE INTERNAL COMPILER CODE

Symbol	Octal	Decimal	Symbol	Octal	Decimal
Space	00	00	5	40	32
A *or* a	01	01	6	41	33
B *or* b	02	02	7	42	34
C *or* c	03	03	8	43	35
D *or* d	04	04	9	44	36
E *or* e	05	05	,	45	37
F *or* f	06	06	;	46	38
G *or* g	07	07	.	47	39
H *or* h	10	08	:	50	40
I *or* i	11	09	}	51	41
J *or* j	12	10	{	52	42
K *or* k	13	11	(	53	43
L *or* l	14	12	)	54	44
M *or* m	15	13	[	55	45
N *or* n	16	14	]	56	46

O *or* o	17	15	$=$	57	47
P *or* p	20	16	$\neq$	60	48
Q *or* q	21	17	$>$	61	49
R *or* r	22	18	$\geq$	62	50
S *or* s	23	19	$<$	63	51
T *or* t	24	20	$\leq$	64	52
U *or* u	25	21	$\rightarrow$	65	53
V *or* v	26	22	$+$	66	54
W *or* w	27	23	$-$	67	55
X *or* x	30	24	$\times$	70	56
Y *or* y	31	25	$/$	71	57
Z *or* z	32	26	$\mid$	72	58
0	33	27	$\cup$	73	59
1	34	28	$\cap$	74	60
2	35	29	$_8$	75	61
3	36	30	$\uparrow$	76	62
4	37	31			

The string of resulting compiler code, called the *symbol string*, must be packed several symbols per word into an appropriate area of the computer memory.

In a production type (or reasonably finished) compiler, many additional functions of a supplementary nature are usually performed by the load program. For instance, the load program may be used to delete the comments and the redundant words IF, DO, GO TO, and FOR. It may also delete all but the initial space in any string of spaces, and it can readily convert all carriage returns to spaces, in order that phrases may be broken between words for continuation on the next line. Further, the load program may be written so that the first symbol tells it whether the program being loaded is a new program, or a correction to an old one, and whether or not the version of the compiler being used corresponds to the expectations of the person who wrote or typed the program. In addition, the load program may be used to determine whether the Neliac symbol string is to be stored in a standard location, or in some special area designated by the computer operator or the programmer.

These features of production type compilers may be examined in detail later in the text. In the present chapter, on the other hand, a much less sophisticated load program will be developed. The load program which will be derived in this chapter is not intended to employ any advanced programming techniques, but instead to demonstrate the basic requirements that must be met, and to use only those concepts that should apply to all computers.

In the next three chapters the attempt to derive a compiler sufficiently powerful to compile itself, yet simple enough to demonstrate only the fundamental points, will necessitate several restrictions. Perhaps the most noticeable will be the limitation on the number of Current Operator-Next Operator combinations employed. By keeping this number small, fewer generators will be required later. In achieving this objective, *for statements, bit handling*, and *nested comparisons* will be avoided. In addition, operands will be restricted to five significant characters, but this should scarcely be noticeable, since lower-case letters without significance will be permitted.

Such restrictions serve a dual purpose. First, they allow the basic functions to be followed without confounding them with the valuable but less essential sophistications to be added later. Second, they provide those fundamental portions of a compiler which will prove adequate to compile itself. Such a compiler will therefore frequently be referred to as a *basic*, or even a *Bootstrap* compiler.

The noun list of this basic load program is given in the following example:

EXAMPLE 37.
Upper Case Flag,
Symbol String First Address $= 10_8$,
Load Buffer,
Buffer,
CLEAR $= 0$,
SET $= 1$,
TWO $= 2$,
Upper Case $= 39$,
Lower Case $= 47$,
STOP $= 35$,
End Of Symbol String,
Symbol,
Symbol Size $= 100_8$,
Symbols Per Word $= 5$,
FULL,
Nearly Full,
Lower Case Code(64) $=$

00,	20,	00,	15,	00,	08,	14,	13,	00,	12,
18,	07,	09,	00,	03,	22,	05,	26,	04,	02,
19,	25,	06,	24,	01,	23,	10,	36,	21,	17,
11,	27,	00,	00,	39,	00,	38,	00,	49,	00,
58,	00,	28,	00,	52,	16,	41,	00,	35,	00,
32,	00,	31,	00,	33,	00,	30,	00,	34,	00,
29,	59,	61,	00,						

Upper Case Code(64) $=$

00,	20,	00,	15,	00,	08,	14,	13,	00,	12,
18,	07,	09,	00,	03,	22,	05,	26,	04,	02,
19,	25,	06,	24,	01,	23,	10,	43,	21,	17,
11,	44,	00,	00,	53,	00,	40,	00,	37,	00,
48,	00,	54,	00,	50,	16,	42,	00,	56,	00,
46,	00,	45,	00,	51,	00,	47,	00,	57,	00,
55,	60,	62,	00;						

Many of the nouns used have meanings which are not completely apparent. For example, *Upper-Case Flag* is a noun whose numerical value will be set at zero whenever the most recent case shift has been to lower case, or to one whenever an upper-case shift was most recently encountered.

Symbol String First Address is a noun whose value is set at the discretion of the compiler writer, or in more sophisticated cases is given a standard value which is used only when the computer operator or the programmer does not specify a special value.

Load Buffer is a word used to hold the numerical value representing the incoming paper tape frame. The code, of course, is that of Table III.

Buffer, on the other hand, is a word used to hold decoded symbols until enough of them have been collected to be packed away into a memory cell in the *Symbol String.*

CLEAR, SET, and TWO are defined as zero, one and two respectively in order to simplify the basic or Bootstrap compiler by avoiding Arabic numerals in the body of the compiler program.

Upper-Case, Lower-Case, and STOP give the tape code, or Table III, values which the load program will have to recognize.

End Of Symbol String is the address at which the Neliac Symbol String ends after all tape frames have been loaded and decoded, and the resultant symbols stored in the memory area starting at *Symbol String First Address.*

Symbol is the noun which holds the most recently decoded Neliac symbol. *Symbol Size,* on the other hand, is the numerical value of the space occupied by a single symbol. Its value is 100 in decimal computers, or 100_8 in octal machines.

Symbols Per Word is the second machine-dependent parameter, insofar as its numerical value must be set for the number of symbols, or powers of 100, which will fill a single cell of the computer upon which the compiler will run. For 48-bit machines this value is 8, for 36-bit machines it would be 6, while for 10-decimal digit machines or 30-bit binary machines it is 5.

Full is a noun whose value is to be computed from *Symbol Size* and *Symbols Per Word,* and used to test whether or not a *Buffer* is filled with symbols.

Lower-Case Code and *Upper-Case Code* are the lists which serve as the heart of the load program. They have been formed by combining Table III and Table IV in such a way that when the numerical value of the tape code, Table III, is used as an index, the numerical value of the internal compiler code for that symbol will be obtained directly. The technique employed can be illustrated quite easily. Suppose, for instance, that the *Upper-Case Flag* was set, or in other words that it contained a one. Then suppose that the letter A was being read from punched tape. On the tape, an A is indicated by the code number 24. This 24 is brought into the *Load Buffer*. From the Load Buffer the 24 is transferred to the index J. By examining the list of numbers making up *Upper Case Code*, it can be seen that the internal compiler code for the letter A, which is 01, is entry number 24. In other words, the value of Upper-Case Code[24] is 01, thus giving an A. Again, if the tape character being read in had been a 19, as it would have been if the letter B had been typed, then entry number 19 in both Upper-Case Code and Lower-Case Code would have to be a 02, since the internal compiler code of Table IV for either a B *or* a b is an 02.

Example 38 gives the body of the load program, and has been derived to follow the Noun List of Example 37. While the basic compiler being developed in this and the next few chapters will operate only if the lower-case letter introduced here for clarity are omitted from the punched tape, any production type compiler will accept them and treat them merely as longer words. It will be left as an exercise for the student to show that by changing only the numerical values of the list Lower-Case Code in Example 37, this load program can be made to eliminate all lower-case letters from any input tape, including those punched exactly as in Examples 37 and 38.

Two subroutines, *Start Reading Device* and *Read One Frame*, which are called upon by the algorithm of Example 38, are given separately in Example 39. These subroutines have been written to include machine language, in order that an input-output package could be delayed until the basic compiler had been completed. The combination of Example 37, 38, and 39 constitute the complete basic load program.

EXAMPLE 38.

Load Program:	1
CLEAR → Upper Case Flag, CLEAR → Buffer,	2
Symbol String First Address → I,	3
Symbol Size → FULL, Symbols Per Word → N,	4
Set Full Buffer Size:	5
FULL × Symbol Size → FULL, N − SET → N,	6
if N = TWO: FULL / Symbol Size → Nearly Full;	7
if not, Set Full Buffer Size.	8
Start Reading Device,	9
Read Next Frame:	10
Read One Frame,	11
Decode Character,	12
if Symbol = CLEAR: ;	13
if not, Store Symbol In String.	14
if Load Buffer = Upper Case: SET → Upper Case Flag,	15
Read Next Frame.	16
if not, ;	17
if Load Buffer = Lower Case: CLEAR → Upper Case Flag,	18
Read Next Frame.	19
if not, ;	20
if Load Buffer = STOP: Finish Loading.	21
if not, Read Next Frame.	22
Store Symbol In String:	23
if Buffer < Nearly Full: Buffer × Symbol Size →	24
Buffer, Symbol + Buffer → Buffer;	25
if not, Buffer × Symbol Size → Buffer,	26
Symbol + Buffer → [I], I + SET → I,	27
CLEAR → Buffer;	28
Read Next Frame.	29
Finish Loading:	30
if Buffer = CLEAR: I → End of Symbol String,	31
Process Noun List Program.	32

if not, ;   33
Pack Last Frame: 34
  if Buffer < Nearly Full: Buffer × Symbol Size →   35
    Buffer;   36
  if not, Buffer × Symbol Size → [I],   37
    CLEAR → Buffer, I + SET → I;   38
  Finish Loading.   39
Decode Character: 40
  { Load Buffer → J,   41
    if Upper Case Flag = CLEAR: 42
      Lower Case Code[J] → Symbol; 43
    If not, Upper Case Code[J] → Symbol;}.. 44

In this example, lines 1 through 3 merely initialize the program by clearing or resetting various parameters which might have been left containing undesired values at the completion of some prior operation. Lines 4 through 8 represent a machine-independent method of finding the numerical value of the word *Full.* This word, when compared with the numerical content of the buffer, will be used to determine whether or not there is space left in the Buffer to pack in another symbol. Lines 9 and 11 call upon the two subroutines which will be found in the next example. Line 10 serves as an entry point to which the flow may return.

Line 12 assumes that the subroutine *Read One Frame* has placed a paper tape character punched according to the code of Table III in the Load Buffer, and calls upon the subroutine of lines 40 through 44 to decode it, and to place the result in the noun *Symbol.*

Line 13 checks to see whether the decoding process produced an actual symbol, or instead resulted in a zero. If an actual symbol resulted, the process goes to the verb *Store Symbol In String.* If not, however, it starts checking the Load Buffer itself, to see if it could have held one of the case shifts or a stop, three characters which decode as zero symbols. If such is the case, one of the alternatives on lines 15, 18, or 21 is called upon.

Lines 23 through 28 are written to pack the applicable number of *Symbols Per Word* into the buffer. Whenever the buffer is packed, its contents are transferred into the next available memory cell in the *Symbol String*, and the buffer is cleared. Since the tally I is used to maintain the record on the status of the Symbol String, its value is increased by one by line 27.

Lines 34 thru 39 are written to handle those cases in which the buffer contains less than the allowable number of symbols when the stop code is reached. After packing the symbols in the last word of the Symbol String in the left-most positions, the process exits through line 32 to the *Process Noun List Program*.

The two subroutines called *Start Reading Device* and *Read One Frame* are completely machine-dependent, making use of actual machine-language instructions. On many computers the first is not needed at all, and the second consists of a single machine-language instruction. A few machines, however, require several instructions to accomplish the operation. In all cases, the coding manual of the particular machine would specify them precisely. The next example shows the machine language for one of the computers which requires several instructions, the Univac M-460 Countess.

EXAMPLE 39.

Start Reading Device:

{ 13 100_8 0, 13 000_8 161_8, 13 300_8 0,

70 000_8 1000_8, 13 300_8 10031_8, 13 300_8 0,

70 000_8 1000_8, 13 300_8 10033_8,},

Read One Frame:

{ 17 130_8 Load Buffer,

DELAY: 63 100_8 DELAY,}..

These two machine-language subroutines take the place of the single statement:

, { FLEX > Load Buffer <}

which could not be used at this stage because the Bootstrap compiler does not contain input or output statements.

As noted earlier, many additional features may be added to a load program. In the event that a truly *one-pass* compiler is being written, such that the entire compilation process is to be completed, one step at a time, between the loading of individual characters, then of course the load program would not employ a Symbol String at all.

The advantage to be derived from increasing the amount of processing which is accomplished while the source material is being entered into the computer lies in the fact that it exploits the high internal computing speeds which are often coupled with slow input speeds on present day computers. While many Neliac compilers do not employ the one-pass concept, some of them do. In any event, the Bootstrap or basic compiler is adequate for compiling the changes which are required.

CHAPTER 6

PROCESSING NOUN LISTS

After the Load Program has converted all of the tape or card characters from the code of Table III into the compiler symbols according to the code of Table IV and stored them in the Symbol String, the next operation involves the process which reads the noun list or dimensioning statement and allocates computer storage cells to all nouns and noun lists. This same process must insert any numerical values specified for a given noun into the computer memory cell allocated to that noun.

Current Operator-Operand-Next Operator combinations are used only in processing the body of the program, and not in the processing of a noun list. Accordingly, the basic dimensioning program will serve to demonstrate the techniques used when the operands, or nouns, are the primary objects in compilation.

Since the first semicolon in a program always designates the end of the noun list, that symbol will serve as the signal which will terminate the process.

The next example presents the list of 19 nouns which the *Process Noun List Program* requires. These are in addition to a few of the nouns used by this program and already given in the noun list that formed part of the load program.

EXAMPLE 40.

Object Program First Address $= 2100_8$,

Noun Name Róll(250),
Noun Address Roll(250),
NumbeR,
A NumbeR = 27,
An Operator = 37,
COMMA = 37,
LEFT Paren = 43,
EQUAL = 47,
SEMIColon = 38,
Nr of Nouns Named,
Noun Buffer,
List Length,
Word,
Divisor,
Canceling Term,
Negative Coefficient,
TEN = 10,
Scratch Pad;

The *Object Program First Address* can be set at any location the compiler writer desires, provided only that it is in a part of the computer memory which does not interfere with the compiler itself. In a production type compiler it would be treated as a variable capable of being reset by the computer operator, or even by an auto monitor program.

Noun Name Roll and *Noun Address Roll* have, in this example, been limited to 250 entries each. While this number would be inadequate for most compilers, it will suffice in the basic one. It is only necessary for the compiler to keep track, in the Noun Name Roll and the Noun Address Roll, of the initial entry of any subscripted noun. For example, despite the fact that the noun list of Example 40 itself will require the allocation of 417 words of computer memory, the compiler only needs to keep track of the 19 nouns listed.

The noun *NumbeR* is needed to serve as a buffer to hold the individual digits of a number as they are read from the Symbol

String one at a time. *A NumbeR* is used as a class limit or boundary in connection with Table IV. By setting A NumbeR = 27, it is then possible to determine whether or not an. unknown symbol of Table IV is a letter simply by determining whether or not it is less than 27.

Similarly, by defining *An Operator* as 37, any symbol which is less than *An Operator* must be a number or a letter.

The four nouns COMMA, LEFT Paren, EQUAL, and SEMIColon are operators which the Process Noun List Program must be able to recognize. Consequently, their numerical values, again from Table IV, must be available.

Nr of Nouns Named is used to keep track of the number of entries in the Noun Name Roll and the Noun Address Roll. *Noun Buffer* is, as its name implies, a place to put symbols while the letters of a noun are being assembled. *List Length* is used to hold the information on an individual noun in the dimensioning statement or noun list. For instance, it would be set to 250 while processing Noun Address Roll in Example 40.

The remaining six nouns in Example 40 all are required by a subroutine called *Find Next Symbol,* which will be needed in processing the noun list or dimensioning statement. Although *Word,* TEN, and even *Scratch Pad* are self-explanatory, the other three are not. In order to understand them, it might be well to look back at the process called *Store Symbol In String* in Example 38, and to reexamine the way in which multiplication and the comparison with the word FULL were used in the packing process. In order to retain machine independence, the unpacking process is written as almost the exact reverse, using division and a canceling term. The only real difference results from the fact that some binary computers use a one in the highest order, or leftmost bit to indicate that the following number is negative. In order to take account of this possibility, the Process Noun List Program will need a *Negative Coefficient* as well as a *Divisor* and a *Canceling Term.* Their precise use will be shown in Example 41.

Examples 40 and 41, when combined, will yield a basic program for processing a noun list, but it should be noted that they do not include any capability to handle such important items as the dimensioning of part-words, words longer than the number of *Symbols Per Word*, or floating-point numbers. All of these items will be developed later in the text.

EXAMPLE 41.

Process Noun List Program:	1
Symbol String First Address → I,	2
Object Program First Address → J,	3
CLEAR → K, CLEAR → Word,	4
FULL − SET → Negative Coefficient,	5
Examine Symbol String:	6
Find Next Symbol,	7
if Symbol < A NumbeR: Read The Noun.	8
if not, Test The Operator.	9
Read The Noun:	10
Symbol → Noun Buffer,	11
Continue Reading Noun:	12
Find Next Symbol,	13
if Symbol < An Operator: ;	14
if not, Process The Noun.	15
if Noun Buffer < FULL: Noun Buffer × Symbol Size →	16
Noun Buffer, Noun Buffer + Symbol → Noun Buffer;	17
if not, ;	18
Continue Reading Noun.	19
Test The Operator:	20
if Symbol = COMMA: Examine Symbol String.	21
if not, ;	22
if Symbol = LEFT Paren: Find List Length.	23
if not, ;	24
if Symbol = EQUAL: Set One Value.	25
if not, ;	26
if Symbol = SEMIColon: K − SET → K, K →	27
Nr of Nouns Named, Compile Body.	28
if not, Examine Symbol String.	29

Process the Noun:	30
J → Noun Address Roll[K],	31
Noun Buffer → Noun Name Roll[K],	32
K + SET → K, J + SET → J,	33
Test The Operator.	34
Find List Length:	35
Find Next Symbol,	36
J − SET → J,	37
Read A Number,	38
NumbeR → List Length,	39
Find Next Symbol,	40
if Symbol = EQUAL: Set Values.	41
if not, J + List Length → J;	42
if Symbol = SEMIColon: Test The Operator.	43
if not, Examine Symbol String.	44
Set One Value:	45
Find Next Symbol,	46
J − SET → J,	47
Read A Number,	48
NumbeR → [J], J + SET → J,	49
if Symbol = SEMIColon: Test The Operator.	50
if not, Examine Symbol String.	51
Set Values:	52
Find Next Symbol,	53
Read A Number,	54
NumbeR → [J], J + SET → J,	55
List Length − SET → List Length,	56
if List Length = CLEAR: Test The Operator.	57
if not, Set Values.	58
Find Next Symbol:	59
{ if Word = CLEAR: [I] → Word,	60
I + SET → I, FULL → Divisor;	61
if not, go to Positive Word.	62
if CLEAR < Word: go to Positive Word.	63
if not, go to Negative Word.	64

Positive Word:	65
Word / Divisor → Symbol,	66
Symbol × Divisor → Cancelling Term,	67
Word — Cancelling Term → Word,	68
if SET < Divisor: Divisor / Symbol Size →	69
Divisor;	70
if not, ;	71
Exit Find Next Symbol.	72
Negative Word:	73
CLEAR — Word → Word, Word/ Divisor → Symbol,	74
Symbol × Divisor → Cancelling Term,	75
Word — Cancelling Term → Word,	76
Negative Coefficient — Word → Word,	77
Symbol Size — SET → Scratch Pad,	78
Scratch Pad — Symbol → Symbol,	79
Divisor / Symbol Size → Divisor,	80
Exit Find Next Symbol:,}..	81

In Example 41, line 1 is *Process Noun List Program,* the name of the program, which was entered or jumped to from line 32 of Example 38. Lines 2 through 5 perform the *Housekeeping Chores,* setting values of parameters which will be needed later. Setting the value of the *Negative Coefficient* by subtracting unity, or SET, from the value of FULL is a subtle trick required only for those computers which use the highest-order binary digit as a negative sign. It will be explained in connection with the routine Negative word on lines 73 through 80.

Examine Symbol String, on lines 6 through 9, is the basic routine of Example 41, and is the one to which the process returns again and again. It first makes use of the subroutine *Read Next Symbol* to "unpack" the next symbol from the symbol string, and to place it in the word *Symbol,* where it can be tested and examined.

The first test, on line 8, makes use of the way that Table IV is organized to separate the letters from the numbers and operators on the basis of their numerical values. Since, in Example 40, the word *A Number* was given the numerical value 27, any symbol which is less than *A Number* will obviously have to be a letter. Because a noun cannot legally start with a number, a single two-way test is adequate here. If the symbol is less than 27, then the first letter of a noun has been found, while if it is not, an operator has been reached. In the first case, the process jumps to *Read The Noun* on line 10, and in the second case it goes to *Test The Operator* on line 20.

Read The Noun, on lines 10 thru 20, first takes the symbol which has already been found to be the first letter of a noun, and inserts it into the Noun Buffer. A repetitive process is then set up which, on line 14, tests to see whether or not an operator has been reached. If the numerical value of the symbol is not less than *An Operator,* or 37, then an operator must have been encountered, all of the letters of the noun must have been read, and the process goes from line 15 to *Process The Noun* on line 30. If, on the other hand, the latest symbol is still a letter, the test on line 16 determines whether or not there is room for another letter in the *Noun Buffer.* If the Noun Buffer is full, but the symbol is still a letter, the repetitive process continues reading, but having no place to put any more letters, it merely ignores them. As long as there is room in the Noun Buffer for additional letters, however, the letters already stored there are moved to the left by multiplying by 100 (decimal or octal, as the case requires) and the new letter is added. In production type compilers, of course, more than one computer word is reserved for each name. Several methods which accomplish this function may be examined later in the text.

Process The Noun, jumped to from line 15, can be seen on lines 30 thru 34. Since the tally or index J contains the memory location of the next cell of computer memory available for the object program, this is the location being assigned to the noun being processed. By inserting this value as the K*th* entry in the *Noun Address Roll,* and also inserting the name of the noun into the *Noun Name Roll,* any later routine in the compiler can find the memory allocation corresponding to that noun. After advancing both J and K, this routine returns to *Test The Operator,* because the symbol which terminated the *Read The Noun* routine must have been an operator.

Test The Operator, on lines 20 through 29, needs to recognize only four operators in the basic compiler; the comma, the left parenthesis, the equality sign, and the semicolon. Whenever a comma is encountered by the test on line 21, it must have been reached in one of only two possible ways. Either it is a comma which immediately follows a noun, or it is the last of a series of commas following the numerical values in a list. In either event, the next requirement is to *Examine the Symbol String.* At this point, the next symbol will have to be a letter.

Whenever the test on line 23 reveals a left parenthesis, it must indicate that a number of memory cells are to be reserved for a list, and that the actual number of cells required will be the next entry in the noun list being compiled. Consequently, the process must go to the routine called *Find List Length* on line 35. The latter routine will take account of the subsequent right parenthesis automatically, and also test to determine whether or not any numerical values have been included. As a result, the routine *Test The Operator* will never encounter either a right parenthesis or an equality sign which is being used with more than one numerical value.

It follows, then, that if an equality sign is detected by the test on line 25, a single numerical value must be involved. The process is therefore directed to the routine called *Set One Value* on line 45.

If the operator being tested is neither a comma, a left parenthesis, nor an equality sign, it must be a semicolon, and no further test is required. In order to allow for later expansion of the basic compiler, however, the test on line 27 is included. When the semicolon which denotes the end of the noun list has been reached, the total number of nouns must be recorded for later use. The tally K, which has been used to keep track of the number of individually named nouns, will already have been advanced. One is therefore subtracted from it before entering it into *Number of Nouns Named* for later use. At this stage, the Process Noun List Program is completed, and the instruction on line 28 directs it to the program called *Compile Body*, which will be discussed in the next chapter.

The role of *Find List Length* on lines 35 through 44 required first that it regain the address of the computer cell allocated to the noun currently being processed. This is done by subtracting one from the tally J, which had previously been advanced to the next available cell. After reading the number between the parentheses, a test is made to determine whether or not a group of numerical values has been included in the program being compiled. If so, the process goes to the routine *Set Values*, but if not the number of blank cells required is merely added to the tally J, so that it again holds the count of the next available location in the object program. Since it is possible to have reached the end of the noun list in this routine, the test on line 43 must be included.

The routine called *Set One Value* is the first which actually inserts anything into the object language program. Since the tally J had previously been advanced to the next available space, one must be subtracted from it before the actual insertion of a numerical value, and it must be restored afterward.

The subroutine called *Read A Number*, given in Example 42, will have left the numerical value desired in the word *NumbeR*, and since the subscript notation used without a noun refers to the absolute address in the computer, the process of insertion of the required number into the final compiled object program is accomplished merely with the phrase NumbeR→[J],.

Set Values is quite similar to *Set One Value*, but must repeat the process until all values in a list have been treated. If *Set One Value* had been written as a subroutine, *Set Values* could readily have utilized it.

There are only two basic subroutines used by the Process Noun List Program. They are the short subroutine called *Read A Number* given in Example 42, and the somewhat more complex *Find Next Symbol* given in lines 59 through 81.

The subroutine *Find Next Symbol* would be considerably less complicated if the basic compiler were not required to apply equally well to that class of computers in which the highest order bit not only determines the sign, but also becomes filled whenever the number itself becomes too large. In order to understand the operation of this subroutine, it might be well to consider the following case. Suppose that *Word* was initially clear, and that the next word in the symbol string held the letters EDCBA, or more precisely, their numerical equivalents, 05 04 03 02 01. In this case the phrase, [I]→Word, would leave 0504030201 in *Word*, and since this is greater than 0, or CLEAR, the process would go to the entry *Positive Word*. There, dividing 0504030201 by 0100000000 would give 0000000005, which would be inserted in *Symbol*, giving an E. All of the original letters, EDCBA, however, would still be present in *Word*. In order to remove the letter E from *Word*, the number 0500000000 must be subtracted from it. This number can be obtained merely by multiplying the value of *Divisor* by the *Value of Symbol*. In line 67, this number is stored in *Canceling Term*, and in line 68 it is subtracted, leaving, in this case, the number 00 04 03 02 01 in *Word*, and the E has been eliminated. In removing the next letter, or D, a smaller Divisor will be needed. Accordingly, the current value of *Divisor* is itself divided by *Symbol Size*, or 100, to give a new value of 00 01 00 00 00 for the Divisor, and the process leaves the subroutine with the numerical equivalent of the E, or 05, in *Symbol*.

The next time that the subroutine is called upon, since 00 04 03 02 01 is not equal to CLEAR, the process goes directly to the routine *Positive Word*. *Word*, with a current value of 00 04 03 02 01, when divided by 00 01 00 00 00, the current value of *Divisor*, gives a value of 00 00 00 00 04, or D, for insertion into the word *Symbol*. This process is quite straightforward, and could be continued until all of the letters, EDCBA, had been separately unpacked.

If the process encountered a combination like →B−A+, or 65 02 67 01 66, however, some computers would handle the numerical values as negative, in which case CLEAR would not be less than *Word*. In that event, the process goes to *Negative Word*, where it is subtracted from zero, and becomes 12 75 10 76 11. Divding by 01 00 00 00 00 gives a 12 for *Symbol*, a value which will have to be corrected. *Symbol* multiplied by *Divisor*, however, gives 00 00 00 00 12 × 01 00 00 00 00, or 12 00 00 00 00, the proper value for the *Canceling Term*. Subtracting it, *Word* then equals 00 75 10 76 11. At this point the *Negative Coefficient*, which had been formed by subtracting one from *Full* to give 00 77 77 77 77, is used as a base from which to subtract *Word*. The result is 00 02 67 01 66, from which it can be seen that the lower symbols have been restored. In order to restore the 12 in the noun *Symbol* to the proper value of 65, it is necessary to subtract one from *Symbol Size*, or 100, giving 00 00 00 00 77 in *Scratch Pad*, and then to subtract the 12 from that. This restores the value of 65 to *Symbol*, the divisor is then adjusted, and the process leaves the subroutine. Since the leading bits of *Word* are now zeros, it will no longer be treated as a negative number by any computer.

The subroutine *Read A Number*, shown in the next example, is a much less complex routine. Since it is always entered with a digit in the word *Symbol*, the first task is to store it in the word *NumbeR*. First, of course, the digit must be converted from its coded form, that of Table IV, to its true value by subtracting 27, or *A Number*, from it. Next, a repetitive process is set up which will read the next symbol. If this is another digit, all previous digits must be multiplied by 10 and the new digit added. Only after all digits have been read — as indicated by the fact that an operator has been entered into the word *Symbol* — will the process leave the subroutine.

Since in some cases it will be necessary to be able to read numbers in either the decimal or the octal number systems, *Read A Number* has been made capable of handling both. Merely by including lines 3, 6, 13, and 15 all numbers can be read as octal. Of course, any number which must be read is either decimal or octal, and not both. However, it is not always known which system it is in until after it has been read. Therefore it is thought more convenient to read in both systems and select the proper answer after the system has been identified.

EXAMPLE 42.
Octal Number,

```
EIGHT = 8,
Sub 8 = 61;
Read A Number:                                              1
  { Symbol — A NumbeR → NumbeR,                             2
    NumbeR → Octal Number,                                  3
  Read Digits:                                              4
    Find Next Symbol,                                       5
    if Symbol = Sub 8: Octal Number → NumbeR,              6
        Read Digits.                                        7
    if not, ;                                               8
    if Symbol < An Operator: ;                              9
    if not, Exit Read A Number.                            10
    Symbol — A NumbeR → Scratch Pad,                       11
    NumbeR × TEN → NumbeR,                                 12
    Octal Number × EIGHT → Octal Number,                   13
    NumbeR + Scratch Pad → NumbeR,                         14
    Octal Number + Scratch Pad → Octal Number,             15
    Read Digits.                                           16
  Exit Read A Number:,}..                                  17
```

CHAPTER 7

CO-NO TABLES

A method of compiling or translating based upon the treatment of two consecutive operators and the intervening operand as a single unit is used throughout the Neliac family of compilers. As mentioned earlier, the use of such a unit allows context to play a role, so that the meaning of a single operator is not necessarily as restricted as it would perforce be if each operator were interpreted individually. The triplets themselves may include any of the compiler symbols whose numerical equivalent in Table IV is equal to or greater than a comma as operators, and any noun, verb, or numerical parameter as the intervening operand.

During the compilation process, the compiler program which is translating the body of a source program advances through the source program in regular steps. Each step consists of transferring the previous *Next Operator* to the *Current Operator* position, finding the new Next Operator, processing the intervening operand, and then transferring control to the generator required by the particular CO–NO combination. This generator in turn obtains and retains any information which will be required later, and then inserts the appropriate machine-language instructions into the object program.

The program that transfers control to the proper generator depends upon the existence of a matrix or table of Current Operator-Next Operator combinations. The formation of a CO–NO table is quite simple, and can readily be illustrated by using the body or logic portions of the Load Program of Chapter 5 and the Process Noun List Program of Chapter 6.

An examination of the load and process noun list programs as given in Examples 38, 39, 41 and 42 will show that not all of the operators defined in Table IV have thus far been used in the basic compiler. By arranging those which do occur into the rows and column headings of a matrix, the framework of Table V can be formed. By designating the entries along the side as Current Operators, and those along the top as Next Operators, the table can be used to count and tabulate actual occurrences as they are encountered in the examples.

By starting with the first and second operators in Example 38, the colon followed by the right arrow; then the second and third operators, or right arrow and comma, and continuing in this way, all of the combinations which have been used will have been counted. In Table V, those combinations which have not been used have been left blank, while those combinations which were encountered have either a numerical or an alphabetical entry.

Although there are 60 unique combinations of two operators occurring in the examples, study of them will show that only 14 different operations are needed in translating them.

For example, the operator combinations of comma-comma, period-comma, colon-comma, right brace-comma, semicolon-semicolon, period-semicolon and colon-semicolon all imply that the object program instructions or machine-language commands for a return jump must be compiled and inserted into the object program by a generator. Since all of these combinations lead to the same generator, they carry the same number in Table V. On the other hand, some combinations that do occur will not be reached directly, in which case the letters NR will appear in the table.

TABLE V

CO–NO TABLE BASED UPON THE COMBINATIONS OF
EXAMPLES 38, 39, 41 AND 42

Next Operator

Current Operator	,	;	.	:	}	{	[	]	=	<	→	+	−	×	/	8
,	1		3	4	5				8	8	9	9	9	9	9	10
;		1	3		5		7		8	8	9	9				
.	1	1	3	4					8	8		9	9			
:	1	1	3			6+	7		8		9	9	9	9	9	10
}	1		3													
{									8		9					10
[							NR									
]	NR	NR									NR					
=				NR												
<				NR												
→	2	2					7									
+												11				
−												12				
×												13				
/												14				
8	NR														NR	

NR = not reached directly, 6+ = reached via 4.

The combination of an arrow and either a comma or a semicolon, on the other hand, always signifies that the result of the previous calculation is to be stored in the operand between them.

Any punctuation, or even a right brace, when followed by a period is invariably the signal for the generation of a direct transfer or straight jump. The generator called upon must therefore provide the machine instructions for the jump to the entry point which is named by the operand found between the current and the next operator.

Whenever a colon follows any punctuation, it can only mean that a verb — an entry point — is to be defined, with the intervening operand as the label.

The occurrence of a right brace following any of the operators involving punctuation can only denote that the end of a subroutine has been reached.

The occurrence of a left brace as a Next Operator can follow only a colon as the CO, and therefore indicates that the verb, entry point or label which has just been defined is to be treated as a subroutine. This suggests that the routine which was called upon to generate an entry point after finding a Current Operator-Next Operator combination of punctuation-colon might well have a *Look-Ahead* feature. Merely examining the next symbol after every punctuation-colon combination to see if it is a left brace can determine whether a straight entry or a subroutine entry is to be compiled at that point.

The occurrence of a left bracket, of course, signifies that subscripting is needed, no matter what other operator the left bracket follows. Because of this fact, the role of the subscripting generator is somewhat different from the others. Since the left bracket can be followed only by a right bracket, the generator which processes any subscripting can perform its function solely on the basis of finding a left bracket in the Next Operator position, and while doing so it can be allowed to remove both the left and the right bracket from considerations as a Current Operator. For example, the Current Operator-Next Operator combination arrow-left bracket occurring in the routine *Process the Noun* in Example 41 leads to subscripting of the word *Noun Address*. As soon as this has been done, the original arrow can be retained as the Current Operator, and the subsequent comma treated as the Next Operator.

Consequently, in Table V, the two rows having brackets as Current Operators and the column which has a right bracket as a Next Operator might all be omitted.

The occurrence of either an equality or a less-than sign, $=$ or $<$, following punctuation or a left brace heralds the reaching of the first indication of a comparison or *If Statement*. Since a comparative sign is followed only by a colon, the latter can be treated automatically, somewhat like the right bracket in subscripting. In addition to generating the initial instructions required for a comparison, a *Comparison Flag* must be set, in order that the regular process of advancing through the CO–NO combinations can also test for the terminations of true and false alternatives at all likely places.

Whenever an arithmetic operator follows a left brace or a punctuation operator, the intervening operand must be entered into a working register by the compiled program. First, however, the working register must be cleared. Consequently, all 14 of these combinations occurring in the examples of Chapters 5 and 6 must be set up to call upon the simple *Clear and Add* generator.

One of the rather different operators is the octal sign. Whenever it occurs as the Next Operator following punctuation or a left brace, it indicates that the intervening operand is to be treated as an octal number. When it occurs as the Current Operator, followed by either a comma or another octal sign, it indicates that a machine-language instruction has been expressed. For a decimal machine, this case requires that the previous operand be recovered and reconverted from octal to decimal by the machine-language generator.

The only additional operators or operator combinations represented in Table V are those which require addition, subtraction, multiplication or division. Since these all occur only in combination with a right arrow as the next operator, they are extremely simple, although each does require its own separate generator.

While the examples cited make use of only 60 of the 676 possible combinations in the CO–NO table, their implementation will permit the operation and self-compilation of the basic compiler. The production type compilers obviously make use of far more combinations. Even these leave many combinations unused. Unused combinations should lead to fault routines designed to assist in program checking. They may, however, be implemented whenever an extension to the Neliac language is desired.

The 60 combinations used in Table V lead to only 14 actual generators. This ratio increases slightly in the more powerful working compilers.

It has perhaps been noted that the numerical values in Table V refer to the various distinct generators required. In summary form, these are:

1. Generate return jump.
2. Generate store instruction.
3. Generate straight jump.
4. Define entry point or label.
5. End subroutine.
6. Start subroutine.
7. Set subscript.
8. Set comparison.
9. Generate clear and add.
10. Transfer machine language.
11. Generate addition.
12. Generate subtraction.
13. Generate multiplication.
14. Generate division.

The enumeration of the functions to be performed by the 14 generators which must be available to be called upon by the compilation process should suffice temporarily. The detailed description of these generators will therefore be deferred until the next chapter, and the remainder of this chapter will be devoted to the process whereby the generators are selected.

After compilation of the allocation of computer memory storage for the noun list, the compiling process must proceed to examine the Current Operator-Operand-Next Operator triplets, proceed to the proper generator, insert into the object program the necessary machine language, and advance to the next triplet.

Example 43 illustrates this process. It can be seen that the noun list for this program consists primarily of operators with their numerical values as given in the internal compiler code of Table IV. These will be used in finding proper generator entries corresponding to Table V.

EXAMPLE 43.
Current Operator,
Next Operator,
Operand Buffer,
Index Designator,
Period = 39,
COLON = 40,
Left BrackeT = 45,
LEFT Brace = 42,
ARROW = 53,
PLUS = 54,
TIMES = 56,
DIVide = 57;

Compile Body:	1
CLEAR → Index Designator,	2
COMMA → Next Operator,	3
Find Next Symbol,	4
Advance:	5
CLEAR → Operand Buffer,	6
Advance Again:	7
if Symbol < An Operator:	8
Read The Operand,	9
Advance Again.	10
if not, Next Operator → Current Operator,	11
Symbol → Next Operator,	12
Find Generator.	13
Read The Operand:	14
{ Symbol → Operand Buffer,	15
Continue With Operand:	16
Find Next Symbol,	17
if Symbol < An Operator: ;	18
if not, Exit Read The Operand.	19
if Operand Buffer < FULL:	20
Operand Buffer × Symbol Size → Operand Buffer,	21
Operand Buffer + Symbol → Operand Buffer;	22

if not, ;	23
Continue With Operand.	24
Exit Read The Operand:,},	25
Find Generator:	26
if Current Operator < PLUS: go to Test A.	27
if not, go to Test B.	28
Test A:	29
if Next Operator < LEFT Paren: go to Test A1.	30
if not, go to Test A2.	31
Test B:	32
if Current Operator < TIMES: go to Test B1.	33
if not, go to Test B2.	34
Test A1:	35
if Next Operator < COLON: go to Test A11.	36
if not, go to Test A12.	37
Test A2:	38
if Next Operator < ARROW: go to Test A21.	39
if not, go to Test A22.	40
Test B1:	41
if Current Operator = PLUS: go to Generator 11.	42
if not, go to Generator 12.	43
Test B2:	44
if Current Operator = TIMES: go to Generator 13.	45
if not, go to Generator 14.	46
Test A11:	47
if Next Operator < Period: go to Test A111.	48
if not, go to Generator 3.	49
Test A12:	50
if Next Operator = COLON: go to Generator 4.	51
if not, go to Generator 5.	52
Test A21:	53
if Next Operator < EQUAL: go to Generator 7.	54
if not, go to Generator 8.	55
Test A22:	56
if Next Operator = SUB 8: go to Generator 10.	57

if not, go to Generator 9.   58
Test All: 59
  if Current Operator < ARROW: go to Generator 1.   60
    if not, go to Generator 2.   61

The program logic of Example 43, starting after the noun list, first must clear the *Index Designator* and preset the *Next Operator*. By having line 3 place a comma in the Next Operator, the special use of the semicolon as a signal that the termination of the noun list had been reached does not need to be provided for in the CO–NO table.

Line 4, which calls upon the subroutine called *Find Next Symbol* in Example 41, will change the contents of Symbol from the semicolon with which it entered *Compile Body* to the first symbol of the body or program logic.

There are two different entries to the basic advance routine: *Advance,* and *Advance Again* (lines 5 and 7). These are the routines to which the process will return after each generator has completed its function. Two are required because some of the generators will have completed the use of the current operand, while others, like the subscripting generator, for example, will not have done so.

The comparison of line 8 determines whether or not the most recently read symbol has a numerical value of less than 37. If so, it must be a letter or a number, and therefore the first symbol of an operand. In this case the subroutine called *Read The Operand* on lines 14 through 25 is called upon. *Read The Operand* will place the entire operand in the Operand Buffer, and it will place the operator which follows the operand in the noun *Symbol* before returning the flow to line 10 and thence to line 7.

When an operator is found by the comparison on line 8, the operators are advanced. The previous *Next Operator* replaces the *Current Operator*, and the newly found operator, temporarily held in the noun *Symbol*, becomes the new Next Operator.

The entire routine called *Find Generator* is merely a series of cascaded comparisons which depend upon the contents of the Current

Operator and the Next Operator to determine which generator is required. It was necessary to write this routine in a most cumbersome fashion for the basic or Bootstrap compiler, as contrasted with most other compilers. The use of nested comparisons would of course have simplified the routine, as would the use of the Boolean *And* and *Or*. The use of part word or *Bit Notation*, combined with a method for computing the proper index for a switch type jump, would allow an even greater increase in the efficiency of the operation. Since the basic compiler uses only 14 generators, however, efficiency of the *Find Generator* routine loses its usual importance.

GENERATORS

As mentioned in earlier chapters, the actual generators that perform the function of inserting the final machine-language instructions into the object program must themselves be machine-dependent. Even so, however, the general function performed by each generator must be accomplished for any computer. Consequently, the degree of machine dependence is usually quite small, and in no case is it necessary to resort to *Crutch Coding* or machine language to implement a generator. Instead, the numerical value of each of the necessary components of the pertinent instructions in the repertoire of a given computer can be named and placed in the noun list of the generator which will need them.

In those cases in which a single generator must provide a large number of instructions, the whole set of such instructions can be maintained in the noun list in skeletal form so that the generator merely completes and transfers them as a block into the object program. This process makes use of a relatively large amount of computer memory, however, and the alternative has certain advantages. This alternative, of course, is the standard practice used in shorter generators, whereby all instructions are constructed individually as required.

[12] The complete repertoire of Countess instructions may be examined in Appendix D.

Each of the 14 generators listed in the preceding chapter will be discussed in detail in the following pages. While an attempt to maintain almost complete machine independence has determined procedures in all cases, this process has not always been successful. Consequently, alternative solutions are discussed, and in some cases presented in detail. The numerical values of the various machine-language instructions and their component parts have been included in the noun lists merely as an assurance that all routines have been machine-tested. For this purpose the repertoire of the Univac M-460 Countess has been employed[12].

Generator 1, The Return Jump

Generator 1, which is called upon whenever punctuation is followed by a comma or a semicolon, must generate the machine-language instructions for a return jump or control transfer to whatever subroutine is named by the intervening operand. It must do this despite the fact that the subroutine named by the operand may not have been defined until later in the source program. At this point it should be kept clearly in mind that Generator 1 is not intended to generate the subroutine instructions themselves, but only the transfer instructions to them.

Let us first assume that the computer involved has a return-jump instruction in its repertoire, which will transfer control from the main program to the second instruction of the subroutine, after placing the address from which it transferred into the address portion of the first instruction of the subroutine. If so, only one machine-language instruction, *Return Jump*, will be needed by this generator. The noun list for such a generator is shown in Example 44.

EXAMPLE 44.

Return Jump $= 65\ 000\ 00000_8$,

Operand Address,

Function,

Instruction For Object Program,

Return Entry Name Roll(250),

Return Entry Address Roll(250),
Nr of Return Entry Names,
Missing Name Return Entry Roll(250),
Missing Address Needed Return Entry Roll(250),
Nr of Missing Return Entry Names,
Comparison Flag;

In addition to the machine-language instruction, the noun list must contain a noun to hold the *Operand Address,* and for both *Function* and *Instruction For Object Program.* The latter is intended to hold not only the machine-language operation code, but the machine-language address portion of the instruction as well. A roll or list of subroutines, called *return entry names,* together with a parallel roll of their addresses, must be maintained during compilation. Since these rolls must occasionally be scanned or searched, it is also worthwhile to keep track of the number of entries in them, in the noun *Nr of Return Entry Names,* so that the unused portion of a list may be eliminated in the searching process.

As has been pointed out, this generator should take care of those cases in which a subroutine is called upon before it has been defined. A subroutine that has not yet been defined can not yet have its name and address in the return entry roll. An incomplete instruction must therefore be inserted into the object program, and the information saved that will be needed to find it. This instruction can then be completed when the subroutine itself is reached in the compilation process.

The information required consists of the address in the object program from which the return jump was made, together with the name of the missing subroutine. Two additional rolls or lists, called *Missing Name Return Entry Roll* and *Missing Address Needed Return Entry Roll* are reserved in the noun list for this purpose. Again, to avoid the necessity of searching all of the 250 cells reserved for these lists, a noun is reserved for the count of actual entries, and called *Nr of Missing Return Entry Names.*

Since this generator may be called upon when a semicolon is the next operator, and since a semicolon may signify not only that a return jump is being made but also that either the true or the false alternative of a comparison statement has been reached, the noun *Comparison Flag* has also been included in the noun list. While Generator 1 performs no function with respect to comparison statements, it will direct the flow to Generator 8, which does, when the Comparison Flag is set.

Example 45 gives the program logic of Generator 1. It correctly assumes that the name of the operand in the Current Operator-Operand-Next Operator triplet is in the Operand Buffer at the time the generator is entered.

EXAMPLE 45.

Generator 1:	1
CLEAR → K,	2
if Operand Buffer = CLEAR:	3
Test Comparison Flag.	4
if not, ;	5
Search Return Entry Roll:	6
if Return Entry Name Roll[K] = Operand Buffer:	7
Return Entry Address Roll[K] → Operand Address;	8
if not, Check Return Entry Roll.	9
Set Return Jump:	10
Return Jump → Function,	11
Insert Instruction,	12
Test Comparison Flag:	13
Find Next Symbol,	14
if Comparison Flag = SET: ;	15
if not, Advance.	16
if Next Operator = SEMIColon: Handle Comparison.	17
if not, Advance.	18
Check Return Entry Roll:	19
if K < Nr of Return Entry Names: K + SET → K,	20
Search Return Entry Roll.	21
if not, Generate Missing Address Return Jump.	22
Generate Missing Address Return Jump:	23

Nr of Missing Return Entry Names → K,   24
Operand Buffer → Missing Name Return Entry Roll[K],   25
J → Missing Address Needed Return Entry roll[K],   26
K + SET → Nr of Missing Return Entry Names,   27
CLEAR → Operand Address,   28
Set Return Jump.   29
Insert Instruction: 30
{ Function + Index Designator →   31
        Instruction For Object Program,   32
    Instruction For Object Program +   33
        Operand Address → [J],   34
    J + SET → J,   35
    CLEAR → Index Designator,}..   36

The routine called *Search Return Entry Roll* on lines 6 through 9 attempts to find the required subroutine by comparing the name in the Operand Buffer with the names of all previously compiled subroutines. If it finds coincidence line 8 then inserts the corresponding address from the Return Entry Address Roll into the Operand Address. In this case the concept of parallel or synchronized lists merely implies that a particular value of a subscript (K in this case) must reference information about the same item, despite the fact that the type of information depends upon the list itself.

The process then goes directly to *Set Return Jump,* unless the subroutine required had not yet been compiled. In the latter event, the process goes to *Generate Missing Return Jump* before going to the routine *Set Return Jump.*

Line 24 of that routine merely sets the index K at the value of the first empty cell in both *Missing Name Return Entry Roll* and the parallel *Missing Address Needed Return Entry Roll.* The tally is advanced by line 27, after the instruction on line 25 has stored the name in the proper roll. Line 26 makes use of the fact that the index J is being used throughout the compilation process to keep track of machine-language addresses as they are used in the object program. Since the current value of J is always identical to the address of the next machine-language intruction to be generated, it is the proper value to place in the roll which is used to maintain a record of incomplete instructions. Also, since no new operand address will have been found in this case, line 28 merely clears any previous one still held by that noun.

Set Return Jump, the routine on lines 10 through 12, places the needed computer operation code in the noun Function, and calls upon the subroutine *Insert Instruction*, on line 30. The latter is a general-purpose subroutine used by most of the generators. It combines the *Function*, and the *Index Designator* if there is one, with the Operand Address into a complete computer command or instruction for the object program. It then inserts this complete instruction into the next vacant cell of the machine-language program which is being compiled.

After the return-jump instruction has been inserted, the routine *Set Return Jump* calls upon the subroutine *Find Next Symbol* of Example 41, in preparation for returning the process to the routine called *Advance* in the main *Compile Body* program. Prior to doing so, however, a test is made on lines 13 through 15 to see whether or not the end of a comparison alternative has also been reached. In that case a straight jump to a part of Generator 8 called *Handle Comparison* will be made. If not, the process returns directly to the routine *Advance* of Example 43.

If a given computer did not have a complete return-jump instruction in its repertoire, it would have been necessary to extend line 11 of *Set Return Jump* slightly. This will be illustrated for the case in which only a straight-jump instruction is available. First, let all subroutines be written or compiled such that the first instruction contains a straight jump to an address which is unspecified, the second command begins the subroutine itself, and the last instruction is a straight jump to the address of the subroutine's own first instruction. In that case the object program, rather than the compiler, would need to be set up to add the address to which the subroutine should return to the first instruction of the subroutine. This could be achieved by compiling the following instructions:

1. Enter the working register with the contents of a cell in the

object program containing a jump instruction.
2. Add the contents of a cell in the object program which contains the address for return.
3. Store the result in the first address of the subroutine.
4. Jump past the cells used as storage.
5. Jump to the subroutine address plus one.

The result might look like the program logic of Example 46, where the entire example would replace line 11 of Example 45.

EXAMPLE 46.
Operand Address → Scratch Pad,
Clear and Add → Function,
J + FOUR → Operand Address,
Insert Instruction,
ADD → Function,
J + FOUR → Operand Address,
Insert Instruction,
Store Working Register → Function,
Scratch Pad → Operand Address,
Insert Instruction,
JUMP → Function,
J + THREE → Operand Address,
Insert Instruction,
JUMP → Function,
CLEAR → Operand Address,
Insert Instruction,
J + TWO → [J], J + SET → J,
JUMP → Function,
Scratch Pad + SET → Operand Address,
Insert Instruction,

The operation of the example above infers, of course, that the additional nouns used would have been included in the noun list of

Example 44.
Generator 2, Generate Store Instructions

Where the current operator is a right arrow and the next operator is a comma or a semicolon, the requirement of the program indicates that there must be generated the machine-language instruction which stores the content of the working register into the cell allocated to the noun specified as the operand. While this is quite a simple operation, it would be even more simple if it were not for the requirements of indexing or subscripting. Indexing can influence Generator 2 in either of two ways. The first and most usual way results from the fact that the noun which may be the operand may have been subscripted. In that case, the Current Operator-Next Operator combination arrow-left–bracket would have been encountered, and the process would have gone to Generator 7. In Generator 7 the proper value of the index would have been placed in the *Index Designator,* the following right bracket would have been cleared, and the comma or semicolon substituted for the Next Operator. Only after that would the *Find Generator* routine have sent the process to Generator 2. Since the Index Designator would have been properly set, no difficulties would have been encountered, and no special action would have been required.

However, the second way in which indexing may affect Generator 2 is much more direct, and does require special action. It may be that the operand is itself an index, instead of a noun. If so, the Operand Buffer will not coincide with any name in the noun list, and a different instruction will be required in the object program.

While the implementation of indexing is somewhat more difficult on computers which do not have index registers, called *B-Registers* or *B-Boxes,* this particular problem does not arise with them. Instead, the letters I, J, K, L, M, and N must always be treated by the compiler as nouns, and it must automatically enter them into the noun list itself.

The noun list and program logic of Generator 2 is given in Example 47, while two of the subroutines which it and other generators employ are given separately in Examples 48 and 49.

EXAMPLE 47.

Store Working Register $= 15\ 030\ 00000_8$,
Store Index $= 12\ 070\ 00000_8$,
Index Flag,
Index Entry Position;

Generator 2:	1
Search Noun Roll,	2
if Index Flag = SET: Store The Index.	3
if not, Store In Noun.	4
Store The Index:	5
Obtain Index Entry,	6
Store Index + Index Entry Position → Function,	7
CLEAR → Operand Address,	8
Finish 2nd Generator.	9
Store In Noun:	10
Store Working Register → Function,	11
Finish 2nd Generator:	12
Insert Instruction,	13
Find Next Symbol,	14
if Comparison Flag = SET: ;	15
if not, Advance.	16
if Next Operator = SEMIColon: Handle Comparison.	17
if not, Advance.	18

The first two nouns of Example 47 are the only machine-language instruction codes required. The noun *Index Flag* is set at either zero or one by the subroutine called *Search Noun Roll*. A one indicates that the operand is indeed an index, while a zero indicates that it is a noun. The noun *Index Entry Position* is used by the subroutine called *Obtain Index Entry* in conjunction with the *Store Index* instruction. It is applicable only to those computers having index registers as a component of their circuitry.

Computers without index registers do not need to have the function implemented at all, since in those computers a compiler does not have to differentiate between a noun and an index. It is interesting to note at this point that the use of an index as a pronoun is quite different from its use as an adjective or adverb.

Line 2 of Generator 2 calls upon the subroutine *Search Noun Roll* much as Generator 1 used the one called *Search Return Entry Roll*. Upon returning from the subroutine, the address associated with the noun whose name is in the Operand Buffer will have been placed in the Operand Address. If the operand was an index, on the other hand, the Index Flag will have been set. Accordingly, the program branches on lines 3 and 4. If the operand was an index, the routine on lines 5 through 8 places the needed information in the noun *Function*, and clears the operand address. It then transfers control to the routine *Finish 2nd Generator*. In the more usual case, that of a noun, the process goes directly from line 4 to lines 10 and 11, and thence to *Finish 2nd Generator*.

The latter routine inserts the required instruction in the object program and then calls upon the subroutine *Find Next Symbol*. At this point it will, like Generator 1, perform a test to determine whether or not the Next Operator also signals the termination of one of the alternatives of a comparison. If so (again like Generator 1), it goes directly to the part of Generator 8 called *Handle Comparison*. If that is not the case, its task has been completed, and the process is returned to the routine *Advance*.

The next two examples will show the details of the two new subroutines employed.

EXAMPLE 48.

Top Index = 15,	
Low Index = 8;	
Search Noun Roll:	1
{ CLEAR → K,	2
CLEAR → Index Flag,	3
Check Noun Roll:	4
if Noun Name Roll[K] = Operand Buffer:	5
Noun Address Roll[K] → Operand Address,	6
Exit Search Noun Roll.	7
if not, ;	8

if K < Nr of Nouns Named: K + SET → K,	9
Check Noun Roll.	10
if not, CLEAR → Operand Address;	11
if Operand Buffer < Top Index: ;	12
if not, Exit Search Noun Roll.	13
if Low Index < Operand Buffer: SET → Index Flag;	14
if not, ;	15
Exit Search Noun Roll:,}..	16

The subroutine *Search Noun Roll* of Example 48 is used by those generators whose Current Operator-Next Operator combinations imply that the intervening operand is a noun rather than a verb.

The two nouns *Top Index* and *Low Index* have been given values corresponding to the numerical values of the letters H and O in Table IV, in order that the index letters I, J, K, L, M, and N can be identified. Lines 4 through 11 have been written to find the address of the operand if it is a noun. If it is not, lines 12 through 15 determine whether or not the operand is an index, and set the Index Flag accordingly.

EXAMPLE 49.

Index Entry Class = 00 100 00000$_8$;

Obtain Index Entry:	1
{ Operand Buffer − Low Index → Scratch Pad,	2
Scratch Pad × Index Entry Class →	3
Index Entry Position,}..	4

The subroutine *Obtain Index Entry* of Example 49 is one which is required for those computers having a positional notation for specifying which index is to be used with the *Enter Index* operational code. By subtracting Low Index, or 8, from the numerical value of the letter, the letter I becomes a 1, J becomes 2, and so forth. Here again, this subroutine is not needed in compilers for those computers which do not have index registers.

Generator 3. Straight Jumps or Unconditional Transfers

Whenever a punctuation symbol is the current operator and a period is the next operator, a straight jump or unconditional transfer is required. The only exception occurs when a double period, signifying the end of a program, is reached. In either case the routine called *Find Generator* sends the process to Generator 3.

The nouns required for Generator 3 are shown in Example 50, and the program logic in Example 51.

EXAMPLE 50.

JUMP = 61 000 00000$_8$,

Stop Command = 61 400 00000$_8$,

Entry Name Roll(250),

Entry Address Roll(250),

Nr of Entry Names,

Missing Entry Name Roll(250),

Missing Entry Address Needed Roll(250),

Nr of Missing Entry Names;

Two more machine-language operational codes are required in the noun list. The first specifies a straight jump or unconditional transfer, the second provides the computer stop instruction. In the same way that Generator 1 required two sets of parallel lists for maintaining a record of compiled and not-yet-compiled subroutine information, Generator 3 requires lists and count numbers for direct entry point information. Accordingly, *Nr of Entry Names* is used to keep the count of the number of entries in both the *Entry Name Roll* and its parallel *Entry Address Roll*. Similarly, *Nr of Missing Entry Names* is used to maintain the record of entries in the *Missing Entry Name Roll* and its parallel *Missing Entry Address Needed Roll*.

Example 51 shows the details of the program logic by means of which Generator 3 produces the required machine language for the object program.

EXAMPLE 51.

Generator 3:	1
if Operand Buffer = CLEAR: Check Stop.	2
if not, ;	3
CLEAR → K,	4

Search Entry Roll:	5
if Entry Name Roll[K] = Operand Buffer:	6
Entry Address Roll[K] → Operand Address;	7
if not, Check Entry Roll.	8
Set Jump:	9
JUMP → Function,	10
Insert Instruction,	11
NOTE Comparison flag:	12
Find Next Symbol,	13
if Comparison Flag = SET: Handle Comparison.	14
if not, Advance.	15
Check Entry Roll:	16
if K < Nr of Entry Names: K + SET → K,	17
Search Entry Roll.	18
if not, Generate Jump to Missing Address.	19
Check Stop:	20
if Current Operator = Period: Generate Stop.	21
if not, NOTE Comparison Flag.	22
Generate Jump to Missing Address:	23
Nr of Missing Entry Names + SET → K,	24
K → Nr of Missing Entry Names,	25
Operand Buffer → Missing Entry Name Roll[K],	26
J → Missing Entry Address Needed Roll[K],	27
·CLEAR → Operand Address,	28
Set Jump.	29
Generate Stop:	30
Stop Command → [J], DBUG..	31

In addition to the generation of jump instructions, Generator 3 must handle the case of a double period indicating the termination of a program. Since it is legal to have two periods as adjacent operators in either a comparison statement or a switch, as well as in a termination signal, these cases must be separated.

The difference in usage can be determined on the basis of the presence or absence of an operand between periods. Accordingly, the first comparison (line 2 of Example 51) determines this point.

At this stage, however, the Current Operator may have been some punctuation other than a period, even though the Next Operator could be only a period. Consequently, if the comparison of line 2 is found to be true, the process is directed to *Check Stop* on line 20.

If the Operand Buffer had contained the name of an entry point, or verb, in the test on line 2, then the process would have continued to *Search Entry Roll* on line 5.. The routine *Search Entry Roll* on lines 5 through 8, together with *Check Entry Roll* on lines 16 through 19, determines whether or not the entry point to which the jump is required is one which has already been compiled.

If it is, then line 6 will find its name in the *Entry Roll*, and line 7 will transfer the address at which it was compiled in the object program to the noun *Operand Address*, and the process will go to the routine *Set Jump*. If it has not yet been compiled, this fact will be apparent after all names in the entry roll have been examined, and line 19 will direct the process to the routine called *Generate Jump to Missing Address*.

This routine, on lines 23 through 29, has two functions. First, it adds the name of the uncompiled entry point to the *Missing Entry Name Roll*, so that when that entry point is finally being compiled later on, the generator compiling it can determine that there was a prior need for it. Second, this routine places the object program address at which the entry point was needed, J, in the parallel list called *Missing Entry Address Needed Roll*. After clearing the Operand Address of any prior entry, the process goes from line 29 to the entry point called *Set Jump* of line 9.

Set Jump calls upon the subroutine *Insert Instruction* to complete the compilation, and prepares to transfer the process back to the main flow at *Advance*. Before doing so, however, it is necessary to determine whether or not the Next Operator, a period, could also have signaled the end of an alternative in a comparison statement. If so, the Comparison Flag will have been set, and the process will transfer from Generator 3 to the routine *Handle Comparison*, which is a part of Generator 8.

Generator 4. Generate an Entry Point or Label

Punctuation followed by a colon indicates one of two possibilities—either a direct entry point or a subroutine is being defined.

These two cannot be distinguished at this point, but depend upon
the next symbol. If the symbol following the colon is a left brace,
then a subroutine is being defined. Conversely, if the symbol is
anything but a left brace, a direct entry point is being defined. In
either case, the Find Generator routine will have sent the process
to Generator 4. Generator 4, as shown in Example 52, must therefore test the next symbol. If a subroutine is involved, the process is
directed away from Generator 4 and sent immediately to Generator
6. The test is shown on lines 3 through 5.

EXAMPLE 52.

Generator 4:	1
Find Next Symbol,	2
if Symbol = LEFT Brace:	3
LEFT Brace → Next Operator,	4
go to Generator 6.	5
if not, ;	6
Nr of Entry Names → K,	7
Operand Buffer → Entry Name Roll[K],	8
J → Entry Address Roll[K],	9
K + SET → Nr of Entry Names,	10
CLEAR → L,	11
Check Previously Needed Entry Names:	12
if Missing Entry Name Roll[L] = Operand Buffer:	13
Missing Entry Address Needed Roll[L] → M,	14
[M] + J → [M],	15
CLEAR → Missing Entry Name Roll[L];	16
if not, ;	17
if L < Nr of Missing Entry Names: L + SET → L,	18
Check Previously Needed Entry Names.	19
if not, ;	20
Advance.	21

For direct-entry points, line 7 inserts the proper location of the first vacant space in the parallel lists into the index K. Line 8 then stores the name of the entry point in the *Entry Name Roll*.

Line 9 stores the value of J, the address of the point in the object program at which the entry point is being defined, into the corresponding cell of the *Entry Address Roll*.

Obviously it is possible that the entry point which is being defined by Generator 4 might already have been called upon by an earlier part of the program, such that Generator 3 would have compiled an incomplete jump to it. Consequently, it is necessary at this point to examine the Missing Entry Name Roll to see if this might have happened. Lines 12 through 19 accomplish this task, and also complete any unfinished jump instructions which are discovered. In particular, line 14 inserts the address of the incomplete jump instruction into the index M. Since the only element which that instruction lacked was the address to which to jump, an address that has now established as the present value of J, line 15 completes the correction. Since the entry point may have been employed more than once, the entire Missing Entry Name Roll is scanned before returning to the major routine *Advance*.

It is interesting to note that this generator does not produce any new machine-language instructions, even though it may complete several earlier ones. Consequently it follows that the number of instructions in an object program will not be increased by a liberal use of entry points or labels in the original program.

Generator 5, Terminating Subroutines

A right brace as a Next Operator signifies the end of a subroutine. Since the basic or Bootstrap compiler allows for only one subroutine at a time, and does not need or allow for *For Statements* or loops, the generator required is very simple. Example 53 shows the program logic of Generator 5. No new nouns are required.

EXAMPLE 53.

Generator 5:	1
Nr of Return Entry Names → K,	2
Return Entry Address Roll[K] → Operand Address,	3

JUMP → Function,	4
Insert Instruction,	5
Find Next Symbol,	6
Advance.	7

The last subroutine to have been initiated must be the one that is being terminated whenever this generator is called upon. Therefore its name must be the last entry in the Return Entry Name Roll, and the *Nr of Return Entry Names* must be its item index in that list and in the Return Entry Address Roll as well. The latter item must be the object program address of the first instruction in the subroutine, which is the location of the instruction that Generator 6 would have produced to return control to the main program. Therefore it is the point to which the last instruction in the compiled subroutine must jump. Line 2 of the generator therefore obtains the item number of the last entry, line 3 transfers the address of that entry to the Operand Address, and lines 4 through 7 complete the instruction, insert it into the object program, and then return the process to the routine *Advance*.

Whenever it is desired to extend the basic or Bootstrap compiler to allow for the compilation of an unlimited number of subroutines written within other subroutines, it is only necessary to replace line 2 of Example 53 with:

Nr of Return Entry Names — Nr of Subroutines
    Being Compiled → K,
Nr of Subroutines Being Compiled — SET →
    Nr of Subroutines Being Compiled,

and to add the lines:

Nr of Subroutines Being Compiled + SET →
    Nr of Subroutines Being Compiled,

to Generator 6. In addition, it would also be necessary to make certain that an initial value of minus one was entered as the value of the noun *Nr of Subroutines Being Compiled* at the beginning of compilation.

Further, when a generator for *For Statements* or loop control is to be added, a *Loop Flag* must be included. The Loop Flag should be increased by one upon the initiation of compilation of each loop. Since subroutines may be called upon from within a loop, but are never defined inside one, the test:

$$\text{if Loop Flag} \neq \text{CLEAR:}$$

would be sufficient to direct the process away from generator 5 to the loop generator.

Generator 6, Generating Subroutine Entrances

Generator 6, which initiates subroutines or re-entry points, is not reached directly from the *Find Generator* routine, but instead from Generator 4, after it has been determined that a re-entry, rather than a direct-entry point is involved.

The program for Generator 6 is shown in the following example.

EXAMPLE 54.

Generator 6:	1
Nr of Return Entry Names + SET → L,	2
L → Nr of Return Entry Names,	3
Operand Buffer → Return Entry Name Roll[L],	4
J → Return Entry Address Roll[L],	5
CLEAR → K,	6
Check Missing Return Entry Names:	7
if Missing Name Return Entry Roll[K] = Operand Buffer:	8
Missing Address Needed Return Entry Roll[K] → M,	9
[M] + J → [M],	10
CLEAR → Missing Name Return Entry Roll[K];	11
if not, ;	12
if K < Nr of Missing Return Entry Names:	13
K + SET → K, Check Missing Return Entry Names.	14
if not, ;	15
JUMP → [J], J + SET → J,	16
Find Next Symbol,	17
Advance.	18

The first operation performed by this generator is that of updating the *Return Entry Name Roll* and the corresponding *Return Entry Address Roll*, which it does on lines 2 through 5.

The other operation to be performed is that of searching the *Missing Return Entry Name Roll* in order to find out whether or not the subroutine being compiled at this point has been called upon earlier in the object program. If so, line 9 finds the address of the return-jump instruction which could not have included the address of the subroutine. Line 10 corrects the omission. Line 11 is included only to assist with program testing after compilation, at which time the *Missing Name Return Entry Roll* should be completely clear. Lines 13 and 14 merely make certain that the roll is completely scanned.

Instead of making the usual call upon the subroutine *Insert Instruction* to place the needed jump command in the first instruction of the subroutine being compiled, line 16 performs this operation directly. This is permissible since subscripting is not involved, and no operand address is needed.

Generator 7, Subscripting

Generator 7, which handles subscripting, depends in large measure upon whether or not the computer for which it is being implemented has index registers. If so, it can be written quite simply, as shown in the following example.

EXAMPLE 55.

Index Position = 100 00000$_8$;

Generator 7:	1
Find Next Symbol,	2
Symbol — Low Index → Scratch Pad,	3
Scratch Pad × Index Position → Index Designator,	4
Find Next Symbol,	5
Find Next Symbol,	6
Current Operator → Next Operator,	7
Advance Again.	8

In Example 55, advantage is taken of the fact that the only symbol which can legally follow a left bracket is one of the letters

I, J, K, L, M, or N. As can be seen in Table V, their numerical values are 9, 10, 11, 12, 13, and 14. Since the noun *Low Index* has been given the value 8, subtracting it from the index in line 3 gives a numerical value corresponding to one of the index registers in the computer itself. In order to shift it to the required position before adding it to a machine-language instruction, line 4 multiplies it by *Index Position,* which must contain a 1 in the proper position, with all other digits zero. The result is then stored in the Index Designator for use by the subroutine Insert Instruction.

Since the basic compiler permits only a single letter as an index, the next symbol, as obtained by line 5, can be nothing else than a right bracket. Because the right bracket yields no information in this case it is ignored, and line 6 calls up the next symbol.

At this point the generator has performed its function of subscripting, but the operand in the original triplet has not been acted upon. By the simple expedient of removing all traces of both brackets, the process will be in condition to treat the modified triplet made up of the original Current Operator, the original Operand, and a new Next Operator. However, because the routine *Advance* would eliminate the original Current Operator by shifting the Next Operator to that word, line 7 cancels that impending operation. Further, since a direct jump to *Advance* would be followed by a clearing of the Operand Buffer, the jump is made instead to the routine *Advance Again.*

The modification which would be required to permit a constant to be used as an index is quite simple. Between lines 2 and 3 of Example 55 the following test might be inserted:

if Symbol > 26: Treat Increment.
if not, ;

and the entry label:

Complete 7th Generator:

would be needed between lines 5 and 6. Three more lines:

Treat Increment:
Read A Number, NumbeR → Address Increment,

Complete 7th Generator.

would be needed at the end. In addition, the subroutine Insert Instruction of Example 45 would need to have the term *Address Increment* added to *Instruction For Object Program*, thereby adding it to *Operand Address* before storing the instruction in [J]. *Address Increment* should subsequently be cleared.

Generator 8, Set Comparison

Basically, when the relational or comparison generator, Generator 8, is called upon it must generate the machine language that will enter the working register with the term on the left of the comparison symbol and subtract it from the term on the right. Then, depending upon which comparison symbol was used, it must generate the machine language that will continue with the true alternative for one state of the working register, but jump around the true alternative for another. Having done this, it should return the process to *Advance* for standard compilation of all expressions constituting the true alternative. After the end of the true alternative has been reached, either by Generator 1 or by Generator 3, Generator 8 must be called upon again to generate a jump around the false alternative. Thereupon the process should be returned once more to *Advance* for regular compilation of the expressions which constitute the false alternative. When the end of the false alternative has been reached by Generator 1 or 3, Generator 8 must again be called upon, this time in order to complete the instruction which will jump the object program around the false alternative.

The noun list for this generator is given in Example 56, where it can be seen that five additional computer operational codes have been required. These are the codes for entering a number into the working register, for adding an index, for subtracting, and for jumping or branching upon finding either a positive or a nonzero register. In addition, the object program locations at which jump commands must be inserted before the destinations of the jumps are known must all be preserved. The nouns *False Comparison Entry Needed* and *Continue Comparison Entry Needed* have been defined for this purpose.

EXAMPLE 56.

Clear And Add = 11 030 00000$_8$,
Add Index = 11 000 00000$_8$,
SUBtract = 21 030 00000$_8$,
Jump With Nonzero Register = 60 500 00000$_8$,
Jump With Positive Register = 60 600 00000$_8$,
False Comparison Entry Needed,
Continue Comparison Entry Needed;

The program logic for the complete comparison generator is given in Example 57.

EXAMPLE 57.

Generator 8:	1
Search Noun Roll,	2
if Index Flag = SET: Use Index.	3
if not, Use Noun.	4
Use Index:	5
Operand Buffer — Low Index → Scratch Pad,	6
Scratch Pad × Index Position → Index Designator,	7
Add Index → Function,	8
CLEAR → Index Flag,	9
CLEAR → Operand Address,	10
Continue 8th Generator.	11
Use Noun:	12
Clear And Add → Function,	13
Continue 8th Generator:	14
Insert Instruction,	15
Find Next Symbol,	16
Read The Operand,	17
Next Operator → Current Operator,	18
Symbol → Next Operator,	19
Search Noun Roll,	20

SUBtract → Function,	21
Insert Instruction,	22
J → False Comparison Entry Needed,	23
SET→ Comparison Flag,	24
if Current Operator = EQUAL: Set Equal Comparison.	25
if not, Set Less-Than Comparison.	26
Set Equal Comparison:	27
Jump With Nonzero Register → [J],	28
J + SET → J,	29
Find Next Symbol,	30
Advance.	31
Handle Comparison:	32
if False Comparison Entry Needed = CLEAR:	33
Set Continue Comparison.	34
if not, Set False Comparison.	35
Set False Comparison:	36
False Comparison Entry Needed → M,	37
CLEAR → False Comparison Entry Needed,	38
J → Continue Comparison Entry Needed,	39
JUMP → [J], J + SET → J,	40
[M] + J → [M],	41
Advance.	42
Set Continue Comparison:	43
Continue Comparison Entry Needed → M,	44
CLEAR → Continue Comparison Entry Needed,	45
CLEAR → Comparison Flag,	46
[M] + J → [M],	47
Advance.	48
Set Less Than Comparison:	49
Jump With Positive Register → [J],	50
J + SET → J,	51
Find Next Symbol,	52
Advance.	53

Generator 8, by calling upon the routine named *Search The Noun Roll* in line 2, determines whether or not the operand to the left of the comparison sign is a normal noun, or instead is a lone index. If the operand had been a noun which was subscripted by an index, the *Index Designator* would have been set by Generator 7. If it is a noun, then the comparison on lines 3 and 4 will send the process to the routine *Use Noun* on line 12, instead of to the routine *Use Index* on line 5. If it is an index, as, for instance, line 7 of Example 38 is, then it will be in the Operand Buffer when the process reaches line 6. At this stage the processing is identical to that of lines 3 and 4 of Example 55, where the numerical value of the index is obtained, shifted, and placed in the Index Designator. Line 8 places the proper machine operation code in *Function*, lines 9 and 10 clear the Index Flag and the unneeded Operand Address, and the process shifts to line 14.

Whenever the left side of the comparison is a noun, on the other hand, line 13 alone accomplishes the needed task, by placing a *Clear And Add* machine operation code in the noun *Function*. The call upon the subroutine *Insert Instruction* on line 15 then places whichever instruction had been stored in Function directly into the program being compiled. As a result, the object program will place the term on the left of the comparison sign in the working register.

At this point most generators would return to *Advance*, because a new Current Operator-Operand-Next Operator combination is to be treated. In this case, however, the next combination will still be a part of the *If Statement*, so Generator 8 continues to treat it. Line 17 calls upon the subroutine *Read The Operand* of Example 43, which will obtain the right-hand term of the comparison. Line 18 and 19 adjust the Current Operator-Next Operator combination, which at this stage must hold the colon as the Next Operator.

The machine-language instruction which will subtract the right-hand term from the left-hand term is compiled by the directions of lines 20, 21, and 22. The jump instruction which the object program will need as its next command will not yet have been determined, since it will be a conditional jump and will depend upon which comparison symbol was used. The location at which it must be inserted is obviously given by the current value of J. Accordingly, it will be saved for future use by line 23. Line 24 sets the indicator so that Generators 1 and 3 can determine whether or not any expression they compile is inside a comparison statement.

The type of comparison being compiled is determined by the test of lines 25 and 26, since only two possibilities were provided for in Table V. For those cases in which the equality sign was used, the comparative statement will always be true whenever the working register is reduced to zero by subtracting one term from the other. Because the action to be taken in the true case will follow immediately, it must be jumped over in the false case. Therefore line 28 is written to insert the *Jump With Non Zero Register* command into the object program. The address to which the jump will be made will have to be inserted later. Meanwhile, the process returns to *Advance*, in order that the material which constitutes the orders to be followed in the true case can be compiled in the standard way.

In the event that the *Less Than* symbol had appeared in the comparison, lines 49 through 53 would have been used instead of those of lines 27 through 31. In either case the process returns to *Advance* after inserting two complete and one incomplete machine-language instructions into the object program, and after setting the *Comparison Flag* in the compiler.

After compiling the true alternative of the comparison with whichever generators are needed, the process will eventually encounter either a period or a semicolon. At that time it will return to the routine *Handle Comparison* which starts on line 32. It will also return to this routine at the completion of the false alternative, so this routine must be written in such a way that it can determine which case is involved. This is accomplished with the test on line 33. The noun *False Comparison Entry Needed* was used on line 23 to hold a needed address. If that address has not yet been used, then it follows that the first termination is the one being encountered, so the process is directed to line 36. If the address has already been used and the noun cleared, then the second termination has been reached, so the process is transferred to line 43.

The routine called *Set False Comparison* on line 36 places the address of the object program instruction which jumped over the true alternative in the tally M with line 37, and then clears the noun which held it with line 38. At this stage the next instruction to be compiled should be one which transfers the object program around the false alternative. Since the false alternative cannot as yet have been compiled, its length cannot yet be known and the address to which the jump should be made cannot yet be known either. The address from which the jump will be made is known, however, because it is the current value of the tally J. Line 39 therefore preserves it, while line 40 inserts an incomplete jump instruction and advances J.

At this point, J holds the address to which the object program should jump if the comparison were false, and the tally M·holds the address from which that jump should be made. Accordingly, the logic on line 47 takes the incomplete jump instruction, adds the previously missing address to it, and returns it to its original location. Thereupon, the process leaves Generator 8 and returns to the routine *Advance*.

Again, after the other generators have compiled all of that part of the program constituting the false alternative, a period or a semciolon will be encountered. The process will then return once more to the routine *Handle Comparison* in Generator 8. This time, though, the *False Comparison Entry Needed* noun will already have been cleared, and the process will therefore go to the routine named *Set Continue Comparison* starting on line 43.

At this stage, the entire comparison or *If Statement* will have been compiled, with the exception of the incomplete instruction intended to transfer the object program from the end of that portion constituting the true alternative to the first instruction after the last instruction of the false alternative. Lines 44 through 47 complete that prior jump instruction, and clear the noun used to hold its address. Also, since the comparison statement is now completely compiled, the Comparison Flag is cleared, and the process returned to *Advance*.

Generator 8 as written in this example does not produce as

efficient an object program as possible, for it does not check to see whether or not the true alternative ends with a period. If it does, then the jump around the false alternative is obviously never going to be used, and should be suppressed.

Generator 9, Enter the Working Register

Whenever a punctuation type operator is followed by an arithmetic operator, the object program must clear the working register and insert the value held by the operand. If the operand is an index, then the *Add Index* computer operation code must be generated. This requires that the numerical designation of the particular index be found and placed in the index designator. The program logic for this generator is given in the following example.

EXAMPLE 58.

Generator 9:	1
Search Noun Roll,	2
if Index Flag = SET: Bring From Index.	3
if not, Bring From Noun.	4
Bring From Index:	5
Operand Buffer — Low Index → Scratch Pad,	6
Scratch Pad × Index Position → Index Designator,	7
Add Index → Function,	8
CLEAR → Operand Address,	9
CLEAR → Index Flag,	10
Finish 9th Generator.	11
Bring From Noun:	12
Clear And Add → Function,	13
Finish 9th Generator:	14
Insert Instruction,	15
Find Next Symbol,	16
Advance.	17

The six lines, 1, 2, 13, 15, 16, and 17 would have sufficed for this generator if the indices had been treated as nouns. It is only in those cases in which a computer has index registers that they are treated separately, in order that the full speed of the computer can be utilized.

Generator 10, Transfer Machine Language

Whenever a punctuation symbol is followed by an octal symbol, two possibilities exist. Either an octal number is to be entered into the working register, or a machine-language instruction has been encountered in the source-language program. To differentiate between these two possibilities, it is necessary to examine the next symbol. If the next symbol is an operator, then an octal number is to be treated. If instead the next symbol is a letter or a number, then a machine-language instruction has been found. In the basic compiler of this example, however, arabic numerals have not been used in the program logic, so that Generator 10 does not need to include such a test. Instead, it can proceed immediately upon the assumption that a machine-language instruction has been found in the source program, as it does in Example 59.

The task which this generator must perform is obviously so simple that it might be expected that the generator itself would be trivial. All that is required of it is to effect the transfer, unchanged, of a set of digits from the source program to the object program, and to find and add the address of a noun or verb if one has been used. Strangely enough, the first of these two requirements necessitates as many instructions as the second. The reason for this is apparent when one remembers that both the paper-tape code for characters and the internal compiler code for symbols must allocate two digits for each character or symbol. Consequently, if a source program contained a machine language instruction such as:

$$, 60 \ 531_8 \ \text{NAME},$$

then the Operand Buffer would not actually contain the number 60531 when the Current Operator-Next Operator combination of COMMA-SUB8 was reached, but instead it would contain the internal compiler code version of this operand. From Table IV it can be seen that the operand buffer in this case would actually hold the number 41 33 40 36 34, where the code value of zero is 33. Even after a 33 is subtracted from each pair of digits, the number still is 06 00 05 03 01. A further complication, first noted in the discussion of load programs, arises in those computers which treat the highest order bit as a sign bit. In this generator, however, a different method of handling this problem will be employed.

EXAMPLE 59.

Machine Language Factor $= 1\ 00000_8$,
Negative Mask $= 40\ 00\ 00\ 00\ 00_8$,
Correction Mask $= 05\ 00\ 00\ 00\ 00_8$,
Final Mask $= 00\ 33\ 33\ 33\ 33_8$,
Positive Mask $= 33\ 33\ 33\ 33\ 33_8$,
Hundreds(5) $= 1, 100_8, 10000_8, 1000000_8, 100000000_8$,
Tens(5) $= 1, 10_8, 100_8, 1000_8, 10000_8$;

Generator 10:	1
if Operand Buffer < CLEAR:	2
Operand Buffer − Negative Mask → Operand Buffer,	3
Operand Buffer + Correction Mask → Operand Buffer,	4
Operand Buffer − Final Mask → Operand Buffer;	5
if not, Operand Buffer − Positive Mask → Operand Buffer;	6
Symbols Per Word → M,	7
CLEAR → N,	8
Continue 10th Generator:	9
M − SET → M,	10
Hundreds[M] → Scratch Pad,	11
Operand Buffer / Scratch Pad → Scratch Pad,	12
Tens[M] × Scratch Pad → L,	13
L + N → N,	14
Hundreds[M] × Scratch Pad → Scratch Pad,	15
Operand Buffer − Scratch Pad → Operand Buffer,	16
if M = CLEAR: ;	17
if not, Continue 10th Generator.	18
N → Operand Buffer,	19
Operand Buffer × Machine Language Factor → Function,	20
Find Next Symbol,	21
if Symbol < A NumbeR:	22
Read The Operand,	23

Search Noun Roll,	24
Search Entry Roll 1;	25
if not, Read A Number,	26
NumbeR → Operand Address;	27
Insert Instruction,	28
Symbol → Next Operator,	29
Find Next Symbol,	30
Advance.	31
Search Entry Roll 1:	32
{CLEAR → K,	33
Search Entry Roll 2:	34
if Entry Name Roll[K] = Operand Buffer:	35
Entry Address Roll[K] → Operand Address,	36
Exit Search Entry Roll.	37
if not, ;	38
if K < Number of Entry Names:	39
K + SET → K, Search Entry Roll 2.	40
if not, ;	41
Exit Search Entry Roll:,},	42

The noun list contains one mask which consists of as many 33's as there are symbols in a word, and three other partial masks to handle the negative word problem.

Since it would seem more than mildly absurd to insist upon too great a degree of machine independence in this particular generator, the tables of tens and hundreds in the noun list are not computed by the compiler, even though it would have been quite simple to have arranged it so.

The first 6 lines of Example 59 are required to convert the initial contents of the Operand Buffer back from internal compiler code to the required numerical values, but these are still spaced twice as far apart as they should be. It is interesting to note that if the problem of negative values were not present, line 6 alone would have sufficed for this operation.

In order to repack a number such as 06 00 05 03 01 into the required form, 60531, the instructions on lines 7 through 19 are used. In this area, the tallies L and N are merely used as additional scratch pads, a practice which would not be adequate for any computer in which the word length exceeded twice the length of its index registers.

Line 20 merely serves to shift the machine-language instruction into its required position for insertion into the object program.

Lines 21 and 22 examine the first symbol of the machine-language operand as it appears in the source language. If this operand is also in pure machine language, then it will of course be a number, and lines 26 and 27 will place it in the *Operand Address.* If the Operand is a name, the call on the subroutine Read The Operand of line 23 will place it in the Operand Buffer. Since it may be either a noun or a verb, both the noun roll and the entry roll must be searched for its address. Looking back at Generator 3, it is seen that the routine *Search Entry Roll* included there was not written as a subroutine, hence it is not available here. Consequently, the subroutine on lines 32 through 42 must be included. By this time the student should be able to simplify Generator 3 by substituting one call upon the subroutine and a single test for success for all of the material on the eight lines; 5, 6, 7, 8, 16, 17, 18 and 19 of Example 51.

Returning to Example 59, it should be apparent that by the time line 28 is reached the complete machine-language instruction will be contained in the two parts, *Function* and *Operand Address,* regardless of the form in which it was originally given.

Because both the subroutines *Read A Number* and *Read The Operand* terminate with the next operator in the word *Symbol,* this generator actually extends its coverage beyond the simple Current Operator-Next Operator combination. Lines 29 and 30 are required to compensate for this fact, before line 31 returns the process to the main stream of the compilation process.

It is perhaps of interest to note that the primary aim of most assemblers, which is to keep track of memory locations, or addresses, could be accomplished with the *Load Program,* the *Process The Noun List* program, and the single generator of this example.

Generator 11, Addition

Whenever the plus operator is followed by a right arrow, the value of the operand is to be added to the value already in the working register. The simple logic required is shown in the following example.

EXAMPLE 60.

FOUR = 4,

ADD = 20 030 00000$_8$;

Generator 11:	1
Search Noun Roll,	2
if Index Flag = SET: go to Generator 11A.	3
if not, ;	4
ADD → Function,	5
Insert Instruction,	6
Find Next Symbol,	7
Advance.	8
Generator 11A:	9
Store Working Register → Function,	10
J + FOUR → Operand Address,	11
Insert Instruction,	12
Operand Buffer − Low Index → Scratch Pad,	13
Scratch Pad × Index Position → Scratch Pad,	14
Add Index + Scratch Pad → Function,	15
CLEAR → Operand Address,	16
Insert Instruction,	17
ADD → Function,	18
J + TWO → Operand Address,	19
Insert Instruction,	20
JUMP → Function,	21
J + TWO → Operand Address,	22
Insert Instruction,	23
J + SET → J,	24
Find Next Symbol,	25
Advance.	26

For the simple case in which the operand is a noun, lines 2, 5, and 6 suffice to compile the single machine-language instruction required.

If the operand is an index, however, several instructions will be needed, unless, of course, the repertoire of the computer contains an instruction which will add the contents of an index directly to the contents of a working register. Since most of them do not, it is usually necessary to store the contents of the working register temporarily somewhere in the object program. This is done to allow the object program itself to bring in the contents of the index register.

Lines 10, 11, and 12 therefore provide the object program instruction which will store the current contents of the working register in a cell which is four cells ahead of the instruction. The next object program instruction, compiled by lines 13 through 17, will transfer the contents of the proper index register to the working register. Lines 18, 19, and 20 then compile the instruction which will add the previous contents of the working register as stored in the program ahead, to the new contents. A jump over the temporary storage cell in the object program is then provided by lines 21, 22, and 23. Since no instruction is inserted where the cell is reserved for temporary storage, the object program instruction counter, J, must be advanced separately, as in line 24. Thereupon, the process is complete and the flow returns to the routine Advance.

Generator 12, Subtraction

The CO–NO combination of MINUS-ARROW calls for the compilation of a simple subtract instruction. Example 61 shows the few details required.

EXAMPLE 61.

Generator 12:	1
Search Noun Roll,	2
SUBtract → Function,	3
Insert Instruction,	4
Find Next Symbol,	5
Advance.	6

Generator 13, Multiplication

The Current Operator-Next Operator combination of Multiply-Right Arrow indicates that the object program instructions for integer multiplication must be compiled. In some computers this will require one or two shift instructions as well as the simple multiplication command. Such a case is illustrated in Example 62, where the shift instructions are included in the noun list.

EXAMPLE 62.

MULTiply = 22 030 00000$_8$,
Shift Before Dividing = 03 000 00036$_8$,
Shift After Dividing = 07 000 00036$_8$;

Generator 13:	1
Shift Before. Dividing → [J],	2
J + SET → J,	3
Search Noun Roll,	4
MULTiply → Function,	5
Insert Instruction,	6
Shift After Dividing → [J],	7
J + SET → J,	8
Find Next Symbol,	9
Advance.	10

Since the basic compiler being used in this example contained no cases in which the operand in a multiplication was a lone index, the program logic to handle that eventuality has not been included in this generator. It would be basically the same as that of Generator 11 in Example 60, however.

Generator 14, Division

Generator 14 is called upon whenever a CO–NO combination of *Divide-Right Arrow* is encountered by the *Find Generator* routine. The program is virtually identical to that of multiplication in Example 62. The details of the program logic are given in the following example.

EXAMPLE 63.

DIVide $= 23\ 030\ 00000_8$;

Generator 14:	1
Shift Before Dividing → [J],	2
J + SET → J,	3
Search Noun Roll,	4
DIVide → Function,	5
Insert Instruction,	6
Shift After Dividing → [J],	7
J + SET → J,	8
Find Next Symbol,	9
Advance.	10

With the foregoing set of 14 generators, and the programs of Chapters 5, 6, and 7, it is possible to compile programs, provided that they are written in a sort of Basic Neliac or Basic Algol. More importantly, however, this Basic Compiler will compile itself, and has often done so. Consequently, any of the extensions to the simple generators presented here which are desired can be written, compiled and added to the basic compiler.

CHAPTER 9

COMPILING COMPILERS
AND COMPILING SYSTEMS

The examples given in Chapters V through VIII, when combined, constitute a compiler having the capacity for recompilation. That is, if an initial version is once converted to machine code, either by compilation on an existing compiler or by hand coding, then that version contains everything required to convert the combined examples directly to machine code. While the method by which this is accomplished may be self-evident, it will be described here for the sake of completeness.

At the same time, the process of describing the procedures that must be followed in order to compile the basic compiler is intended to reveal those points at which its limitations must be eliminated if it is to develop into a complete compiler system. Since the machine independence of the language in no way depends upon the manner in which these system features are implemented, they will be pursued only in general terms.

By examining Example 38 it can be seen that the basic compiler can compile only one program at a time. This results from the fact that no method has been provided to retain values of the tallies I and J at the end of one program for use at the beginning of the next. In compiling the first compiler this problem can be overcome by combining all of the examples into one program. This requires combining all noun lists into a single list at the beginning of the program—an obvious disadvantage which would have to be eliminated before the compiler could become part of a system. On the other hand, upon completion of compilation of a group of programs, many nouns will have new values, many lists will have new entries, and areas of memory will contain symbol strings, word lists, and the object programs themselves. If normal programming techniques had been used in the writing of the compiler, all of these values would have been reset to their original condition at the start of any portion of the compiler which made use of them. In the case of a compiler, however, this standard procedure would prevent the compilation of the group of programs as a single unit. An additional routine is therefore needed. This routine, called *Clear Name Lists*, should be entered before the routine *Load Program*, and should be an optional starting point for the compiler itself. A simple routine capable of serving this purpose is shown in Example 64.

EXAMPLE 64.

Clear Name Lists:

for I = 0(1)249

{ 0 → Return Entry Name Roll[I] →

Return Entry Address Roll[I] →

Missing Name Return Entry Roll[I] →

Missing Address Needed Return Entry Roll[I] →

Entry Name Roll[I] →

Entry Address Roll[I] →

Missing Entry Name Roll[I] →

Missing Entry Address Roll[I] },

0 → Nr of Return Entry Names →

Nr of Missing Return Entry Names →

Nr of Entry Names →

Nr of Missing Entry Names,

for I = 10(1)2000{ 0 → [I],},

Load Program.

Returning to the process of compiling the compiler, let it be assumed that a hand-coded version exists in one part of the computer memory, and that it is sufficiently far removed from the areas reserved for the *Symbol String* and the *Object Program First Address* to avoid interference. Placing a paper-tape copy of the merged examples to Chapters 5 through 8 in the paper-tape reader and starting the hand-coded compiler will then result in a new compiler being generated in an area beginning at the location specified by the contents of the noun *Object Program First Address*.

At this point it is always advisable to test the newly compiled compiler by additional compilations. In order to do so, the values of the nouns *Symbol String First Address* and *Object Program First Address* must be changed, in order that the compiler not interfere with itself.

Here two further limitations are encountered that must be eliminated in a production type compiler. First, a method must be provided for readily changing the two addresses involved, preferably under the control of a monitor type program. Second, and even more obviously, there must be included a method whereby the compiler can tell the programmer the addresses at which it has compiled all of the nouns and verbs in his program.

Writing a routine which will accomplish this is quite simple, for all that is required is to have the compiler print the contents of the parallel list sets:

1. Noun Name Roll with Noun Address Roll
2. Return Entry Name Roll with Return Entry Address Roll
3. Entry Name Roll with Entry Address Roll

The addition of an optional capability to alphabetize the lists before printing them is a nice touch which has been implemented in some compilers.

Returning again to the recompilation process, it is probably best at this point to dump a copy of the basic compiler as compiled by the hand-coded version and to retain this copy for comparison with another copy to be compiled subsequently. Here again a feature which should be incorporated into a production type compiler can be noted. Despite the fact that the compilation process is so fast that Neliac compilers are usually used in the "Compile-and-Run" mode, there are conditions under which it is desirable to preserve the machine-language code of a compiled program. Usually this is done by transferring the program to either magnetic or punched tape. Such a program is not intended to be printed, but only to be reloaded into the computer. It should therefore employ a format more economical of time than those required for printers or electric typewriters. On punched tape the "Bioctal" format fits this requirement, and allows each frame to hold two octal digits, rather than the one character per frame described in Chapter 5. A complete compiler system therefore needs to include the optional ability to issue compiled programs in some such form. Since they are not to be printed, however, the system needs the further ability to verify such outputs. A solution to this part of the problem which is quite straightforward is to provide for a "Comparison Load," whereby any dumped program can be immediately reloaded, and each word compared with the original word still held in memory. If no discrepancies are found, then the "dump" is proved to be good.

After dumping a copy of the compiled basic compiler and altering the Symbol String and Object Program addresses as required, the basic compiler is again loaded and compiled, this time by the compiled version of the compiler. Next, the compiler which has just been used is wiped out, or replaced by zeros, in order to make room for yet another compilation in precisely the same area. This last compilation should yield an identical program in the area from which the earlier program dump was made. Using a comparison load with the previous dump will then confirm the fact that the compiler reproduces itself perfectly, a quality which is necessary (but not always sufficient) in establishing the fact that it contains no logical errors. The basic compiler, as well as those presented in the appendices, will do this because all of the errors which originally prevented it have been removed. It is a truism of computer programming, however, that all but the shortest programs do contain initial errors. While the proper choice of a programming language tends to reduce the number of such initial errors drastically, no language has yet been found which will completely eliminate them.

Consequently, a compiler system should contain routines which assist in detecting such errors. While the details will not be discussed here, the general requirements will be outlined. Looking back at line 31 of Example 51, the generator which handles the terminal double period, one finds a straight jump to the as yet unwritten routine DBUG. This routine should examine the two lists, Missing Entry Name Roll and Missing Name Return Entry Roll. If there are any remaining entries in either roll, this routine should print them together with the corresponding values from the Missing Entry Address Needed Roll or the Missing Address Needed Return Entry Roll. Further, the routine *Find Generator* should be expanded to provide jumps to fault routines whenever unimplemented or "illegal" Current Operator-Next Operator combinations are encountered in a program. While it is still a matter of considerable uncertainty, it appears desirable to write these fault routines in such a way that compilation does not cease upon finding a fault. In that way additional errors can usually be detected with the least possible use of computer time. Even if this technique is not used, the fault routines should at least return the compiler to the processing of any remaining uncompiled programs.

Having noted that a compiling system should assist in the detection of errors, it is only natural to extend this to a provision for assistance in their correction. One of the most frequent problems encountered in this regard arises when a large major program, consisting of many individual programs of a single page each, is to be extended or altered. The "brute force" method of reloading all of the original individual programs, and merely substituting for the few to be altered, is much too cumbersome. Instead, a method whereby an entire Symbol String can be preserved, with the ability to add a new program, or even to substitute for an old one of different length directly into the original Symbol String, has proved to be a valuable facility. Another technique which has proved useful in the correction of errors is a device for replacing a small part of a single program, again making the replacement directly into the Symbol String. This device operates in the following way. First, a portion of the original program immediately prior to the material to be altered and sufficiently long to be unique is copied on an input device. Then the corrected portion is typed. Finally, a part of the material immediately following the text to be corrected is also copied, again only enough to make it unique. The routine which handles this type of correction merely decodes the correction copy and searches the Symbol String for the first identical part of the string. It then moves the remaining Symbol String further along in memory, and adds the new material. It then starts at the other end of the Symbol String and searches for the part which is identical to the last line of the correction copy. As soon as this is found, the string from that point to the end is repacked. Even this correction technique has a disadvantage, though, unless an additional feature is provided. The disadvantage lies in the fact that after a few short corrections have been made, the documentation deteriorates. Since the documentation consists of the "hard copy" of the Neliac statement of the program itself, this problem is most difficult to solve. However, a contribution of John E. White [13] has provided a solution, by giving the compiler the capability of reconverting a symbol string to a properly spaced and legible statement of the program in the Neliac language. Appendix A itself shows the form in which the results from this routine appear.

A further feature which is useful in a complete compiler system is the capability of a program being compiled to call upon functions, subroutines, routines or complete programs already compiled and waiting at known addresses in the computer memory. This feature can readily be added by writing a routine which will be entered ahead of the Process Noun List Program, and which will accept only a program in a special form consisting solely of the names and addresses required. This feature can also be examined in the compiler given in Appendix A.

[13] Written as a portion of Neliac C, in Appendix A.

CHAPTER 10

INPUT-OUTPUT

The subject of Input-Output includes the methods by means of which compiled programs can be made to accept data from paper tapes, punched cards, or magnetic tape and to issue answers to be printed on high-speed printers or one-line electric typewriters. This subject has purposely been avoided in earlier chapters for a number of reasons.

First of these is the basic fact that the pure Algol language itself contains no input or output statements. Instead it tacitly assumes that this area is inherently machine-dependent, and that the best solution to the problem therefore lies in the use of special subroutines or procedures hand-tailored to the peripheral equipment available to an individual computer. This point of view has sufficient merit to have been initially accepted and has now proven reasonably satisfactory.

Further, many users prefer to adapt the input-output packages from other systems. Therefore the Neliac system of input-output, even though it is fundamentally machine-dependent, can scarcely be considered as an integral part of the language.

The third reason for dealing with this area as a separate entity arises because the basic compiler does not require it, and since the group of generators required is fairly lengthy, their implementation is best left until after the basic compiler is well understood.

From the foregoing it should be apparent that it is not necessary to master, or even to agree with, the material in this chapter in order to understand, to use, and even to implement either Algol or the Neliac language.

As explained in Chapter 4, one of the principles upon which the Neliac language is based is the assumption that all inherent meaning in the language itself should be restricted to symbolic operators or combinations of such operators, and that the user of the language should retain complete freedom to define any word to mean precisely what he wants it to mean. Fundamentally this principle is maintained in the Neliac approach to a machine-independent input-output system.

Output

Two basic types of output must be handled. First, there must be an ability for the writer of a program to specify any words, phrases, or symbols he wants to have printed verbatim. This has been referred to as Form 1. Second, there must be an ability to call for the printing of the numerical values of nouns and noun arrays. This will be referred to as Form 2. While statements which combine these two will be needed, they do not constitute a separate class.

By giving a secondary meaning to the comparison symbols *Less Than*, <, and *Greater Than*, >, and having that meaning depend upon the context in which they are used, a type of quotation mark can be realized. By using these quotation marks in various ways, at least three different meanings can be conveyed.

An examination of Table V shows that the Current Operator-Next Operator combination of punctuation followed by a left brace is not used. Consequently, the *Find Generator* routine can be extended slightly so that it will direct the flow to an additional generator, called *Generate Input Output*.

If, for instance, a Form 1 statement such as:

$$, \{ \; << \; || \; P \; | \; Q \; | \; R \; | \; S \; || \; >> \; \}$$

appeared in a program, the first two operators would be sufficient to transfer the flow to the input-output generator. From that point until the right brace was reached, all earlier rules regarding the meanings of operators would not need to apply. The second CO–NO combination, *left brace-less than,* would be adequate to signal that the output portion of the generator was needed. At this point if the fourth operator is another "less than" symbol, which signifies that a verbatim printing is required, the process can then be directed accordingly. If the fourth operator had not been a second "less than" symbol, but instead had been part of a Form 2 statement, such as:

$$,\{ \; < \; || \; T \; | \; U \; | \; V \; | \; W \; || \; > \; \}$$
$$,\{ \; < \; || \; T[I] \; \uparrow \; \uparrow \; \uparrow \; > \; \}$$

or $\qquad ,\{ \; < \; | \; T[0 \rightarrow J] \; | \; U[0 \rightarrow J] \; \uparrow \; > \; \}$

the output of numerical values of nouns or arrays would have been intended. In no case is it necessary to find an operand between these first three operators.

In implementing Form 2 output statements, an additional important problem must be solved. This is the problem of *format,* or the manner in which numerical data are to be presented. This involves more than the mere spacing of rows and columns of figures, since even the number of digits in a number, the number system to be used, and the choice of scientific or fixed-point notation must be under the control of the user. In the Neliac output system, the compiler must obtain this type of information from the noun list, rather than from the output statement itself.

The following table illustrates the form into which numbers must be converted depending upon the use of zeros in the noun list. It can be noted that the number of zeros specifies the number of digits to be printed, except that a single zero specifies not one, but all available digits. There is no way to call for the printing of a single digit directly, but since leading zeros are suppressed, it can be done indirectly.

TABLE VI

DETERMINATION OF OUTPUT FORMAT FROM NOUN LIST ENTRIES

Form in Noun List	Form in Print-Out	Comments
A $= 0_8$,	1234567012345_8	
B $= 00_8$,	45_8	
C $= 000_8$,	345_8	
D $= 0000$,	7890	No decimal point or sign
E $= 000.00$,	$+931.72$	Integer arithmetic with arbitrary decimal point
F $= 000.00 \times 0$,	$+931.72$	Floating point arithmetic with true decimal point
G $= O \times 0$,	$+.1234567890 \times 10\uparrow +123$	Floating point
H $= 0000 \times 00$,	$+.1234 \times 10\uparrow +23$	

Whether or not there should be suppression of the sign when it is positive, and of leading zeros in a full octal number, appears to be immaterial.

It is interesting to speculate upon the applicability of the technique of Table VI to that class of computers having no specified word length. In such computers, might not the user specify his desired precision in the same way, letting the compiler itself furnish some standard whenever only single zeros were encountered?

Returning to the output statement itself, the compiler must also respond to the notation used to specify line spacing, paging, and termination of output. This notation consists of a comma, semicolon, and period, respectively, placed after the final quotation mark and before the right brace.

Commas found in this position signal the need for the compiler to generate the instructions for as many blank line feeds or carriage returns as there are commas, while a semicolon signals the need to advance to a new page. The period should be treated as an end-of-file or as a signal to turn off equipment depending upon the circumstances.

Form 3 statements, used for input, reverse the order of the quotation marks, as:

$$, \{> Y <\}$$

and will be discussed later.

Before studying the details of the process, it should be noted that the absolute sign, | , which is used here to indicate spacing, must have only a relative meaning, since the number of spaces on a line of output will vary from one type of printing device to another. Further, it should be apparent that if a given installation operates with a policy of "off-line" use of printers, reached via magnetic tape or other output from the computer itself, then the compiler input-output generators should reflect this policy without concerning the program writers using the system.

While it is not the intention here to examine input-output generators in great detail, they do tend to be sufficiently different from others that a few techniques will be illustrated. In order to do so, the basic compiler of the previous chapters will be utilized. Accordingly, lines 53, 54, and 55 of Example 43 can be replaced by the following text.

EXAMPLE 65.

Test A 21:
  if Next Operator < EQUAL: go to Test A 211.
  if not, go to Generator 8.

Test A 211:
  if Next Operator = LEFT Brace: go to Generate Input Output.
  if not, go to Generator 7.

The generator itself could then be divided into various parts, with the first as simple as the following example.

EXAMPLE 66.

Generate Input Output:
  Find Next Symbol,
  if Symbol = Less Than: go to Generate Output.
  if not, Generate Input.

Generate Output:
  Find Next Symbol,
  if Symbol = Less Than: Generate Heading.
  if not, Generate Data.

The next example will follow the process for the particular case in which a verbatim printing is specified, the *Generate Heading* routine. Since this particular generator would not normally be added until such features as loops and partial word capability had been implemented, their availability will be assumed. Nevertheless, only a basic version of the generator will be shown.

The problem to be solved by this generator can be stated quite simply. First, the generator must examine the message to be printed, counting separately the spacing symbols and the symbols in the textual material. Because relative spacing is used, the value of a space symbol must be calculated by the compiler. This can only be done after the complete message has been tabulated and compared with the number of characters available on a line of the printing device. It must then provide storage in the object program to retain the message, complete with absolute spacing, for use at "run-time." Because of the spacing uncertainty, each symbol cannot be stored directly into the object program as the message is read. Consequently, a temporary storage area must be maintained elsewhere during the compilation process.

Furthermore, the internal compiler code is most unlikely to coincide with the code of any printer, so that an encoding process must be performed before the characters in the message can be stored in the object program. This encoding task will be simplified in the next example by assuming that an on-line electric typewriter is the printer of choice.[14]

After converting the message to proper form, and storing it in the object program, the generator must produce the instructions necessary to select the printer and operate it as required. The number of instructions required for this purpose varies greatly from one computer to another, and may be fairly sizable. The most obvious way to handle this problem is to place these instructions, or at least their invariant parts, in the noun list of the generator as an

[14] In the general case this should not be true. Ordinarily, the word FLEX is inserted between the left brace and the less-than sign if electric typewriter printing is intended. Nevertheless, if a program containing the word FLEX is compiled on a machine not having one, the machine language instructions for high-speed printer output will automatically be generated instead.

array. At compilation time these instructions can be modified as required, and transferred as a block into the object program.

While this technique is adequate to perform the task, and is used in Example 67, it should be considerably refined for regular use. Possible refinements will be treated later.

The noun list of this example can be considered in two parts. The first 24 nouns are those which would be required for any computer, while the array called *Heading Code* will have both its number of entries and their numerical values determined by the particular computer involved.

EXAMPLE 67.

Less Than = 51,
Greater Than = 49,
Absolute Sign = 58,
Heading Count,
Heading Space Count,
Heading Word Count,
Heading Store First Address = 2000_8,
Heading Store Last Address,
Heading Skip Address Needed,
Line Length = 60,
Space = 04,
Spacing,
Save Word,
New Word,
Save Divisor,
Save Symbol,
Store Symbol Counter,
Last Case Flag,
Save L,
Save K,
Save I,
Save M,
Save N,
Heading Code(38) =

16 110 00000$_8$,   16 210 00000$_8$,   12 100 00000$_8$,
12 200 00000$_8$,   17 040 00000$_8$,   52 000 00160$_8$,
13 070 00000$_8$,   50 000 00160$_8$,   13 070 00000$_8$,
13 300 10012$_8$,   70 000 40000$_8$,   12 030 00001$_8$,
13 300 00000$_8$,   13 300 10013$_8$,   70 000 40000$_8$,
12 030 00001$_8$,   17 140 00000$_8$,   17 040 00000$_8$,
50 000 00003$_8$,   13 070 00000$_8$,   12 200 00000$_8$,
11 031 00000$_8$,   62 100 00000$_8$,   13 170 00000$_8$,
02 000 00006$_8$,   16 200 00000$_8$,   27 000 00004$_8$,
60 200 00000$_8$,   12 202 00001$_8$,   60 100 00000$_8$,
12 200 00000$_8$,   16 140 00000$_8$,   21 000 00014$_8$,
60 400 00000$_8$,   12 101 00001$_8$,   60 100 00000$_8$,
12 110 00000$_8$,   12 210 00000$_8$;

Generate Heading:

J → Heading Skip Address Needed,

JUMP → [J], J + 1 → J,

Heading Store First Address → L,

O → L → Heading Count → Heading Space Count,

Read Headings:

Find Next Symbol,

if Symbol = Greater Than: Find Relative Spacing.

if not, ;

if Symbol = CLEAR: Read Headings.

if Symbol = Exponent Sign: Ten + Heading Space Count →
Heading Space Count, Retain Symbol.

if not, ;

if Symbol = Absolute Sign: 1 + Heading Space Count →
Heading Space Count;

if not, 1 + Heading Count → Heading Count;

Retain Symbol:

[L] → Buffer,

if Buffer < Nearly Full: Buffer × Symbol Size +
Symbol → [L];

if not, Buffer × Symbol Size + Symbol → [L],
L + 1 → L, O → [L];

Read Headings.

Find Relative Spacing:
  if Heading Count + Heading Space Count > Line Length:
      1 → Spacing;
  if not, (Line Length − Heading Count) / Heading
      Space Count → Spacing;
Preset To Convert:
  FULL → New Divisor,
  0 → New Word,
  L + 1 → Heading Store Last Address,
  Heading Store First Address → L,
Obtain Heading Symbols:
  Find Next Heading Symbol,
  if Symbol = Exponent Sign: Store Many Spaces,
      Test Midway Point.
  if not, ;
  if Symbol = Absolute Sign: Store Spaces,
      Test Midway Point.
  if not, ;
  Convert To Flex,
  if Last Case Flag = Upper-Case Flag: Store Symbol;
  if not, Store Case Change;
Test Midway Point:
  if L = Heading Store Last Address: Compile Heading.
  if not, Obtain Heading Symbols.
Compile Heading:
  Heading Skip Address Needed → M,
  [M] + J → [M],
  J + 4 → Heading Code[0](0→14) → Heading Code[36](0→14),
  J + 6 → Heading Code[1](0→14) → Heading Code[37](0→14),
  J + 21 → Heading Code[35](0→14),
  M + 1 → Heading Code[21](0→14),
  J + 22 → Heading Code[22](0→14) →
      Heading Code[29](0→14),
  J + 30 → Heading Code[27](0→14),
  J + 36 → Heading Code[33](0→14),
  Heading Word Count − 1 → Heading Code[32](0→14),
  for M = 0(1)35

{ Heading Code[M] → [J], J + 1 →J, },

Reset NO:

  Find Next Symbol,

  if Symbol = Right Brace: COMMA → Next Operator,
    Advance.

  if not, Reset NO.

Find Next Heading Symbol:

  { I → SAVE I, Word → Save Word, Divisor → Save Divisor,
    New Word → Word, New Divisor → Divisor, L → I,
    Find Next Symbol,
    I → L, Save I → I, Word → New Word, Divisor →
      New Divisor,
    Save Word → Word, Save Divisor → Divisor,},

Convert To Flex:

  { for K = 0(1)63

    { if Upper Case Code[K] = Symbol: K → Scratch Pad,
        1→ Upper Case Flag;

      if not, ;

      if Lower Case Code[K] = Symbol: K → Scratch Pad,
        0 → Upper Case Flag;

      if not, ; },

    Scratch Pad → Symbol,},

Store Symbol:

  { if Store Symbol Counter = 0: Symbol → [J](0→5);;

    if Store Symbol Counter = 1: Symbol → [J](6→11);;

    if Store Symbol Counter = 2: Symbol → [J](12→17);;

    if Store Symbol Counter = 3: Symbol → [J](18→23);;

    if Store Symbol Counter = 4: Symbol → [J](24→29),
        0 → Store Symbol Counter, J + 1 → J,
        Heading Word Count + 1 → Heading Word Count;

    if not, Store Symbol Counter + 1 → Store Symbol
        Counter; } ,

Store Case Change:

  { Symbol → Save Symbol,

    if Upper Case Flag → Last Case Flag = Set:
        Upper Case → Symbol;

if not, Lower Case → Symbol;
Store Symbol,
Save Symbol → Symbol,
Store Symbol, },
Store Spaces:
{ for N = 1(1)Spacing
{ Space → Symbol, Store Symbol, },},
Store Many Spaces:
{ Spacing × 10 → Spacing,
Store Spaces,
Spacing / 10 → Spacing, }. .

While most of Example 67 should be self-explanatory, it does make use of a few techniques which might require further explanation. The routine called *Compile Heading*, for instance, takes advantage of the way in which bit notation operates to leave the invariant parts of the array called *Heading Code* undisturbed.

Similarly, the negative-word problem encountered so often in earlier generators is avoided completely with the use of bit notation, as shown in the subroutine called *Store Symbol*. On the other hand, the previously written subroutine called *Find Next Symbol* is exploited by the subroutine *Find Next Heading Symbol*. This requires that all dynamic variables in the first subroutine be preserved, while a new set is substituted. After the first subroutine has been used by the second, the dynamic variables from the second must then be replaced by those from the first.

The methods shown in Example 67, as mentioned earlier, would require considerable refinement for any serious use. The most obvious deficiency lies in the fact that while only a few of the 38 Heading Code instructions require modification to suit an individual case, they are all inserted every time that the generator is called upon. Instead, the compiler would be made to treat them as a subroutine which it would insert only once, and thereafter insert a set of modifying instructions and a return jump to the subroutine. Another deficiency, which is not as serious in this generator as it would be in other output generators, concerns the length of the

Heading Code array. The very length of such arrays may become too great for the available memory space. A possible solution to this problem might lie in devising a method whereby the compiler could hold only the Symbol String corresponding to the Heading Code array, and then compile that into temporary storage within the compiler only when it was needed.

The *Generate Data* routine is somewhat more complex, since it must include in the object program a subroutine for the conversion of binary fixed or floating-point numbers to decimal, as well as the instructions for looping whenever the contents of lists are to be printed. Interaction of, and extensions to both generators are required if a statement of the form:

$$,\{ \;<<\; \| \; \text{ANSWER} \; | \; = \; | \; > \; Y \; < \; | \; \text{VOLTS} \; \| \; >>;\}$$

is to be handled.

Looking back at the examples, it can be seen that any operand inserted between the comma and the left brace will be ignored. Therefore it is permissible to write a phrase, such as *Print Headings,* or even *Schreiben Sie die Namen* there if desired.

An operand inserted between the left brace and the first comparative sign, on the other hand, should be read and compared with a list of any alternatives available to a given computer. If the requested one is not found, the generator should automatically substitute the instructions for the device of choice of the particular installation.

As an instrument for automation or Real-Time Control, the ability to specify output to any control device in this way is quite useful.

Input

The use of Form 3 to specify input to a computer is fairly straightforward. Basically all that is required is a generator which will compile the instructions given in Example 39 in machine language.

Example 68 shows the details of a simple generator to read one word at a time from punched tape into a Control Data Corporation 1604 computer.

EXAMPLE 68.

CARD = 51 49 41 52 20 20 20 20$_8$,

FLEX 1 = 66 43 65 27 20 01 20 20$_8$,

FLEX 8 = 66 43 65 27 20 10 20 20$_8$,

INPUT CODE(8) =

740	11200	100	00000$_8$,	200	00001	741	00000$_8$,
750	00000	500	00000$_8$,	571	00000	747	00011$_8$,
040	00077	501	00000$_8$,	050	00006	431	00000$_8$,
541	00007	750	00000$_8$,	531	00000	200	00000$_8$,

FACTOR = 1 000 00000$_8$,

LIMIT;

GENERATE INPUT OUTPUT:

  FIND OPERATOR,

  PRESENT OPERATOR = LESS THAN: GENERATE OUTPUT.
    GENERATE INPUT.

  GENERATE INPUT:

OPERAND = FLEX 1 U OPERAND = FLEX 8: GENERATE
  FLEX INPUT.;

OPERAND = CARD: GENERATE CARD INPUT. GENERATE
  MT INPUT.

GENERATE FLEX INPUT:

  OPERAND = FLEX 8: GENERATE FLEX WORD INPUT.
    GENERATE FLEX FRAME INPUT.

GENERATE FLEX WORD INPUT:

  FILL UPPER HALF WORD,

  747 00011$_8$ → [I](0→23), I + 1 → I,

  INPUT CODE[0] + I + 11 → [I], I + 1 → I,

  INPUT CODE[1] + I + 2 → [I], I + 1 → I,

  INPUT CODE[2] + FACTOR × I + FACTOR × 10 →
    [I], I + 1 → I,

  I + 8 → LIMIT,

  FOR I = I(1)LIMIT { 0 → [I]}

  INPUT CODE[3] + FACTOR × I − FACTOR →
    [I], I + 1 → I,

  INPUT CODE[4] → [I], I + 1 → I,

INPUT CODE[5] + I − 11 → [I], I + 1 → I,
INPUT CODE[6] + I − 1 → [I], I + 1 → I,
FIND OPERATOR,
FIND ADDRESS,
INPUT CODE[7] + FACTOR × I − FACTOR × 5 +
    ADDRESS → [I], I + 1 → I,
PRESENT OPERATOR ≠ LESS THAN: FAULT;;
FIND OPERATOR,
PRESENT OPERATOR ≠ RIGHT BRACE: FAULT;;
0 → HALF WORD FLAG, COMMA → PRESENT OPERATOR,
OPERATOR ENTRY. .

CHAPTER 11

DECOMPILING WITH D-NELIAC

For several years it has been apparent that those computer programs written in machine-dependent languages represented large investments in time which were lost whenever a change in computers was required. Even though a change to a machine-independent language was made, all programs written before the change still require complete rewriting if they are to remain in use.

If, however, such programs could be computer-converted to the Neliac language, then they would be in a form adaptable to recompilation upon any other computer having a Neliac compiler. Furthermore, if the translator were to be capable of accepting the machine-language programs of a given computer as input, then it would not matter whether the program had originally been written in machine language, in an assembly system, or any possible problem-oriented compiler system.

While it would be premature to infer that this objective can be met with complete satisfaction, the Donnelly D-Neliac system [15] as produced by J. K. Donnelly and Herman Englander has already established that such an approach is highly feasible, and preliminary versions now exist for both the Remington Rand Univac M-460

[15] J. K. Donnelly, "A Decompiler for the Countess Computer," *Navy Electronics Laboratory Technical Memorandum 427*, Sept., 1960.

Countess computer and for the Control Data Corporation 1604 computer. A recent version of the former is given in complete detail in Appendix D.

To understand the workings of a decompiler, consider the following case, in which Example 69 shows the source material, a machine-language version of a program which has been written, tested, and rendered operational on the M-460 Countess.

EXAMPLE 69.

Address	ff	jkb	yyyyy	Address	ff	jkb	yyyyy
10100	00	000	00000	10142	07	000	00036
10101	00	000	00000	10143	03	000	00036
10102	00	000	00000	10144	23	030	10106
10103	00	000	00000	10145	14	030	10107
10104	00	000	00000	10146	61	010	10131
10105	00	000	00000	10147	10	030	10103
10106	00	000	00000	10150	26	030	10100
10107	00	000	00000	10151	22	030	10106
10110	00	000	00000	10152	14	030	10107
10111	00	000	00000	10153	10	030	10100
10112	00	000	00000	10154	27	630	10103
10113	00	000	00000	10155	65	000	10113
10114	10	030	10103	10156	11	030	10100
10115	35	030	10100	10157	10	030	10106
10116	61	010	10113	10160	27	000	00001
10117	00	000	00000	10161	04	430	10103
10120	10	000	00005	10162	61	000	10165
10121	26	030	10100	10163	65	000	10117
10122	27	730	10106	10164	61	000	10166
10123	61	000	10126	10165	65	000	10131
10124	65	000	10113	10166	61	000	10167
10125	61	000	10130	10167	12	100	00000
10126	10	030	10103	10170	10	000	00170
10127	34	030	10100	10171	40	031	10103
10130	61	010	10117	10172	07	000	00073
10131	00	000	00000	10173	41	031	10100

10132	10	030	10106	10174	07	000	00072
10133	26	030	10103	10175	14	031	10107
10134	07	000	00036	10176	71	100	00002
10135	03	000	00036	10177	61	000	10170
10136	23	030	10106	10200	10	030	10103
10137	26	030	10107	10201	14	030	10106
10140	22	030	10100	10202	61	400	10000
10141	26	030	10103				

The program of Example 69 was then accepted by the Decompiler of Appendix D, which found all of the absolute addresses used as nouns or verbs, and assigned arbitrary names to them. The program logic itself was then decoded into the equivalent Neliac statements, as shown in Example 70.

EXAMPLE 70.

4
A STORE,
Q STORE,
AA(3),
AB(3),
AC,
AD(4), ;

START: (AA + AB) $\times$ AC $\rightarrow$ AD ,
AB − AA $\geq$ 0: ;
   SUB B,
AB $\rightarrow$ A STORE,
AC − 1 $\rightarrow$ Q STORE,
Q STORE $\geq$ AA $\cap$ A STORE < AA : ;
   ENT E.
SUB A,
ENT A.
ENT E: SUB C,
ENT A: ENT B.
ENT B: 0 $\rightarrow$ i,
i = i(1)2{ AA[i] (3 $\rightarrow$ 6) + AB[i] (2 $\rightarrow$ 5) $\rightarrow$ AD[i] , } ,

```
AA → AC,
HALT.
SUB C: { (((AC + AA)/ AC + AD )× AB + AA)/ AC → AD, } .
SUB B: { AB − AA → AB , } .
SUB A: { 5 + AB − AC < 0: ;
    ENT D.
SUB B,
ENT C.
ENT D: AB + AA → AB ,
ENT C: } .
HALT: . .
```

In addition to producing the Neliac version solely from the machine-coded version of the program, the decompiler also produced a listing of the various names which it assigned, as shown in Example 71.

EXAMPLE 71.

```
SUB A 0 10117
  ENT A 0 10166
  ENT B 0 10167
  SUB B 0 10113
  ENT C 0 10130
  ENT D 0 10126
  ENT E 0 10165
  SUB C 0 10131
  START 0 10147
AA 3 10103
AB 3 10100
AC 3 10106
AD 3 10107
```

where an initial zero denotes a verb and a 3 indicates a noun.

It may be noted that in a case of this kind there is no inherent meaning in the names assigned to nouns or verbs, except perhaps to the first and last of the verbs. If the original documentation has been adequate, so that the comments accompanying the original program has been sufficiently informative to allow a person to provide meaningful names for given addresses, the decompiler will accept and use them.

As can be seen from a study of Appendix D, in the event that a machine-language combination is encountered for which no decompilation instructions have been written it can still convert them to the Neliac machine-language form, and then continue. Strangely enough, working with decompilers has emphasized one of the limitations in the bit-handling capabilities of the Neliac language. This limitation consists of the inability to specify any but contiguous bits in a part word, a feature sometimes used in masking for logical operations.

In addition to its primary mission of translating non-Neliac programs into the Neliac language, D-Neliac has also proved useful in another way. This secondary use has been in the area of error detection. Since a program will appear in different words, and with several of the details handled differently if it is decompiled after having been compiled, the paraphrased version is sometimes helpful in the detection of errors in logic. A classic example is a case in which an occasionally used regression-analysis program was found to fault in certain circumstances. Since the program had originally been coded in machine language by a mathematician no longer available, the fault was so subtle that it had not been found, even after considerable searching. Upon decompilation, however, it was immediately apparent that a misuse of an index occasionally occurred.

A final pair of examples will show the decompilation of one of the utility routines long in use on the Countess for loading flexowriter coded punched tape. This particular routine calls upon other subroutines outside the area being decompiled, so that while the decompiler named them, it obviously could record only their locations, and not their contents. The numerical values for the Flexowriter codes in Table III correspond with results in this case, too, of course. The first example shows the raw program as fed to the D-Neliac program, the second shows the Neliac program which it produced', while the third shows the *Name List* which it also furnished.

EXAMPLE 72.

Address	ff	jkb	yyyyy	Address	ff	jkb	yyyyy
00522	00	000	00000	00565	12	130	00130
00523	65	000	00352	00566	10	030	00132
00524	65	000	00211	00567	14	031	00000
00525	16	030	00130	00570	61	000	00526
00526	16	030	00131	00571	65	000	00346
00527	16	030	00132	00572	12	500	00007
00530	12	300	00000	00573	10	030	00130
00531	10	030	00130	00574	27	515	00133
00532	27	500	00051	00575	61	000	00541
00533	61	000	00571	00576	72	500	00573
00534	10	030	00130	00577	11	530	00130
00535	27	500	00045	00600	61	000	00571
00536	61	000	00571	00601	10	030	00130
00537	65	000	00346	00602	27	500	00004
00540	61	000	00526	00603	61	000	00571
00541	10	003	00000	00604	10	030	00130
00542	27	700	00005	00605	27	500	00057
00543	61	000	00553	00606	61	000	00571
00544	10	030	00131	00607	10	030	00130
00545	05	000	00003	00610	27	500	00047
00546	14	030	00467	00611	61	000	00571
00547	10	005	00000	00612	10	030	00130
00550	26	030	00467	00613	27	500	00077
00551	14	030	00131	00614	61	000	00571
00552	61	000	00561	00615	10	030	00130
00553	10	030	00132	00616	27	400	00042
00554	05	000	00003	00617	61	000	00526
00555	14	030	00467	00620	65	000	00346
00556	10	005	00000	00621	10	030	00130
00557	26	030	00467	00622	27	400	00042
00560	14	030	00132	00623	61	000	00526

00561	12	303	00001	00624	65	000	00265
00562	10	003	00000	00625	65	000	00363
00563	27	400	00017	00626	61	010	00522
00564	61	000	00571	00627	00	000	00000

EXAMPLE 73.

5

;

START: { SUB A,

SUB B,

O → aa,

ENT A: 0 → ab,

0 → ac.

0 → k,

aa − 51_8 ≠ 0: ;

    ENT B.

aa − 45_8 ≠ 0: ;

    ENT B.

SUB C,

ENT A.

ENT D: k − 5 < 0: ;

    ENT F.

ab × 2↑3 → ad,

m + ad → ab,

ENT E.

ENT F: ac × 2↑3 → ad,

m + ad → ac,

ENT E: 1 + k → k,

k − 17_8 = 0: ;

    ENT B.

ab → i,

ac → [i],

ENT A.

ENT B: SUB C,

7 → m,

m = m(1)0{ aa − ae[m](0 → 14) ≠ 0: ;

    ENT D. } ,

aa $\neq$ 0: ;
   ENT B.
aa $-$ 4 $\neq$ 0: ;
   ENT B.
aa $-$ 57_8 $\neq$ 0: ;
   ENT B.
aa $-$ 47_8 $\neq$ 0: ;
   ENT B.
aa $-$ 77_8 $\neq$ 0: ;
   ENT B.
aa $-$ 42_8 $=$ 0: ;
   ENT A.
SUB C,
aa $-$ 42_8 $=$ 0: ;
   ENT A.
SUB D,
SUB E, } .

. .

EXAMPLE 74.
SUB A   0 352
SUB B   0 211
SUB C   0 346
ENT A   0 526
ENT B   0 571
SUB D   0 265
SUB E   0 363
ENT C   0 522
ENT D   0 541
ENT E   0 561
ENT F   0 553
START   0 522
AA   3 130
AB   3 131
AC   3 132
AD   3 467
AE   3 133

NELIAC C

In order to illustrate methods and techniques which could not be covered in earlier chapters, a complete production type compiler will be reproduced in this appendix. Neliac C, which operates on the Remington Rand Univac M-460 Countess—a computer with 32,000 words of magnetic core memory, a word size of 30 bits, and an average execution time of approximately 20 microseconds—has been chosen for this purpose for a number of reasons. First, it has been developed entirely by the bootstrapping method, having grown from a basic compiler like the one described in the text entirely in its own language. Second, it illustrates in complete detail all of those supplementary features referred to in the text, including both the additional generators and an error-testing capability, as well as various utility routines. In addition, it demonstrates the use of "level arithmetic" as required for algebraic grouping, as well as the methods required for a computer which does not include a floating point capability in the hardware itself.

Because the compiler has been developed over a period of time, with several people contributing to it at different stages of its development, many of the words used in it do not coincide exactly with those in the text. For example, the word *Flowchart* in Neliac C is merely a synonym for *Symbol String*, while the word *Character* sometimes agrees with the usage in the text, but more often refers to *Symbol* instead. Despite certain anachronisms, it produces quite efficient machine code, at a rather high rate of speed.

Neliac C is not intended as a final solution, however, as ways obviously can still be found to improve virtually every routine within it. When improved methods are found, however, as they have often been, they are merely substituted and recompiled, yielding an improved version.

In order to make this compiler somewhat easier to follow, its internal compiler code and its complete CO-NO table are shown in Tables VII and VIII. The compiler itself is presented in the form resulting from its own Dump A Flowchart routine, as printed by an ANalex high-speed printer having the complete Neliac character set.

TABLE VII

THE INTERNAL COMPILER CODE OF NELIAC C

Symbol	Octal	Decimal	Symbol	Octal	Decimal
Space	00	00	5	40	32
A *or* a	01	01	6	41	33
B *or* b	02	02	7	42	34
C *or* c	03	03	8	43	35
D *or* d	04	04	9	44	36
E *or* e	05	05	8	45	37
F *or* f	06	06	,	46	38
G *or* g	07	07	;	47	39
H *or* h	10	08	.	50	40
I *or* i	11	09	:	51	41
J *or* j	12	10	(	52	42
K *or* k	13	11	)	53	43
L *or* l	14	12	[	54	44
M *or* m	15	13	]	55	45
N *or* n	16	14	{	56	46
O *or* o	17	15	}	57	47
P *or* p	20	16	=	60	48
Q *or* q	21	17	≠	61	49
R *or* r	22	18	≥	62	50
S *or* s	23	19	<	63	51

T *or* t	24	20		$\leq$	64	52
U *or* u	25	21		$>$	65	53
V *or* v	26	22		$\rightarrow$	66	54
W *or* w	27	23		$+$	67	55
X *or* x	30	24		$-$	70	56
Y *or* y	31	25		/	71	57
Z *or* z	32	26		$\times$	72	58
0	33	27		Color Shift	73	59
1	34	28		|	74	60
2	35	29		$\cup$	75	61
3	36	30		$\cap$	76	62
4	37	31		$\uparrow$	77	63

TABLE VIII

THE CURRENT OPERATOR-NEXT OPERATOR TABLE FOR NELIAC C

Next Operator

	,	;	.	:	(	)	[	]	{	}	=	≠	≥	<	≤	>	→	+	−	/	×	$_8$	∪	∩	↑
,	4	4	3	29	6	4	23		21	4	10	10	10	10	10	10	10	11	11	17	13	10			
;	4	4	3	29	6	4	23		21	4	10	10	10	10	10	10	10	11	11	17	13	10			
.	4	4	3	29	6	4	23		21	4	10	10	10	10	10	10	10	11	11	17	13	10			
:	4	4	3	5	6	4	23		21	4	10	10	10	10	10	10	10	11	11	17	13	10	10	10	
(					6	20	23										20	7	7	17	13				
)		9				8	23		21	9	9	9	9	9	9	9	9	8	8	18	14		9	9	
[								25						22		22			24	24					
]																									
{	4	4	3	29	6	4	23			4	10	10	10	10	10	10	10	11	11	17	13	10			
}																									
=		1	1				23											1	1	1	1	1	1	1	
≠		1	1				23											1	1	1	1	1	1	1	
≥		1	1				23											1	1	1	1	1	1	1	
<		1	1				23								1			1	1	1	1	1	1	1	
≤		1	1				23											1	1	1	1	1	1	1	
>		1	1				23											1	1	1	1	1	1	1	
→	19	19	19	19	26	19	23				19	19	19	19	19	19	19	19	19	19	19	19	19	19	
+				10	6	10	23	25	21		10	10	10	10	10	10	10	11	11	17	13	10	10	10	
−				12	6	12	23	25	21		12	12	12	12	12	12	12	12	12	17	13		12	12	
/				16	6	16	23				16	16	16	16	16	16	16	16	16	16	16		16	16	
×				15	6	15	23				15	15	15	15	15	15	15	15	15	15	15		15	15	
$_8$																									
∪					6		23				10	10	10	10	10	10	10	11	11	17	13	10		10	
∩					6		23				10	10	10	10	10	10	10	11	11	17	13	10		10	
↑																									

 0. Fault
 1. Initiate relation control
 2. Fault
 3. Generate straight jump
 4. Generate return jump
 5. Check partial word
 6. Check for algebra
 7. Check for negative loop increment
 8. Check for loop limits
 9. Clear temp list
10. Generate add or enter
11. Generate add
12. Generate subtract
13. Generate multiply
14. Generate multiply quantity or expression
15. Generate multiply or enter
16. Generate divide
17. Generate divide or enter
18. Generate divide quantity or expression
19. Generate store
20. Initiate loop control
21. Set exit conditions
22. Generate IO
23. Initiate subscript
24. Modify subscript
25. Set subscript
26. Save current operator
27. Generate add or enter
28. Initiate relation control
29. Generator exit.

The version presented here is one written by Lt. John E. White and Ensign Arthur Lemay, whose cooperation in preparing it is greatly appreciated.

5
name part 1(1000_8), name part 2(1000_8), name part 3(1000_8),
OPERAND LIST: | name dumped flag(27 → 29), name temp flag(27 → 29),
name k desig(18 → 20), name address(0 → 14), |(1000_8),
NAME MASK: | name mask length(0 → 4), name mask lower limit(5 → 9),
list length(10 → 21), matrix width(22 → 28),
name floating flag(29 → 29), |(1000_8),
undefined name 1(200_8), undefined name 2(200_8), undefined name 3(200_8),
| undefined name location(15 → 29), mask record(0 → 14), |(200_8),
address corr list(200_8),
| first obj prog address(15 → 29), sequence number(0 → 14), |,
| current obj prog last address(15 → 29), program entry address(0 → 14), |,
OBJ PROG LIMITS:
| obj prog first addr(15 → 29), obj prog last addr(0 → 14), |(100_8),
FLOCHART LIMITS:
| flochart first addr(15 → 29), flochart last addr(0 → 14), |(100_8),
| name index(0 → 14), entrance addr(15 → 29), |(100_8), floating entrance,
| debug flag(15 → 29), glossary flag(0 → 14), |, key(4), bias,
| final seq nr(0 → 14), entrance flag(15 → 29), |,
first comparison(20), correction(20), second comparison(20),
| ts ready flag(0 → 14), ts address record(15 → 29), |(20),
| tc offset(15 → 29), tc reg flag(0 → 14), |(50),
| tc mask flag(15 → 29), level list(0 → 14), |(50),
TEMP LIST: | temp list function(24 → 29), |(50),
ADDRESS LIMITS: | first address(15 → 29), last address(0 → 14), |,
exit condition list(25),
| temp fc storage(15 → 29), temp pc storage(0 → 14), |,
| flo chrt addr storage(15 → 29), comparison lockout flag(0 → 14), |,
operand, previous operand, operand storage(4),
LOAD BUFFER:
| first frame load buffer(0 → 5), last frame load buffer(24 → 29),
upper load buffer(15 → 29), lower load buffer(0 → 14), |(3),
DUMP BUFFER:
| first frame dump buffer(0 → 5), last frame dump buffer(24 → 29),
upper dump buffer(15 → 29), lower dump buffer(0 → 14), |(3),
NAME BUFFER: | first frame name buffer(0 → 5), upper name buffer(15 → 29),
last frame name buffer(24 → 29), |(3),
FLOWCHART BUFFER: | first frame flowchart buffer(0 → 5), |,
temp fb storage, function code, j designator, k designator,
b designator, number accumulator(2), mask accumulator, full operand,
operand flag, | current operator(0 → 14), temp co storage(15 → 29), |,
| next operator(0 → 14), present character(15 → 29), |,
| flex code character(0 → 14), compiler code character(15 → 29), |,
a function, q function, | offset(0 → 14), op offset(15 → 29), |,
| level(0 → 14), reg flag(15 → 29), |,
| op reg flag(0 → 14), tl reg flag(15 → 29), |,
| space flag(0 → 14), back space flag(15 → 29), |,
| frame counter(0 → 14), character counter(15 → 29), |,
| carriage return counter(0 → 14), carriage return flag(15 → 29), |,
| comparison counter(0 → 14), comparison type(15 → 29), |,
| true alt address(0 → 14), false alt address(15 → 29), |,
| correction length(0 → 14), lessless comparison(15 → 29), |,
| clear flag(0 → 14), zero flag(15 → 29), |,
| temp list index(0 → 14), comparison level(15 → 29), |,
| lower loop limit(0 → 14), upper loop limit(15 → 29), |(2),
| punch on flag(0 → 14), flex on flag(15 → 29), |,
| title flag(0 → 14), load type(15 → 29), |,
| loop control flag(0 → 14), exit condition counter(15 → 29), |,
| partial word flag(0 → 14), negative flag(15 → 29), |,

```
| divide inst address(0 → 14), case flag(15 → 29),   |,
| octal flag(0 → 14), neg number flag(15 → 29),   |,
| name found flag(0 → 14), unknown operand flag(15 → 29),   |,
| type name flag(0 → 14), right shift flag(15 → 29),   |,
| shift flag 1(0 → 14), shift flag(15 → 29),   |,
BIT LIMITS: | lower bit limit(0 → 14), upper bit limit(15 → 29),   |,
| last lower bit limit(0 → 14), last upper bit limit(15 → 29),   |,
| bit limit flag(0 → 14),   |,
| manual entry flag(0 → 14), end relation symbol(15 → 29),   |,
first shift, second shift, temp skip storage(2),
| temp name flag(0 → 14), optional end of line(15 → 29),   |,
| punctuation(0 → 14), clear temp list flag(15 → 29),   |,
| move back flag(0 → 14), skip flag(15 → 29),   |,
| punctuation counter(0 → 14), colon counter(15 → 29),   |,
| print flag(0 → 14), end of line count(15 → 29),   |,
| dimn lower bit limit(0 → 14), constant flag(15 → 29),   |,
| function co(0 → 14), function flag(15 → 29),   |,
| define function flag(0 → 14), floating point flag(15 → 29),   |,
| repeat counter(0 → 14), reverse comparison flag(15 → 29),   |,
temporary storage(10), comparison list; . .
```

```
5
title constant(133) = 14111120013₈, 30110416038₈, 54031520012₈, 30062254068₈,
0300000000₈, 24050312018₈, 04310312368₈, 14061304248₈, 15301620008₈,
14061534018₈, 04033401158₈, 34010426038₈, 12073001048₈, 20121203128₈,
14111120138₈, 30110422148₈, 07200624148₈, 03061406138₈, 04240130018₈,
20072006018₈, 06300720048₈, 11142401048₈, 03172012268₈, 11033100008₈,
03152012308₈, 01031204208₈, 12120312048₈, 12202420018₈, 07142424148₈,
06130430118₈, 01201206308₈, 01141720008₈, 30342714118₈, 14301225048₈,
06300720048₈, 11142404048₈, 03172012268₈, 11033100008₈, 16052016368₈,
04243407048₈, 20121203128₈, 45451603548₈, 06034545578₈, 45454726118₈,
03311605308₈, 12010404578₈, 45470630078₈, 20041114248₈, 01042234078₈,
15454500008₈, 04570404048₈, 45040404048₈, 04040404048₈, 16303401148₈,
03066161618₈, 61616161508₈, 50505050508₈, 50454526038₈, 11110331148₈,
06130406308₈, 07202404348₈, 06222026148₈, 06202245458₈, 01122030018₈,
20220430248₈, 04263411118₈, 04313012228₈, 04261427208₈, 22041506018₈,
34062220268₈, 14062022048₈, 12033401148₈, 06200404008₈, 45325734078₈,
12030204018₈, 03042612038₈, 07040404048₈, 24011230148₈, 13050104328₈,
34071504018₈, 03042434238₈, 12033401148₈, 06200404008₈, 06201114308₈,
16042611208₈, 27042207158₈, 05241504008₈, 06201114308₈, 16042314038₈,
16013011048₈, 22340715008₈, 34242022048₈, 01311416208₈, 45472420358₈,
04061204048₈, 12033401148₈, 06200406308₈, 07200404048₈, 04040323328₈,
44151203138₈, 12300704048₈, 04261103318₈, 16053012018₈, 04040404048₈,
20060112308₈, 06162045578₈, 45454706038₈, 01570462478₈, 04110330228₈,
31031222048₈, 04300104008₈, 45130303228₈, 06201114308₈, 16041406008₈,
16123401168₈, 05041603228₈, 20042630348₈, 11010000008₈, 33160307078₈,
20060144048₈, 45242001048₈, 23524407038₈, 06042374448₈, 22300120048₈,
34061401048₈, 16300606038₈, 20150104038₈, 12222012048₈,
07142424148₈, 06130412148₈, 13050104238₈, 12301620008₈,
| obj prog std last address(15 → 29), std program entry address(0 → 14),   |,
| set(0 → 14), standard compiling location(15 → 29),   | = 7,
STD ADDRESSES: | object prog std first address(15 → 29),
flo cht storage std first address(0 → 14) |, beginning of flowcharts,
end of flowcharts, shift q right function = 1000 00000₈,
MONITOR FUNCTION: shift a right function = 2000 00000₈,
shift aq right function = 3000 00000₈, compare function = 4000 00000₈,
shift q left function = 5000 00000₈, shift a left function = 6000 00000₈,
shift aq left function = 7000 00000₈, enter q function = 10000 00000₈,
enter a function = 11000 00000₈, enter b function = 12000 00000₈,
```

```
ENTER C FUNCTION: external function = 13000 00000₈,
store q function = 14000 00000₈, store a function = 15000 00000₈,
store b function = 16000 00000₈, store c function = 17000 00000₈,
add function = 20000 00000₈, sub function = 21000 00000₈,
multiply function = 22000 00000₈, divide function = 23000 00000₈,
add repl function = 24000 00000₈, sub repl function = 25000 00000₈,
q add function = 26 000 00000₈, q sub function = 27000 00000₈,
load a add q function = 30000 00000₈,
load a sub q function = 31000 00000₈, repl add q function = 34000 00000₈,
repl sub q function = 35000 00000₈, repl add one function = 36000 00000₈,
repl sub one function = 37000 00000₈, enter log prod function = 40000 00000₈,
add log prod function = 41000 00000₈, sub log prod function = 42000 00000₈,
substitute function = 53000 00000₈, repl substitute function = 57000 00000₈,
arithmetic jump function = 60000 00000₈,
straight jump function = 61000 00000₈, input jump function = 62000 00000₈,
output jump function = 63000 00000₈, return jump function = 65000 00000₈,
terminate input function = 66000 00000₈,
terminate output function = 67000 00000₈, repeat function = 70000 00000₈,
inc loop cntrl function = 71000 00000₈, dec loop cntrl function = 72000 00000₈,
buffer in function = 73000 00000₈, buffer out function = 74000 00000₈,
j desig(8) = , 100 00000₈, 200 00000₈, 300 00000₈, 400 00000₈,
500 00000₈, 600 00000₈, 700 00000₈,
k desig(8) = , 10 00000₈, 20 00000₈, 30 00000₈, 40 00000₈,
50 00000₈, 60 00000₈, 70 00000₈,
b desig(8) = , 1 00000₈, 2 00000₈, 3 00000₈, 4 00000₈, 5 00000₈,
6 00000₈, 7 00000₈,
io j desig(14) = , 4000000₈, 10000000₈, 14000000₈, 20000000₈,
24000000₈, 30000000₈, 34000000₈, 40000000₈, 44000000₈,
50000000₈, 54000000₈, 60000000₈, 64000000₈,
| comma(15 → 29), semicolon(0 → 14) | = 4600047₈,
| period(15 → 29), colon(0 → 14) | = 5000051₈,
| left paren(15 → 29), right paren(0 → 14) | = 5200053₈,
| left brace(15 → 29), right brace(0 → 14) | = 5600057₈,
| left bracket(15 → 29), right bracket(0 → 14) | = 5400055₈,
| equal sign(15 → 29), less than(0 → 14) | = 6000063₈,
| not equal sign(15 → 29), greater than(0 → 14) | = 6100065₈,
| right arrow(15 → 29), plus(0 → 14) | = 6600067₈,
| minus(15 → 29), divide(0 → 14) | = 7000071₈,
| multiply(15 → 29), color shift(0 → 14) | = 7200073₈,
| temp name sign(15 → 29), absolute(15 → 29), crutch(15 → 29),
crutch code(15 → 29), or(0 → 14) | = 7400075₈,
| and(15 → 29), octal sign(0 → 14) | = 7600045₈,
| exponent sign(15 → 29), an operator(0 → 14) | = 7700046₈,
| punct area minus 1(15 → 29), punct area plus 1(0 → 14) | = 4500052₈,
| a number(15 → 29), a letter(0 → 14) | = 3300032₈;
neliac dimn part2: .  .
```

```
5
R|LEX CODE: fle|x code letter(27) = 04₈, 30₈, 23₈, 16₈, 22₈, 20₈, 26₈,
13₈, 05₈, 14₈, 32₈, 36₈, 11₈, 07₈, 06₈, 03₈, 15₈, 35₈, 12₈, 24₈, 01₈, 34₈,
17₈, 31₈, 27₈, 25₈, 21₈,
flex code number(10) = 37₈, 52₈, 74₈, 70₈, 64₈, 62₈, 66₈, 72₈, 60₈, 33₈,
on|line flex code operator(27) = 0450610304₈, 0000044604₈,
4744615746₈, 0000044204₈, 4744615742₈, 0004474657₈,
0047425704₈, 0000000450₈, 0000005004₈, 0411231250₈,
5012231204₈, 0000044404₈, 4754615744₈, 5013012050₈,
5011202450₈, 5011012050₈, 5013120150₈, 5030120350₈,
0000045404₈, 0000045604₈, 0447545704₈, 0447275704₈,
5016240550₈, 50₈, 0437615404₈, 4727610357₈, 4754615057₈,
o|ff line flex code operators(27) = 76₈, 47465704₈, 4404₈,
4204₈, 47445704₈, 473357₈, 473757₈, 476457₈, 476257₈,
```

```
47565704₈, 456₈, 447705704₈, 447505704₈, 447545704₈,
447665704₈, 045404₈, 044604₈, 447425704₈, 447525704₈,
447745704₈, 447725704₈, 447605704₈, 2, 50₈, 47504₈, 447755704₈,
477657₈;
START FLEX:
| 17040₈0, 13100₈0, 17100₈0, 50000₈163₈, 13300₈0, 13070₈0,
70000₈100₈, 13300₈10026₈, 13300₈0, 70000₈10000₈, 13300₈10013₈,
13300₈0, 70000₈100₈, 13300₈10012₈, 13300₈0, set → flex on flag,  |,
START PUNCH:
| 13100₈0, 13000₈163₈, 13300₈0, 70000₈10000₈, 13300₈10023₈,
13300₈0, 70000₈10000₈, 13300₈10022₈, punch leader, 0 → flex on flag,  |,
PUNCH LEADER:
| 1 → punch leader(15 → 29), 1 = 200(1)0| 13100₈0, delay output,  |,
punch leader(15 → 29) → 1,  |,
START READER:
| 13100₈0, 13000₈161₈, 13300₈0, 70000₈10000₈, 13300₈10031₈,
13300₈0, 70000₈10000₈, 13300₈10033₈ |,
TURN OFF FLEX:
| 70000₈10000₈, 13300₈10014₈, 13300₈0, 13300₈10016₈, 0 → flex on flag,  |,
TURN OFF PUNCH:
| 43₈ → dump buffer, print, punch leader, 13300₈0, 70000₈10000₈,
13300₈10024₈, 13300₈0, 13300₈10026₈ |,
TURN OFF READER:
| 13000₈160₈, 13300₈0, 70000₈10000₈, 13300₈10034₈, 13300₈0, 13300₈10036₈ |,
PRINT:
| m → print(15 → 29), m = 4(1)0| dump buffer x 2↑6 → dump buffer,
first frame dump buffer = 15₈ ∩ flex on flag = 0:
     55₈ → first frame dump buffer; ;
first frame dump buffer ≠ 0: 13130₈dump buffer, delay output; ;  |,
print(15 → 29) → m,  |,
TYPE LIMITS: | start flex, carriage return lower case, print limits,  |,
PRINT LIMITS:
| address limits → dump buffer[1], dump five numbers, space,
dump five numbers,  |,
DUMP A TITLE:
| 1 → dump a title(15 → 29),
1 = lower loop limit(1)upper loop limit| title constant[1] →
dump buffer, print,  |, dump a title(15 → 29) → 1,  |,
DUMP ONE NUMBER:
| 1 → dump one number(15 → 29), dump buffer[1] x 2↑3 → dump buffer[1],
dump buffer[1](0 → 2) + 27 → 1, decode and print,
dump one number(15 → 29) → 1,  |,
DUMP FIVE NUMBERS:
| k → dump five numbers(15 → 29), k = 4(1)0| dump one number,  |,
dump five numbers(15 → 29) → k,  |,
DECODE AND PRINT: | flex code[1] → dump buffer, print,  |,
CONVT AND PRINT COMPILER CODED WORD:
| k → convt and print compiler coded word(15 → 29),
1 → decode and print(15 → 29),
k = 4(1)0| read any character, present character → 1,
flex on flag = 0 ∩ a letter < present character < an operator:
     lower case, decode and print, upper case; decode and print;  |,
convt and print compiler coded word(15 → 29) → k,
decode and print(15 → 29) → 1,  |,
READ ONE WORD:
| k → read one word(15 → 29), k = 4(1)0| read one frame,
load buffer → last frame load buffer[1],
load buffer[1] x 2↑6 → load buffer[1],  |,
read one word(15 → 29) → k,  |,
```

READ ONE FRAME: | 17130₈load buffer, delay input, |,
WRITE NAME BUFFER:
| i → write name buffer(15 → 29),
i = 0(1)2| name buffer[i] → flowchart buffer, 5 → frame counter,
convt and print compiler coded word, |,
write name buffer(15 → 29) → i, |,
TYPE CHECK SUM ERROR:
| start flex, carriage return upper case,
38 → lower loop limit, 40 → upper loop limit, dump a title,
turn off flex, |,
WRITE NAME:
| name part 1[n] → name buffer, name part 2[n] → name buffer[1];
name part 3[n] → name buffer[2], write name buffer, |,
WRITE UNDEFINED NAME:
| undefined name 1[n] → name buffer, undefined name 2[n] → name buffer[1],
undefined name 3[n] → name buffer[2], write name buffer, |,
DELAY OUTPUT: | d|elay: 62100₈delay. |,
DELAY INPUT: | d|elay 1: 63100₈delay 1. |,

CARRIAGE RETURN:
| 45₈ → dump buffer, print,
1 + carriage return counter → carriage return counter, |,
SPACE: | 04 → dump buffer, print, |,
LOWER CASE: | 57₈ → dump buffer, print, |,
UPPER CASE: | 47₈ → dump buffer, print, |,
CARRIAGE RETURN LOWER CASE: | carriage return, lower case, |,
CARRIAGE RETURN UPPER CASE: | carriage return, upper case, |,
CHECK KEY SETS:
| 0 → key[1] → key[2] → key[3], 65100₈key 1 set, 65200₈key 2 set,
65300₈key 3 set, |,
K|EY 1 SET: | set → key[1], |,
K|EY 2 SET: | set → key[2], |,
K|EY 3 SET: | set → key[3], |,
CLEAR INDICES: | 0 → i → j → l → k → m → n, |,
STORE FLOWCHART PARAMETERS:
| flowchart buffer → temp fb storage, frame counter → temp fc storage,
present character → temp pc storage, j → flochrt addr storage, |,
RESTORE FLOWCHART PARAMETERS:
| temp fb storage → flowchart buffer, temp fc storage → frame counter,
temp pc storage → present character, flochrt addr storage → j, |,
DUMP THE DATE:
| date ≠ 0: title constant[123] → dump buffer, print,
    lower case, date[1] / 10 → temporary storage[1],
    print bit limit, date → dump buffer, print; ; |. .

5
d|o1 = 41700₈, g|o 2 = 7170024₈, 1|f 1 = 110600₈, 1|f 2 = 11060016₈,
1|f 3 = 172446₈, c|omment 1 = 5203171515₈,
c|omment 2 = 5200031715₈, f|or 1 = 6172200₈,
| c|ompiler code upper case(15 → 29),
c|ompiler code lower case(0 → 14) |(64) =,
2400024₈, , 1700017₈, , 1000010₈, 1600016₈, 1500015₈, , 1400014₈,
2200022₈, 700007₈, 1100011₈, 2000020₈, 300003₈, 2600026₈,
500005₈, 3200032₈, 400004₈, 200002₈, 2300023₈, 3100031₈,
600006₈, 3000030₈, 100001₈, 2700027₈, 1200012₈, 5200044₈,
2500025₈, 2100021₈, 1300013₈, 5300033₈, , 6600050₈, , 5100047₈,
4600065₈, , 6100074₈, , 6700034₈, , 6200064₈, 2000020₈, 5600057₈, ,
7200043₈, , 5500040₈, , 5400037₈, , 6300041₈, , 6000036₈, ,

7100042₈, , 7000035₈, 7600075₈, 7700045₈, ,
| s|ingle compiler code(15 → 29), d|ouble compiler code(0 → 14) |(22) =
7461₈, 6174₈, 6106071₈, 6107160₈, 6107460₈, 6106074₈, 7501767₈,
7506717₈, 7503367₈, 7506733₈, 7601772₈, 7707161₈, 7607217₈,
7603372₈, 7607233₈, 5466₈, 6654₈, 7706171₈, 3303371₈, 3307133₈,
3301771₈, 3307117₈;
LOAD FLOWCHARTS:
m = 0: flo cht storage std first address → m; ;
m → beginning of flowcharts, 1 ≠ 0: 1 → end of flowcharts; ;
i ≠ 0: set date; ;
LOAD NEXT FLOWCHART: 0 → sequence number,
k ≠ 0: k → sequence number, 8 → load type, correct flowchart, ;
    i = 59(1)0| 0 → first comparison[i], |, start reader,
    0 → case flag → compiler code char → back space flag,
    0 → space flag → load buffer[1] → load buffer[2] →
    carriage return counter.
R|EAD LEADER:
read one frame, load buffer = 0: read leader. ;
5 → frame counter, m → first address,
j = 9(1)0| flex code number[j] = load buffer: | j → load type,
    load type < 7: 0 → [m], m + 1 → m, 0 → [m]; ;
    read next frame. |; ; |, read leader.
RE|AD NEXT FRAME:
read one frame, decode, compiler code char ≠ 0: enter buffer. ;
load buffer = 47₈: set → case flag; ;
load buffer = 57₈: 0 → case flag; ;
load buffer = 45₈: reset loading index. ;
load buffer = 04₈: set space flag. ;
load buffer = 61₈: set → back space flag; ;
load buffer = 43₈: exit. ; read next frame.
R|ESET LOADING INDEX:
6 < load type < 9:
    | 1 + carriage return counter → carriage return counter = 1:
        12500₈first comparison[1]; final packing;
    carriage return counter = 2: 12500₈correction[1]; ;
    carriage return counter = 3: 12500₈second comparison[1]; ; |; ;
S|ET SPACE FLAG:
space flag ≠ 0: read next frame. ;
set → space flag, enter memory, read next frame.
E|NTER BUFFER:
load type = 4 ∩ compiler code char = greater than:
    comma → compiler code char; 0 → space flag,
repeat counter ≠ 0:
    | repeat counter - 1 → repeat counter ≠ 0 ∩
    a letter < compiler code character < an operator: ;
        | back space flag ≠ 0 ∩ load buffer[1](6 → 11) = 33₈:
            octal sign → load buffer[1](6 → 11),
            33₈ → first frame load buffer[1];
        octal sign → first frame load buffer[1], 0 → repeat counter;
        enter memory, |; |; ;
compiler code char → first frameload buffer[1], enter memory,
back space flag = 0: read next frame. ; 0 → back space flag,
load buffer[1](6 → 17) → temporary storage,
k = 21(1)0| double compiler code[k] = temporary storage:
    substitute. ; |,
temporary storage(6 → 11) = not equal sign:
    temporary storage x 2↑6 + temp name sign → load buffer[1](6 → 17);
    | temporary storage(0 → 5) = not equal sign:

temp name sign → load buffer[1](6 → 11); ; |; read next frame.
S|UBSTITUTE:
single compiler code[k] → load buffer[1](6 → 17),
k < 2: | 6 → repeat counter, load buffer[1](18 → 23) < an operator ∩
    load buffer[1](24 → 29) < an operator:
        comma → load buffer[1](6 → 17); ; |; ;
14 < k < 17: 200 → repeat counter; ; read next frame.
E|XIT:
final packing, turn off reader, m ≠ 0: m + 1 → m; ;
0 → [m], m + 1 → m → last address, 0 → [m], check key sets,
move back flag ≠ 0: m → 1, address limits → address limits[1],
    flochrt addr storage → j, end of flowcharts → k, move flowchart. ;
6 < load type < 9: correct flowchart, address limits → address limits[1],
    RETURN TO LOAD:
    end of flowcharts → last address,
    beginning of flowcharts → first address, type limits,
    address limits[1] → address limits,
    end of flowcharts → m, continue.
3 < load type < 6: ; start flex, 106 → lower loop limit,
    108 → upper loop limit, dump a title;
C|ONTINUE:
m → end of flowcharts, type limits, carriage return,
turn off flex, clear indices, end of flowcharts → m,
key[2] ≠ 0: clear name list and stop. 61400_8 load next flowchart.
D|ECODE:
| load buffer → k, case flag = 0:
    compiler code lower case[k] → compiler code character;
    compiler code upper case[k] → compiler code character; |,
E|NTER MEMORY:
| load buffer[2](18 → 23) → temporary storage,
last frame load buffer[2] → [m](0 → 5) = 0:
    | 0 < temporary storage < octal sign ∩
    0 < temporary storage[1] < octal sign: ; pack buffers. |; ;
frame counter - 1 → frame counter = 0: 5 → frame counter, m + 1 → m,
    0 → [m]; [m] × 2↑6 → [m];
last frame load buffer[2] → temporary storage[1],
P|ACK BUFFERS:
load buffer[2] × 2↑6 → load buffer[2],
last frame load buffer[1] → first frame load buffer[2],
load buffer[1] × 2↑6 → load buffer[1],
0 → first frame load buffer[1].
temporary storage[1] < an operator: check for comments. ;
load buffer[2](6 → 29) = do1: 0 → load buffer[2](12 → 29); ;
load buffer[2] = go2 ∩ load buffer[1](18 → 29) = 1700_8:
    0 → load buffer[2] → last frame load buffer[1]; ;
load buffer[2] = if2 ∩ load buffer[1](12 → 29) = if3:
    0 → load buffer[2] → load buffer[1](12 → 29); ;
load buffer[2](6 → 29) = if1: 0 → load buffer[2](12 → 29); ;
load buffer[2] = for1: 0 → load buffer[2]; ;
C|HECK FOR COMMENTS:
load buffer[2] = comment1 ∪ load buffer[2] = comment2:
    0 → load buffer[1] → load buffer[2]; skip deletion.
D|ELETE COMMENTS:
read one frame, decode,
compiler code character = right paren: read next frame. ;
load buffer = 47_8: set → case flag; ;
load buffer = 57_8: 0 → case flag; ; delete comments. s|kip deletion: |.
F|INAL PACKING:

| f|p|: enter memory, load buffer[2] = 0 ∩ load buffer[1] = 0: ; fp|.
F|P2:
[m] ≠ 0 ∩ [m](24 → 29) = 0: [m] x 2↑6 → [m], fp2. ;
6 < load type < 9 ∩ first comparison[1](0 → 14) = 0:
    (first comparison[1](24 → 29) - 27) x 2↑3 +
    first comparison[1](18 → 23) - 27 → sequence number,
    0 → first comparison[1],
    carriage return counter - 1 → carriage return counter; ;
5 → frame counter, |. load flowcharts and stop: , . .

5;
CORRECT FLOWCHART:
| 12100₈first comparison, end of flowcharts → k,
j = k(1)k + 40| 0 → [j], |.
sequence number ≠ 0: | beginning of flowcharts → j,
    n = 1(1)sequence number| s|kip zeros: j + 1 → j,
    [j] = 0: skip zeros. ; j → first address ≥ end of flowcharts:
        print flowchart error. ; find flowchart limits, |,
    load type = 8: | r|eplace flowchart: first address - 1 → m,
        end of flowcharts → k, [j + 1] = 0: j + 1 → j; ;
        j + 1000₈ → i → flochrt addr storage, move flowchart. |; ;
    first address → lower loop limit[1],
    last address → upper loop limit[1], |;
    beginning of flowcharts → lower loop limit[1],
    end of flowcharts → upper loop limit[1];
F|IND CORRECTION AREA:
l = 1(1)5| 1 → lower loop limit + 19 → upper loop limit, shift left,
j = lower loop limit[1](1)upper loop limit[1]| [i + 1] = [j]:
    check other words; ; |, |, print flowchart error.
F|IND END CORRECTION AREA:
12600₈second comparison, i ≥ n: find split location. ;
k → first address - 1 → lower loop limit[1],
load type = 8: find flowchart limits, replace flowchart. ;
m → temporary storage[1], n → 1, find correction area.
F|IND SPLIT LOCATION:
j - 1 → last address, 1 → shift flag 1,
i - 20 → lower loop limit + 18 → upper loop limit,
temporary storage[1] → i, count empty frames, shift flag ≠ 0:
    i = 1(1)shift flag| shift left, |; ;
l = end of flowcharts(77776₈)last address| [1] → [1 + 21], 0 → [1], |,
first address → k, temporary storage[1] → m, [m] → [k],
last address + 21 → k, second comparison → [k],
n = 1(1)19| correction[n] = 0: set length. ; |.
S|ET LENGTH:
n → correction length, first address → k,
lower loop limit → m + 19 → upper loop limit, pack or repack flowcharts,
first address + correction length - 1 → i → k, count empty frames,
last address + 21 → m, end of flowcharts + 21 → upper loop limit,
shift flag = shift flag 1: pack or repack flowcharts, exit. ;
shift flag - shift flag 1 → temporary storage < 0: shift right. ;
m → lower loop limit, i = 1(1)temporary storage| shift left, |,
pack or repack flowcharts, exit.
S|HIFT RIGHT:
0 - temporary storage → temporary storage,
1 + upper loop limit → upper loop limit,
j = 1(1)temporary storage| n = upper loop limit(77776₈)m -
1| [n](0 → 5) → [n + 1](24 → 29), [n] / 2↑6 → [n], |, |,
pack or repack flowcharts,
E|XIT: k = k(1)0| [k - 2] ≠ 0: final exit. ; |.

F|INAL EXIT:
k → end of flowcharts, find flowchart limits, 65100₈dump a flowchart, |.
P|ACK OR REPACK FLOWCHARTS:
| [m] + [k] → [k],
m = m + 1(1)upper loop limit| k + 1 → k, [m] → [k], |, |.
S|HIFT LEFT:
| n = lowerloop limit(1)upper loop limit| [n] x 2↑6 → [n],
[n + 1](24 → 29) → [n](0 → 5), |, |.
C|HECK OTHER WORDS:
| j → k, m = 1 + 2(1)1 + 18| k + 1 → k, [m + 1] = 0:
    find end correction area. ; [m] ≠ [k]: exit check. ; |,
e|xitcheck: |.
C|OUNT EMPTY FRAMES:
| [1] → temporary storage[2], m = 1(1)5| temporary storage[2](0 → 5) ≠ 0:
    m → shift flag - 1 → shift flag, exit cef. ;
temporary storage[2] / 2↑6 → temporary storage[2], |,
5 → shift flag, e|xit cef: |.
FIND FLOWCHART LIMITS:
| j = first address(- 1)beginning of flowcharts| [j] = 0:
    j + 1 → first address, find end. ; |.
F|IND END:
j = j + 1(1)end of flowcharts| [j] = 0: j - 1 → last address,
    exit ffl. ; |, e|xit ffl: |. .

5;
MOVE FLOWCHART:
j → first address, k → last address,
load type ≠ 8 ∩ move back flag = 0: type limits; ;
last address → k, i → first address. i ≥ j: move up. ;
j - 1 → temporary storage, j = j(1)k| [j] → [i], 0 → [j], i + 1 → i, |,
i - 1 → last address → end of flowcharts, exit.
M|OVE UP:
i - j → temporary storage + k → 1 → last address → end of flowcharts,
k = k(- 1)j| [k] → [1], 0 → [k], 1 - 1 → 1, |,
E|XIT:
load type = 8: | [m - 1] ≠ 0: m + 1 → m; ;
    7 → move back flag, 0 → k, load next flowchart. |; ;
move back flag ≠ 0: | 0 → move back flag,
    1 = 1(1)0| [1 - 2] ≠ 0: | 1 → end of flowcharts, check key sets,
        key[1] ≠ 0: address limits[1] → address limits,
            dump a flowchart; ; return to load. |; ; |, |; ;
type limits, space, space, temporary storage → upper dump buffer[1],
dump five numbers, turn off flex, clear indices, . .

5;
DUMP A FLOWCHART:
| start punch, 1 = 200₈(1)0| 0 → exit condition list[1], |,
first address → j, read next character, store flowchart parameters,
carriage return lowercase, 50₈ → last frame dump buffer[1],
dump one number, date ≠ 0: 118 → lower loop limit, 119 → upper loop limit,
    space, uppercase, dump a title, dump the date,
    37₈ → dump buffer, print; ; carriage return lower case,
0 → upper loop limit, set → name found flag,
E|NTER:
character counter + 1 → character counter ≥ end of line count ∩
print flag ≠ 0: return carriage, indent, 1 → character counter,
    56 → end of line count, 0 → print flag → punctuation counter →
    case flag → optional end of line, store flowchart parameters; ;
S|TART:

```
print flag ≠ 0: print character. ;
right brace < present character < right arrow: 0 → name found flag; ;
present character = right paren ∩ current operator = left paren ∩
punctuation counter ≠ 0 ∩ skip flag = 0: reset. ;
current operator ≠ left bracket ∩ right arrow < present character <
exponent sign: character counter → optional end of line; ;
present character = right arrow ∩ current operator ≠ left paren:
     character counter → optional end of line; ;
current operator = colon ∩ present character ≠ right brace ∩
present character ≠ period ∩ present character ≠ comma:
   colon counter + 1 → colon counter, reset. ;
constant flag = 0: | temporary storage[4] ≥ an operator ∩
     a letter < present character < octal sign: set → constant flag; ;  |;
     | present character = period: octal sign → present character; ;  |;
punct area minus 1 < present character < colon ∩ function flag = 0:
     | current operator = left paren: set → function flag;
       set → name found flag,
       character counter → punctuation counter; |; ;
present character = right paren ∩ current operator ≠ left paren ∩
current operator ≠ right arrow: 0 → function flag; ;
present character = right brace:
     character counter → punctuation counter; ;
present character = right brace ∪ present character = left brace:
     | set → name found flag,
     punctuation counter ≠ 0: set → skip flag; ;  |; ;
present character < octal sign ∪ present character = temp name sign:
     | character counter + upper loop limit ≥ 56 ∩
     current operator ≠ left paren: | punctuation counter = 0:
           | optional end of line = 0:
                character counter → punctuation counter;
                optional end of line → punctuation counter;  |; ;
     reset. |; | skip flag ≠ 0:
     | punct area minus 1 < current operator < colon ∪
     current operator = left brace ∪
     current operator = left bracket: reset. ;  |; ;  |;  |;
current operator → temporary storage[1], 0 → constant flag,
present character → current operator; print flag = 0: margin control. ;
P|RINT CHARACTER:
present character = temp name sign ∩ case flag ≠ 0:
     575047₈ → dump buffer, print, look ahead. ;
present character → 1 ≥ octal sign: | 27 + 1 → 1,
     present character → current operator = colon:
     comma → current operator; ;  |;
     | 1 ≥ a number ∩ case flag ≠ 0: lower case, decode and print,
     uppercase, look ahead. ;  |; decode and print,
[j - 1] = 0: exit. ; look ahead.
M|ARGIN CONTROL:
comparison type ≠ 0: | present character = period ∪
     present character = semicolon:| character counter → punctuation counter,
     1 + comparison counter → comparison counter,
     comparison counter ≥ 2: set → skip flag; ;  |; ;
     present character = right brace ∪     present character = colon ∪
     present character = left brace: comparison type - comparison counter →
     comparison type, 0 → comparison counter; ;
     comparison type = comparison counter:
          0 → comparison type → comparison counter; ;  |; ;
L|OOK AHEAD:
present character → temporary storage[4], read any character, enter.
R|ESET:
```

colon counter < 2 ∩'punctuation counter ≠ 0:
    punctuation counter → end of line count;
    | 0 → colon counter, name found flag ≠ 0:
    ' | temporary storage[1] = left brace: go on. ;
        set → case flag, return carriage, uppercase,
        carriage return counter = 28: return carriage; ; indent, |;
    2 + comparison type → comparison type,
    G|O ON:
    comma → current operator, character counter - 1 → punctuation counter,
    margin control. character counter - 1 → end of line count, |;
set → print flag, 0 → character counter → skip flag,
restore flowchart parameters, start.
I|NDENT:
| comparison type - comparison counter → upper loop limit,
upper loop limit(0 → 0) ≠ 0: 1 + upper loop limit → upper loop limit; ;
upper loop limit × 2 → upper loop limit ≥ 1:
    1 = 1(1)upper loop limit| space, |; ; |,
R|ETURN CARRIAGE:
| carriage return, carriage return counter ≥ 29:
    1 = 3(1)0| carriage return, |, 0 → carriage return counter; ; |,
E|XIT: turn off punch, |. .

5;
NELIAC FLEX DUMP:
check key sets, start flex, carriage return upper case,
key[1] ≠ 0: title 1; title 2; 61400₈select output equipment.
S|ELECT OUTPUT EQUIPMENT:
0 → carriage return counter, key[1] = 0: turn off flex, start punch,
    carriage return upper case, dump the date, carriage return, title 1; ;
carriage return, 1 = first address(1)last address| [1] = 0:
    | key[2] ≠ 0: set → zero flag, check next word. ;
    0 → dump buffer[1], dump one number, i(0 → 2) = 0:
        n = 10(1)0| space, |, dump address. dump next word. |; ;
zero flag ≠ 0: return carriage; ;
[1] → dump buffer[1], dump one number, dump one number, space,
dump one number, dump one number, dump one number, space,
upper dump buffer[1] = 0: | dump one number,
    i(0 → 2) = 0 ∪ zero flag ≠ 0: n = 3(1)0| space, |; ; |;
    dump five numbers; zero flag = 0 ∩ i(0 → 2) ≠ 0: dump next word. ;
D|UMP ADDRESS:
space, 1 → upper dump buffer[1], dump five numbers,
zero flag = 0: return carriage; ; 0 → zero flag.
D|UMP NEXT WORD:
return carriage, c|heck next word: |.
key[1] ≠ 0: turn off flex; turn off punch; clear indices,
T|ITLE 1:
| 83 → lower loop limit, 85 → upper loop limit, dump a title,
i → first address, j → last address,
carriage return lower case, print limits, carriage return, |.
T|ITLE 2: | title constant[86] → dump buffer, print, space, title 1, |.
R|ETURN CARRIAGE:
| carriage return, carriage return counter ≥ 58:
    n = 7(1)0| carriage return, |, 0 → carriage return counter; ; |. .

5;
NELIAC BIO DUMP:
start flex, carriage return upper case, 86 → lower loop limit,
90 → upper loop limit, dump a title, i → first address,
j → last address, type limits, turn off flex, 61400₈dump.

D|UMP:
start punch, 77₈ → dump buffer, print, bio dump, 0 → temporary storage,
1 - first address(1)last address| [i] + temporary storage →
temporary storage, [i] → dump buffer[1], bio dump, |,
temporary storage → dump buffer[1], bio dump, turn off punch, clear indices,
B|IO DUMP:
| n - 4(1)0| dump buffer[1] x 2↑6 → dump buffer[1],
13130₈dump buffer[1], delay output, |, |. neliac bio dump and stop: . .

5;
NELIAC BIO LOAD:
start reader, set addresses, 0 → temporary storage,
1 - first address(1)last address| read one word,
load buffer[1] → [i] + temporary storage → temporary storage, |,
read one word, turn off reader, temporary storage ≠ load buffer[1]:
    type check sum error, exit. ;
type limits, turn off flex, check key sets,
key[1] - 0: first address → beginning of flowcharts,
    last address → end of flowcharts; ; clear indices,
SET ADDRESSES: | read one word, read one word,
R|EAD LEADER:
read one frame, load buffer ≠ 0: read one word; read leader.
load buffer[1] → address limits, |.
E|XIT: neliac bio load and stop: . .

5;
COMPARISON LOAD:
start reader, set addresses, 0 → title flag,
1 - first address(1)last address| read one word,
[i] ≠ load buffer[1]: print error; ; |,
turn off reader, start flex, title flag ≠ 0: type check sum error;
    title constant[111] → dump buffer, print, space,
    title constant[90] → dump buffer, print, type limits, turntoff flex;
clear indices, neliac bio dump and stop.
P|RINT ERROR:
| set → title flag, check key sets, key[1] ≠ 0: exit print error. ;
shift from reader to flex, carriage return lower case,
title constant[109] → dump buffer, print, [i] → dump buffer[1],
dump five numbers, space, dump five numbers,
title constant[110] → dump buffer, print,
1 → upper dump buffer[1], dump five numbers,
carriage return, title constant[90] → dump buffer, print,
space, load buffer[1] → dump buffer[1], dump five numbers,
space, dump five numbers, carriage return,
shift from flex to reader, e|xit print error: |.
SHIFT FROM READER TO FLEX:
| 13300₈10036₈, 17130₈temporary storage, 13100₈0, start flex, |.
SHIFT FROM FLEX TO READER:
| turn off flex, 13130₈temporary storage, 13300₈10031₈, 13000₈161₈, |. .

5
m|onth(13) - , 447323006₈, 447262023₈, 447073012₈, 447301512₈,
447073025₈, 447323406₈, 447323411₈, 447303413₈, 447242015₈,
447031601₈, 447060317₈, 447222016₈, date(2);
SET THE DATE: set date, clear indices,
SET DATE: | 0 → date, month[1] → date, j → date[1], |. .

5;
CHECK NELIAC LOAD:

0 → temporary storage,
1 - [5](1)n| [i] + temporary storage → temporary storage |,
turn off reader, [n + 1] ≠ temporary storage: type check sum error;
  | check key sets,   key[1] ≠ 0: k + 3 → k, mag tape handler; ;
  start flex, 112 → lower loop limit, 113 → upper loop limit,
  carriage return upper case, dump a title, turn off flex,
  n - 7677₈(1)0| 0 → name part 1[n], |, clear indices,
  check key sets, key[2] ≠ 0: load flowcharts and stop. ;
  key[1] ≠ 0: 61400₈rru tape handler; ; neliac bio load and stop. |.

5;
CLEAR NAME LISTS:
n - 7677₈(1)0| 0 → name part 1[n], |, clear indices, start flex,
date - 0: 120 → lower loop limit, 123 → upper loop limit,
    dump a title, 65400₈set date; ;
carriage return upper case, dump the date, turn off flex,
clear indices, check key sets, key[3] ≠ 0: store names and stop. start
    compiling and stop. clear name list and stop: . .

5
I|O NAME: e|xt function - 530240522₈, r|elease interrupt - 2205140506 ,
J|ump active - 1225152001₈, t|erminate buffer - 2405221511₈,
b|uffer - 225060605₈, m|onitor buffer - 1517161124₈,
d|elay - 405140131₈, | max io index(0 → 14), perm io index(15 → 29), |,
| less(0 → 14), greater(15 → 29), | - 6500063₈;
DECLARE NAMES:
J ≠ 0: J → flochart first address; flocht storage std.first address →
    flochart first address → J; 0 → frame counter,
comma → current operator → present character,
colon → next operator, J → flochart first address[1],
1 → sequence number → type name flag,
perm io index → max io index → k, 0 → io list[k], set → offset,
R|EAD NAME LIST:
present character - period: read next character, exit. ;
read next character, present character < a number: | read the name,
    R|EENTER:
    present character ≠ colon: set link or io type. ;
    offset - 0: increment io index; ; read next character,
    present character - 27 → n < 8: k desig[n] → k designator,
        read next character, read a number, number accumulator → 1,
        process the name, read name list. ;
    present character ≠ left paren: dn fault. ;
    name buffer + 4000000000₈ → io list[k],
    name buffer[1] + 4000000000₈ → io list[k + 1],
    name buffer[2] + 4000000000₈ → io list[k + 2], .k + 3 → k,
    0 → io list[k], read next character, read a number,
    number accumulator → io list[k](15 → 29),
    increment io index, 0 → space flag, read name list. |; ;
present character - less ∪ present character - greater:
    1 → space flag; | present character - left paren: 11₈ → space flag;
    0 → space flag; |; read name list.
S|ET LINK OR IO TYPE:
space flag ≠ 0: | present character - left paren: read next character,
        10₈ + space flag → space flag, read a number;
        0 → number accumulator;
        n - 6(1)0| name buffer - io name[n]: n + space flag → operand,
        set io list. ; |, dn fault. |;
| searth io list, 0 → number accumulator,
n ≠ 0: n + 31₈ → operand; dn fault. |;

S|ET IO LIST:
offset ≠ 0: operand → io list[k](15 → 29), 0 → offset;
        operand → io list[k](0 → 14), set → offset;
7 < operand < 30₈: increment io index, number accumulator → io list[k]; ;
offset ≠ 0: increment io index; ; 0 → space flag, read name list.
E|XIT:
offset = 0: increment io index; ;
perm io index = 0: max io index → perm io index; ;
max io index + io list → upper dump buffer[1], start flex,
carriage return lower case, dump five numbers, turn off flex,
j → temporary storage - 1 → flochart last address[1],
777₈ → sequence number, 0 → obj prog limits[1] → offset,
clear indices, temporary storage → j, start compiling and stop.
D|N FAULT: 9 → lower loop limit, 13 → upper loop limit, type the fault,
F|IND NEXT DECLARATION:
read next character, present character = period: read name list. ;
present character = colon: reenter. find next declaration.
I|NCREMENT IO INDEX:
| k + 1 → k → max io index, 0 → io list[k], set → offset, |,
SEARCH IO LIST:
| 0 → skip flag, n = max io index(- 1)2| io list[n] = - 1:
    | skip flag ≠ 0: 0 → skip flag, look at next word,
        set → skip flag; |; ;
io list[n] ≥ 0 ∪ skip flag ≠ 0: look at next word. ;
name buffer + 4000000000₈ = io list[n - 2] ∩ name buffer[1] +
4000000000₈ = io list[n - 1] ∩ name buffer[2] +
4000000000₈ = io list[n]: exit search. ;
l|ook at next word: |, e|xit search: |,
store names and stop: . .

5;
DUMP NAME LISTS:
select output equipment, 0 → title flag,
D|UMP UNDEFINED NAMES:
n = 177₈(1)0| undefined name 1[n] ≠ 0:
    | title flag = 0: print title |; ;
    write undefined name, space, space, lower case,
    undefined name location[n] → upper dump buffer[1],
        dump five numbers, carriage return uppercase, |; ; |,
key[1] ≠ 0: turn off flex, 65400₈select output equipment; ;
D|UMP DEFINED NAMES:
print title 2, 0 → name index,
k = 777₈(1)0| name part 1[k] = 0: set → name dumped flag[k];
    name index + 1 → name index; |,
C|ALCULATE DUMP INDICES:
k = 49(1)0| 0 → first comparison[k], |,
k = 49(1)0| find name, m + 1 → first comparison[k](15 → 29), |,
k = 49(1)0| find name, m + 1 → first comparison[k](0 → 14), |,
D|UMP:
k = 49(1)0| carriage return uppercase, set → shift flag,
first comparison[k](15 → 29) → n = 0: exit. dump name;
0 → shift flag, first comparison[k](0 → 14) → n ≠ 0: dump name; ; |,
k = 15(1)0| carriage return, |,
first comparison(0 → 14) = 0 ∪ name index = 0: exit. ;
calculate dump indices.

F|IND NAME:
| name index - 1 → name index < 0: dump. ;
key[3] = 0: | 100000₈ → temporary storage,

```
                  n - 777₈(1)0| 'name address[n] < temporary storage ∩
                name dumped flag[n] - 0: n → m,
                     name address[n] → temporary storage; ;  |,  |;
                | repl sub q function → temporary storage[1],
                  n - 777₈(1)0| temporary storage[1] ≥ name part 1[n] ∩
                name dumped flag[n] - 0: n → m,
                     name part 1[n] → temporary storage[1]; ;  |,  |;
        set → name dumped flag[m],  |,
        D|UMP NAME:
        | n - 1 → n, write name, space, lower case,
        name k desig[n] → dump buffer[1](27 → 29), dump one number,
        space, name address[n] → upper dump buffer[1],
        dump five numbers, dump bit limits,  |,
        D|UMP BIT LIMITS:
        | name mask length[n] ≠ 0: space, space, 2 → m,
             name mask lower limit[n] / 10 → temporary storage[1],
             print bit limit, space,
             (name mask length[n] + name mask lower limit[n] - 1) / 10 →
             temporary storage[1], print bit limit;
                | name mask[n] < 0: space, space, 2615₈ → dump buffer, print,
                  5 → m; 9 → m;  |;
        shift flag ≠ 0 ∩ first comparison[k](0 → 14) ≠ 0: upper case,
             m - m(1)0| space |; ; 0 → m |,
        PRINT BIT LIMIT:
        | k → print bit limit(15 → 29), 15030₈temporary storage,
        k - 1(1)0| temporary storage[k] + 27 → 1, decode and print,  |,
        print bit limit(15 → 29) → k,  |,
        P|RINT TITLE 1:
        | set → title flag, carriage return uppercase,
        51 → lower loop limit, 62 → upper loop limit, dump a title,  |,
        P|RINT TITLE 2:
        | n - 777₈(1)0| 0 → name dumped flag[n],  |,
        carriage return upercase, dump the date,
        46 → lower loop limit, 49 → upper loop limit, dump a title,  |,
        S|ELECT OUTPUT EQUIPMENT:
        | check key sets, key[1] ≠ 0: start flex; start punch;  |,
        E|XIT:
        key[1] ≠ 0: turn off flex; turn off punch; check key sets,
        clear indices, key[2] ≠ 0: 61410₈program entry address. ;
        dump name lists and stop: . .


        5
        m|ag tape routine - | print operator error, write, read,
        rewind, pass ahead, pass back,  |,
        | 1|ast block(15 → 29), bl|ock nr(0 → 14),  |(4) - 1, 1, 1, 1;
        RRU TAPE HANDLER: mag tape handler,
        MAG TAPE HANDLER:
        | i → first address, j → last address, j → sequence number,
        k / 2↑8 → load type / 2↑4 → n ≥ 4: print operator error. ;
        1 ≠ 0: 1 → last block[n]; ; 0 → move back flag,
        last block[n] - 0: start flex, carriage return lower case,
             2420012364₈ → dump buffer, print, print block nr. ;
        k(0 → 11) → function code → k ≥ 6: print operator error. ;
        interogate unit status, load buffer[1] - 12₈ ∪ load buffer[1] - 16₈:
             repeat. 1 - 32000(1)0| ,  |; mag tape routine[k], exit.
        I|NTEROGATE UNIT STATUS:
        | r|epeat: 17300₈0, 13000₈160₈, 50010₈ + load type → dump buffer[1],
        13310₈dump buffer[1], 0 → dump buffer[1], 13000₈120₈,
        17330₈load buffer[1], load buffer[1] - load type → load buffer[1],
```

```
7 < load buffer[1] < 17₈: ; print unit error.
load buffer[1] = 13₈:
    | k = 3 ∪ k = 5: 1 → block nr[n], exit. exit ius.  |; ;
load buffer[1] = 12₈ ∪ load buffer[1] = 16₈:
    | 3 < function code < 6 ∪ move back flag ≠ 0: exit ius. ;  |; ;
load buffer[1] = 14₈: | k = 5 ∪ k = 3: exit ius. print unit error.  |; ;
load buffer[1] ≠ 10₈: repeat. ; e|xit ius:  |.
W|RITE:
| r|ewrite: last address - first address → dump buffer < 0:
    print operator error. ;
0 → temporary storage[1], block nr[n] → upper dump buffer,
initiate output, write one word,
i = first address(1)last address| [1] → dump buffer, write one word,
dump buffer + temporary storage[1] → temporary storage[1],  |,
temporary storage[1] → dump buffer, write one word,
1 = 32000(1)0|  , |, 5 → k, read or int check sum,
1 = 32000(1)0|  , |, clear flag = 0: block nr[n] + 1 → last block[n],
    1 → j, pass ahead; ; check key sets, key[1] ≠ 0: exit. ;
initiate output, initiate output, initiate output, rewrite.  |.
R|EAD:
| 0 → function code, sequence number = 0: read on. ;
sequence number - block nr[n] → j → move back flag < 0:
    0 - move back flag → j, pass back; pass ahead;
R|EAD ON:
block nr[n] ≥ last block[n]: print operator error. ;
4 → k, read or int check sum, type limits, print block nr.  |.
R|EWIND: | 1 → block nr[n], initiate input, exit.  |.
P|ASS AHEAD:
| 4 → k, block nr[n] + j → block nr[n] ≥ last block[n] + 1:
    block nr[n] - j → block nr[n], print operator error. ; pass,  |.
P|ASS BACK:
| 5 → k, block nr[n] - j → block nr[n], pass,
interogate unit status, 1 = 32000(1)0|  , |,  |.
P|ASS:
| j ≠ 0: | i = j( - 1)1| initiate input,
    move back flag = 0 ∩ i = 1: exit. ;
    interogate unit status, load buffer[1] ≠ 16₈: repeat. ;  |,  |; ;
0 → move back flag,  |.
R|EAD OR INT CHECK SUM: | 0 → case flag,
S|TART AGAIN: initiate input, read a word, function code ≠ 0: go on. ;
upper load buffer → block nr[n] ≠ sequence number ∩
sequence number ≠ 0: 1 + block nr[n] → block nr[n],
    print operator error. ;
lower load buffer + first address → last address ≥ 100000₈:
    1 + block nr[n] → block nr[n], print operator error. ;
G|O ON:
0 → temporary storage, i = first address(1)last address| read a word,
function code = 0: load buffer → [i]; ;
load buffer + temporary storage → temporary storage,  |,
read a word, function code = 0: | check key sets,
    key[1] = 0: first address → beginning of flowcharts,
        last address → end of flowcharts; ;
    1 + block nr[n] → block nr[n], load buffer → temporary storage[1],  |;
temporary storage[1] ≠ temporary storage:
    | type check sum error, function code = 0:
        | case flag + 1 → case flag ≥ 3: print unit error. ;
        1 → j, j → move back flag, pass back, 4 → k, start again.  |;
        k → clear flag;  |; 0 → clear flag;  |.
I|NITIATE INPUT:
| interogate unit status, load buffer[1] = 16₈: repeat. ;
560₈ → dump buffer[1], start tape unit,  |.
```

I|NITIATE OUTPUT: '
| 1 → k, interogate unit status, 760₈ → dump buffer[1],
start unit, |.
S|TART TAPE UNIT:
| 17300₈0, 13000₈0, 13030₈dump buffer[1], 17400₈0,
50000₈ + load type + k → dump buffer[1], 13310₈dump buffer[1],
1 = 20(1)0| , |, 17300₈0, |.
W|RITE ONE WORD:
| 13430₈dump buffer, m = 10(1)0| 1 = 22400(1)0| 63400₈continue. |, |,
print unit error. c|ontinue: |.
R|EAD A WORD: | d|elay 1: 63400₈delay 1. 17430₈load buffer, |.
P|RINT OPERATOR ERROR:
04000₈0, start flex, 24 → lower loop limit, 27 → upper loop limit,
carriage return upper case, dump a title, print block nr.
P|RINT UNIT ERROR:
start flex, 124 → lower loop limit, |28 → upper loop limit,
carriage return upper case, dump a title, print block nr.
E|XIT: start flex,
P|RINT BLOCK NR:
load type × 2↑8 → upper dump buffer[1], carriage return lower case, dump
one number, block nr[n] → n, space, print sequence number,
E|XIT 1: turn off flex, clear indices, |. .

5;
FLOWCHART DUMP:
m ≠ 0: m → beginning of flowcharts; ; 1 ≠ 0: 1 → end of flowcharts; ;
0 → title flag,
D|UMP:
j = 0: beginning of flowcharts → j, n → sequence number;
      0 → sequence number; 1 = sequence number(1)0| s|kip zeros:
[j] = 0: j + 1 → j, skip zeros. ;
j → first address ≥ end of flowcharts: exit. ;
find flowchart limits, |, check key sets,
key[2] = 0: dump a flowchart; ; key[1] ≠ 0: punch limits; type limits;
n + 1 → n, space, space, print sequence number,
key[1] ≠ 0: dump. ; exit.
P|UNCH LIMITS:
| title flag = 0: start punch, set → title flag; ;
carriage return lower case, print limits, |.
PRINT FLOWCHART ERROR:
start flex, 43 → lower loop limit, 45 → upper loop limit,
dump a title, upper case, title constant[13] → dump buffer,
print, 0 → address limits[1], return to load.
E|XIT:
0 → m → 1 → 1 → j, title flag ≠ 0: turn off punch; turn off flex; .

5;
DEBUG SCAN:
1 = 0: standard compiling location → 1; ;
j = .0: obj prog std last address → j; ;
i = 1(1)j| [i] = straight jump function ∪ [i] = return jump function:
    fault 9. ; [i](15 → 29) = 61000₈ ∩ [i](0 → 14) ‒ bias → k ≠ 0:
    | [k] = 0 ∪ [k] = straight jump function: fault 10. ; |; ;
l|oop exit: |. check key sets, turn off flex, clear indices,
key[2] ≠ 0: dump name lists and stop. exit.
F|AULT 9:
start flex, carriage return upper case, 69 → lower loop limit,
72 → upper loop limit, dump a title,

```
n = 177₈(1)0| undefined name location[n] = 1:
    write undefined name, continue. ;  |,
C|ONTINUE: write address, loop exit.
F|AULT 10:
start flex, carriage return upper case,
77 → lower loop limit, 82 → upper loop limit, dump a title,
n = 777₈(1)0| name address[n] - bias = k: write name, go on. ;  |,
k → upper dump buffer[1], dump five numbers,
G|O ON: write address, loop exit.
W|RITE ADDRESS:
| 73 → lower loop limit, 76 → upper loop limit, dump a title,
i → upper dump buffer[1], dump five numbers,  |. e|xit: . .


5;
TYPE FLOWCHART:
0 → frame counter, set → manual entry flag,
type the flowchart, clear indices,
TYPE THE FLOWCHART:
| start flex, 43 → lower loop limit, 45 → upper loop limit,
dump a title, j → first address, manual entry flag ≠ 0: type one line. ;
sequence number → n, print sequence number,
T|YPE ONE LINE:
carriage return, carriage return,
n = 7(1)0| convt and print compiler coded word,  |, check key sets,
manual entry flag ≠ 0 ∩ key[1] ≠ 0: type one line. ;
j → last address, type limits, turn off flex, 0 → manual entry flag,  |. .


5;
START COMPILING:
1 → final seq nr, sequence number = 777₈: 1 → sequence number;
    0 → sequence number; m = 0: standard compiling location → m; ;
check key sets, key[1] ≠ 0: start flex, 93 → lower loop limit,
    105 → upper loop limit, dump a title, turn off flex; ;
CONTINUE COMPILING:
i ≠ 0: i → obj prog first address;        object prog std first address →
    obj prog first address → i;
j ≠ 0: j → flochart first address; flocht storage std first address →
    flochart first address → j;
k ≠ 0:    k → obj prog last address → current obj prog last address;
    obj prog std last address → obj prog last address →
    current obj prog last address;
n ≠ 0: n → program entry address;
    std program entry address → program entry address; m = 0: 1 → m; ;
i - m → bias, m → 1, 1 + sequence number → sequence number → m,
13405₈0, j < 1 < end of flowcharts: fault 1. ;
i < j < obj prog last address: flochart first address - 1 →
    current obj prog last address; ;
1 = i(1)current obj prog last address| 0 → [1],  |,
1 + bias → obj prog first address[m] ≠ temporary storage[4]:
    i → first obj prog address; ;
1 = 777₈(1)0| 0 → first comparison[1],   |,
j → flochart first address[m], process dimensions,
i → entrance flag → type name flag,
present character → next operator, 0 → operand, advance.
start compiling and stop: . .


5;
PROCESS DIMENSIONS:
| comma → current operator, colon → next operator,
k desig[3] → k designator,
```

E|NTRY A:
read next character, 0 → back space flag,
E|NTRY B: 0 → manual entry flag,
present character < a number: | read the name, process the name,
    operand → k, partial word flag = 0: 1 + 1 → 1,
    1 → number accumulator → list length[k]; ; |; ;
present character = period: initialize floating operation,
    1 + number accumulator → 1, entry a. ;
present character = comma: entry a. ; present character = left paren:
    | e|ntry c: read next character,
    a letter < present character < an operator: read a number; fault 3.
    present character = right arrow:
        number accumulator → name mask lower limit[k], entry c. ;
    partial word flag = 0: number accumulator → list length[k]; ;
    present character = multiply: read next character,
        read a number, number accumulator → matrix width[k] ×
        list length[k] → number accumulator; ;
    present character = right paren:
        | partial word flag = 0: 1 + number accumulator - 1 → 1;
        | number accumulator + 1 - name mask lower limit[k] →
        name mask length[k] = 15: | name mask lower limit[k] = 0:
            1 → name k desig[k], 0 → name mask[k]; ;
        name mask lower limit[k] = 15:
            2 → name k desig[k], 0 → name mask[k]; ; |; ;
        name mask[k] ≠ 0: check previous call; ; entry a. |;
    read next character, a letter < present character < an operator:
        number accumulator → temporary storage, read a number,
        number accumulator × (matrix width[k] + 1) →
        back space flag, temporary storage → number accumulator; ;
    decrement name addresses, entry b. |; fault 3. |; ;
present character = colon ∩ partial word flag = 0: 1 - 1 → 1, entry a. ;
present character = left brace: set → partial word flag, entry a. ;
present character = right brace: 0 → partial word flag, 1 + 1 → 1,
    1 → number accumulator, entry a. ;
present character = equal sign: | 1 → temporary storage,
    read next character, 1 - number accumulator → 1,
    check subsequent operator, first comparison = period ∪
    first comparison = multiply: initialize floating operation,
        temporary storage + number accumulator → temporary storage,
        1 → floating point flag; ; 0 → back space flag,
    present character = left brace: set → manual entry flag,
E|NTRY D: read next character; ;
    present character < a number ∩ manual entry flag ≠ 0:
        0 → k designator, period → next operator, read the name,
        process the name, 0 → floating point flag, operand +
        k designator → [1], colon → next operator,
        k desig[3] → k designator; ;
    present character = minus: set → negative flag,
        read next character; 0 → negative flag;
    a letter < present character < an operator:
        read a number, number accumulator → [1]; ;
    floating point flag ≠ 0: number accumulator[1] → [1 + 1],
        1 + 1 → 1; ; 1 + 1 → 1, 0 → number accumulator[1],
    present character = right brace: entry a. ;
    present character = comma: entry d. ;
    temporary storage → 1, 0 → floating point flag, entry b. |; ;
present character = right paren ∩ define function flag ≠ 0: exit. ;
define function flag ≠ 0: entry a. ;
present character = left bracket: | read next character,

0 → k designator, read the name, process the name,
k desig[3] → k designator, read next character, 30 → shift flag,
I|NSERT CODES: present character ≠ right bracket:
    | [i] × 2↑6 + present character → [i],
    shift flag - 6 → shift flag = 0: 30 → shift flag, 1 + i → i; ;
    read next character, insert codes. |; ;
[i] × 2↑shift flag → [i], i + 1 → i, [i - 1] ≠ 0: i + 1 → i; ;
0 → shift flag, entry a. |; ;
present character ≠ semi colon: fault 3. ;
E|XIT:
floating entrance = 7: i + bias + k desig[1] → floating entrance,
    period → next operator, k = 16(1)26| 0 → name buffer[1] →
    name buffer[2], (- k) × 2↑24 → name buffer, process the name,
    i + 1 → i |, colon → next operator; ;
reconcile name lists(1), 0 → k designator → unknown operand flag, |.
C|HECK PREVIOUS CALL:
| n = 177₈(1)0| name part 1[k] = undefined name 1[n] ∩
name part 2[k] = undefined name 2[n] ∩
name part 3[k] = undefined name 3[n]:
    store flowchart parameters, start flex, carriage return upper case,
    write name buffer, space, 63 → lower loop limit,
    68 → upper loop limit, dump a title, turn off flex,
    restore flowchart parameters, exit cpc. ; |, e|xit cpc: |,
D|ECREMENT NAME ADDRESSES:
| k ≠ 0: | k - 1 → n, n = n(1)0| name address[n] = name address[k]:
    name address[n] - back space flag → name address[n],
    name mask[k](10 → 29) → name mask[n](10 → 29); ; |, |; ;
name address[k] - back space flag → name address[k], |,
I|NITIALIZE FLOATING OPERATION:
| floating entrance = 0: 7 → floating entrance; ;
1 → name floating flag[k], decrement name addresses,
check previous call, |. .

5;
ADVANCE: advance and return, jump to generator.
ADVANCE 1: advance 1 and return, jump to generator.
ADVANCE AND RETURN:
| next operator → current operator,
operand → previous operand, 0 → operand, advance 1 and return, |,
ADVANCE 1 AND RETURN:
| read next character,
present character ≥ a number: check for an operator. ;
read the name, present character → next operator,
name buffer(0 → 23) = 0 ∩ 10000₈ < upper name buffer < 17000₈:
    set b designator. ; 0 → b designator → k designator,
process the name, set next operator.
S|ET B DESIGNATOR:
name buffer × 2↑6 - 8 → n, b desig[n] → b designator,
0 → name buffer → type name flag, set next operator.
C|HECK FOR AN OPERATOR: present character ≥ an operator ∩
present character ≠ octal si gn:. set next operator. ;
read a number, number accumulator → operand,
operand(15 → 29) ≠ 0 ∪ floating point flag ≠ 0: enter a constant; ;
S|ET NEXT OPERATOR: present character → next operator,
b designator + k designator + operand + full operand +
unknown operand flag → operand flag, |,
ENTER A CONSTANT:
| n = 177₈(1)0| mask record[n] = 0: make a new constant. ;
mask record[n] → m, [m] = number accumulator:
    | floating point flag ≠ 0 ∩ number accumulator[1] ≠ [m + 1]: ;

m + bias → operand, exit eac. |; ; |,
M|AKE A NEW CONSTANT:
floating point flag ≠ 0: straight jump function → function code,
   i + bias + 3 → operand, assemble next command, record constant. ;
[i - 1](24 → 29) → temporary storage,
constant flag ≠ 0 ∪ temporary storage ≥ 60₈ ∪
11₈ < temporary stor age < 14₈ ∪ 15₈ < temporary storage < 20₈:
   add function → function code, 0 → operand, assemble next command; ;
i ≠ entrance flag: [i - 1] + j desig[1] → [i - 1];
   entrance flag + 1 → entrance flag;
n = 777₈(1)0| name address[n] - bias = 1:
   | 1 + name address[n] → name address[n], |; ; |,
R|ECORD CONSTANT:
n = 177₈(1)0| mask record[n] = 0: 1 → mask record[n], exit loop. ; |,
E|XIT LOOP:
number accumulator → [i], i + bias → operand → constant flag, i + 1 → i,
floating point flag ≠ 0: number accumulator[1] → [1], i + 1 → i; ;
E|XIT EAC: k desig[3] → k designator, |. .

5
f|ractional part. d|ummy(20) = 77777 77702₈, 15574 67755₈,
77777 77706₈, 10456 02764₈, 77777 77711₈, 12571 43561₈,
77777 77714₈, 15327 74515₈, 77777 77720₈, 10306 75720₈,
77777 77723₈, 12370 55304₈, 77777 77726₈, 15066 70566₈,
77777 77732₈, 10142 23351₈, 77777 77735₈, 12172 70244₈,
77777 77740₈, 14631 46315₈, t|s. i|ndex fp, f|p number accumulator. ;
READ NEXT CHARACTER: | e|xtract next frame:
frame counter - 1 → frame counter < 0: [j] → flowchart buffer,
   j + 1 → j, 4 → frame counter; ;
flowchart buffer x 2↑6 → flowchart buffer,
flowchart buffer(0 → 5) → present character = 0: extract next frame. ; |,
READ ANY CHARACTER:
| frame counter - 1 → frame counter < 0: [j] → flowchart buffer,
   j + 1 → j, 4 → frame counter; ;
flowchart buffer x 2↑6 → flowchart buffer,
flowchart buffer(0 → 5) → present character, |,
READ A NUMBER: | read an integer,
present character = period: | store flowchart parameters,
   read next character, a letter < present character < octal sign ∩
   floating point flag = 0: set → floating point flag; ;
   restore flowchart parameters, |; ; floating point flag = 0:
   | negative flag ≠ 0: number accumulator → → number accumulator,
      0 → negative flag; ; exit ran. |; ;
number accumulator → fp number accumulator,
present character = period: | read next character,
   n = 9(1)0| present character - 27 → ts, fractional part[n + 1] ×
   ts + fp number accumulator → fp number accumulator,
   read next character, a letter < present character < octal sign: ;
      check for exponent. |,
   R|EAD TO END: a letter < present character < octal sign:
      read next character, read to end. ; |; ;
C|HECK FOR EXPONENT:
negative flag ≠ 0: - index fp[2] → index fp[2], 0 → negative flag; ;
present character = multiply ∩ floating point flag = 1:
   | read next character, present character = minus: read next character,
      fractional part[10] → ts; 10. 0 → ts; read an integer,
   number accumulator ≠ 0:
      n = 1(1)number accumulator| fp number accumulator ×
      ts → fp number accumulator, |; ; |; ;
index fp[1] → number accumulator,
index fp[2] → number accumulator[1], e|xit ran: |

```
R|EAD AN INTEGER: | 0 → number accumulator → number accumulator[1],
R|EAD NEXT FRAME:
number accumulator × 2↑3 + present character _ 27 → number accumulator,
number accumulator[1] × 10 + present character _ 27 →
number accumulator[1], read next character,
a letter < present character < octal sign: read next frame. ;
present character = octal sign: | read next character,
    present character < an operator ∪ present character = left bracket:
        copy machine code. ; |;
    number accumulator[1] → number accumulator; |,
READ THE NAME:
| 0 → name buffer → name buffer[1] → name buffer[2],
m = 0(1)2| n = 4(1)0| name buffer[m] × 2↑6 → name buffer[m],
present character → first frame name buffer[m], read next character,
present character = temp name sign: set → temp name flag,
    read next character; ;
present character ≥ an operator: pack the name buffer. ; |, |,
D|ISCARD INSIGNIFICANT CHARACTERS: read next character,
present character ≥ an operator: exit read a name.
    discard insignificant characters.
P|ACK THE NAME BUFFER: n ≠ 0:
    n = n(77776₈)1| name buffer[m] × 2↑6 → name buffer[m],  |; ;
E|XIT READ A NAME: glossary flag ≠ 0 ∩ type name flag = 0:
    _ name buffer → name buffer; ;  |. .


5;
PROCESS THE NAME:
| n = 0(1)777₈| name buffer = name part 1[n] ∩
name buffer[1] = name part 2[n] ∩
name buffer[2] = name part 3[n]: set → name found flag,
    exit name list search. ; 0 → name found flag, |,
E|XIT NAME LIST SEARCH:
next operator = left paren ∩ loop control flag = 0:
    | check subsequent operator, first comparison = right arrow:
        continue. ; current operator < left paren: | 0 → character counter,
        L|OOK ON: present character = left paren:
            character counter + 1 → character counter; ;
        present character = right paren:
            character counter _ 1 → character counter; ;
        read next character, character counter ≠ 0: look on. ;
        present character = colon: set → define function flag,
            restore flowchart parameters, colon → next operator,
            check jump around, continue. ; |; ;
    restore flowchart parameters, set → function flag →
    unknown operand flag, 0 → operand, exit process the name. |; ;
C|ONTINUE:
next operator ≠ colon ∪ right brace < current operator < or:
    set operand. ; name found flag ≠ 0: n → temporary storage,
    start flex, store flowchart parameters,
    carriage return upper case, write name buffer, space,
    91 → lower loop limit, 92 → upper loop limit,
    dump a title, lower case, space, i + bias → first address,
    j → last address, print limits, space, sequence number → n,
    print sequence number, turn off flex, restore flowchart parameters,
    temporary storage → n, enter name list. ;
n = 0(1)777₈| name part 1[n] = 0: enter name list. ; |. fault 4.
E|NTER NAME LIST:
name buffer → name part 1[n], name buffer[1] → name part 2[n],
name buffer[2] → name part 3[n], k designator → operand list[n], i +
```

bias → name address[n], set → operand list[n](15 → 17),
temp name flag ≠ 0 ∪ name buffer < 0: set → name temp flag[n]; ;
define function flag = 3: 1 → name temp flag[n]; ;
n → operand, sequence number → 1, type name flag ≠ 0:
   n + 1 → name index[1]; ; 0 → type name flag,
define function flag = 7: | n → process the name(15 → 29),
   3 → define function flag, process dimensions,
   process the name(15 → 29) → name index → 1,
   n = 0(1)name index| name address[n] = name address[1] ∩
   name k desig[n] = 0: 1 + bias → name address[n]; ⌐ |,
   read next character, present character → next operator,
   advance. |; ; exit process the name.
E|NTER UNDEFINED NAME LIST: n = 0(1)177₈| undefined name 1[n] = 0:
   name buffer → undefined name 1[n], name buffer[1] → undefined name 2[n],
   name buffer[2] → undefined name 3[n], 1 → undefined name location[n],
   n + 1 → unknown operand flag, 0 → operand,
   exit process the name. ; |. fault 7.
S|ET OPERAND: name found flag = ∪ operand list[n](15 → 17) ≠ 0:
   enter undefined name list. ; name address[n] → operand,
name k desig[n] → k designator(18 → 20),
name mask[n] < 0: set → floating point flag; 0 → floating point flag;
name mask length[n] ≠ 0: name mask lower limit[n] → lower bit limit,
   name mask length[n] + name mask lower limit[n] - 1 →
   upper bit limit, set → partial word flag; ;
E|XIT PROCESS THE NAME: 0 → temp name flag, |,
CHECK JUMP AROUND: | i = entrance flag: 0 → entrance flag;
  | add function → a function, exit condition counter → m,
  set simple exit, exit condition list[m](24 → 29) = 6:
    | exit condition list[m] → k, straight jump function +
    i + bias = [k]: exit condition counter + 1 →
     exit condition counter → m; ; |; ; |; |. .

5;
FAULT: 0 → lower loop limit, 4 → upper loop limit, type the fault,
generator exit.
FAULT 1: 5 → lower loop limit, 8 → upper loop limit, exit.
FAULT 2: 9 → lower loop limit, 13 → upper loop limit, exit.
FAULT 3: 14 → lower loop limit, 19 → upper loop limit,
present character → next operator, type the fault, advance.
FAULT 4: 20 → lower loop limit, 23 → upper loop limit, exit.
FAULT 6:
| 28 → lower loop limit, 31 → upper loop limit, type the fault, |,
FAULT 7: 32 → lower loop limit, 37 → upper loop limit,
E|XIT: type the fault, exit entry from fault.
TYPE THE FAULT: | start flex, store flowchart parameters,
carriage return upper case, dump a title, 41 → lower loop limit,
42 → upper loop limit, dump a title, current operator → 1,
decode and print, space, space, next operator → 1, decode and print,
j - 4 → j, 0 → frame counter, type the flowchart, restore flowchart
parameters, |. .

5;
GENERATOR EXIT:
unknown operand flag ≥ 120₈ ∩ comparison level = 0 ∩
temp list index = 0: reconcile name lists(0); ;
0 → unknown operand flag → operand flag → first shift →
second shift → shift flag → shift flag1,
floating point flag ≠ 0 ∩ next operator = right arrow:

100_8 + op reg flag → op reg flag → tc reg flag[0]; ;
clear temp list flag $\neq$ 0 ∪ function flag $\neq$ 0:
   0 → floating point flag; ; next operator $\neq$ right brace: advance. ;
I|NTERPRET EXIT CONDITION LIST:
exit condition counter - 1 → exit condition counter < 0: fault. ;
exit condition counter → m, exit condition list[m](0 → 23) → a function,
exit condition list[m](24 → 29) → l, exit condition routine[l],
exit condition list[m - 1](24 → 29) = 6 ∩ exit condition counter $\neq$ 0:
   interpret exit condition list. ; comma → next operator, advance.
E|XIT CONDITION ROUTINE: release comparison lockout, set simple exit,
purge formal parameter names, set decrement loop functions,
set increment loop functions, set unknown increment loop functions,
set jump around subroutine,
SET SIMPLE EXIT: | next operator = right brace ∪
a function(15 → 29) = j desig[4](15 → 29):
   | k = 777_8(1)0| name address[k] - bias = i: set exit jump,
     exit sse. ; |, |; ; [1 - 2](24 → 29) → temporary storage,
11_8 < temporary storage < 14_8 ∪ 15_8 < temporary storage < 20_8: ;
   | [1 - 2](21 → 23) $\neq$ 0: set exit jump, exit sse. ; |;
second comparison $\neq$ 0: | k = second comparison(1)1| [k](0 → 14) -
   bias = i: set exit jump, exit sse. ; |, |; ;
[1 - 1](21 → 29) = 610_8 ∪ 613_8 < [1 - 1](21 → 29) < 620_8: ; set exit jump,
   exit sse. exit condition list[m + 1](24 → 29) = 6:
   | exit condition list[m + 1](0 → 14) → k,
   [k](0 → 14) - bias = i: set exit jump; ; |; ;
E|XIT SSE: a function(15 → 29) = k desig[1](15 → 29) ∩ entrance flag = 0 ∩
exit condition counter = 0: i → entrance flag; ; |,
S|ET EXIT JUMP: | a function(0 → 14) = 0:
   | k = 777_8(1)0| name address[k] - bias = i: name address[k] +
     1 → name address[k]; ;, exit condition counter → m,
   shift a left function + 1 → exit condition list[m],
   exit condition counter + 1 → exit condition counter → m, |; ;
a function(0 → 23) + straight jump function → [i], i + 1 → i, |,
P|URGE FORMAL PARAMETER NAMES:
| k = 777_8(1)0| name temp flag[k] = 1: purge name; ; |,
set simple exit, |,
S|ET DECREMENT LOOP FUNCTIONS:
| dec loop cntrl function + a function → [i], i + 1 → i, |,
S|ET INCREMENT LOOP FUNCTIONS:
| inc loop cntrl function + a function → [i], i + 1 → i,
interpret exit condition list. |,
S|ET UNKNOWN INCREMENT LOOP FUNCTIONS:
| a function - 1 → m, i → undefined name location[m],
interpret exit condition list. |,

R|ELEASE COMPARISON LOCK OUT: | 0 → comparison lockout flag, |,
S|ET JUMP AROUND SUBROUTINE: | a function → 1, i + bias → [l](0 → 14), |,
ASSEMBLE NEXT COMMAND:
| function code + j designator + k designator + b designator +
operand → [i], i + 1 → i, i ≥ current obj prog last address: fault 1. ;
0 → function code → j designator → k designator → b designator, |.
CHECK HALF WORD: | upper bit limit = 14 ∩ lower bit limit = 0:
   k desig[1] → k designator, 0 → partial word flag → bit limits; ;
upper bit limit = 29 ∩ lower bit limit = 15: k desig[2] → k designator,
   0 → partial word flag → bit limits; ;
b designator + k designator + operand → full operand, |. .

5 ;
COPY MACHINE CODE: number accumulator → function code(15 → 29).

present character < a number: read the name,
    present character → next operator, process the name, 0 → k designator.;
present character < an operator: read a number,
    number accumulator → operand; ;
present character ≠ left bracket: read on. ; read next character,
8 < present character < 15:
    present character - 8 → function code(15 → 17), read next character; ;
present character < a number: crutch code fault. ;
present character → temp pc storage - minus ∪
present character - plus: read next character; ;
present character < an operator: | read a number, temp pc storage - minus:
    0 - number accumulator → number accumulator; ;
    operand + number accumulator → operand(0 → 14), |; ;
present character ≠ right bracket: crutch code fault. ; read next character,
R|EAD ON: partial word flag ≠ 0 ∪ present character - left paren:
    0 → partial word flag → lower bit limit → upper bit limit,
    crutch code fault. ;
assemble next command, present character → next operator,
punct area minus 1 < present character < punct area plus 1:
    complete relation control. generator exit.
C|RUTCH CODE FAULT: 114 → lower loop limit, 117 → upper loop limit,
    type the fault,
F|IND NEXT STATEMENT:
punct area minus 1 < present character < punct area plus 1:
    read on. read next character, find next statement. .

5;
STORE TEMP COMMAND:
| temp list index → 1 ≠ 0: | tc reg flag[1 - 1] → reg flag,
    tc offset[1 - 1] → offset ≠ lower bit limit ∪
    tc reg flag[1 - 1] + tl reg flag - 106₈: align part words; ; |; ;
lower bit limit → offset, store word, |,
STORE WORD: | function code + j designator + k designator +
b designator + operand → temp list[1],
0 → function code → j designator → k designator → b designator,
level → level list[1], tl reg flag → tc reg flag[1],
offset → tc offset[1], 1 + 1 → temp list index → 1, |,
PART WORD COMMAND: | a function → function code, 7 → tl reg flag,
store temp command, check for undef name, set tl mask, |,
FULL WORD COMMAND: | tl reg flag - 0: op reg flag → tl reg flag; ;
tl reg flag - 7: a function → function code;
    q function → function code, 77₈ → tl reg flag;
store temp command, check for undef name, 0 → bit limits[1], |,
ALIGN PART WORDS: | 0 → j designator → k designator → b designator,
function code + full operand → full operand, shift aq left function →
function code, reg flag + tl regflag - 106₈: 30 → operand; 60 → operand.
operand - lower bit limit + offset → operand ≥ 61:
    operand - 60 → operand; ; store word, reg flag → tc reg flag[1 - 1],
full operand → operand, |,
STORE AND ADD TS: | zeroize op offset, store current sum,
partial word flag → temporary storage[3](0 → 14), 0 → partial word flag,
unknown operand flag → temporary storage[3](15 → 29),
0 → unknown operand flag, lower bit limit → temporary storage,
0 → lower bit limit, k desig[3] → k designator,
bit limits[1] → temporary storage[2], set add inst,
temporary storage → lower bit limit, temporary storage[2] → bit limits[1],
temporary storage[3](0 → 14) → partial word flag,
temporary storage[3](15 → 29) → unknown operand flag, |,
OP STORE PART WORD: | op reg flag → temporary storage[1] ≠ 0:
    zeroize op offset, store current sum, operand → operand storage[2]; ;

0 → k designator → b designator, set op mask, unknown operand flag ≠ 0:
    unknown operand flag - 1 → n, 1 → undefined name location[n]; ;
enter log prod function → function code, reset operand,
assemble next command, last lower bit limit → op offset,
zeroize op offset, 0 → bit limits[1], 7 → op reg flag,
compile op shift, store current sum, operand → operand storage[1],
temporary storage[1] ≠ 0: enter q function → function code,
    k desig[3] + operand storage[2] → operand → [1],
    release ts, assemble next command, 77₈ → op reg flag, ; ;
k desig[3] + operand storage[1] → full operand → operand, |,
ZEROIZE OP OFFSET:
| op offset ≠ 0: shift aq left function + 60 - op offset → [1],
    1 + 1 → 1, 0 → op offset; ; |,
CHECK FOR UNDEF NAME: | unknown operand flag → tc mask flag[1 - 1],
 0 → unknown operand flag, |. .

5;
TRANSFER TEMP COMMAND:
| temp list index - 1 → temporary storage < 0: exit. ;
op reg flag ≠ 0: | temp list index → 1, tc offset[1 - 1] → offset,
    op reg flag → reg flag, lower bit limit → temporary storage[3],
    op offset → lower bit limit ≠ offset ∪ op reg flag +
    tc reg flag[1 - 1] = 106₈: 1 + temporary storage → temporary storage,
        tl reg flag → temporary storage[4], tc reg flag[1 - 1] →
        tl reg flag, align part words, temporary storage[4] →
        tl reg flag; ; temporary storage[3] → lower bit limit, |; ;
1 = temporary storage(1)0| level list[1] ≥ level:
    | level list[1 - 1] < level ∩ temp list[1](15 → 29) = 07000₈: ;
        | temp list[1] → [1] ≠ 0:
            | [1 - 1] - [1] = compare function: decrement i(1); ;
            [1 - 2] - j desig[1] - [1 - 1] - [1] = compare function:
                decrement i(2); ;
            [1 - 2] = [1] ∩ [1 - 1] - [1 + 1] = 6: decrement i(3); ;
            [1 - 5] = [1] ∩ [1 - 4] - [1 - 2] - [1 - 1] - [1 + 1] = 6:
                decrement i(6); ; [1] = 07000 00036₈ ∩ op reg flag = 77₈:
                load a add q function → [1]; ;
            0 → constant flag, tc reg flag[1] → op reg flag,
            tc offset[1] → op offset, tc mask flag[1] ≥ 2000₈:
                tc mask flag[1] - 2000₈ + i + bias → [1](0 → 14),
                0 → tc mask flag[1]; ;
            tc mask flag[1] = 777₈: enter mask record;
            | tc mask flag[1] ≥ 1000₈: | store current sum,
                1 - 1 → 1, tc mask flag[1] - 1000₈ → n,
                floating point flag = 0: operand + k desig[3] → operand; ;
                operand → temp list[n](0 → 20), |;
                | tc mask flag[1] ≠ 0: tc mask flag[1] - 1 → n,
                    i → undefined name location[n];
                release ts; |; |; 1 + 1 → 1. |; ; |;
        C|LEAR TEMP COMMAND: 0 → temp list[1] → level list[1] →
        tc mask flag[1] → tc offset[1], 0 → tc reg flag[1],
        i ≥ current obj prog last address: fault 1. ;
        1 → temp list index = 0: 0 → tl reg flag; ; |; ; |.
E|XIT: 0 → bit limits[1], |.
D|ECREMENT I(a): | release ts, n = 0: exit di. ;
a = 2 ∪ a = 6: 0 → ts address record[n] → ts ready flag[n]; ;
a = 3 ∪ a = 6: 1 + 1 → 1; ; 1 - a → n, n = n(1)1| 0 → [n], |,
1 - a → 1, clear temp command. e|xit di: |,
STORE CURRENT SUM: | 0 → j designator → b designator → k designator,

floating point flag $\neq$ 0: enter b function + j desig[7] → [i],
   return jump function + floating entrance + 6 → [i + 1], 1 → m;
   | op reg flag = 7: store a function → [i]; store q function → [i];
   4 → m, |; n = 19(- 1)|| 0 < ts ready flag[n] < m + 1:
ts address record[n] + bias → operand + k desig[m - 1] + [i] →
[i], 0 → ts ready flag[n], exit 1. ; ts address record[n] = 0:
 | s|et new ts: floating point flag $\neq$ 0: 1 + 2 → 1,
   straight jump function + 1 + bias + 3 → [i],
   1 + 1 → 1 → ts address record[n] + bias → operand + [i - 3] →
   [i - 3]; 1 + 1 → 1 → ts address record[n] + bias → operand +
   j desig[1] + k desig[3] + [i - 1] → [i - 1];
  set → constant flag, exit 1. |; ; |. set new ts.
E|XIT 1: 1 + 1 → 1, floating point flag $\neq$ 0: 1 + 1 → 1,
  [i - 4] - [i - 2] ∩ [i - 1] - [i - 3] - 6: 1 - 4 → 1,
   0 → [i] → [i + 1] → [i + 2] → [i + 3]; ; |;
  | [i - 1] - [i - 2] = compare function: 1 - 2 → 1, 0 → [i] → [i + 1]; ; |;
0 → op reg flag, |.
RELEASE TS: | 0 → n, [i](0 → 14) $\neq$ 0:
  | n = 19(1)0| [i](0 → 14) - bias = ts address record[n]:
   | floating point flag $\neq$ 0: 1 → ts ready flag[n];
   4 → ts ready flag[n]; exit 2. |; ; |,
  e|xit 2: |; ; |. .

5;
MASK ROUTINES:
SET OP MASK: | set up positive mask, assemble next command,
mask accumulator $\neq$ 0: mask accumulator → [i],
  enter mask record, 1 + 1 → 1; ; |.
SET TL MASK: | temp list index → 1,
upper bit limit - lower bit limit → temporary storage,
last upper bit limit - last lower bit limit = temporary storage ∩
level list[1 - 3] = level: | temp list function[1 - 2] $\neq$ 07: 1 + 1 → 1; ;
  temp list function[1 - 3] = 10₈: | 0 → temp list[1 - 3],
   tc mask flag[1 - 4] = 777₈:
    0 → temp list[1 - 4] → tc mask flag[1 - 4]; ; |; ; |; ;
set up positive mask, enter mask in temp list, |.
SET TL NEG MASK: | set up negative mask, enter mask in temp list, |.
S|ET UP POSITIVE MASK: | build a mask,
last upper bit limit < 15: 0 → mask accumulator, exit epm. ;
last upper bit limit - 29 ∩ last lower bit limit < 15:
  operand + k desig[4] → operand, 0 → mask accumulator,
  exit epm. ; set up full mask, e|xit epm: |.
S|ET UP NEGATIVE MASK:
| build a mask, - mask accumulator → mask accumulator,
mask accumulator(0 → 14) → operand(0 → 14),
last upper bit limit < 14: operand + k desig[4] → operand,
  0 → mask accumulator, exitenm. ; last upper bit limit = 29 ∩
last lower bit limit < 15: 0 → mask accumulator, exit enm. ;
set up full mask, e|xit enm: |.
S|ET UP FULL MASK: | k desig[3] → operand(0 → 23),
m = 1(1)177₈| mask record[m] → n $\neq$ 0 ∩ [n] = mask accumulator:
  operand + bias + n → operand, 0 → mask accumulator, exit efm. ; |,
operand + j desig[1] → operand, e|xit efm: |.
E|NTER MASK IN TEMP LIST: | temp list index → 1,
mask accumulator $\neq$ 0: operand → operand[3], mask accumulator → operand,
  store word, 777₈ → tc mask flag[1 - 1], operand[3] → operand; ;
store word, |.
ENTER MASK RECORD:
| m = 1(1)177₈| mask record[m] = 0: 1 → mask record[m], exit emr. ; |,

E|XIT EMR: 1 + bias → [1 - 1](0 → 14), |.
B|UILD A MASK: | 0 → mask accumulator,
1 = lower bit limit(1)upper bit limit| mask accumulator × 2 +
1 → mask accumulator, |, lower bit limit ≠ 0:   '
    1 = 1(1)lower bit limit| mask accumulator × 2 → mask accumulator, |; ;
bit limits → bit limits[1], 0 → bit limits → partial word flag,
enter q function + mask accumulator(0 → 14) → operand, |. .

5;
SHIFT ROUTINES: COMPILE OP ENTER AND SHIFT:
| op reg flag = 77₈: enter a function → function code,
    7 → reg flag; enter q function → function code, 77₈ → reg flag;
reset operand, 0 → unknown operand flag,
assemble next command, enter op shift, |.
COMPILE OP SHIFT:
| first shift ≠ 0: op reg flag → reg flag, enter op shift; ; |.
COMPILE TL SHIFT: | e|nter tl shift: first shift ≠ 0: | invert shifts,
    0 → operand → k designator → b designator, first shift →
    q function + 01000 00000₈ → a function, partial word flag ≠ 0:
        7 → tl reg flag; ; unknown operand flag → temporary storage[1],
    shift flag → unknown operand flag, full word command,
    shift flag| → shift flag, second shift → first shift,
    0 → second shift, reset operand, temporary storage[1] → unknown operand
    flag, enter tl shift. |; ; |.
E|NTER OP SHIFT: | 0 → case flag → k designator → b designator,
E|NTER SHIFT: [1 - 1](24 → 29) = 22₈ ∪ case flag ≠ 0:
    02000 00000₈ + first shift → first shift, 0 → case flag; ;
reg flag = 7: 01000 00000₈ + first shift → operand; first shift → operand;
shift flag ≠ 0: shift flag - 1 → n, 1 → undefined name location[n]; ;
assemble next command, second shift → first shift ≠ 0: 0 → second shift,
    shift flag | → shift flag, enter shift. |.
INVERT SHIFTS: | second shift ≠ 0: second shift → temporary storage[4],
    shift flag | → temporary storage[5], shift flag → shift flag |,
    temporary storage[5] → shift flag, first shift → second shift,
    temporary storage[4] → first shift; ; |,
CHECK FOR PART WORD OR SHIFT:
| partial word flag ≠ 0: check for divide shift, op store part word;
    | first shift ≠ 0: | check for divide shift, compile op enter and shift,
        op reg flag → temporary storage = 77₈: 7 → op reg flag; ;
        store current sum, k desig[3] + operand → operand → full operand,
        temporary storage → op reg flag, |; ; |; |,
CHECK FOR DIVIDE SHIFT: | temp list index → 1,
temp list[1 - 1] = divide function: set divide shift inst; ; |,
CHECK FOR SHIFT: | first shift ≠ 0: check for part word or shift; ; |. .

5
c|o logical index(25) = 4050426130₈, 4050426130₈, 4050426130₈,
1050426170₈, 44420300₈, 51041400₈, 320000000₈, 4040426130₈,
40000002₈, 400000002₈, 40000002₈, 2040000002₈, 400000002₈, 40000002₈,
442000000₈, 1250426100₈, 250470100₈, 40200100₈, 40100100₈,
40426100₈, 40426100₈, n|o logical index(25) = 2000020₈, 2000020₈,
2000010₈, 50023110420₈, 400000102₈, 1006310420₈, 40000000₈, 200000000₈,
10000000₈, 2000020₈, 2313000₈, 2313000₈, 22313000₈, 2022313000₈,
2313000₈, 22313000₈, 6313002₈, 102314602₈, 102314602₈, 3700002₈,
2360002₈, , 2000₈, 10023110028₈, 1002311002₈;
JUMP TO GENERATOR:
k designator + b designator + operand → full operand +
unknown operand flag → operand flag,
next operator = equal sign ∪ next operator = less than:

check ahead; ; minus' < next operator < color shift:
| check subsequent operator, first comparison = exponent sign:
    | check half word, first shift = 0: current operator →
        temp co storage, full operand → operand storage[3],
        unknown operand flag → operand storage[2],
            0 → unknown operand flag; full operand → first shift(0 → 23),
            unknown operand flag → shift flag, 0 → unknown operand flag;
        0 → k designator → b designator, advance. |; ; |; ;
next operator = exponent sign: record shift. ;
current operator = exponent sign: | first shift(0 → 23) = 0 ∩
    shift flag = 0: full operand → first shift(0 → 23),
        unknown operand flag → shift flag; full operand →
        second shift(0 → 23), unknown operand flag → shift flag |;
    operand storage[3] → full operand, reset operand,
    operand storage[2] → unknown operand flag,
    temp co storage → current operator, |; ;
punct area minus 1 < current operator < punct area plus 1 ∪
crutch < current operator < exponent sign:
    current operator → punctuation; 0 → punctuation;
next operator = colon ∪ next operator = and ∪ next operator = or:
    next operator → end relation symbol; | next operator = less than ∩
    less less comparison ≥ 2: next operator → end relation symbol;
    0 → end relation symbol; |;
right brace < next operator < plus ∪ next operator = end relation symbol:
    set → clear temp list flag; 0 → clear temp list flag;
current operator - 38 → n, next operator - 38 → 1, co logical index[n] →
co logical index[n], 40034₈no logical index, 15030₈temporary storage,
n = 0(1)29| temporary storage(0 → 0) ≠ 0: generator[n]. ;
temporary storage / 2↑1 → temporary storage, |, fault.
G|ENERATOR: fault. initiate relation control. fault. generate straight jump.
generate return jump. check partial word. check for algebra.
check for neg loop increment. check for loop limits. clear temp list.
generate add or enter. generate add. generate subtract.
generate multiply. generate mult quant. generate mult or enter.
generate divide. generate div or enter. generate div quant.
generate store. initiate loop control. set exit conditions.
generate io. initiate subscript. modify subscript. set subscript.
save current operator. generate add or enter. initiate relation control.
generator exit.
R|ECORD SHIFT: current operator = multiply:
    shift q left function → function code; shift q right function →
    function code; first shift = 0: function code → first shift;
    function code → second shift;
0 → k designator → b designator → function code, advance.
CHECK SUBSEQUENT OPERATOR: | store flowchart parameters,
R|EAD ON: read next character,
present character → first comparison < an operator: read on. ;
restore flowchart parameters, |,
C|HECK AHEAD: | store flowchart parameters,
L|OOK SOME MORE: read next character,
punct area minus 1 < present character < punct area plus 1 ∪
present character = or ∪ present character = and: exit check. ;
present character = less than ∩ less less comparison = 0:
    1 → less less comparison, exit check. ;
present character ≠ left brace: look some more. ; set → loop control flag,
E|XIT CHECK: restore flowchart parameters, |. .

5;
INITIATE RELATION CONTROL:
loop control flag ≠ 0: save current operator. ;

operand flag ≠ 0 ∩ next operator = left paren:
  save current operator. ; transfer temp commands, next operator = and:
    and → comparison type; ; next operator = or:
    or → comparison type; ; check half word,
less less comparison flag → n ≠ 0: process compare function[n]. ;
right brace < current operator < right arrow:
  | current operator - 44 → n ≥ 8: set → reverse comparison flag,
    n - 2 → n; ; J desig[n] → J designator |; ;
next operator ≠ colon ∩ next operator ≠ and ∩ next operator ≠ or:
  calculate quantity. ; first shift ≠ 0 ∪ partial word flag ≠ 0:
  calculate quantity. ; temp skip storage[1] ≠ 0:
  | temp skip storage[1] → full operand → operand flag,
  reset operand, 0 → temp skip storage[1], reverse comparison flag = 0:
    | set → reverse comparison flag, op offset ≠ 0: op offset +
      30 → op offset, 77₈ → op reg flag; ; |;
    0 → reverse comparison flag; |; ;
zeroize op offset, 0 → bit limits[1], [i - 1](24 → 29) →
temporary storage[7], operand flag ≠ 0 ∪ reverse comparison flag ≠ 0 ∪
temporary storage[7] = 22₈ ∪ temporary storage[7] = 23₈ ∪
temporary storage[7] = 12₈ ∪ temporary storage[7] = 65₈:
  subtract and skip. ;
temporary storage[7] = 26₈ ∪ temporary storage[7] = 27₈ ∪
op reg flag ≠ 77₈: set skip condition. ;
[i - 1](24 → 29) = 10₈: enter a and skip. ; J designator ≥ J desig[6]:
  J designator - J desig[4] → J designator, set skip condition. ;
S|UBTRACT AND SKIP: level + 1 → level, floating point flag = 0:
  | reverse comparison flag = 0: op reg flag → t1 reg flag,
    q sub function → q function, sub function → a function,
    full word command; load a sub q function → function code,
    77₈ → t1 reg flag, store temp command; |;
  | J designator(15 → 29) + 60000₈ + enter a function → [i],
  i + 1 → i, 0 → J designator, reverse comparison flag = 0:
    set floating call(7); set floating call(8);
  enter floating operand, |; transfer temp commands,
level - 1 → level, 0 → reverse comparison flag,
S|ET JUMP TO NEGATIVE:
1 + comparisoncounter → comparison counter → 1, 1 → correction[1],
straight jump function → [1], 1 + 1 → 1,
next operator = colon: comparison level x 10 → m,
  comparison level + 1 → comparison level, 0 → comparison list[m],
  comparison counter → comparison list[m + 1](15 → 29),
  comparison type → comparison list[m + 1](0 → 14), 1 → 1,
  n = m + 2(1)m + 9| correction[1] → comparison list[n],
  correction[1 + 1] → comparison list[n](15 → 29), 1 + 2 → 1, |,
  0 → comparison counter → comparison lockout flag; ;
0 → op reg flag, generator exit.
E|NTER A AND SKIP: 01000 00000₈ + [i - 1] → [i - 1],
S|ET SKIP CONDITION: J designator + [i - 1] → [i - 1],
0 → J designator, set jump to negative.
P|ROCESS COMPARE FUNCTION: fault. save second quantity.
store second quantity. enter third quantity. enter compare command.
S|AVE SECOND QUANTITY: next operator ≠ less than ∪ partial word flag ≠ 0 ∪
first shift ≠ 0: 2 → less less comparison flag, calculate quantity. ;
full operand → temp skip storage, zeroize op offset, 0 → bit limits[1],
3 → less less comparison flag, 0 → k designator → b designator,
generator exit.
S|TORE SECOND QUANTITY:
zeroize op offset, 0 → bit limits[1], store current sum,
operand + k desig[3] → temp skip storage,
3 → less less comparison flag, generator exit.

E|NTER THIRD QUANTITY:
partial word flag $\neq$ 0 $\cup$ first shift $\neq$ 0: entry a. ;
next operator $\neq$ colon $\cap$ next operator $\neq$ and $\cap$ next operator $\neq$ or:
    e|ntry a: 4 $\rightarrow$ less less comparison flag, calculate quantity. ;
    op reg flag = 77_8:
        | $[i - 1](24 \rightarrow 29)$ = 10_8: 01000 00000$_8$ + $[i - 1]$ $\rightarrow$ $[i - 1]$;
            shift aq left function + 30 $\rightarrow$ $[i]$, $i + 1 \rightarrow i$; |; ;
    enter q function $\rightarrow$ function code, assemble next command,
    E|NTER COMPARE COMMAND: temp skip storage$[1]$ $\neq$ 0 $\cap$ op reg flag = 7:
        op offset + 30 $\rightarrow$ op offset, zeroize op offset; ;
    $[i - 1](18 \rightarrow 20)$ = 0 $\cap$ $[i - 1](24 \rightarrow 29)$ $\neq$ 22_8 $\cap$ $[i - 1](24 \rightarrow 29)$ $\neq$ 23_8 $\cap$
    $[i - 1](24 \rightarrow 29)$ $\geq$ 10_8: $[i - 1](0 \rightarrow 14)$ - 1 $\rightarrow$ $[i - 1](0 \rightarrow 14)$;
        q sub function + 1 $\rightarrow$ $[i]$, $i + 1 \rightarrow i$; temp skip storage$[1]$ $\neq$ 0:
        | temp skip storage$[1]$ = J desig$[1]$: 0 $\rightarrow$ temp skip storage$[1]$; ;
        enter a function + temp skip storage$[1]$ $\rightarrow$ $[1]$,
        release ts, $i + 1 \rightarrow i$ |; ; compare function + J desig$[4]$ +
temp skip storage $\rightarrow$ $[i]$, release ts, $i + 1 \rightarrow i$, 0 $\rightarrow$ bit limits$[1]$ $\rightarrow$
less less comparison flag $\rightarrow$ temp skip storage, 0 $\rightarrow$ temp skip storage$[1]$,
set jump to negative.
    C|ALCULATE QUANTITY: zeroize op offset, 0 $\rightarrow$ bit limits$[1]$,
    temp skip storage$[1]$ = 0: | $[i - 1](24 \rightarrow 29)$ = 10_8:
        | J designator + $[i - 1](0 \rightarrow 23)$ $\rightarrow$ temp skip storage$[1]$ = 0:
          J desig$[1]$ $\rightarrow$ temp skip storage$[1]$; ;
        $i - 1 \rightarrow i$, 0 $\rightarrow$ $[i]$, 0 $\rightarrow$ op reg flag $\rightarrow$ J designator |;
    J designator $\rightarrow$ temp skip storage$[1]$, store current sum,
    temp skip storage$[1]$ + k desig$[3]$ + operand $\rightarrow$
    temp skip storage$[1]$, full operand $\rightarrow$ operand; |; ;
colon $\rightarrow$ current operator $\rightarrow$ punctuation, jump to generator. .

5;
COMPLETE RELATION CONTROL:
next operator $\neq$ period $\cap$ next operator $\neq$ semicolon: generator exit. ;
 comparison level = 0 $\cup$ comparison lockout flag $\neq$ 0:
    generator exit. ; (comparison level - 1) x 10 $\rightarrow$ 1,
comparison list$[1](15 \rightarrow 29)$ $\rightarrow$ m = 0: straight jump function $\rightarrow$ $[i]$,
    1 $\rightarrow$ comparison list$[1](15 \rightarrow 29)$, $i + 1 \rightarrow i$, generator exit. ;
comparison list$[1 + 1](0 \rightarrow 14)$ $\rightarrow$ comparison type,
comparison list$[1 + 1](15 \rightarrow 29)$ $\rightarrow$ comparison counter, 1 $\rightarrow$ k,
n = 1 + 2(1)1 + 9| comparison list$[n](0 \rightarrow 14)$ $\rightarrow$ correction$[k]$,
comparison list$[n](15 \rightarrow 29)$ $\rightarrow$ correction$[k + 1]$, k + 2 $\rightarrow$ k, |,
comparison counter $\rightarrow$ n, correction$[n]$ $\rightarrow$ second comparison $\rightarrow$ n,
$i - 1$ = m: | $i - 3$ = n: move true alternative; m $\rightarrow$ false alt address,
    n + 1 $\rightarrow$ true alt address, $i - 1 \rightarrow i$ + bias + $[n]$ $\rightarrow$ $[n]$; exit. |;;
n + 1 = m: | $i - 2$ = m: move false alternative; change skip condition,
    $i - 1 \rightarrow i$ + true alt address + bias + $[n]$ $\rightarrow$ $[n]$,
    move false alt(1); exit. |; ;
$[m + 1](21 \rightarrow 29)$ = 610_8 $\cap$ m + 4 + bias $\neq$ $[m + 1](0 \rightarrow 14)$:
    move false alternative, exit. ;
$[n + 1](21 \rightarrow 29)$ = 610_8 $\cap$ n + 4 + bias $\neq$ $[n + 1](0 \rightarrow 14)$:
    move true alternative, move false alt(2), exit. ;
m + 1 $\rightarrow$ false alt address + bias + $[n]$ $\rightarrow$ $[n]$, 1 + bias + $[m]$ $\rightarrow$ $[m]$,
n + 1 $\rightarrow$ true alt address.
E|XIT: comparison counter $\rightarrow$ 1, 0 $\rightarrow$ correction$[1]$,
comparison counter - 1 $\rightarrow$ comparison counter = 0: exit 1. ;
1 = 1(1)comparison counter| correction$[1]$ $\rightarrow$ n,
comparison type = and: false alt address + bias + $[n]$ $\rightarrow$ $[n]$;
    | comparison type = or: true alt address + bias + $[n]$ $\rightarrow$ $[n]$,
        change skip condition; fault 6; |; 0 $\rightarrow$ correction$[1]$, |.
E|XIT 1: comparison level - 1 $\rightarrow$ comparison level,

```
exit condition counter → m ≠ 0: | m - 1 → m,
    m - m(1)0| exit condition list[m](15 → 29) - 0:
       | exit condition list[m] - comparison level:
          set → comparison lockout flag; ; exit 2.  |; ;  |,  |; ;
E|XIT 2: 0 → false alt address → comparison type → comparison counter →
[i] → [i + 1] → true alt address, 7 → constant flag, generator exit.
M|OVE TRUE ALTERNATIVE: | change skip condition, [n + 1] → [n],
i - 2 → i → false alt address, n → true alt address,
change undefined name location(1),  |.
M|OVE FALSE ALTERNATIVE:
| n → false alt address, n + 1 → true alt address, i - 2 → i,
[m + 1] → [n], i + 1 - n → temporary storage, m → n,
change undefined name location(temporary storage),  |.
M|OVE FALSE ALT(a): | n + 1 → false alt address,
m - m + 1(1)i + 1| a → k, n < [m](0 → 14) - bias < 1 + 3:
    | 60₈ < [m](24 → 29) < 70₈ ∪ [m](24 → 29) - 72₈ ∪ [m](15 → 20) - 30₈:
       [m - 1](24 → 29) → temporary storage,
       [m - 1](21 → 23) ≠ 1 ∪ 11₈ < temporary storage < 14₈ ∪
       15₈ < temporary storage < 20₈ ∪ temporary storage ≥ 60₈: ;
          dont change. temporary storage - 77₈ ∪ temporary storage - 0:
             | straight jump function + bias + 3 - [m - 2]:
                dont change. ;  |; ;  |;
       | [m](15 → 29) ≠ 12700₈: dont change. ;
       [m + 1](9 → 29) ≠ 1100060₈ ∩ [m + 1](15 → 29) ≠ 65010₈:
          dont change. ;  |;
    1 - 19(1)0| [m](0 → 14) - bias - ts address record[1]:
       ts address record[1] - k → ts address record[1]; ;  |,
    [m](0 → 14) - k → [m](0 → 14), d|ont change: |; ;
m - a → k, [m] → [k],  |, change undefined name location(1),  |,
CHANGE SKIP CONDITION:
| [n - 1](15 → 29) - 65010₈: [n - 3](6 → 6) + 1 → [n - 3](6 → 6);
    [n - 1](21 → 21) + 1 → [n - 1](21 → 21);  |.
C|HANGE UNDEFINED NAME LOCATION(b):
| 1 - 177₈(1)0| n < undefined name location[1] < 1 + 2:
    undefined name location[1] - b → undefined name location[1]; ;  |,
1 - 777₈(1)0| n < name address[1] - bias < 1 + 2:
name address[1] - b → name address[1]; ;  |,  |. .


5;
JUMP GENERATORS: GENERATE STRAIGHT JUMP:
operand flag - 0: | current operator - period: exit compilation.
       complete relation control.  |; ;
k designator - k desig[3]: k desig[1] → k designator; ;
straight jump function → function code,
assemble next command, complete relation control.
GENERATE RETURN JUMP: function flag - 7:
       | operand flag ≠ 0: 0 → t1 reg flag, set enter inst,
          transfer temp command; set → clear flag; colon counter → n,
       1 → address corr list[n], floating point flag ≠ 0:
          2 → address corr list[n](15 → 29), punctuation counter + 2 →
          punctuation counter; 1 →.address corr list[n](15 → 29),
          punctuation counter + 1 → punctuation counter;
       restore name buffer, k desig[3] → k designator, generate store.  |; ;
function flag - 3: | operand flag - 0:
          punctuation counter + 1 → punctuation counter, colon counter -
          1 → n, address corr list[n](15 → 29) + 1 →
          address corr list[n](15 → 29), check for function end. ;
       colon counter → n, 1 → address corr list[n],
       floating point flag ≠ 0: 2 → address corr list[n](15 → 29),
```

punctuation counter + 2 → punctuation counter;
1 → address corr list[n](15 → 29), punctuation counter + 1 →
punctuation counter; bit limits → temporary storage[1],
0 → bit limits → b designator, unknown operand flag →
temporary storage(15 → 29), partial word flag → temporary storage(0→14),
0 → unknown operand flag, restore name buffers,
0 → partial word flag, k desig[3] → k designator, 0 → tl reg flag, set
enter inst, reset operand, temporary storage → partial word flag,
temporary storage[1] → bit limits, temporary storage(15 → 29) →
unknown operand flag, generate store. |; ;
operand flag ≠ 0: | return jump function → function code,
   k designator = k desig[3]: k desig[1] → k designator; ;
   assemble next command, |; ; complete relation control.
CHECK PARTIAL WORD: partial word flag ≠ 0 ∪ first shift ≠ 0:
   generate add or enter. generator exit.
RESET OPERAND: | full operand(0 → 14) → operand,
full operand(15 → 17) → b designator(15 → 17), full operand(18 → 20) →
k designator(18 → 20), full operand(21 → 23) → j designator(21 → 23), |. .

5;
ARITHMETIC GENERATORS:
CHECK FOR ALGEBRA: operand flag ≠ 0: save current operator. ;
current operator = divide: generate div by quantity. ;
current operator = plus ∪ current operator = minus:
   | op reg flag ≠ 0: store and add ts; ; check for negation,
   2 + level → level. generator exit. |; ;
current operator = multiply: generate mult by quant. ;
current operator = left paren: 2 + level → level; 3 + level → level;
generator exit.

CHECK FOR NEG LOOP INCREMENT:
loop control flag = 0: level - 1 → level, generate add. ;
next operator = minus: set → neg number flag; 0 → neg number flag;
current operator → next operator, previous operand → operand,
generator exit.
CHECK FOR LOOP LIMITS: loop control flag ≠ 0: advance. ;
transfer temp commands, compile op shift, level - 2 → level,
transfer temp commands, generator exit.
CLEAR TEMP LIST:
transfer temp commands, compile op shift, level - 3 → level,
transfer temp commands, next operator = end relation symbol:
   initiate relation control. generator exit.
CHECK FOR NEGATION: | current operator = minus:
   | floating point flag ≠ 0: set floating call(5);
      store a function + k desig[4] → a function, store q function →
      q function, 0 → operand, full word command; |; ; |.
SET ADD INST: | floating point flag ≠ 0:
   set floating call(1), enter floating operand;
   | partial word flag ≠ 0: add log prod function → a function,
      part word command; add function → a function,
   q add function → q function, full word command; |; |,
SET ENTER INST: | floating point flag ≠ 0:
   set floating call(0), enter floating operand;
   | partial word flag ≠ 0: enter log prod function → a function,
      part word command; enter a function → a function,
   enter q function → q function, full word command; |; |,
SET MULTIPLY INST: | floating point flag ≠ 0:
   set floating call(3), enter floating operand; 77ₐ → tl reg flag,
   multiply function → q function, full word command; |,

INITIATE DIVIDE INST: | floating point flag $\neq$ 0: set floating call(4),
 enter b function + j desig[7] → function code; divide function →
 function code; 0 → operand, 77_8 → tl reg flag, store temp command,
1 - 1 → divide inst address; |.
SET DIVIDE SHIFT INST: | floating point flag = 0:
 shift aq right function → function code, 30 → operand,
 store temp command, 7 → tc reg flag[1 - 1] → tl reg flag; ; |.
SET FLOATING CALL(a): | temp list index → 1,
return jump function + floating entrance + a → temp list[1],
level → level list[1], 77_8 → tl reg flag → tc reg flag[1],
offset → tc offset[1], 1 + 1 → temp list index → 1, |.
ENTER FLOATING OPERAND: | 0 → k designator → operand(18 → 20),
b designator → a function $\neq$ 0: operand(0 → 14) → q function,
 77_8 → tl reg flag, enter b function + j desig[7] → function code,
 0 → b designator → operand, store word, store q function →
 function code, k desig[1] → k designator, store word,
 2001_8 → tc mask flag[1 - 1], q add function → function code,
 q function → operand, store word, shift q left function →
 function code, 1 → operand, store word, enter q function →
 function code, a function → operand, store word; enter b function +
 j desig[7] → function code, store word; check for undef name, |. .

5;
GENERATE ADD OR ENTER:
current operator $\neq$ plus: 1 + level → level; ; check half word,
next operator = right arrow ∩ operand flag = 0: set → clear flag,
 advance. ; op reg flag $\neq$ 0: check for shift, set add inst;
 compile tl shift, set enter inst; clear temp list flag $\neq$ 0:
 level - 1 → level, transfer temp commands; ;
next operator = end relation symbol:
 initiate relation control. generator exit.
GENERATE ADD: check half word, current operator $\neq$ plus:
 1 + level → level; ; check for shift, set add inst, generator exit.
GENERATE SUBTRACT: check half word,
clear temp list flag $\neq$ 0: level - 1 → level; ; op reg flag = 0:
 | temp list index - 1 → 1, floating point flag $\neq$ 0:
 | temp list function[1 - 1] = 65_8: temp list[1 - 1] - 1 →
  temp list[1 - 1]; temp list[1 - 5] - 1 → temp list[1 - 5]; |;
 | temp list[1](24 → 29) = 10_8: | tc mask flag[1 - 1] = 777_8:
  40_8 → temp list[1 - 2](24 → 29);
  40_8 → temp list[1 - 1](24 → 29); |;
 | temp list[1](24 → 29) = 20_8: 11_8 → temp list[1](24 → 29);
  10_8 → temp list[1](24 → 29); |; |; |; ;
transfer temp commands, check for shift, floating point flag $\neq$ 0:
 set floating call(2), enter floating operand;
 | partial word flag $\neq$ 0: sub log prod function → a function,
  part word command; sub function → a function,
 q sub function → q function, full word command; |;
transfer temp commands, next operator = end relation symbol:
 initiate relation control. generator exit.
GENERATE MULTIPLY: check half word,
current operator = left paren: level - 1 → level; ;
op reg flag $\neq$ 0: store and add ts, reset operand;
check for part word or shift, current operator = plus ∪
current operator = minus: level + 1 → level; level + 2 → level;
set multiply inst, check for negation, generator exit.
GENERATE MULT QUANT: transfer temp commands, compile op shift,
level - 1 → level, transfer temp commands, generator exit.
GENERATE MULT BY QUANT: op reg flag $\neq$ 0: zeroize op offset,

store current sum, k desig[3] → k designator, set multiply inst; ;
level + 1 → level, generator exit.
GENERATE MULT OR ENTER: check half word,
op reg flag ≠ 0: check for part word or shift, set multiply inst;
    compile tl shift, set enter inst; clear temp list flag ≠ 0:
    level - 2 → level; ; next operator = right paren ∪
next operator = plus ∪ next operator = minus: level - 1 → level; ;
transfer temp commands,
CHECK FOR DIVIDE TO FOLLOW: next operator = divide: | initiate divide inst,
    current operator = divide: set divide shift inst; ; |; ;
next operator = end relation symbol:
    initiate relation control. generator exit.
GENERATE DIVIDE: check half word, check for part word or shift,
divide inst address → 1, floating point flag ≠ 0:
    | b designator ≠ 0: n = 1 + 1(1)temp list index| temp list[n] →
        temp list[n + 4], tc mask flag[n] → tc mask flag[n + 4],
        0 → tc mask flag[n], tc reg flag[n] → tc reg flag[n + 4],
        level list[n] → level list[n + 4], tc offset[n] →
        tc offset[n + 4], |, temp list index. + 4 → divide inst address,
        1 → temp list index, enter floating operand,
        divide inst address → temp list index, exit gen div.
        0 → full operand(18 → 20), full operand + j desig[7] →
        full operand; |; ; full operand → temp list[1](0 → 23),
unknown operand flag → tc mask flag[1],
E|XIT GEN DIV: 0 → divide inst address → j designator → k designator →
b designator, transfer temp commands, clear temp list flag ≠ 0:
    level - 2 → level; ; next operator = plus ∪ next operator = minus ∪
next operator = right paren: level - 1 → level; ;
check for divide to follow.
GENERATE DIV OR ENTER: check half word,
0 → j designator → k designator → b designator,
op reg flag ≠ 0: store and add ts; ; lower bit limit →
temporary storage(0 → 14), 0 → lower bit limit,
current operator = punctuation: 2 + level → level; 1 + level → level;
unknown operand flag → temporary storage(15 → 29), 0 → unknown operand flag, 7
77₈ → tl reg flag, check for negation, initiate divide inst,
set divide shift inst, first shift ≠ 0: | invert shifts,
    first shift(18 → 29) = 0100₈ ∩ shift flag = 0:
        divide inst address + 1 → 1, first shift(0 → 17) +
        temp list[1](0 → 17) → temp list[1](0 → 17), second shift →
        first shift, shift flag 1 → shift flag, 0 → second shift; ;
    compile tl shift, |; ; reset operand, temporary storage(0 → 14) →
lower bit limit, temporary storage(15 → 29) → unknown operand flag,
set enter inst, generator exit.
GENERATE DIV QUANT: transfer temp commands, compile op shift,
level - 1 → level, transfer temp commands, initiate divide inst,
[1 - 1](24 → 29) ≠ 22₈: set divide shift inst; ; generator exit.
GENERATE DIV BY QUANTITY:
op reg flag ≠ 0: check for divide shift, zeroize op offset,
    store current sum, k desig[3] → k designator, set enter inst; ;
temp list index → 1, 0 → tc offset[1 - 1], store q function →
function code, store temp command, 77₈ → tc reg flag[1 - 1] →
tl reg flag, divide inst address + 1000₈ → tc mask flag[1 - 1],
0 → bit limits[1], 0 → divide inst address, level + 1 → level,
generator exit. .

5;
GENERATE STORE: bit limit flag ≠ 0: set upper bit limit. ;
check half word, transfer temp commands, floating point flag ≠ 0:
    | clear flag ≠ 0: store b function + full operand → [1],

```
          1 + 1 → 1, full operand + 1 → full operand, store zero,
          full operand - 1 → full operand, 1 - 1 → 1,
          enter q function → [1], 1 + 1 → 1, 77₈ → op reg flag; ;
     set floating call(6), enter floating operand,
     op reg flag < 100₈ ∩ function flag = 0: 77₈ → tl reg flag,
          set floating call(9); ; exit.  |; | op reg flag ≥ 100₈:
          return jump function + floating entrance + 10 → [1],
          1 + 1 → 1, 77₈ → op reg flag; ;  |; partial word flag ≠ 0:
     | [1 - 1] = enter q function ∩ lower bit limit = op offset: 1 - 1 → 1;;
     clear flag ≠ 0: 0 → clear flag, enter a function → [1],
          lower bit limit → op offset, 1 + 1 → 1,
          7 → op reg flag → tl reg flag; ;
     next operator ≥ colon: enter q function → function code,
          0 → j designator → k designator → b designator → operand,
          7 → tl reg flag, store temp command, substitute function →
          function code, store temp command, full operand → operand; ;
     7 → tl reg flag, repl substitute function → function code,
     store temp command, check for undef name, set tl neg mask,
     0 → partial word flag, exit.  |; ;
loop control flag ≠ 0: check for index arithmetic.
operand + k designator + unknown operand flag = 0 ∩ b designator ≠ 0:
     | next operator < colon ∪ next operator = right brace:
          | n = 177₈(1)0| 1 - 1 = undefined name location[n] ∪ 1 -
          2 = undefined name location[n]: check for enter b.  ;  |,
          check for index arithmetic.  |; check for enter b.  |; ;
clear flag ≠ 0: store zero, enter q function → [1],
     77₈ → op reg flag → tl reg flag, 1 + 1 → 1; ; condense previous
commands.
C|HECK FOR INDEX ARITHMETIC: [1 - 2](0 → 14) = 0 ∩ [1 - 2](18 → 29) = 1000₈:
     | [1 - 1](15 → 29) = 26000₈: set inc b inst. ;
     [1 - 1](15 → 29) = 27000₈:
          | [1 - 1](0 → 14) = 1 ∩ [1 - 2](0 → 23) = b designator: 0 → [1 - 2],
          arithmetic jump function + bias + 1 - 2 → k designator,
          set inc b inst. ; [1 - 1](15 → 29) - 6000₈ → [1 - 1](15 → 29),
          [1 - 2](15 → 29) + 1000₈ → [1 - 2](15 → 29), 7 → op reg flag,
          check for enter b.  |; ;  |; ;
[1 - 2](15 → 29) = 10000₈ ∩ [1 - 1](18 → 29) = 2600₈ ∩
[1 - 1](0 → 14) = 0: set inc b inst. ;
C|HECK FOR ENTER B: b designator → b designator,
clear flag ≠ 0: | next operator ≠ right arrow: 0 → clear flag; ;
     set enter b inst.  |; ; op reg flag = 77₈:
     | right brace < next operator < or: set enter b from a reg. ;
     [1 - 1](24 → 29) = 10₈: 1 - 1 → 1, enter b function → function code,
          [1](0 → 20) → operand, 77₈ → tl reg flag, set store inst. ;  |; ;
SET|ENTER B FROM A REG: 7 → tl reg flag, k desig[7] → k designator,
S|ET ENTER B INST: enter b function → function code, set store inst.
S|ET INC B INST: 1 - 2 → 1, enter b function → function code,
b designator × 2↑6 → b designator,
[1](0 → 23) + [1 + 1](0 → 23) → operand, set store inst.
C|ONDENSE PREVIOUS COMMANDS: op reg flag = 77₈: store q function →
     function code, 77₈ → tl reg flag; store a function →
     function code, 7 → tl reg flag;
unknown operand flag ≠ 0: set store inst. ;
add function + full operand = [1 - 1]:
     add repl function → function code, 1 - 1 → 1, set store inst. ;
sub function + full operand = [1 - 1]:
     sub repl function → function code, 1 - 1 → 1, set store inst. ;
q add function + full operand = [1 - 1]: | repl add q function →
     function code, 1 - 1 → 1, enter q function + 1 = [1 - 1]:
```

```
                repl add one function → function code, i - 1 → 1; ;
         set store inst.  |; ;
n - 177₈(1)0| 1 - 1 - undefined name location[n]: set store inst. ;  |,
enter q function + full operand = [1 - 2]:
   | q sub function + 1 = [1 - 1]:
         repl sub one function → function code, 1 - 2 → 1, set store inst. ;
   q add function + 1 = [1 - 1]: repl add one function →
         function code, 1 - 2 → 1, set store inst. ;
   [1 - 1](24 → 29) = 27₈: [1 - 1](0 → 23) + enter q function → [1 - 2],
         1 - 1 → 1, repl sub q function → function code, set store inst. ;
   [1 - 1](24 → 29) = 26₈: [1 - 1](0 → 23) + enter q function → [1 - 2],
         1 - 1 → 1, repl add q function → function code, set store inst. ;  |; ;
right brace < next operator ∪ [1 - 1](18 → 29) ≠ 1000₈ ∪
[1 - 1](0 → 14) ≠ 0 ∪ [1 - 1](15 → 17) = 0: set store inst. ;
n - 177₈(1)0| 1 - 1 = undefined name location[n]: set store inst. ;  |,
store b function → function code, 1 - 1 → 1, [1](15 → 17) →
j designator(21 → 29), function flag = 7: colon counter → n,
         address corr list[n] - 1 → address corr list[n]; ;
S|ET STORE INST: store temp command, check for undef name,
EX|IT: transfer temp commands, 0 → [1], function flag ≠ 0:
   | next operator = semicolon: restore name buffers,
         return jump function → function code,
         assemble next command, 3 → function flag; ; 0 → op reg flag,
   check for function end.  |; ; compile op shift,
load a add q function < [1 - 1] < enter log prod function:
   7 → op reg flag; ; next operator < colon ∪ next operator = right brace:
   0 → op reg flag → tl reg flag → level + offset → op offset,
   0 → floating point flag, complete relation control. ;
next operator = end relation symbol: initiate relation control. ;
next operator = plus ∪ next operator = minus: 1 + level → level; ;
next operator = multiply ∪ next operator = divide: 2 + level → level; ;
next operator = divide: initiate divide inst, set divide shift inst; ;
generator exit.
S|TORE ZERO: | next operator ≠ right arrow: 0 → clear flag; ;
next operator < colon ∪ next operator = right brace ∪
next operator = right paren ∪ next operator = right arrow:
   store b function → function code, set store inst. ;  |, . .


5;
INITIATE LOOP CONTROL: next operator = right arrow: set lower bit limit. ;
first shift ≠ 0: compile tl shift, set enter inst, generator exit. ;
operand → loop control flag, check half word,
partial word flag ≠ 0: fault. ;
[1 - 1](15 → 17) = m → set loop control(0 → 14), 1 - 1 → 1,
enter q function → function code, 0 → operand,
temp co storage = equal sign ∩ previous operand → operand +
unknown operand flag + k designator = 0 ∩ [1] -
b designator = enter q function: 0 → b designator,
   generator exit. ; assemble next command, temp co storage ≠ equal sign:
   | temp co storage = plus: q add function → function code;
       q sub function → function code; previous operand → operand,
   assemble next command,  |; ; b desig[m] → b designator,
0 → operand, generate store.
SET EXIT CONDITIONS: exit condition counter → m,
colon ≥ current operator ∩ comparison level ≠ 0:
   comparison level → exit condition list[m], exit condition counter +
   1 → exit condition counter, exit to advance. ;
loop control flag ≠ 0: set loop control. ; define function flag = 0:
   check jump around; ; shift q right function + 1 + bias +
```

```
k desig[1] → exit condition list[m],
exit condition counter + 1 → exit condition counter,
define function flag ≠ 0: 0 → define function flag,
    exit condition list[m] + shift q right function →
    exit condition list[m]; ; i + 1 → i,
E|XIT TO ADVANCE: comma → next operator, advance.
S|ET LOOP CONTROL: 0 → m, current operator = plus:
    previous operand + operand(0 → 14) → full operand(0 → 14) →
    operand(0 → 14); ; current operator = minus:
    previous operand - operand(0 → 14) → full operand(0 → 14) →
    operand(0 → 14); ; 0 → op reg flag, exit condition counter → 1,
operand flag = 0: | loop control flag - 1 → loop control flag ≥ 1:
    set a reg decb; 0 → exit condition list[1];
    exit condition list[1] + shift aq right function + 1 + bias +
    j desig[m] → exit condition list[1], |; | neg number flag ≠ 0:
        loop control flag + 1 → loop control flag, set a reg dec b;
    | loop control flag ≥ 2: add function + j desig[1] → [1],
        i + 1 → i, enter b function + j desig[m] → b desig[m] +
        loop control flag - 1 → [1], i + 1 → i, - 1 → exit condition list[1];
        0 → exit condition list[1];  |;
    exit condition list[1] + shift q right function + 1 + bias →
    exit condition list[1], exit condition counter + 1 →
    exit condition counter → 1, compare function + j desig[m] +
    full operand → exit condition list[1], unknown operand flag ≠ 0:
        exit condition counter + 1 → exit condition counter → 1,
        unknown operand flag + shift q left function →
        exit condition list[1]; ; 0 → b designator → k designator,  |;
0 → loop control flag → neg number flag, exit condition counter +
1 → exit condition counter, exit to advance.
S|ET A REG DEC B: |  - 3 → exit condition list[1],
straight jump function + 1 + bias + 4 → [1], 1 + 1 → i,
enter a function + b desig[m] → [1], i + 1 → i,
sub function + loop control flag → [1], i + 1 → i,
enter b function + k desig[7] + j desig[m] → [1], i + 1 → i,  |,
INITIATE SUBSCRIPT: current operator → temp co storage,
floating point flag → temp co storage(12 → 14), 0 → floating point flag,
k designator = 0: k desig[3] → k designator; ; advance.
MODIFY SUBSCRIPT:
previous operand + operand(0 → 14) → operand(0 → 14), advance.
SET SUBSCRIPT: floating point flag ≠ 0: fault. ;
temp co storage(12 → 14) → floating point flag ≠ 0:
    operand(0 → 14) x 2 → operand(0 → 14); ; current operator = minus:
    previous operand - operand(0 → 14) → operand(0 → 14);
    previous operand + operand(0 → 14) → operand(0 → 14);
temp co storage(0 → 11) → current operator, advance 1.
SAVE CURRENT OPERATOR: current operator → temp co storage,
function flag = 0: advance. ; op reg flag ≠ 0: zeroize op offset,
    store current sum; ; operand → temporary storage[8],
current operator → function co, 0 → colon counter, 1 + level → level,
name buffer → first comparison[1], name buffer[1] → first comparison[2],
name buffer[2] → first comparison[3], comma → next operator,
generator exit.
SET LOWER BIT LIMIT: partial word flag ≠ 0:
    lower bit limit → dimn lower bit limit; 0 → dimn lower bit limit;
operand + dimn lower bit limit → lower bit limit,
set → partial word flag → bit limit flag,
previous operand → operand, advance.
SET UPPER BIT LIMIT: operand + dimn lower bit limit → upper bit limit,
temp co storage → current operator,
previous operand → operand, 0 → bit limit flag, advance 1.
```

RESTORE NAME BUFFERS: | first comparison[1] → name buffer,
first comparison[2] → name buffer[1], first comparison[3] → name buffer[2],
process the name, colon counter → n,
address corr list[n](15 → 29) = 2: set → floating point flag; ; |,
CHECK FOR FUNCTION END: store flowchart parameters, read next character,
present character = right paren ∩ next operator = comma:
    present character → next operator; restore flowchart parameters;
next operator = right paren: | function flag = 7: restore name buffers,
        return jump function → function code, assemble next command; ;
    0 → function flag, n = 0(1)colon counter| address corr list[n] → m,
    [m](0 → 14) - punctuation counter → [m](0 → 14)
    punctuation counter - address corr list[n](15 → 29) →
    punctuation counter, 0 → address corr list[n], |,
    function co → current operator, check subsequent operator,
    0 → unknown operand flag,
    punct area minus 1 < current operator < punct area plus 1:
        | punct area minus 1 < first comparison < punct area
        plus 1 ∪ first comparison = right brace: level - 1 → level,
            0 → k designator → b designator → j designator →
            operand → floating point flag, advance 1. ; |; ;
    store current sum, operand → temporary storage[7],
    temporary storage[8] → operand → [1] ≠ 0:
        k desig[3] → k designator + operand → full,operand,
        release ts, set enter inst, transfer temp commands; ;
    temporary storage[7] → operand, k desig[3] → k designator,
    level - 1 → level, advance 1. |; restore flowchart parameters,
    colon counter + 1 → colon counter; generator exit. .

5;
EXIT COMPILATION: comparison level ≠ 0: fault 6; ;
exit condition counter ≠ 0: 129 → lower loop limit,
    132 → upper loop limit, type the fault; ; sequence number → n,
1 ≠ entrance flag:
    program entry address → k + bias → a function → entrance addr[n],
    straight jump function + entrance flag + bias → [k],
    program entry address + 1 → program entry address,
    j desig[4] + a function → function, 77776₈ → m, set simple exit; ;
reconcile name lists(0), 1 - 1 → current obj prog last address +
bias → obj prog last address[n], j - 1 → flo chart last address[n],
0 → title flag → type name flag,
k = 777₈(1)0| name temp flag[k] ≠ 0: purge name; ; |,
name index[n] - 1 → 1, name part 1[1] = 0: 0 → name index[n]; ;
P|URGE NAME: | 0 → name part 1[k] → name part 2[k] → name part 3[k] →
operand list[k] → name mask[k], |, check key sets, sequence number → n,
glossary flag = 7: purge name(15 → 29) → j,
    print sequence number(15 → 29) → glossary flag, 0 → flochart limits[n],
    sequence number - 1 → sequence number, check for end of flowchart. ;
key[1] ≠ 0: start flex, print run info, turn off flex; ;
floating entrance - bias → m ≠ 0 ∩ [m] = 0: j → purge name(15 → 29),
    neliac dimn part 2 + 1 → j, glossary flag →
    print sequence number(15 → 29), set → glossary flag, continue. ;
C|HECK FOR END OF FLOWCHART: j + 4 ≥ end of flowcharts:
    | sequence number < final seq nr(0 → 8):
        | final seq nr + 2 - final seq nr(0 → 11) → k,
        sequence number → temporary storage[4], 0 → j → 1,
        flocht storage std first address → 1, mag tape handler,
        temporary storage[4] → sequence number,
        upper loop limit = 27 ∪ upper loop limit = 128:
            type last address, 0 → 1, 61400₈rru tape handler. ;
        continue. |; ; check key sets, key[3] = 0: exit. ;

n = $177_8(1)0$| undefined name 1[n] ≠ 0:
   initiate library search. ; |, exit.
I|NITIATE LIBRARY SEARCH: n = $177_8(1)0$| undefined name 1[n] < 0:
   - undefined name 1[n] → undefined name 1[n]; ; |,
13000_81174_8, 13300_840047_8, 47030_80, 17330_80,
13300_840042_8, 47030_80, 17330_80, 13200_80,

WAIT FOR C2: 62200_8wait for c?,
77777_8 × 2↑15 + flochart first address[1] → temporary storage,
75530_8temporary storage, temporary storage(0 → 14) →
end of flowcharts,
W|AIT FOR FIRST WORD: 63500_8wait for first word,
W|AIT FOR SECOND WORD: 63500_8wait for second word,
W|AIT FOR THIRD WORD: 63500_8wait for third word,
MONITOR: 12610_85, 11036_877776_8, 60500_8monitor, 13000_80,
[n - 3] = 0: terminate search. ;
end of flowcharts → temporary storage → j, n → end of flowcharts,
LOOK FOR NAME OF LIBRARY ROUTINE: read next character,
present character ≠ semicolon: look for name of library routine. ;
read next character, read the name,
n = $177_8(1)0$| name buffer = undefined name 1[n] ∩
name buffer[1] = undefined name 2[n] ∩
name buffer[2] = undefined name 3[n]: end of flowcharts →
temporary storage, 13000_81174_8, wait for first word. ; |,
temporary storage → [5](0 → 14) → end of flowcharts,
13000_81174_8, wait for first word.
T|ERMINATE SEARCH: 13000_81174_8, - 1 → [5], temporary storage -.
4 ≥ flochart first address[1]: flochart first address[1] → j,
77_8 → glossary flag, continue. ;
EXIT ENTRY FROM FAULT: E|XIT:
0 → glossary flag → final seq nr → debug flag, punch run info,
program entry address - 1 → programentry address,
S|TOP: check key sets, first obj prog address → i,
current obj prog last address + 1 → j, type last address,
key[2] ≠ 0: 61400_8debug scan. 61400_8stop. |; ;
C|ONTINUE: sequence number = 77_8: punch run info, 0 → sequence number; ;
current obj prog last address + 1 → m + bias → temporary storage[4],
program entry address → n, obj prog last address → k,
key[2] ≠ 0: continue compiling. ; 61400_8continue compiling.
P|UNCH RUN INFO: | 1 → n, start punch, carriage return upper case,
dump the date, 93 → lower loop limit, 105 → upper loop limit,
dump a title, print run info, turn off punch,
n = 1(1)77_8| 0 → flochart limits[n] → entrance addr[n] →
name index[n], |, |,
PRINT SEQUENCE NUMBER:
| n → last frame dump buffer[1], dump one number, dump one number, |,
P|RINT RUN INFO:
| n = n(1)77_8| flochart limits[n] ≠ 0: | carriage return, space,
  space, print sequence number, space, space, space, space,
  uppercase, n → temporary storage[1],
  name index[n] → n ≠ 0: n - 1 → n, write name; n = 14(1)0| space, |;
  temporary storage[1] → n, lower case, space, space,
  obj prog limits[n] → address limits, print limits, space, space,
  space, flo chart limits[n] → address limits, print limits,
  entrance addr[n] ≠ 0: space, space, space,
    entrance addr[n] → upper dump buffer[1],
    dump five numbers; ; |; ; |, |.
R|ECONCILE NAME LISTS(c):
| 1 = $777_8(1)0$| operand list[1](15 → 17) ≠ 0 ∩ name k desig[1] ≥ c:

| 0 → operand list[1](15 → 17),
m - 177₈(1)0| name part 1[1] - undefined name 1[m] ∩
name p art 2[1] - undefined name 2[m] ∩
name part 3[1] - undefine d name 3[m]: | undefined name location[m] → k,
    name address[1] + [k](0 → 14) x 2↑15 / 2↑15 → [k](0 → 14),
    [k](18 → 20) = 0: name k desig[1] → [k](18 → 20); ;
    0 → undefined name 1[m] → undefined name 2[m] →
    undefined name 3[m] → undefined name location[m]; |; ; |, |; ;|,
T|YPE LAST ADDRESS:
| 98 → lower loop limit, 100 → upper loop limit, start flex,
dump a title, current obj prog last address + 1 → upper dump buffer[1],
dump five numbers, turn off flex, |. .

5;
STORE CONSTANTS: 0 → std addresses, 1 → object prog std first address,
j → flo cht storage std first address, k → obj prog std last address,
m → standard compiling location, n → std program entry address,
clear indices, clear namelist and stop. .

5
| c|hannel(15 → 29), i|o index(0 → 14) |, s|ubscript 1, s|ubscript 2;
GENERATE IO: unknown operand flag → n ≠ 0:
    0 → undefined name 1[n - 1] → undefined name location[n - 1] →
    unknown operand flag; ; search io list, n = 0: io fault; ;
n + 1 → n,
L|INK ENTRY:
io list[n](15 → 20) → channel, n + 1 → n → io index, set → offset,
S|ET NEXT OPERATION: next operator ≠ less ∩ next operator ≠ greater ∩
next operator ≠ right bracket: advance and return,
    set next operation. ; io index → n,
offset ≠ 0: io list[n](15 → 29) → operand storage, 0 → offset;
    io list[n](0 → 14) → operand storage, set → offset;
operand storage = 0: exit. ; operand storage < 20₈:
    | next operator = right bracket: exit. ; next operator = less:
    0 → space flag; 1 → space flag; 0 → unknown operand flag,
    advance and return, k designator → temporary storage[1],
    0 → subscript 1 → subscript 2 → k,
    next operator = left bracket: | operand flag ≠ 0: 0 → skip flag;
        k desig[3] → temporary storage[1], 1 → skip flag;
        R|PT: 0 → k designator,
    unknown operand flag → temporary storage[1](0 → 14),
    0 → unknown operand flag, advance and return,
    b designator + operand ≠ operand flag:
        | skip flag = 0: io fault; skip subscript. |; ;
    temporary storage[1](0 → 14) → unknown operand flag,
    0 → skip flag, operand + b designator → subscript 1[k],
    previous operand → operand + subscript 1 → operand flag,
    0 → b designator, next operator = right arrow: 1 → k, rpt. ;
    S|KIP SUBSCRIPT: next operator ≠ right bracket: io fault;
        read next character,
        present character → current operator → next operator; |; ;
operand storage ≥ 10₈: | operand flag + unknown operand flag = 0:
        extract next cell for operand;
        io index + 1 → io index, set → offset; |; ;
temporary storage[1](15 → 29) → k designator(15 → 29), |;
| operand storage ≥ 30₈: modify index for link.
0 → space flag, extract next cell for operand; |;
C|ONTINUE:
channel → n, 0 → a function, operand storage(0 → 2) → m, io generator[m].

I|O GENERATOR: io fault, generate ext function. generate rels interrupt.
generate jump active. generate terminate buffer.
generate buffer. generate monitor buffer. generate delay.
G|ENERATE EXT FUNCTION: k designator = 0 ∩ unknown operand flag = 0:
 operand → number accumulator, enter a constant; ;
channel → n, io j desig[n] → j designator,
space flag = 0: external function → function code;
 store c function → function code,
k desig[3] → k designator, subscript 1 → b designator, set io inst.
G|ENERATE RELS INTERRUPT:
arithmetic jump function → function code, operand flag ≠ 0:
 j desig[1] → j designator; ; subscript 1 → b designator, set io inst.
G|ENERATE JUMP ACTIVE:
space flag ≠ 0: input jump function → function code;
 output jump function → function code; io j desig[n] →
j designator, subscript 1 → b designator, set io inst.
G|ENERATE TERMINATE BUFFER:
space flag ≠ 0: terminate input function → function code;
 terminate output function → function code;
io j desig[n] → j designator, set io inst.
G|ENERATE MONITOR BUFFER: monitor function → a function,
G|ENERATE BUFFER: skip flag ≠ 1: | enter q function → function code,
 k desig[4] → k designator, assemble next command, 0 → operand,
 subscript 1 → b designator ≠ 0: load a add q function → function code,
  assemble next command, store a function → function code;
 store q function → function code;
 k desig[1] + 77₈ → k designator, assemble next command,
 subscript 2 → b designator ≠ 0: q add function → function code,
  assemble next command, store q function → function code;
  | subscript 1 ≠ 0: store a function → function code;
 store q function → function code; |; 77₈ → operand,
 k desig[2] → k designator, assemble next command,
 k desig[3] → k designator, |; ; space flag ≠ 0:
buffer in function + a function → function code; buffer out function +
a function → function code; io j desig[n] → j designator, set io inst.
G|ENERATE DELAY:
enter b function → function code, j desig[7] → j designator,
assemble next command, dec loop cntrl function → function code,
j desig[7] → j designator, 1 + bias → operand, set io inst.
M|ODIFY INDEX FOR LINK:
operand storage - 30₈ → n, io index → io list[n](0 → 14),
channel → io list[n](21 → 26), offset → io list[n](14 → 14), link entry.
S|ET IO INST: assemble next command, operand storage < 20₈ ∪
current operator = left bracket: advance and return; ;
C|HECK FOR END: next operator = comma: read next character,
 present character → next operator; ; io index → n,
io list[n + 1] < 0 ∩ io list[n + 2] < 0 ∩ io list[n + 3] < 0 ∩
io list[n + 4] ≥ 0 ∩ offset ≠ 0: | b|ack down:
 io list[n - 1] ≥ 0 ∪ io list[n - 2] ≥ 0 ∪ io list[n - 3] ≥ 0:
  n - 1 → n, back down. ; io list[n](0 → 13) → io index ≠ 0:
  io list[n](14 → 14) → offset, io list[n](21 → 26) → channel,
  0 → io list[n](0 → 14), io index → n;
  | e|xit: next operator = right bracket:
   | current operator = less ∪ current operator = greater:
    0 → offset → skip flag → space flag, comma →
    next operator, generator exit. ; |; ; io fault, |; |; ;
offset ≠ 0: n + 1 → n → io index; 0 → offset;
0 → skip flag → space flag, set next operation.
I|O FAULT: | 9 → lower loop limit, 13 → upper loop limit, type the fault,
F|IND END: present character → temporary storage, read next character,

```
present character = comma: read next character; ;
present character = right bracket:
     | temporary storage = less ∪ temporary storage = greater:
          0 → offset, comma → next operator, generator exit. ;   |; ;
present character = period ∩ temporary storage = period:
     exit compilation. find end.   |,
E|XTRACT NEXT CELL FOR OPERAND:
| io index + 1 → n → io index, io list[n](0 → ?8) → operand,
set → offset, 0 → k designator → temporary storage[1],   |, io list: . .
```

NELIAC 704

In order to demonstrate the methods employed when the character set is restricted to that available with IBM card equipment, a compiler written for such use is given in this appendix. It should be noted, however, that IBM has recently made available an expanded character set for its 026 key punch, which will print and punch 26 letters, 10 numbers, and 17 of the remaining 26 symbols required. Such a key punch, especially if coupled with an SC 3000 or an ANalex high-speed printer, both of which have the entire set, should make a real improvement in both the legibility and ease of use of the language.

Table IX shows both the substitute symbols used in this compiler, as well as those that will still be required with the expanded set.

TABLE IX

CHARACTER SET SUBSTITUTIONS REQUIRED WITH STANDARD
AND WITH MODIFIED IBM EQUIPMENT

| Symbol | Substitution | | Comments |
	Modified	Standard	
;		$	semicolon
:		CLN	colon
[	LBK	LBK	left bracket
]		RBK	right bracket

{		LBR	left brace
}		RBR	right brace
=		EQU	for comparisons only
≠	NEQ	NEQ	not equals
≥	GEQ	GEQ	greater than
<	LSS	LSS	less than
≤	LEQ	LEQ	less or equal
>		GTR	greater than
→		=	for assignments only
×		＊	multiplication
|		ABS	not implemented
U	OR	OR	Boolean OR
∩	AND	AND	Boolean AND
↑		EXP	exponent
8		OCT	if used as octal number sign
8		MCH	if used preceding machine code

The cooperation of Professor Harry Huskey in providing the compiler listing presented here is greatly appreciated.

```
( COMMENT CLN MASTER DECK , LOWER COMPILER , JANUARY 25, 1961 )
$ START COMPILE CLN ZERO = I , CLEAR ALL NAME . . .

        ( COMMENT CLN NAME LIST DIMENSIONING STATEMENT)          00   0010
        NAME WORD 1 (1024),                                      00   0020
        NAME WORD 2 (1024),                                      00   0030
        NAME WORD 3 (1024),                                      00   0040
        NAME LOCATION (1024),                                    00   0050
        UNDEFINED NAME 1 (512),                                  00   0080
        UNDEFINED NAME 2 (512),                                  00   0090
        UNDEFINED NAME 3 (512),                                  00   0100
        UNDEFINED LOC (512),                                     00   0110
$ COMMAND LIST CLN ,                                             00   0130
        ADD CLN  MCH 0400000 0,                                  00   0140
        ALS CLN  MCH 0767000 0,                                  00   0150
        ANA CLN MCH  4320000 0,                                  00   0160
        ARS CLN  MCH 0771000 0,                                  00   0170
        CAL CLN MCH 45000000,                                    00   0171
        CAS CLN  MCH 0340000 0,                                  00   0180
        CLA CLN  MCH 0500000 0,                                  00   0190
        CLM CLN  MCH 0760000 0,                                  00   0200
        CLS CLN· MCH 0502000 0,                                  00   0210
        COM CLN  MCH 0760000 6,                                  00   0220
        DVP CLN  MCH 0221000 0,                                  00   0230
        FAD CLN MCH 0300000 0,                                   00   0240
        FDP CLN  MCH 0241000 0,                                  00   0250
        FMP CLN  MCH 0260000 0,                                  00   0260
        FSB CLN  MCH 0302000 0,                                  00   0270
        HTR CLN  MCH 0000000 0,                                  00   0280
        LDQ CLN MCH  0560000 0,                                  00   0290
        LLS CLN  MCH 0763000 0,                                  00   0300
        LRS CLN  MCH 0765000 0,                                  00   0310
        LXA CLN  MCH 0534000 0,                                  00   0320
        LXD CLN  MCH 4534000 0,                                  00   0330
        MPY CLN  MCH 0200000 0,                                  00   0340
        ORA CLN  MCH 4501000 0,                                  00   0350
        PAX  CLN  MCH 0734000 0,                                 00   0360
        PDX CLN  MCH 4734000 0,                                  00   0370
        PXD CLN  MCH 4754000 0,                                  00   0380
        SLW CLN  MCH 0602000 0,                                  00   0390
        STA CLN  MCH 0621000 0,                                  00   0400

        STD CLN  MCH 0622000 0,                                  00   0410
        STO CLN  MCH 0601000 0,                                  00   0420
        STQ CLN  MCH 4600000 0,                                  00   0430
        STZ CLN  MCH 0600000 0,                                  00   0440
        SUB CLN  MCH 0402000 0,                                  00   0450
        SXD CLN  MCH 4634000 0,                                  00   0460
        TMI CLN  MCH 4120000 0,                                  00   0470
        TNZ CLN  MCH 4100000 0,                                  00   0480
        TRA CLN  MCH 0020000 0,                                  00   0490
        TSX CLN  MCH 0074000 0,                                  00   0500
        TXH CLN  MCH 3000000 0,                                  00   0510
        TXI CLN  MCH 1000000 0,                                  00   0520
        TXL CLN  MCH 7000000 0,                                  00   0530
        TZE CLN  MCH 0100000 0,                                  00   0540
        FLOATING CONSTANT CLN  MCH 2330000 0,                    00   0550
        FLOATING TEN CLN  MCH 2045000  0,                        00   0560
        OCTAL LIMIT CLN  MCH 1000000 0,                          00   0570
        DECIMAL LIMIT CLN  MCH 0631463 OCT  14630,               00   0580
        ERROR CODE CLN  MCH 2551514 OCT 65160,                   00   0590
        MCH 2346242 OCT 56060,                                   00   0600
```

```
         LABELS CLN   MCH 6060603 OCT 11360,                              00   0610
               MCH 6060606 OCT 06073,                                     00   0620
               MCH 6041136 OCT 06060,                                     00   0630
               MCH 6060607 OCT 36042,                                     00   0640
               MCH 1360606 OCT 06060,                                     00   0650
               MCH 6073602 OCT 34613,                                     00   0660
               MCH 6060607 OCT 36045,                                     00   0670
               MCH 4613606 OCT 06073,                                     00   0680
               MCH 6043216 OCT 26360,                                     00   0690
               MCH 4521442 OCT 51360,                                     00   0700
    RECORD CLN MCH 00000000, MCH 00000000, MCH 00000000, MCH 00000000,    26   0310
               MCH 00000000, MCH 00000000, MCH 00000000, MCH 00000000,    26   0320
               MCH 00000000, MCH 00000000, MCH 00000000, MCH 00000000,    26   0330
               MCH 77000000, MCH 77000000,                                26   0340
               LAST NAME CLN MCH 0000000 0,                               00   0710
                             MCH 0000000 0,                               00   0720
                             MCH 0000000 0,                               00   0730
               PROGRAM NAME CLN   MCH 6060606 OCT 06060,                  00   0740
                                  MCH 6060606 OCT 06060,                  00   0750
                                  MCH 6060606 OCT 06060,                  00   0760
                                  MCH 6060606 OCT 06060,..                00   0770

     (COMMENT CLN MASTER DIMENSIONING STATEMENT )                         00   0790
    SIMPLE DIMENSION LIST CLN ADDRESS,                                    00   0800
               ADDRESS FLAG,                                              00   0810
               ADDRESS PAST ,                                             00   0820
               ADDRESS TEMP,                                              00   0830
               ANDFLAG,                                                   00   0831
               ARGUMENT STACK (20),
               BRACE FLAG,                                                00   0832
               CHAR,                                                      00   0840
               CLEAR SYMBOL FLAG,                                         00   0850
               CLEAR ADD FLAG,                                            00   0845
               COMPARATOR,
               COMPARISON FLAG,                                           00   0860
               COMPARISON FLAG 1,                                         00   0870
               COMPARISON LOC (35),                                       00   0880
               COMPARISON LOC 1,                                          00   0890
               CONTROL FLAG ,                                             00   0900
               COUNT,                                                     00   0910
               CURRENT INDEX,                                             00   0920
               CURRENT OP,                                                00   0930
               CURRENT OP TEMP,                                           00   0940.
               DECIMAL INTEGER,                                           00   0950
               DECREMENT,                                                 00   0960
               ENTRANCE ADDRESS,                                          00   0980
    FAULT FLAG=0,
               FLOATER,
               FLOATING FLAG,                                             00   0990
               FLOATING FLAG PAST,
               FLOATING PT STACK (20),                                    00   1000
               FRACTION COUNT,                                            00   1010
               FUNCTION FLAG,                                             00   1020
               HOLDAD (100),
               HOLDOP (100),
               HOLD STACK INDEX,
               IL ADDRESS,                                                00   1025
               IL OP,                                                     00   1026
               INDEX COUNTER,
               INDEX FLAG,                                                00   1030
               INDEX REG,                                                 00   1040
               I TEMP STORE,                                              00   1050
```

```
ITS,                                                              00  1060
J TEMP STORE,                                                     00  1070
J TEMPORARY,
JTS ,                                                             00  1080
K TS,
LOC START,                                                        00  1090
LOC TEMP,                                                         00  1100
LOOP FLAG,                                                        00  1110
LOOP INDEX NUMBER,                                                00  1120
LOOP STORAGE (30),                                                00  1130
MESSAGE,                                                          00  1140
MINUS FLAG,                                                       00  1150

MULT DIV FLAG,                                                    00  1160
NAME BUFFER 1, NAME BUFFER 2, NAME BUFFER 3,                      00  1170
NAME FOUND FLAG,                                                  00  1180
NEXT OP,                                                          00  1190
N TS,                                                             00  1195
NUMBER,                                                           00  1200
NUMBER BUFFER,                                                    00  1210
NUMBER FLAG,                                                      00  1220
OCTAL FLAG,                                                       00  1230
OPERAND,
OPERAND PAST,
ORFLAG,                                                           00  1240
OTS,
OTS2,
PARTIAL WORD FLAG,                                                00  1250
PART WORD 1,                                                      00  1260
PART WORD 2,                                                      00  1270
PART WORD 3,                                                      00  1280
PART WORD STACK(35),                                              00  1290
PEEK SYMBOL,                                                      00  1300
PEEK SYM BUFFER,                                                  00  1310
PEEK SYM COUNT,                                                   00  1320
PREFIX,                                                           00  1330
PRESENT SYMBOL,                                                   00  1340
PREVIOUS SYMBOL,                                                  00  1350
PRINT NAME FLAG,                                                  00  1360
PROGRAM FLAGS COUNT,                                              00  1370
BARF BUFFER ,
  SCALE,                                                          00  1380
  SHIFT FLAG,                                                     00  1390
  STORE FLAG,                                                     00  1400
  SUBROUTINE LOC,                                                 00  1410
  SYMBOL BUFFER,                                                  00  1420
  SYMBOL BUFFER TS,                                               00  1430
   SYMBOL COUNT,                                                  00  1440
  SYMBOL COUNT TS,                                                00  1450
  TAG,                                                            00  1460
    TEMP STORE,
  TEMP STORAGE,                                                   00  1470
  TEMP STORAGE 2,                                                 00  1475
  UNDEFINED LIST LOC,                                             00  1480
  WORD FLAG,                                                      00  1490
  WORD FLAG TS,                                                   00  1500
  WS,
D SIMPLE DIMENSION CLN TS,
  S,,
   ENTRY LOCATION,                                                00  1510
   INPUT PROGR LOC,                                               00  1520
   LOCATION,                                                      00  1530
```

```
      OUTPUT PROGR LOC,  '                              00  1540
      PROGRAM FLAGS LOC,                                00  1550
      SUB MARK LOC,                                     00  1560

      LEFT BRACE           =40 ,
      LEFT PAREN           =41 ,
      LEFT BRACKET         =42 ,
      CRUTCH               =43 ,
      OCTAL                =44 ,
      IFOP                 =45 ,
      EXPONENT             =46 ,
      MULTIPLY             =47 ,
      DIVIDE               =48 ,
      PLUS                 =49 ,
      MINUS                =50 ,
      LESS                 =51 ,
      LESSOR EQUAL         =52 ,
      EQUAL                =53 ,
NOTEQUAL CLN UNEQUAL       =54 ,
      GREATEROR EQUAL      =55 ,
      GREATER              =56 ,
      NOTOP                =57 ,
      ANDOP                =58 ,
      OROP                 =59 ,
      IMPLICATION          =60 ,
      IDENTITY             =61 ,
      ARROW                =62 ,
      FOROP                =63 ,
      STEPOP               =64 ,
      UNTILOP              =65 ,
      WHILEOP              =66 ,
      DOOP                 =67 ,
      THENOP               =68 ,
      ELSEOP               =69 ,
      PERIOD               =70 ,
      COMMA                =71 ,
      RIGHT BRACKET        =72 ,
      SEMICOLON            =73 ,
      COLON                =74 ,
      RIGHT PAREN          =75 ,
      RIGHT BRACE          =76 ,
      TRUETHING            =78 ,
      FALSETHING           =79 ,
      REALOP               =80 ,
      INTEGEROP            =81 ,
      BOOLEANOP            =82 ,
      OWNOP                =83 ,
      VALUEOP              =84 ,
      ARRAYOP              =85 ,
      PROCEDUREOP          =86 ,
      LABELOP              =87 ,
      STRINGOP             =88 ,
      SWITCHOP             =89 ,
      SUBROUTINE MARK      = 92,
      LEFT HOOK            =90 ,
      RIGHT HOOK           =91 ,
      PRINTOP              =126,
      READOP               =127,
    $..

      END CLN ONETAG = 32768,                           00  1630
      FIRST NUMBER = 27,                                00  1660
```

```
FLOAT BIT = OCT 100000,
LAST LETTER = 26,                                          00   1690
LAST NUMBER = 36,
PROGRAM FLAGS CONSTANT = OCT 15000,                        00   1850
SUB MARK CONSTANT = OCT 15001,                             00   1910
DEFINED LIST LOC = -1,                                     00   1930
INDEX (4),                                                 00   1940
INDEX COUNTER ONE = OCT 1000000,
TWO TAG = OCT 200000,                                      00   1960
FOUR TAG = OCT 400000,                                     00   1970

ZERO = 0,                                                  00   1980
ONE = 1,                                                   00   1990
 TWO =2,                                                   00   2000
 THREE =3,                                                 00   2010
 FOUR =4,                                                  00   2020
 FIVE =5,                                                  00   2030
 SIX =6,                                                   00   2040
 SEVEN =7,                                                 00   2050
 EIGHT =8,                                                 00   2060
 NINE =9,                                                  00   2070
 TEN = 10,                                                 00   2080
 ELEVEN = 11,                                              00   2090
 TWELVE = 12,                                              00   2100
 THIRTEEN = 13,                                            00   2110
 FOURTEEN = 14,                                            00   2120
 FIFTEEN = 15,                                             00   2130
 SIXTEEN =16,                                              00   2140
 SEVENTEEN = 17,                                           00   2150
 EIGHTEEN = 18,                                            00   2160
 NINETEEN = 19,                                            00   2170
 TWENTY = 20,                                              00   2180
 TWENTY ONE = 21,                                          00   2190
 TWENTY TWO = 22,                                          00   2200
 TWENTY THREE = 23,                                        00   22 0
TWENTY FOUR = 24,                                          00   2211
  TWENTY SIX = 26 ,
 TWENTY SEVEN = 27,                                        00   2220
 MINUS TWENTY SEVEN = -27,                                 00   2230
 THIRTY ONE = 31,                                          00   2240
 THIRTY FIVE = 35,                                         00   2250
 FIFTY THREE = 53,                                         00   2260
 ONE O ONE = 101,
 TEN TWENTY THREE = 1023,                                  00   2270
 OUTPUTCONSTANT(2)= OCT 40000, OCT 40000,                  00   2280
INPUT CONSTANT = OCT 43100 ,
 END PROG BUFFER = OCT 20000,                              00   2290

 IL INSTRUCTION      = OCT 77000000000,            ILINS 00
 IL MPY              = OCT 11000000000,            ILINS 01
 IL DIV              = OCT 12000000000,            ILINS 02
 IL ADD              = OCT 04000000000,            ILINS 03
 IL CHS (7)          = OCT 14000000000, ......     ILINS 04
 IL COM              = OCT 15000000000,            ILINS 05
 IL ANA              = OCT 36000000000,            ILINS 06
 IL ORA (3)          = OCT 35000000000,            ILINS 07
                       OCT 35000000000,  .         ILINS 08
 IL STO              = OCT 37000000000,            ILINS 09

 IL CLA              = OCT 01000000000,            ILINS 10
 IL CLS              = OCT 02000000000,            ILINS 11
 IL CAM              = OCT 03000000000,            ILINS 12
```

```
IL ADM        ' = OCT 05000000000,              ILINS 13
IL SUB          = OCT 06000000000,              ILINS 14
IL SBM          = OCT 07000000000,              ILINS 15
IL ISB          = OCT 10000000000,              ILINS 16
IL IDV          = OCT 13000000000,              ILINS 17
IL ILF          = OCT 16000000000,              ILINS 18
IL ELF          = OCT 17000000000,              ILINS 19
IL ILB          = OCT 20000000000,              ILINS 20
IL ELB          = OCT 21000000000,              ILINS 21
IL SL           = OCT 22000000000,              ILINS 22
IL RS           = OCT 23000000000,              ILINS 23
IL TRA          = OCT 24000000000,              ILINS 24
IL TNP          = OCT 25000000000,              ILINS 25
IL TRN          = OCT 26000000000,              ILINS 26
IL TNZ          = OCT 27000000000,              ILINS 27
IL TZE          = OCT 30000000000,              ILINS 28
IL TRP          = OCT 31000000000,              ILINS 29
IL TNN          = OCT 32000000000,              ILINS 30
ILREAL          = OCT 33000000000,              ILINS 31
ILINTEGER       = OCT 34000000000,              ILINS 32
IL LXA          = OCT 40000000000,              ILINS 33
IL LXM          = OCT 41000000000,              ILINS 34
IL SXA          = OCT 42000000000,              ILINS 35
IL SXM          = OCT 43000000000,              ILINS 36
RELATION CONSTANT= 30,

    IL OUTPUTER (37)=  OCT 606060606060,                       ILOUT 00
OCT 606060234321, OCT 606060234362, OCT 606060232144, OCT 606060212424,ILOUT 04
OCT 606060212444, OCT 606060626422, OCT 606060622244, OCT 606060316222,ILOUT 10
OCT 606060444363, OCT 606060243165, OCT 606060312465, OCT 606060233062,ILOUT 14
OCT 606060234644, OCT 606060314326, OCT 606060254326, OCT 606060314322,ILOUT 20
OCT 606060254322, OCT 606060606243, OCT 606060605162, OCT 606060635121,ILOUT 24
OCT 606060634547, OCT 606060635145, OCT 606060634571, OCT 606060637125,ILOUT 30
OCT 606060635147, OCT 606060634545, OCT 606051252143, OCT 314563252751,ILOUT 34
OCT 606060465121, OCT 606060214521, OCT 606060626346, OCT 606060436721,ILOUT 40
OCT 606060436744, OCT 606060626721, OCT 606060626744, OCT 606060606060,ILOUT 44.
```

```
$ADVANCE CLN                                                      04  0010
      NEXT OP = CURRENT OP, ADDRESS = ADDRESS PAST,               04  0020
      FLOATING FLAG= FLOATING FLAG PAST,
      ZERO = ADDRESS = ADDRESS FLAG = NAME BUFFER 1 =             04  0030
      NAME BUFFER 2 = NAME BUFFER 3 , OPERAND=OPERANDPAST,        04  0040
ADVANCE 1 CLN                                                     04  0050
      FIND NON ZERO SYM,                                          04  0060
      PRESENT SYMBOL GEQ FIRST NUMBER CLN  ADVANCE 4.$ONE=OPERAND.$  04  0070
      READ NAME, PRESENT SYMBOL = NEXT OP,                        04  0080
      NAME BUFFER 1 * 2 EXP 14 NEQ ZERO CLN ADVANCE 2 .$         04  0090
      NAME BUFFER 1 / 2 EXP 24 = TEMP STORAGE,                    04  0100
      EIGHT LSS TEMP STORAGE LSS FIFTEEN CLN ADVANCE 3 .$        04  0110
ADVANCE 2 CLN                                                     04  0120
      NAME DEFINITION, FIND OP ENTRANCE.                          04  0130
ADVANCE 3 CLN                                                     04  0140
      TEMP STORAGE - EIGHT = ADDRESS, ONE = INDEX FLAG = ADDRESS FLAG,  04  0150
      ZERO = NAME BUFFER 1, FIND OP ENTRANCE.                     04  0160
ADVANCE 4 CLN    ZERO=OPERAND.                                    04 0170
      IF PRESENT SYMBOL LEQ LAST NUMBER CLN
            TEST NUMBER, REQUEST NUMBER, ONE=OPERAND.$$
      PRESENT SYMBOL EQU OCTAL CLN ONE = OCTAL FLAG= OPERAND,     04  0190
      FIND NON ZERO SYM, TEST NUMBER, REQUEST NUMBER $$          04  0200
      PRESENT SYMBOL = NEXT OP, FIND OP ENTRANCE ..               04  0210
```

```
$BUILD PROGRAM FLAGS CLN LBR
    PROGRAM FLAGS COUNT EQU ZERO CLN PROGRAM FLAGS LOC - ONE =          06  0240
    PROGRAM FLAGS LOC = M, ZERO = LBK M RBK , TEN = PROGRAMFLAGSCOUNT$$06  0250
    PROGRAM FLAGS LOC = M, LBK M RBK * 2 EXP 3 +WORDFLAG= LBK M RBK ,   06  0260
    PROGRAM FLAGS COUNT - ONE = PROGRAM FLAGS COUNT, I-ONE=I, RBR ..    06  0270

$CLEAR ALL NAME CLN
 ·   L EQU O(1)6143 LBR ZERO = NAME WORD 1 LBK L RBK RBR ,
    LOAD SOURCE PROGRAM . . .

$COMPARE CLN LBR
    IF RIGHT BRACKET LEQ CURRENT OP CLN W.$
    IF CURRENT OP EQU DIVIDE CLN
        LBR IF NEXT OP GEQ MULTIPLY CLN S.W. RBR $$
    IF CURRENT OP EQU MINUS CLN
        LBR IF NEXT OP GEQ PLUS CLN S.W. RBR $$
        IF LESS LEQ  CURRENT OP LEQ GREATER CLN
        LBR IF NEXT OP GTR GREATER CLN S. W. RBR $$
    IF CURRENT OP GTR ARROW CLN RIGHT.$
LEFT CLN  IF CURRENT OP LEQ NEXTOP CLN S.W.
RIGHT CLN IF CURRENT OP LSS NEXTOP CLN S.W.
S CLN ONE = COMPARATOR, COMPARE EXIT.
W CLN ZERO= COMPARATOR,
 COMPARE EXIT CLN RBR ..

$CRUTCH CODE CLN                                                        13  0010
    PEEK, PEEK SYMBOL - FIRST NUMBER GEQ FOUR CLN ZERO - ONE =          13  0020
    LBK I+1 RBK $ ONE = LBK I+1 RBK $ L EQU O(1)6 LBR FIND NONZEROSYM,  13  0030
    LBK I RBK *2 EXP 3+ PRESENT SYMBOL - FIRST NUMBER= LBK I RBK , RBR  13  0040
    + LBK I RBK *2 EXP 15 = LBK I RBK ,FIND NON ZERO SYM,               13  0050
    PRESENT SYMBOL EQU OCTAL CLN FIND NON ZERO SYM, ONE = OCTAL FLAG $  13  0060
     ZERO=OCTALFLAG$FIRSTNUMBER LEQ PRESENTSYMBOL LEQ LASTNUMBER CLN    13  0070
    FIND NUMBER, FOUR = WORD FLAG, NUMBER BUFFER = ADDRESS,CRUTCH CODE  13  0080
    1.$ READ NAME, NAME DEFINITION, FIVE = WORD FLAG,                   13  0090
    PRESENT SYMBOL NEQ LEFT BRACKET CLN CRUTCH CODE 1.$                 13  0100
    FIND NON ZERO SYM, PRESENT SYMBOL EQU MINUS CLN FIND NON ZERO       13  0110
    SYM, ONE = MINUS FLAG$ ZERO= MINUS FLAG $ PRESENT SYMBOL EQU OCTAL  13  0120
    CLN FIND NON ZERO SYM, ONE = OCTAL FLAG,$$                          13  0130
    FIRSTNUMBER LEQ PRESENT SYMBOL LEQ LAST NUMBER CLN $ FAULT22, FIND  13  0140
    NUMBER, MINUS FLAG EQU ONE CLN ADDRESS +NUMBER BUFFER =ADDRESS $    13  0150
    ADDRESS- NUMBER BUFFER = ADDRESS $ FIND NON ZERO SYM,               13  0160
CRUTCH CODE 1 CLN                                                       13  0170
    ADDRESS + LBK I RBK = LBK I RBK ,                                   13  0180
    MCH 0500001 00, MCH 056000100001, MCH 0763000 0,                    13  0181
    MCH 0601001 0,                      ZERO = LBK I+1 RBK , BUILD PROGRAM 13  0190
    FLAGS, PRESENT SYMBOL NEQ COMMA CLN  FAULT 22.$                     13  0200
    PRESENT SYMBOL = NEXT OP, ZERO = ADDRESS = ADDRESS FLAG,            13  0210
    GENERATE EXIT..                                                     13  0220

$DIMENSION CLN J = JTS,                                                 14  0010
    LBK J RBK = SYMBOL BUFFER, J - ONE =J, FIVE = SYMBOL COUNT,         14  0020
    END - I = LOC START, ONE = WORD FLAG,                               14  0030
DIMENSION A CLN                                                         14  0040
    PRESENT SYMBOL EQU COLON CLN DIMENSION C .$                         14  0050
    PRESENT SYMBOL EQU SEMICOLON CLN DIMENSION F .$ FIND NON ZERO SYM,  14  0060
    PRESENT SYMBOL EQU LEFT BRACE CLN BUILD PROGRAM FLAGS, DIMENSIONE.$ 14  0070
    PRESENT SYMBOL GEQ FIRST NUMBER CLN DIMENSION A.$ READ NAME,        14  0080
    PRESENT SYMBOL EQU LEFT PAREN CLN DIMENSION B.$                     14  0090
    BUILD PROGRAM FLAGS, DIMENSION A.                                   14  0100
DIMENSION B CLN                                                         14 ‹0110
    FIND NON ZERO SYM, PRESENT SYMBOL EQU OCTAL CLN FIND NON ZERO SYM,  14  0120
```

```
    ONE = OCTAL FLAG $$ FIND NUMBER, I-NUMBER BUFFER + ONE = ITS,      14   0130
  L EQU I(-1)ITS LBR BUILD PROGRAM FLAGS, RBR , DIMENSION A.           14   0140
DIMENSION C CLN                                                        14   0150
    FIND NON ZERO SYM, PRESENT SYMBOL EQU LEFT BRACE CLN DIMENSION E.$  14   0160
    READ NAME,                                                         14   0170
DIMENSION D CLN                                                        14   0180
    PRESENT SYMBOL EQU LEFT PAREN CLN UNBUILD PROGRAM FLAGS,           14   0190
    DIMENSION B. DIMENSION A.                                          14   0200
DIMENSION E CLN                                                        14   0210
    FIND NON ZERO SYM, PRESENT SYMBOL NEQ RIGHT BRACE CLN DIMENSIONE.$ 14   0220
    FIND NON ZERO SYM, DIMENSION D.                                    14   0230
DIMENSION F CLN                                                        14   0240
    JTS = J, LBK J RBK = SYMBOL BUFFER, J- ONE=J, FIVE = SYMBOL COUNT, 14   0250
    ONE = CLEAR SYMBOL FLAG, COMMA = CURRENT OP, COLON = NEXT OP,      14   0260
    I= ITEMP STORE, I + ONE = I,                                       14   0270
DIMENSION 1 CLN FIND NON ZERO SYM,                                     14   0280
DIMENSION 2 CLN PRESENT SYMBOL LSS FIRST NUMBER CLN DIMENSION 6.$      14   0290
DIMENSION 3 CLN                                                        14   0300
    PRESENT SYMBOL EQU COMMA CLN DIMENSION 1. ZERO =NUMBER BUFFER =    14   0310
    OCTAL FLAG$ PRESENT SYMBOL EQU COLON CLN PW DIMENSION.$            14   0320
    PRESENT SYMBOL EQU LEFT BRACE CLN PW DIMENSION 1.$                 14   0330
    PRESENT SYMBOL NEQ LEFT PAREN CLN DIMENSION 4, FIND NON ZERO SYM$  14   0340
    PRESENT SYMBOL EQU OCTAL CLN ONE = OCTAL FLAG, FIND NON ZERO SYM.$ 14   0350
    ZERO = OCTAL FLAG $                                                14   0360
    FIRSTNUMBER LEQ PRESENTSYMBOL LEQ LASTNUMBER CLN
       FIND NUMBERS FAULT3.
    PRESENT SYMBOL NEQ RIGHT PAREN CLN FAULT 3.$ I- ONE=I,             14   0380
  L EQU I(1) NUMBER BUFFER LBR I +ONE= I, RBR , FIND NON ZERO SYM,     14   0390
    PRESENT SYMBOL EQU COMMA CLN DIMENSION 1.$                         14   0400
DIMENSION 4 CLN PRESENT SYMBOL EQU ARROW CLN DIMENSION 7.$             14   0410
DIMENSION 5 CLN                                                        14   0420
    PRESENT SYMBOL NEQ SEMICOLON CLN FAULT 4.$                         14   0440
    ZERO = CLEAR SYMBOL FLAG = NAME BUFFER 1 =NAME BUFFER 2      =     14   0440
    NAME BUFFER 3, END-I +ONE NEQ LOC START CLN FAULT 21.$            14   0450
    ITEMP STORE = I, ZERO = ADDRESS PAST, FIND.BRACES 1.              14   0460
DIMENSION 6 CLN READ NAME, NAME DEFINITION,                           14   0470
    ZERO = NUMBER BUFFER, I+ ONE = I,DIMENSION 3 .                     14   0480
DIMENSION 7 CLN I =ITS, NUMBER BUFFER EQU ZERO CLN I- ONE = I $        14   0490
    I- NUMBER BUFFER = I $ PEEK,                                       14   0500
    PEEK SYMBOL LSS FIRST NUMBER CLN FAULT 21 .$                       14   0510

DIMENSION 8 CLN FIND NON ZERO SYM, PRESENT SYMBOL EQU COMMA CLN        14   0520
    DIMENSION 10.$ PRESENT SYMBOL EQU MINUS CLN FIND NON ZERO SYM,     14   0530
    ONE = MINUS FLAG$ ZERO = MINUS FLAG $                              14   0540
    PRESENT SYMBOL EQU OCTAL CLN ONE = OCTAL FLAG, FIND NON ZERO SYM,  14   0550
    DIMENSION 9. ZERO = OCTAL FLAG $ LAST LETTER LSS PRESENT SYMBOL    14   0560
    CLN DIMENSION 9.$     I TS = I, FLOATING DEFINITION TEST, DIMENSION6.14  0570
DIMENSION 9 CLN PRESENT SYMBOL EQU MINUS CLN FIND NON ZERO SYM,        14   0580
    ONE=MINUSFLAG, PRESENT SYMBOL GTR LAST NUMBER CLN                  14   0590
    LBR PRESENT SYMBOL NEQ PERIOD CLN DIMENSION 11. RBR $$             14   0600
    TEST NUMBER, NUMBER BUFFER = LBK I RBK ,                           14   0610
    MINUS FLAG EQU ONE CLN ZERO - LBK I RBK = LBK I RBK $$             14   0620
DIMENSION 10 CLN I + ONE = I, I TS LSS I CLN FAULT 21.$                14   0630
    PRESENT SYMBOL EQU COMMA CLN DIMENSION 8.$ ITS = I,                14   0640
DIMENSION 11 CLN FLOATING DEFINITION TEST, PRESENT SYMBOL EQU LEFT     14   0650
    BRACE CLN PW DIMENSION 1. DIMENSION 5.                             14   0651
PW DIMENSION CLN                                                       14   0660
    I - ONE = I, FIND NON ZERO SYM,                                    14   0670
    PRESENT SYMBOL NEQ LEFT BRACE CLN DIMENSION 6.$                    14   0680
PW DIMENSION 1 CLN                                                     14   0690
    FIND NON ZERO SYM,                                                 14   0700
PW DIMENSION 2 CLN                                                     14   0710
```

```
       PRESENT SYMBOL LSS FIRST NUMBER CLN $ FAULT 3.                   14   0720
       READ NAME, NAME DEFINITION,                                      14   0730
       PRESENT SYMBOL NEQ LEFT PAREN CLN FAULT 3 .$                     14   0740
       ONE = FLOATING FLAG, PARTIAL WORD .                              14   0750
PW DIMENSION 3 CLN                                                      14   0760
       ZERO = FLOATING FLAG, DEFINED LIST LOC = N,                      14   0770
       NUMBER BUFFER - PART WORD 1 + ONE = TEMP STORAGE * 2 EXP 15 +    14   0780
       PART WORD 1 * 2 EXP 21 + NAME LOCATION LBK N RBK = NAME LOCATION 14   0790
       LBK N RBK , FIND NON ZERO SYM, PRESENT SYMBOL EQU COMMA CLN FIND 14   0800
       NON ZERO SYM$$ PRESENT SYMBOL NEQ RIGHT BRACE CLN PW DIMENSION 2.$ 14 0810
       I+ ONE = I, FIND NON ZERO SYM, DIMENSION 3.                      14   0820
FLOATING DEFINITION TEST CLN                                            14   0830
       LBR FLOATING FLAG EQU ONE CLN DEFINED LIST LOC =N, ZERO =FLOATING 14 0840
       FLAG, NAME LOCATION LBK N RBK +ONE *2 EXP 34 = NAME LOCATION     14   0850
       LBK N RBK $$ RBR ..                                              14   0860

$EXEC ROUTINE CLN                                                       16   0010
       I NEQ ZERO CLN I= OUTPUT PROGR LOC, END -I = ENTRY LOCATION $    16   0020
       OUTPUT CONSTANT+ONE=OTS+ONE=OTS2+ONE O ONE=I=OUTPUTPROGRLOC,     16   0030
       ZERO-OTS2=WS,                                                    00   1631
       OUTPUT CONSTANT LBK 1 RBK = ENTRY LOCATION,                      16   0040
       PROGRAM FLAGS CONSTANT = PROGRAM FLAGS LOC $                     16   0050
       INPUT CONSTANT = INPUT PROGR LOC = J,                            16   0060
       SUB MARK CONST = SUB MARK LOC = K.                               16   0070
    L EQU I(-1) END PROG BUFFER LBR ZERO = LBK L RBK RBR .
    CLEAR SIMPLE DIMENSION LIST.
       FIVE = WORD FLAG, TRA = PREFIX, BUILD COMMAND 1,                 16   0100
       ENTRY LOCATION NEQ OUTPUT CONSTANT LBK 1 RBK CLN DIMENSION.$     16   0110
       ZERO = WORD FLAG, L EQU 0(1)7 LBR BUILD PROGRAM FLAGS, RBR ,     16   0120
    DIMENSION.                                                          16   0130

       (COMMENT  THIS SUBROUTINE DOES NOT NEED TO KNOW HOW LONG THE
                 LIST MAY BE.  )
CLEAR SIMPLE DIMENSION LIST CLN LBR                                     16   0140
       CSDL1-CSDL2=CSDL3, L EQU 0(1)CSDL3 LBR ZERO= SIMPLE DIMENSION    16   0150
       LIST LBK L RBK   RBR . RBR .                                     16   0160
CSD1 CLN MCH 0000000 SIMPLE DIMENSION LIST .                           16   0170
CSDL2 CLN MCH 0000000 END SIMPLE DIMENSION .                           16   0180
CSDL3 CLN MCH 0000000 0...                                             16   0190

$FAULT CLN                                                              17   0010
       LBR I = INDEX, J=INDEX LBK 1 RBK ,K=INDEX LBK 2 RBK , L=INDEX    17   0020
       LBK 3 RBK =FAULT FLAG, DEFINED LIST LOC = L,NAME WORD 1 LBK L RBK 17  0030
       = LOCATION, CONVERT TO BCD, MESSAGE =LAST NAME,NAME WORD 2       17   0040
       LBK L RBK = LOCATION, CONVERT TO BCD, MESSAGE =LAST NAME         17   0050
       LBK 32767 RBK , NAME WORD 3 LBK L RBK = LOCATION,CONVERT TO BCD, 17   0060
       MESSAGE = LAST NAME LBK 32766 RBK ,                              17   0070
       GLOUT2,                                                          17   0080
       MCH 3 03770 O ERROR CODE,      (COMMENT  12 CHARACTERS TO PW 40) 17   0090
       MCH 3 05714 U PROGRAM NAME,    (COMMENT  18 CHARACTERS TO PW 20) 17   0100
       MCH 4 00053 O INDEX LBK 3 RBK ,(COMMENT  ERROR CODE   TO PW 43)  17   0110
    MCH 5 00000 0 0,                                                    17   0130
       GLOUT2,                                                          17   0140
       MCH 3 23515 O LABELS,          (COMMENT  60 CHARACTERS TO PW 61) 17   0140
       MCH 3 06007 O LAST NAME,       (COMMENT  18 CHARACTERS TO PW 79) 17   0150
       MCH 4 00050 O CURRENT OP,      (COMMENT  CURRENT OP   TO PW 40)  17   0160
       MCH 4 00060 O NEXT OP,         (COMMENT NEXT OP       TO PW 48)  17   0170
       MCH 4 00014 O INDEX,           (COMMENT I            TO PW 12)   17   0180
       MCH 4 00026 O INDEX LBK 1 RBK ,(COMMENT J            TO PW 22)   17   0190
       MCH 4 00040 O INDEX LBK 2 RBK ,(COMMENT K            TO PW 32)   17   0200
    MCH 5 00000 0 0, RBR ,
FAULT 1 CLN ONE =L, FAULT, FAULT EXIT..                                 17   0220
```

```
FAULT 2 CLN TWO =L, FAULT, F'IND NUMBER LBK 32767 RBK .            17  0230
FAULT 3 CLN THREE =L, FAULT, FAULT EXIT.                           17  0240
FAULT 4 CLN FOUR  =L, FAULT, FAULT EXIT.                           17  0250
FAULT 5 CLN FIVE  =L, FAULT, FAULT EXIT.                           17  0260
FAULT 6 CLN SIX   =L, FAULT, FAULT EXIT.                           17  0270
FAULT 7 CLN SEVEN =L, FAULT, FAULT EXIT.                           17  0280
FAULT 8 CLN EIGHT =L, FAULT, FAULT EXIT.                           17  0290
FAULT 9 CLN NINE  =L, FAULT, FAULT EXIT.                           17  0300
FAULT 10 CLN TEN  =L, FAULT, FAULT EXIT.                           17  0310
FAULT 11 CLN ELEVEN   =L, FAULT, FAULT EXIT.                       17  0320
FAULT 12 CLN TWELVE   =L, FAULT, FAULT EXIT.                       17  0330
FAULT 13 CLN THIRTEEN =L, FAULT, FAULT EXIT.                       17  0340
FAULT 14 CLN FOURTEEN =L, FAULT, FIND BRACES 3A.                   17  0350
FAULT 15 CLN FIFTEEN  =L, FAULT, FAULT EXIT.                       17  0360
FAULT 16 CLN SIXTEEN  =L, FAULT, FAULT EXIT.                       17  0370
FAULT 17 CLN SEVENTEEN =L, FAULT, FAULT EXIT.                      17  0380
FAULT 18 CLN EIGHTEEN =L, FAULT, NAME DEFINITION 1.               17  0390
FAULT 19 CLN NINETEEN =L, FAULT, FAULT EXIT.                       17  0400
FAULT 20 CLN TWENTY   =L, FAULT, FAULT EXIT.                       17  0410
FAULT 21 CLN TWENTY ONE =L, FAULT, FAULT EXIT.                     17  0420
FAULT 22 CLN TWENTY TWO =L, FAULT, FAULT EXIT.                     17  0430
FAULT 23 CLN TWENTY THREE = L, FAULT, FAULT EXIT.                  17  0440
FAULT 24 CLN TWENTY FOUR = L, FAULT, FAULT EXIT.                   17  0441
FAULT 25 CLN LBR L = COMPARISON FLAG 1, 25 = L, FAULT,             17  0442
    COMPARISON FLAG 1 = L, ZERO = COMPARISON FLAG 1, RBR ,         17  0443
FAULT EXIT CLN                                                     17  0450
    N EQU 32767(-1)32765 LBR PROGRAM NAME LBK 32765 RBK = PROGRAM NAME 17  0460
    LBK N+1 RBK , RBR , LOAD SOURCE PROGRAM..                      17  0470

$FIND BRACES CLN                                                   18  0020
    ZERO = PRESENT SYMBOL = NEXT OP = LOOP FLAG = BRACE FLAG,      18  0030
    INPUT PROGR LOC = J, LBK J RBK = SYMBOL BUFFER,                18  0040
    J- ONE = J, FIVE = SYMBOL COUNT.                               18  0050
$FIND BRACES 1 CLN                                                 18  0060
    PRESENT SYMBOL = PREVIOUS SYMBOL, FIND NON ZERO SYM,           18  0070
    PRESENT SYMBOL LEQ LAST NUMBER CLN FINDBRACES1.$NEXTOP=CURRENTOP, 18  0080
    PRESENT SYMBOL = NEXT OP EQU LEFT BRACE CLN FIND BRACES 2 .$   18  0090
    NEXT OP EQU RIGHT BRACE CLN FIND BRACES 3.$                    18  0100
    PRESENT SYMBOL NEQ PERIOD CLN FIND BRACES 1.$                  18  0110
    PREVIOUS SYMBOL NEQ PERIOD CLN FIND BRACES 1.$                 18  0120
    BRACE FLAG EQU ONE CLN FAULT 12 .$                             18  0130
    ONE = PRINT NAME FLAG, OUTPUT PROGR LOC = J,                   18  0140
    END -I+ LBK J RBK = LBK J RBK , INPUT PROGR LOC = J,           18  0150
    LBK J RBK = SYMBOL BUFFER, J-ONE = J, FIVE = SYMBOL COUNT,     18  0160
    SEMICOLON = NEXT OP, ADVANCE.                                  18  0170
FIND BRACES 2 CLN                                                  18  0180
    CURRENT OP EQU RIGHT 'PAREN CLN ONE = LOOP FLAGS ZERO = LOOP FLAGS 18  0190
    PLUS LEQ CURRENT OP LEQ MINUS CLN ONE=LOOP FLAG $$             18  0200
    J=J TEMP STORE, SYMBOL COUNT = SYMBOL COUNT TS, ONE =BRACE FLAG, 18  0210
    SYMBOL BUFFER = SYMBOL BUFFER TS, FIND BRACES 1.              18  0220
FIND BRACES 3 CLN                                                  18  0230
    BRACE FLAG EQU ZERO CLN                                        18  0240
    SYMBOL BUFFER - PRESENT SYMBOL = SYMBOL BUFFER,FAULT 14 .$     18  0250
FIND BRACES 3A CLN                                                 18  0260
    ZERO =BRACE FLAG, LOOP FLAG EQU ONE CLN FIND BRACES 4 .$       18  0270
    J TEMP STORE=J, SYMBOL COUNT TS = SYMBOL COUNT,                18  0280
    SYMBOL BUFFER TS = SYMBOL BUFFER,                              18  0290
    SYMBOL BUFFER /2 EXP 7 *2 EXP 7 +SUBROUTINE MARK = SYMBOL BUFFER, 18  0300
    LEFT BRACE = NEXT OP, ONE = CLEAR SYMBOL FLAG, ADVANCE.        18  0310
FIND BRACES 4 CLN                                                  18  0320
    ZERO = LOOP FLAG,                                              18  0330
    SYMBOL BUFFER /2 EXP 7*2 EXP 7 + RIGHT HOOK = SYMBOL BUFFER,   18  0340
```

```
        RESET SYM BUFFER, J TEMP STORE = J,                              18   0350
        SYMBOL COUNT TS = SYMBOL COUNT,                                  18   0360
        SYMBOL BUFFER TS= SYMBOL BUFFER,                                 18   0370
        SYMBOL BUFFER /2 EXP 7*2 EXP 7 + LEFT HOOK = SYMBOL BUFFER,      18   0380
        RESET SYM BUFFER, FIND BRACES.                                   18   0390
RESET SYM BUFFER CLN                                                     18   0400
LBR RESET SYM BUFFER 1 CLN                                               18   0410
        SYMBOL COUNT -ONE = SYMBOL COUNT LSS ZERO CLN RESET SYM BUFFER 2.$18  0420
        SYMBOL BUFFER /2 EXP 28 = CHAR,                                  18   0430
        SYMBOL BUFFER *2 EXP 7  + CHAR= SYMBOL BUFFER, RESET SYM BUFFER 1.18  0440
        RESET SYM BUFFER 2 CLN                                           18   0450
        SYMBOL BUFFER = LBK J-1 RBK RBR ..                               18   0460


$ FIND NON ZERO SYM CLN                                                  19   0010
    LBR NON ZERO SYMBOL CLN                                              19   0020
        SYMBOL COUNT - ONE = SYMBOL COUNT LSS ZERO CLN                   19   0030
        NON ZERO SYMBOL 2 . $ SYMBOL BUFFER / 2 EXP 28                   19   0040
        = PRESENT SYMBOL , SYMBOL BUFFER * 2 EXP 7 = SYMBOL BUFFER ,     19   0050
        PRESENT SYMBOL EQU ZERO CLN NON ZERO SYMBOL . $                  19   0060
        CLEAR SYMBOL FLAG EQU ZERO CLN                                   19   0070
    SYMBOL BUFFER + PRESENT SYMBOL = SYMBOL BUFFER $$ RBR ,              19   0080
    NON ZERO SYMBOL 2 CLN                                                19   0090
        SYMBOL BUFFER = LBK J - 1 RBK , LBK J RBK = SYMBOL BUFFER ,      19   0100
        J - ONE = J , FIVE = SYMBOL COUNT , NON ZERO SYMBOL ..           19   0110


$ FIND NUMBER CLN                                                        20   0010
    LBR ZERO = NUMBER BUFFER , ONE = NUMBER FLAG ,                       20   0020
    OCTAL FLAG EQU ZERO CLN FIND DEC NUMBER.$                            20   0030
    FIND OCTAL NUMBER CLN                                                20   0040
        NUMBER BUFFER GEQ OCTAL LIMIT CLN FAULT 2 .$                     20   0050
        NUMBER BUFFER * EIGHT + PRESENT SYMBOL - FIRST NUMBER            20   0060
        = NUMBER BUFFER , FIND NON ZERO SYM ,                            20   0070
    FIRST NUMBER LEQ PRESENT SYMBOL LEQ LAST NUMBER CLN                  20   0080
        FIND OCTAL NUMBER .$                                             20   0090
    FIND NUMBER EXIT CLN   ZERO = OCTAL FLAG RBR .                       20   0100
    FIND DEC NUMBER CLN                                                  20   0110
        NUMBER BUFFER GEQ DECIMAL LIMIT CLN FAULT 2 .$                   20   0120
        NUMBER BUFFER * TEN   + PRESENT SYMBOL - FIRST NUMBER            20   0130
        = NUMBER BUFFER , FIND NON ZERO SYM ,                            20   0140
    FIRST NUMBER LEQ PRESENT SYMBOL LEQ LAST NUMBER CLN                  20   0150
        FIND DEC NUMBER . FIND NUMBER EXIT ..                            20   0160


$FIND NUMBER PAST CLN                                                    21   0010
    LBR RESET SYM BUFFER, J TEMP STORE =J, FIVE = SYMBOL COUNT,          21   0020
    SYMBOL BUFFER TS = PRESENT SYMBOL,                                   21   0030
    LBK J-1 RBK = SYMBOL BUFFER, TEMP STORAGE = CLEAR SYMBOL FLAG NEQ    21   0040
    ONE CLN LBR NUMBER PAST 1 CLN SYMBOL COUNT NEQ SYMBOL COUNT TS CLN21  0050
    FIND NON ZERO SYM, NUMBER PAST 1.$ RBR $$ FIND NUMBER, RBR .         21   0060
REQUEST NUMBER CLN LBR                                                   21   0070
    CURRENT OP EQU LEFT BRACKET CLN REQUEST EXIT .$                      21   0080
    CURRENT OP EQU LEFT PAREN CLN REQUEST EXIT .$                        21   0090
    CURRENT OP EQU EXPONENT CLN REQUEST EXIT .$                          21   0100
    MULTIPLY LEQ CURRENT OP LEQ DIVIDE CLN                               21   0110
        LBR PRESENT SYMBOL EQU EXPONENT CLN REQUEST EXIT .$ RBR $$       21   0120
    CURRENT OP EQU RIGHT PAREN CLN REQUEST EXIT .$                       21   0130
    CURRENT OP EQU EQUAL CLN LBR PRESENT SYMBOL EQU LEFT PAREN CLN       21   0140
    REQUEST EXIT .$ RBR $$ NUMBER BUFFER = NAME BUFFER 2, ZERO -ONE      21   0150
    =NAME BUFFER 1, COMMA = NEXT OP, NAME DEFINITION,                    21   0160
REQUEST EXIT CLN , RBR ..                                                21   0170


$FIND OP ENTRANCE CLN
    IF FLOATING FLAG NEQ ZERO CLN CHECK MODE FOR FLOATING $$
```

```
    J=J TEMPORARY, HOLD STACK INDEX=J,
    IF CURRENT OP EQU LEFT PAREN CLN LEFT PAREN ENTRY.$
    IF CURRENT OP EQU RIGHT PAREN CLN RIGHT PAREN ENTRY.$
    IF CURRENT OP EQU LEFT BRACKET CLN LEFT BRACKET ENTRY.$
    IF CURRENT OP EQU RIGHT BRACKET CLN RIGHT BRACKET ENTRY.$
    IF CURRENT OP EQU  ARROW CLN ARROW ENTRY.$
    IF CURRENT OP GTR ARROW CLN PUNCTUATION.$

    COMPARE, IF COMPARTATOR EQU ZERO CLN WEAK, STRONG.

ARROW ENTRY CLN
    IF RESULT EQU ZERO CLN
       LBR IF OPERAND PAST EQU ZERO CLN FAULT12$CLEARADDPAST$ RBR $$
    RESET MODE,ILSTO=PREFIX, MAKECOMMAND1, SET RESULT, EXIT TO ADVANCE.

ASSURE RESULT CLN LBR IF RESULT NEQ ZERO CLN LBR IF OPERAND PAST
    NEQ ZERO CLN CLEARADDPAST$$ RBR $$ RBR ,

CLEAR RESULT CLN LBR ZERO=RESULT, RBR ,

COLLAPSE CLN
    IF J EQU ZERO CLN EXIT TO ADVANCE.$
    HOLDOP LBK J RBK = CURRENT OP, COMPARE,
    IF COMPARATOR EQU ZERO CLN EXIT TO ADVANCE.$
    RECOVER ADDRESS,
    IF CURRENT OP EQU EXPONENT CLN RIGHT EXPONENT.$
    IF CURRENT OP EQU DIVIDE CLN RIGHT DIVIDE.$
    IF LESS LEQ CURRENT OP LEQ GREATER CLN RIGHT RELATION.$
    STRONG 1.

ENTER HOLD CLN ENTER HOLD 1, CLEAR RESULT, EXIT TO ADVANCE.
ENTER HOLD 1 CLN LBR J+ONE=J, CURRENT OP= HOLDOP LBK J RBK ,
                 ADDRESS PAST = HOLDAD LBK J RBK , RBR ,

EXIT TO ADVANCE CLN J=HOLD STACK INDEX, J TEMPORARY=J, ADVANCE.

EXPAND WORK STACK CLN LBR
    WS-ONE=WS=ADDRESS PAST, PUT RESULT IN WORK STACK, RBR ,

LEFT BRACKET ENTRY CLN
    INDEX COUNTER + INDEX COUNTER ONE= INDEX COUNTER
    + ADDRESS PAST = ADDRESS PAST, RIGHT BRACKET=CURRENT OP,
    ENTER HOLD.

LEFT PAREN ENTRY CLN
    RIGHT PAREN = CURRENT OP, ENTERHOLD.

RECOVER ADDRESS CLN LBR
    IF HOLDAD LBK J RBK LSS ZERO CLN
       ZERO-HOLDAD LBK J RBK =ADDRESS,SHRINK WORK STACK$
          HOLDAD LBK J RBK = ADDRESS$
    J-ONE=J, RBR ,..

$RIGHT BRACKET ENTRY CLN
    IF HOLDOP LBK J RBK NEQ RIGHT BRACKET CLN FAULT9.$
    IF RESULT EQU ZERO CLN CLEAR ADD PAST$
    ACCUMULATOR INTO INDEX,
    INDEX COUNTER - INDEX COUNTER ONE = INDEX COUNTER,
    HOLDAD LBK J RBK = ADDRESS PAST,CLEARADDPAST, J-ONE=J, COLLAPSE.

RIGHT PAREN ENTRY CLN
    IF HOLDOP LBK J RBK NEQ RIGHT PAREN CLN FAULT 8.$
```

```
      ASSURE RESULT,
      IF HOLDAD LBK J RBK EQU ZERO CLN J-ONE=J$ FUNCTION ENTRY.
      COLLAPSE.

SET RESULT CLN LBR ONE=RESULT, RBR ,

SHRINK WORK STACK CLN LBR WS+ONE=WS, RBR ,

STRONG CLN
      IF OPERAND EQU ZERO CLN WEAK.$
      IF LESS LEQ CURRENT OP LEQ GREATER CLN LEFT RELATION.$
      IF RESULT EQU ZERO CLN
            LBR IF OPERAND PAST EQU ZERO CLN UNARY.$CLEARADDPAST, RBR $$
      IF CURRENT OP EQU EXPONENT CLN LEFT EXPONENT.$
      IF CURRENT OP EQU MINUS CLN LEFT MINUS.$
      IF CURRENT OP EQU IMPLICATION CLN COMPLEMENT $$
STRONG 1 CLN
      IF CURRENT OP EQU IDENTITY CLN EQUIVALENCE.$
      K=K TS,
      CURRENT OP - EXPONENT= K, IL INSTRUCTION LBK K RBK = PREFIX,
      MAKE COMMAND 1, K TS=K, COLLAPSE.

UNARY CLN
      IF CURRENT OP EQU PLUS CLN EXIT TO ADVANCE.$
      IF OPERAND EQU ZERO CLN ENTER HOLD.$
      IF CURRENT OP EQU MINUS CLN CLEAR SUBTRACT RIGHT, UNARY1.$
      IF   CURRENT OP EQU  NOTOP CLN
            IL CLA=PREFIX, MAKE COMMAND1, COMPLEMENT, UNARY1.$
      FAULT 9,
UNARY1 CLN SET RESULT, COLLAPSE.
UNARY2 CLN
      IF CURRENT OP EQU PLUS CLN EXIT TO ADVANCE.$
      IF CURRENT OP EQU MINUS CLN ENTER HOLD.$
      IF CURRENT OP EQU NOTOP CLN ENTER HOLD.$
      FAULT9.

WEAK CLN
      IF RESULT EQU ZERO CLN
            LBR IF   OPERAND  PAST EQU ZERO CLN UNARY1.$ IF CURRENT OP
                     EQU IMPLICATION CLN CLEARADDPAST, WEAK1$$ RBR $
         WEAK1$
      ENTER HOLD.
WEAK1 CLN LBR
      IF CURRENT OP EQU IMPLICATION CLN   COMPLEMENT $$
      EXPAND WORK STACK,
      IF CURRENT OP EQU MINUS CLN
            PLUS=CURRENT OP,ENTER HOLD1,
                 MINUS=CURRENT OP, ZERO= ADDRESSPAST$
         $ RBR ,

FUNCTION ENTRY CLN   FAULT 7,.

$MAKE COMMAND CLN   MAKE COMMAND1, COLLAPSE.
MAKE COMMAND 1 CLN LBR
      PREFIX+TAG+ADDRESS= LBK I RBK , STEP I, RBR ,
MAKE COMMAND 2 CLN LBR
      PREFIX+TAG+ADDRESSPAST= LBK I RBK , STEP I, RBR ,

ACCUMULATOR INTO INDEX CLN LBR
      IL LXA + INDEX COUNTER = LBK I RBK , STEP I, RBR ,

CLEARADDPAST  CLN LBR ILCLA=PREFIX, MAKECOMMAND2,SET RESULT, RBR ,
```

```
CLEARADDRIGHT CLN LBR ILCLA=PREFIX, MAKECOMMAND1,SET RESULT, RBR ,

CLEAR SUBTRACT RIGHT CLN LBR
     IL CLS = PREFIX, MAKE COMMAND 1 , SET RESULT, RBR ,

COMPLEMENT CLN LBR IL COM= LBK I RBK , STEP I, RBR ,

EQUIVALENCE CLN
     IL STO+OTS= LBK I RBK , STEP I,
     IL ANA=PREFIX, MAKE COMMAND 1,
     IL STO+ OTS2= LBK I RBK , STEP I,
     IL CLA = PREFIX, MAKE COMMAND 1,
     IL ORA + OTS = LBK I RBK , STEP I,
     COMPLEMENT,
     IL ORA + OTS2 = LBK I RBK , STEP I,
     COLLAPSE.

LEFT EXPONENT CLN LDQ=PREFIX, BUILD COMMAND 1,
 LE1 CLN EXPAD=ADDRESS,TSX=PREFIX,FOURTAG=TAG,BUILDCOMMAND1,COLLAPSE.
RIGHT EXPONENT CLN SHIFT TO MQ, CLA=PREFIX, BUILDCOMMAND1,LE1.

LEFT MINUS CLN IL SUB=PREFIX, MAKE COMMAND.

PUT RESULT IN WORK STACK CLN LBR
     IL STO - ADDRESS PAST = LBK I RBK , STEP I, RBR ,

RIGHT DIVIDE CLN   IL IDV=PREFIX, MAKE COMMAND.

STEP I CLN LBR I-ONE=I, RBR ..

SCHECK MODE FOR FLOATING CLN LBR
     IF FLOATER NEQ ZERO CLN CMFF EXIT.S
     FLOAT BIT = FLOATER,
     ILREAL= LBK I RBK , STEP I ,
CMFF EXIT CLN  RBR ,
RESET MODE CLN LBR
     IF FLOATING FLAG EQU FLOATER CLN RESET MODE EXIT.S
     IF FLOATING FLAG EQU ZERO CLN
          ZERO = FLOATER, ILINTEGER=PREFIXS
          FLOAT BIT = FLOATER, ILREAL = PREFIXS
     PREFIX = LBK I RBK , STEP I,
RESET MODE EXIT CLN RBR ,

LEFT RELATION CLN
     IF RESULT NEQ ZERO CLN EXPAND WORK STACKSS
     ENTERHOLD1, CLEARADDRIGHT, RIGHT RELATION.

RIGHT RELATION CLN FAULT 5.


PUNCTUATION CLN
(COMMENT TEMPORARY ONLY 8/8/61 )
     IF CURRENT OP EQU SEMICOLON CLN
          CLEAR RESULT, EXIT TO ADVANCE.S
     MCH 0760000 141,
     MCH 0760000 142,
     MCH 0760000 143,
     MCH 0760000 144,
        MCH 0420000 0,
     MCH 0760000 140,
     LOAD SOURCE..
```

```
COMB 1  (37) =                   OCT 16070      74,      58,      40,
(COMMENT                              ••          CLN      AND      LBR       )
          59,      53,      46,      55,         56,      42,      52,
(COMMENT  OR       EQU      EXP      GEQ         GTR      LBK      LEQ       )
          51,      43,      54,      44,         72,      76,      68,
(COMMENT  LSS      MCH      NEQ      OCT         RBK      RBR      THEN      )
          69,      78,      64,      65,         66,      40,      76,
(COMMENT  ELSE     TRUE     STEP     UNTIL       WHILE    BEGIN    END       )
          83,      80,      85,      87,         84,      57,      126,
(COMMENT  OWN      REAL     ARRAY    LABEL       VALUE    NOT      PRINT     )
          127,     62,      61,      60,         79,
(COMMENT  READ     CEQ      IDN      IMP         FALSE                       )

COMB TABLE 1  (41) =             OCT 1017,         OCT 303622,
(COMMENT                             DO                FOR                   )
  OCT 70745017,    OCT 1617,       OCT 2206,         OCT 143016,
(COMMENT  GOTO            GO              IF                CLN               )
  OCT 43404,       OCT 600422,     OCT 3622,         OCT 244225,
(COMMENT  AND             LBR             OR                EQU               )
  OCT 246020,      OCT 341221,     OCT 345022,       OCT 600413,
(COMMENT  EXP             GEQ             GTR               LBK               )
  OCT 601221,      OCT 604623,     OCT 640610,       OCT 701221,
(COMMENT  LEQ             LSS             MCH               NEQ               )
  OCT 740624,      OCT 1100413,    OCT 1100422,      OCT 240401216,
(COMMENT  OCT             RBK             RBR               THEN              )
  OCT 50604605,    OCT 241105205,  OCT 231201220,    OCT 52161202214,
(COMMENT  ELSE            TRUE            STEP              UNTIL             )
  OCT 56100443005, OCT 4050342216, OCT 1100422,      OCT 745616,
(COMMENT  WHILE           BEGIN           END               OWN               )
  OCT 220240214,   OCT 2221100231, OCT 30010101214,  OCT 54010605205,
(COMMENT  REAL            ARRAY           LABEL             VALUE             )
  OCT 703624,      OCT 40220443424,OCT 220240204,    OCT 141221,
(COMMENT  NOT             PRINT           READ              CEQ               )
  OCT 441016,      OCT 443220,     OCT 14010604605,
(COMMENT  IDN             IMP             FALSE                               )

COMB 2  (5) =                    88,      89,      82,
(COMMENT                         STRING   SWITCH   BOOLEAN                   )
          81,      86,
(COMMENT  INTEGER  PROCEDURE                                                 )

COMB TABLE 2A  (5) =             OCT 46241102216, OCT 46270445003,
(COMMENT                             STRIN            SWITC                  )
  OCT 4170743005, OCT 22161201207, OCT 40220740605,
(COMMENT  BOOLE           INTEG           PROCE                              )

COMB TABLE 2B  (5) =             OCT 07,          OCT 10,
(COMMENT                             G                H                      )
  OCT 216,        OCT 1222,        OCT 41244405,
(COMMENT  AN              ER              DURE                               )
MINUS ONE INDEX = 32767, SEVEN SEVEN = 77, NOTCOMMA = OCT 160745045,
BLANK FLAG = 0, PUNCTUATION FLAG = 0, END FLAG = 0,

$LOAD SOURCE PROGRAM CLN
  I = ITS, INPUT CONSTANT = J, FOUR = SHIFT FLAG,
  ZERO = END FLAG = LBK J RBK ,
LOAD SOURCE CLN
  LOAD SOURCE 1, RECORD EQU CONTROL CLN
    PROCESS CONTROL.
    PROCESS SOURCE.
LOAD SOURCE 1 CLN
  LBR MCH 0762000 130, M EQU 32767(-1)32755
```

```
(COMMENT    RDS-TAPE 2  •                                                        )
       LBR MCH 0700004 RECORD LBK 1 RBK • RBR •
(COMMENT        CPY                                                              )
       MCH 0766000 219• MCH 4760000 10• BST.
(COMMENT  WRS-DELAY            RTT                                               )
       LOAD SOURCE EXIT CLN
          ONE = SCALE• ZERO = SYMBOL COUNT•
          RECORD LBK 32755 RBK = RECORD LBK 32756 RBK • RBR •
BST CLN
    K EQU 0(1)9
       LBR MCH 0764000 130• MCH 0762000 130•
(COMMENT        BST-TAPE 2           RDS-TAPE 2                                   )
          M EQU 32767(-1)32755
          LBR MCH 0700004 RECORD LBK 1 RBK • RBR •
(COMMENT           CPY                                                           )
       MCH 0766000 219• MCH 4760000 10• BST EXIT•
(COMMENT     WRS-DELAY            RTT                                            )
          LOAD SOURCE EXIT•
          BST EXIT CLN
           • RBR • MCH 0000000 BST•
CONTROL CLN MCH 23 46 45 6 OCT 3 51 46•••
(COMMENT BCD - C   O   N       T       R   O                                     )

$PROCESS SOURCE CLN
    END FLAG NEQ ZERO CLN
       ITS = I• TEST ROUTINE•
       $
       GET SOURCE CHARACTER• I GEQ ONE CLN
          CHECK EXCEPTION•
          $
CLEAR BLANK FLAG CLN
    ZERO = BLANK FLAG = PUNCTUATION FLAG•
TEST SHIFT FLAG CLN
    SHIFT FLAG EQU ZERO CLN
       SHIFT EXIT 1•
       $
SHIFT CHARACTER CLN
    LBK J RBK * 2 EXP 7 + CHAR = LBK J RBK • SHIFT FLAG - ONE =
    SHIFT FLAG• PROCESS SOURCE•
SHIFT EXIT 1 CLN
    LBK J RBK * 2 EXP 7 + CHAR = LBK J RBK •
SHIFT EXIT 2 CLN
    J - ONE = J• FOUR = SHIFT FLAG• ZERO = LBK J RBK • PROCESS SOURCE•
SHIFT EXIT 3 CLN
    J - ONE = J• CHAR = LBK J RBK • THREE = SHIFT FLAG• PROCESS SOURCE•

CHECK EXCEPTION CLN
    I EQU FIFTEEN CLN
       CHECK COMMENT•
       $
    I EQU TWELVE CLN
       SET BLANK FLAG•
     $
   :I EQU TEN CLN
       SET PUNCTUATION FLAG•
       $
    BLANK FLAG + PUNCTUATION FLAG EQU ZERO CLN
       TEST SHIFT FLAG•
       $
ENTER SEARCH CLN
    SHIFT FLAG NEQ FOUR CLN
       J - ONE = J $
```

```
         $
         CHAR = LBK J RBK + K EQU 1(1)5
            LBR GET SOURCE CHARACTER, I EQU TWELVE CLN
               ONE = BLANK FLAG, SEARCH LIST 1.
               $
               I EQU TEN CLN
                  SEARCH LIST 3.
                  $
               K EQU FIVE CLN
                  LBR SEARCH LIST 4 CLN
                     M EQU 0(1)4
                        LBR LBK J RBK EQU COMB TABLE 2A LBK M RBK CLN
                           ENTER SEARCH 1.
                           $ RBR +
                        ZERO = BLANK FLAG = PUNCTUATION FLAG,
                        SHIFT EXIT 3. RBR $
               $
            SEARCH LOOP CLN
               LBK J RBK * 2 EXP 7 + CHAR = LBK J RBK , RBR +
ENTER SEARCH 1 CLN
   J - ONE = J, CHAR = LBK J RBK , K EQU 1(1)5
      LBR GET SOURCE CHARACTER, I EQU TWELVE CLN
         ONE = BLANK FLAG, SEARCH LIST 5.
         $
         I EQU TEN CLN
            SEARCH LIST 3.
            $
         K EQU FIVE CLN
            ZERO = BLANK FLAG = PUNCTUATION FLAG, SHIFT EXIT 3.
            $
         SEARCH LOOP 1 CLN
            LBK J RBK * 2 EXP 7 + CHAR = LBK J RBK , RBR +
SEARCH LIST 5 CLN
   LBK J RBK EQU COMB TABLE 2B LBK M RBK CLN
      J + ONE = J, COMB 2 LBK M RBK = CHAR, SEARCH LIST 1A.
      $
      ZERO = PUNCTUATION FLAG, K EQU FIVE CLN
         SHIFT EXIT 2.
         FOUR - K = SHIFT FLAG, PROCESS SOURCE..


$SEARCH LIST CLN
   ZERO = BLANK FLAG = PUNCTUATION FLAG, SHIFT EXIT 2.
SEARCH LIST 1 CLN
   N EQU 0(1)40
      LBR LBK J RBK EQU COMB TABLE 1 LBK N RBK CLN
         LBR N GEQ SIX CLN
            LBR COMB 1 LBK N-4 RBK = CHAR, N LSS NINE CLN
               CHAR = PUNCTUATION FLAG $
               $
               SEARCH LIST 1A. RBR $
            $
            N EQU FIVE CLN
               LBR COLON = PUNCTUATION FLAG = CHAR,
                  SEARCH LIST 1A CLN
                     ZERO = LBK J RBK , SHIFT FLAG EQU FOUR CLN
                        SHIFT CHARACTER.
                        J + ONE = J, TEST SHIFT FLAG. RBR $
               $
            PUNCTUATION FLAG EQU ZERO CLN
               ZERO = BLANK FLAG, SHIFT EXIT 2.
               $
```

```
                  N LSS THREE CLN
                     SEARCH LIST 2.
                     $
                  N EQU THREE CLN
                     GET SOURCE CHARACTER, SEARCH LOOP.
                     $
                  PUNCTUATION FLAG EQU COMMA CLN
                     SEARCH LIST 2.
                     $
                  PUNCTUATION FLAG EQU COLON CLN
                     SEARCH LIST 2.
                     $
                  ZERO = LBK J RBK = SHIFT FLAG, K EQU 1(1)4
                     LBR GET SOURCE CHARACTER, I EQU TWELVE CLN
                        SEARCH LIST 1B CLN
                           ONE = BLANK FLAG, ZERO = PUNCTUATION
                           FLAG, SHIFT EXIT 2.
                        $
                        LBK J RBK + 2 EXP 7 + CHAR = LBK J RBK ,
                        I EQU TEN CLN
                           ZERO = BLANK FLAG, SET PUNCTUATION FLAG.
                           $ RBR ,
                        SEARCH LIST, RBR $
              $ RBR ,
           ZERO = PUNCTUATION FLAG, K EQU FIVE CLN
              SHIFT EXIT 2.
              FOUR - K = SHIFT FLAG, PROCESS SOURCE.
SEARCH LIST 2 CLN
     J + ONE = J, ZERO = BLANK FLAG, SHIFT EXIT 2.
SEARCH LIST 3 CLN
     CHAR = PUNCTUATION FLAG, K EQU FIVE CLN
        SHIFT EXIT 3.
        FOUR - K = SHIFT FLAG, TEST SHIFT FLAG.
SET BLANK FLAG CLN
     ONE = BLANK FLAG, PROCESS SOURCE.

SET PUNCTUATION FLAG CLN
     PUNCTUATION FLAG EQU CHAR CLN
        LBR CHAR EQU PERIOD CLN
           LBR J - ONE = J, COMB 1 = END FLAG = LBK J RBK ,
           LOAD SOURCE. RBR $
        $ RBR $
     $
     CHAR = PUNCTUATION FLAG, ZERO = BLANK FLAG,
     LBK J RBK EQU NOTCOMMA CLN
        SEARCH LIST 2.
        TEST SHIFT FLAG..

PAREN COMM = OCT 122030743215, ENT OF COMM = OCT 243424,
```

```
CHECK COMMENT CLN
    GET SOURCE CHARACTER, I EQU TWELVE CLN
        CHECK COMMENT.
        $
        J - ONE = J, LEFT PAREN = LBK J RBK , CHAR EQU FIFTEEN CLN
            THREE = SHIFT FLAG, ENTER SEARCH.
            $
        CHAR NEQ THREE CLN
            LBR THREE = SHIFT FLAG, SHIFT CHARACTER. RBR $
            $
        LBK J RBK * 2 EXP 7 + CHAR = LBK J RBK , K EQU 1(1)3
            LBR GET SOURCE CHARACTER, I EQU TWELVE CLN
                SEARCH LIST 1B.
                $
                I EQU TEN CLN
                    SHIFT EXIT 1.
                    $
                LBK J RBK * 2 EXP 7 + CHAR = LBK J RBK , RBR ,
            LBK J RBK NEQ PAREN COMM CLN
                SEARCH LIST.
                $
                J - ONE = J, ZERO = LBK J RBK , K EQU 1(1)3
                    LBR GET SOURCE CHARACTER, I EQU TWELVE CLN
                        SEARCH LIST 1B.
                        $
                        I EQU TEN CLN
                            SHIFT EXIT 1.
                            $
                        LBK J RBK * 2 EXP 7 + CHAR = LBK J RBK , RBR ,
                    LBK J RBK NEQ ENT OF COMM CLN
                        SEARCH LIST.
                        $
                        CHECK COMMENT 1 CLN
                            GET SOURCE CHARACTER,
                            CHAR NEQ RIGHT PAREN CLN
                                CHECK COMMENT 1.
                                $
                                J + TWO = J , PROCESS SOURCE..


$GET SOURCE CHARACTER CLN LBR
GET SOURCE ENTRY CLN
    IF SYMBOL COUNT EQU ZERO CLN
        SIX=SYMBOLCOUNT,SCALE+MINUSONEINDEX=SCALE,$$
    SYMBOL COUNT - ONE = SYMBOL COUNT,
(COMMENT LXA SCALE,4        LDQ RECORD,4        ZAC        )
    MCH 0534004 SCALE, MCH 0560004 RECORD, MCH 4754000 0 ,
(COMMENT LGL 6             STQ RECORD,4        COM        PAX,1     )
    MCH 4763000 6, MCH 4600004 RECORD, MCH 0760000 6, MCH 0734001 0,
(COMMENT CAL TABLE-1,1                  PDX ,1        STA CHAR      )
    MCH 4500001 TABLE LBK 1 RBK , MCH 4734001 0, MCH 0621000 CHAR,
    IF I EQU SEVENSEVEN CLN LOADSOURCE1,GETSOURCEENTRY.$ RBR ,

TABLE CLN
(COMMENT O                  1             2             3         )
    MCH 0000000 27, MCH 0000000 28, MCH 0000000 29, MCH 0000000 30,
(COMMENT 4                  5             6             7         )
    MCH 0000000 31, MCH 0000000 32, MCH 0000000 33, MCH 0000000 34,
(COMMENT 8                  9                           =,RT.ARROW )
    MCH 0000000 35, MCH 0000000 36, MCH 0000105 00, MCH 0000000 62,
(COMMENT -, NOT                                                   )
    MCH 0000000 57, MCH 0001050 0 , MCH 0001050 0 , MCH 0001050 0 ,
```

```
(COMMENT +           A                B                C              )
    MCH 0000000 49, MCH 0000020 1 , MCH 0000010 2 , MCH 0000020 3 ,
(COMMENT D           E                F                G              )
    MCH 0000150 4 , MCH 0000030 5 , MCH 0000040 6 , MCH 0000040 7 ,
(COMMENT H           I                +0,12-0,AND      •              )
    MCH 0000000 8 , MCH 0000160 9 , MCH 0000000 58, MCH 0000120 70,
(COMMENT RT. PAREN
    MCH 0000000 75, MCH 0001050 0 , MCH 0001050 0 , MCH 0001050 0 ,
(COMMENT -           J                K                L              )
    MCH 0000000 50, MCH 0000000 10, MCH 0000000 11, MCH 0000050 12,
(COMMENT M           N                O                P              )
    MCH 0000060 13, MCH 0000070 14, MCH 0000110 15, MCH 0000010 16,
(COMMENT Q           R                -0,11-0,OR       S              )
    MCH 0000000 17, MCH 0000100 18, MCH 0000000 59, MCH 0000120 73,
(COMMENT *
    MCH 0000000 47, MCH 0001050 0 , MCH 0001050 0 , MCH 0001050 0 ,
(COMMENT BLANK       /                S                T              )
    MCH 0000120 0 , MCH 0000000 48, MCH 0000010 19, MCH 0000010 20,
(COMMENT U           V                W                X              )
    MCH 0000010 21, MCH 0000010 22, MCH 0000010 23, MCH 0000000 24,
(COMMENT Y           Z                R.M.8-2-0,IMP    •              )
    MCH 0000000 25, MCH 0000000 26, MCH 0000000 60, MCH 0000120 71,
(COMMENT (                                            END RECORD )
    MCH 0000170 41, MCH 0001050 0 , MCH 0001050 0 , MCH 0001150 0,..
```

```
SNAME DEFINITION CLN LBR                                              29  0010
    SEARCH NAME LIST, NEXT OP NEQ COLON CLN FIND ADDRESS.$            29  0020
    IF LESS LEQ CURRENT OP LEQ GREATER CLN FIND ADDRESS.$            29  0030
    NAME FOUND FLAG EQU ONE CLN FAULT 18 .$                          29  0040
    PRINT NAME FLAG EQU ONE CLN PRINT NAME,$$                        29  0050
  DEFINED LIST LOC + ONE = DEFINED LIST LOC = N                        290060
  GTR TEN TWENTY THREE CLN FAULT 19.$                                  290061
NAME DEFINITION 1 CLN                                                 29  0080
    ZERO = CURRENT INDEX,                                             29  0090
    NAME BUFFER 1 = NAME WORD 1 LBK N RBK ,                          29  0100
    NAME BUFFER 2 = NAME WORD 2 LBK N RBK ,                          29  0110
    NAME BUFFER 3 = NAME WORD 3 LBK N RBK , PEEK,                    29  0120
    PEEK SYMBOL EQU SUBROUTINE MARK CLN NAME DEFINITION 4.$          29  0130
    CURRENT OP NEQ LEFT BRACE CLN END -I = LOC TEMP $                29  0140
    END -I +ONE = LOC TEMP $                                         29  0150
NAME DEFINITION 2 CLN                                                 29  0160
    LOC TEMP = NAME LOCATION LBK N RBK ,                             29  0170
    N EQU 0(1) 511 LBR UNDEFINED NAME 1 LBK N RBK NEQ NAME BUFFER1 CLN 29 0180
    NAME DEFINITION 3.$ UNDEFINED NAME 2 LBK N RBK NEQ NAME BUFFER 2  29  0190
    CLN NAME DEFINITION 3 .$ UNDEFINED NAME 3 LBK N RBK NEQ NAME      29  0200
    BUFFER 3 CLN NAME DEFINITION 3.$ UNDEFINED LOC LBK N RBK = L,    29  0210
    ZERO GTR LBK L RBK CLN LBK L RBK -LOC TEMP = LBK L RBK $         29  0220
    LBK L RBK + LOC TEMP = LBK L RBK $ ZERO = UNDEFINED NAME 1       29  0230
    LBK N RBK = UNDEFINED NAME 2 LBK N RBK = UNDEFINED NAME3 LBK N RBK 29 0240
    = UNDEFINED LOC LBK N RBK ,                                      29  0250
NAME DEFINITION 3 CLN RBR ,NAME DEFINITION EXIT.                     29  0260
NAME DEFINITION 4 CLN                                                29  0270
    FIND NON ZERO SYM, SEARCH SUB LIST,                             29  0280
    SUBROUTINE LOC = LOC TEMP, NAME DEFINITION 2.                   29  0290
FIND ADDRESS CLN                                                     29  0300
    NAME FOUND FLAG EQU ZERO CLN FIND ADDRESS 1 $$                   29  0310
NAME DEFINITION EXIT CLN                                             29  0320
    ZERO = NAME BUFFER 1 = NAME BUFFER 2 = NAME BUFFER 3 RBR .      29  0330
FIND ADDRESS 1 CLN LBR                                               29  0340
    N EQU 0(1)511 LBR UNDEFINED NAME 1 LBK N RBK NEQ ZERO CLN       29  0350
    FIND ADDRESS 2.$ NAME BUFFER 1 = UNDEFINED NAME 1 LBK N RBK ,   29  0360
    NAME BUFFER 2 = UNDEFINED NAME 2 LBK N RBK ,                    29  0370
```

```
NAME BUFFER 3 = UNDEFINED NAME 3 LBK N RBK •                    29  0380
I = UNDEFINED LOC LBK N RBK • N= UNDEFINED LIST LOC,FIND ADDRESS3.  29  0390
FIND ADDRESS 2 CLN RBR • FAULT 20.                             29  0400
FIND ADDRESS 3 CLN RBR ••                                      29  0410

$PEEK CLN                                                       34  0010
    LBR SYMBOL COUNT = PEEK SYM COUNT, SYMBOL BUFFER = PEEK SYM    34  0020
    BUFFER, J= J TS,                                           34  0030
PEEK 1 CLN                                                      34  0040
    PEEK SYM COUNT -ONE = PEEK SYM COUNT LSS ZERO CLN PEEK 2.$     34  0050
    PEEK SYM .BUFFER *2 EXP 7= TEMP STORAGE, PEEK SYM BUFFER /2 EXP 28=  34  0060
    PEEK SYMBOL NEQ ZERO CLN $ TEMP STORAGE = PEEK SYM BUFFER, PEEK 1.   34  0070
    J TS = J, RBR •                                            34  0080
PEEK 2 CLN                                                      34  0090
    LBK J RBK =PEEK SYM BUFFER, J-ONE=J, FIVE =PEEK SYM COUNT,PEEK 1..   34  0100

$ PROCESS CONTROL CLN MCH 0760000 OCT 161,                     015 0010
    WRITE TAPE. EXECUTE PROGRAM CLN OUTPUT CONSTANT = I,       015 0020
    CCPRINTLOOP CLN LBK I RBK = TEMP STORAGE, IOH PRINT(1,11,  015 0030
    TEMPSTORAGE), I-1=I, IF TEMP STORAGE EQU OUTPUT CONSTANT   015 0040
    CLN FINISHUP. CCPRINTLOOP.                                 015 0050
    FINISHUP CLN FOR J EQU 0(1)10 LBR LBK I RBK = TEMPSTORAGE,  015 0060
    IOH PRINT(1,11,TEMPSTORAGE), I-1=I. RBR • MCH 0534002 OUTPUT  015 0070
    CONSTANT,                                                  015 0080
MCH 0000002 0 •
WRITE TAPE CLN MCH 0500000 OUTPUT CONSTANT LBK 1 RBK •
MCH 0400000 TRA •  MCH 0601000 OCT 77776 •
FOR L EQU 32767(-1)32730 LBR LOADER LBK L+1 RBK = LBK L+1 RBK RBR •
 MCH 0020000 13 •
LOADER CLN MCH 0534001 0 • MCH 0700001 2 • MCH 5777771 1 •
MCH 0761000 0 • MCH 0760000 0 • MCH 0534001 6 • MCH 0361001 OCT 77777 •
MCH 2000011 6, MCH 0602000 30, MCH 0020000 24, MCH 4760000 10,
MCH C000000 28, MCH 0020000 0, MCH 0760000 0, MCH 0534001 6,
• MCH 0361001 OCT 77777 • MCH 2000011 15 • MCH 0602000 OCT 77777 •
MCH 0534001 6 • MCH 0766000 147 • MCH 0700001 OCT 77777 •
 MCH 7000001 23 • MCH 1777771 20 • EXECUTE PROGRAM.
MCH 0500000 OCT 77777, MCH 0402000 30, MCH 0100000 10,
MCH 0200000 11, MCH 0772000 145, MCH 0020000 11, ••••••••

$READ NAME CLN                                                  36  0010
    LBR ZERO = NAME BUFFER 1 = NAME BUFFER 2 = NAME BUFFER 3 = M,   36  0020
READ NAME 1 CLN                                                 36  0030
    L EQU 0(1)4  LBR NAME BUFFER 1 LBK M RBK * 2 EXP 6         36  0040
    + PRESENT SYMBOL = NAMEBUFFER 1 LBK M RBK • FIND NON ZERO SYM,  36  0050
    PRESENT SYMBOL GTR LASTNUMBER CLN READNAME3.$ RBR •        36  0060
    M + ONE = M NEQ THREE CLN READ NAME 1. $                   36  0070
READ NAME 2 CLN                                                 36  0080
    PRESENT SYMBOL GTR LAST NUMBER CLN READ NAME EXIT.$        36  0090
    FIND NON ZERO SYM, READ NAME 2.                            36  0100
READ NAME 3 CLN                                                 36  0110
    L LSS FOUR CLN FOUR - L = TEMP STORAGE $ READ NAME EXIT.   36  0120
    L EQU 1(1) TEMP STORAGE LBR NAME BUFFER 1 LBK M RBK * 2 EXP 6   36  0130
    = NAME BUFFER 1 LBK M RBK  RBR •                           36  0140
READ NAME EXIT CLN                                              36  0150
    • RBR ••                                                    36  0160

$SEARCH NAME LIST CLN                                           40  0010
    LBR                                                         40  0020
SEARCH NAME LIST ENTRY CLN                                      40  0030
    N EQU 0(1) DEFINED LIST LOC LBR NAME WORD 1 LBK N RBK NEQ NAME  40  0040
    BUFFER 1 CLN                                                40  0041
    SEARCH NAME LIST 1. $                                       40  0050
```

```
       NAME WORD 2 LBK N RBK   NEQ NAME BUFFER 2 CLN SEARCH NAME LIST 1. $ 40   0060
       NAME WORD 3 LBK N RBK   NEQ NAME BUFFER 3 CLN SEARCH NAME LIST 1. $ 40   0070
       ONE = NAME FOUND FLAG,                                            40   0080
       NAME LOCATION LBK N RBK /2 EXP 34 * 2 EXP 15= FLOATING FLAG,       40   0090
       NAME LOCATION LBK N RBK * 2 EXP 3 / 2 EXP 30 = SCALE,              40   0100
        NAME LOCATION LBK N RBK *2 EXP 10 /2 EXP 25 = TEMP STORAGE        40   0110
       NEQ ZERO CLN PART WORD UP. $                                      40   0120
       NAME LOCATION LBK N RBK * 2 EXP 22 / 2 EXP 22 = ADDRESS,           40   0130
       SEARCH NAME EXIT.                                                 40   0140
        SEARCH NAME LIST 1 CLN RBR ,                                     40   0150
       ZERO = NAME FOUND FLAG = ADDRESS, ONE = ADDRESS FLAG,             40   0160
SEARCH NAME EXIT CLN                                                     40   0170
       TAG EQU ONE CLN PARTIAL WORD 2. $ RBR ,                           40   0180
PART WORD UP CLN                                                         40   0190
       TEMP STORAGE / 2 EXP 6 * PART WORD 1,                             40   0200
       TEMP STORAGE * 2 EXP 31 / 2 EXP 31 + PART WORD 1 - ONE =          40   0210
       NUMBER BUFFER, NAME LOCATION LBK N RBK = TEMP STORAGE 2,          40   0220
       SET PART WORD PARAMETERS,                                         40   0230
       TEMP STORAGE 2 * 2 EXP 22 / 2 EXP 22 = ADDRESS,                   40   0240
       ONE = NAME FOUND FLAG, SEARCH NAME EXIT..                         40   0250


SUNBUILD PROGRAM FLAGS CLN                                               50   0170
     LBR PROGRAM FLAGS COUNT + ONE NEQ TEN CLN                           50   0180
         PROGRAM FLAGS COUNT + ONE = PROGRAM FLAGS COUNT,                50   0190
         PROGRAM FLAGS LOC = M, LBK M RBK / 2 EXP 3 = LBK M RBK $        50   0200
         PROGRAM FLAGS LOC + ONE = PROGRAM FLAGS LOC,                    50   0210
         ZERO = PROGRAM FLAGS COUNT $                                    50   0220
         I +ONE = I,                                                     50   0230
     RBR ..                                                              50   0240


SGL OUT 2 CLN    MCH 0020000 OCT 36700,..                                55   0010
```

ONTROL

```
A,B,C,D,E,F,G,H,
$ A+B=C$   A*B+C=D$ A+B*C=D$ A*B-C=D$ A*-B=C$
(A+B)*C=D$
A*B/(A-B)=C$ ((A-B)+B)/C=D..
```

NELIAC 1604

The version of Neliac 1604 presented here is a particularly legible compiler, which demonstrates the improvements in documentation which can be achieved by a careful choice of meaningful terms for nouns and verbs. It was written and tested by S. W. and C. B. Porter.

The first version of Neliac 1604 was written by Lt. K. S. Masterson, Jr.,[16] and debugged, revised and expanded by Professor R. M. Thatcher.[17]

The listing given here is based upon those earlier works, as well as upon Neliac B, a compiler for the Burroughs 220 computer also written by the Porters.[18] The cooperation of these four automatic-programming experts is greatly appreciated.

In order that the flow of the program logic can more readily be followed, the internal compiler code is given in Table X, while Table XI shows the CO-NO matrix used.

[16] K. S. Masterson, Jr., "Compilation for Two Computers with Neliac," *Communications of the Association for Computing Machinery,* Vol. 3, No. 11, Nov., 1960.

[17] Richard M. Thatcher, *The Neliac Compiler Language, CDC 1604 Version,* unpublished document of the U. S. Naval Postgraduate School, Sept., 1960.

[18] S. W. Porter and C. B. Porter, "Neliac B—A Compiler for Burroughs 220 Computer, January 1961 Version," *NEL Technical Memorandum 464,* March, 1961; and "A Compiler for the Control Data Corporation 1604 Computer, September 1961 Version," *NEL Technical Memorandum 500,* Oct., 1961.

TABLE X

INTERNAL COMPILER CODE OF NELIAC-1604

Symbol	Octal	Decimal	Symbol	Octal	Decimal
Space	00	0	5	40	32
A *or* a	01	1	6	41	33
B *or* b	02	2	7	42	34
C *or* c	03	3	8	43	35
D *or* d	04	4	9	44	36
E *or* e	05	5	s	45	37
F *or* f	06	6	,	46	38
G *or* g	07	7	;	47	39
H *or* h	10	8	.	50	40
I *or* i	11	9	:	61	41
J *or* j	12	10	(	52	42
K *or* k	13	11	)	53	43
L *or* l	14	12	[	54	44
M *or* m	15	13	]	55	45
N *or* n	16	14	{	56	46
O *or* o	17	15	}	57	47
P *or* p	20	16	=	60	48
Q *or* q	21	17	$\neq$	61	49
R *or* r	22	18	$\geq$	62	50
S *or* s	23	19	<	63	51
T *or* t	24	20	$\leq$	64	52
U *or* u	25	21	>	65	53
V *or* v	26	22	→	66	54
W *or* w	27	23	+	67	55
X *or* x	30	24	−	70	56
Y *or* y	31	25	/	71	57
Z *or* z	32	26	×	72	58
0	33	27	CS	73	59
1	34	28	|	74	60
2	35	29	U *or* $\oplus$	75	61
3	36	30	∩ *or* $\otimes$	76	62
4	37	31	↑	77	63

TABLE XI

CURRENT OPERATOR-NEXT OPERATOR TABLE FOR NELIAC 1604

Next Operator

	:	{	}	.	;	,	=	≠	>	≥	<	≤	∩	∪	→	+	−	/	×	(	)	[	]	↑	|	s
:	a	b	c	c	c	c	d	d	d	d	d	d	d	d	d	d	d	d	d	e		f		g		
{	a	b	c	c	c	c	d	d	d	d	d	d	d	d	d	d	d	d	d	e		f		g		
}	a	b	c	c	c	c	d	d	d	d	d	d	d	d	d	d	d	d	d	e		f		g		
.	a	b	c	c	c	c	d	d	d	d	d	d	d	d	d	d	d	d	d	e		f		g		
;	a	b	c	c	c	c	d	d	d	d	d	d	d	d	d	d	d	d	d	e		f		g		
,	a	b	c	c	c	c	d	d	d	d	d	d	d	d	d	d	d	d	d	e		f		g		
=	h						i	i	i	i	i	i	i	i						e		f		g		
≠	h						i	i	i	i	i	i	i	i						e		f		g		
>	h						i	i	i	i	i	i	i	i						e		f		g		
≥	h						i	i	i	i	i	i	i	i						e		f		g		
<	h						i	i	i	i	i	i	i	i						e		f		g		
≤	h						i	i	i	i	i	i	i	i						e		f		g		
∩	h						i	i	i	i	i	i	i	i						e		f		g		
∪	h						i	i	i	i	i	i	i	i						e		f		g		
→	j	j	j	j	j	j	j	j	j	j	j	j	j	j	j	j	j	j	j	e		f		g		
+							k	k	k	k	k	k	k	k	k	k	k	k	k	e		f		g		
−							l	l	l	l	l	l	l	l	l	l	l	l	l	e		f		g		
/							m	m	m	m	m	m	m	m	m	m	m	m	m	e		f		g		
×							n	n	n	n	n	n	n	n	n	n	n	n	n	e		f		g		

a. Define Location
b. Generate Input-Output
c. Generate Transfer
d. Load Working Register
e. Partial Word Control
f. Subscript
g. Exponent

h. Finish Comparison
i. Multiple Comparison
j. Store Working Register
k. Addition
l. Subtraction
m. Divide
n. Multiply

As a sort of Table of Contents of Neliac 1604, Table XII has been included. It shows the over-all groupings of the routines, insofar as this can be done.

TABLE XII

NELIAC 1604 ORGANIZATION

LOAD NELIAC PROGRAM

LOAD—SUB Programs 1 through 10

SET COMPILER CONDITIONS

MOD 4c—Sub Programs

32 GENERAL PRINT ROUTINES
37 MAGNETIC TAPE ROUTINES
38 CLEAR STORAGE
42 SET UP INITIAL CONDITIONS
50 PRINT ID PAGE

PROCESS NOUNS

MOD 4c—Sub Programs

12 DEFINE LOCATION
13 DELETE ALGOL WORDS
17 FILL UNDEFINED ADDRESS
18 FIND ADDRESS
19 FIND ALPHA OPERAND
21 FIND FLOATING POINT NUMBER
22 FIND NUMBER ADDRESS
23 FIND NUMBER OPERAND
24 FIND OPERATOR
25 FIND SYMBOL
32, 33 GENERAL PRINT ROUTINES
37 MAGNETIC TAPE ROUTINES
43 STORE
44 STORE CONSTANTS

PROCESS PROGRAM BODY

MOD 4c—Sub Programs

36 PROCESS LOGIC (CO-NO TABLE)

Routines directly used by PROCESS LOGIC

10 ADDITION
11 COMPILE SUBROUTINES
12 DEFINE LOCATION
14 DIVIDE
15 DOWNGRADE BRACE TABLE

16 FAULT
24 FIND OPERATOR
26 GENERATE TRANSFER
27 LOAD WORKING REGISTER
28 COMPARISONS, MULTIPLE and FINISH
29 MULTIPLY
30 PARTIAL WORD CONTROL
45 STORE WORKING REGISTER
46 SUBSCRIPT
47 SUBTRACTION
48 UPGRADE COMPARISONS

Routines indirectly used by PROCESS LOGIC

 9 PROCESS INCOMPLETE VALUE
10 GENERATE ADD COMMAND, CLEAR ADD
11 COMPUTER LANGUAGE
13 DELETE ALGOL WORDS
14 GENERATE DIVIDE COMMAND
17 FILL UNDEFINED ADDRESS
18 FIND ADDRESS
19 FIND ALPHA OPERAND
20 GENERAL COMPARISON ROUTINES
21 FIND FLOATING POINT NUMBER
22 FIND NUMBER ADDRESS
23 FIND NUMBER OPERAND
24 FIND OPERATOR
25 FIND SYMBOL
27 GENERATE LOAD Q COMMAND, FIND MASK
29 GENERATE MULTIPLY COMMAND
30 POST LOOP CONTROL
31 PRE LOOP CONTROL
32, 33 GENERAL PRINT ROUTINES
37 MAGNETIC TAPE ROUTINES
39 GENERAL LOOP ROUTINES
40 SET FALSE COMPARISON
41 SET TRUE COMPARISON

```
5;
LOAD NELIAC PROGRAM:
    752₈ ENTRY 2, FIND TAPE WRITE AREA, ACTIVATE READER,
    SET TAPE AREA TO SPACES, READ INFORMATION PAGE,
    WAIT TO WRITE MAG TAPE, WRITE PART 1, 660 → MAG TAPE INDEX,
    1320 → LAST MAG TAPE INDEX,
E|NTRY 1: 761₈ STOP,
S|TOP: FIND PAGE, WRITE MAG TAPE,
    PAGE NUMBER + 1 → PAGE NUMBER < NUMBER OF PAGES: ENTRY 1.;
    WAIT TO WRITE MAG TAPE, SET TAPE AREA TO SPACES,
    END TAPE FLAG → MAG TAPE AREA → MAG TAPE AREA[660],
    WRITE MAG TAPE, WRITE MAG TAPE, WAIT TO WRITE MAG TAPE,
    751₈ ENTRY 2, EXIT.
E|NTRY 2: RESTORE PAGE, FIND TAPE READ AREA, WAIT TO READ MAG TAPE,
    READ PART 1, SET PRINT BARS TO SPACES, READ MAG TAPE,
    MAG TAPE AREA → NUMBER OF PAGES, 40 → MAG TAPE INDEX,
E|NTRY 3: LIST PAGE, PAGE NUMBER + 1 → PAGE NUMBER ≤ NUMBER OF PAGES:
    READ MAG TAPE, ENTRY 3.;
E|XIT: REWIND READ TAPE,..
```

```
5
ALL SPACES = 20 20 20 20 20 20 20 20₈,
ALPHA FIRST LOCATION(2) = 66 71 51 22 23 20 43 46₈,
63 23 71 46 45 20 20₈, ALPHA PAGES = 47 61 67 65 22 20 20 20₈,
ALPHA PROGRAMS = 47 51 46 67 51 61 44 22₈, CARRIAGE RETURN = 6351₈,
END TAPE FLAG = 17 17 17 17 17 17 17 17₈, ILLEGAL CODE = 4095,
LOWER CASE CODE = 57₈, STOP CODE = 2263₈, UPPER CASE CODE = 47₈,
SYMBOL TABLE(128) =
    4095,       19,    4095,       38,      16,       56,      37,       36,
    4095,       35,      41,       55,      57,     4095,      51,       21,
      53,       25,      52,       50,      18,       24,      54,       23,
      49,       22,      33,        9,      20,       40,      34,       10,
    4095,     4095,      59,    2263₈,      63,     6351₈,      47,     4095,
      62,     4095,       1,     4095,      13,       39,      30,     4095,
       8,     4095,       5,     4095,       4,     4095,       6,     4095,
       3,     4095,       7,     4095,       2,       42,      43,     4095,
    4095,       19,    4095,       38,      16,       56,      37,       36,
    4095,       35,      41,       55,      57,     4095,      51,       21,
      53,       25,      52,       50,      18,       24,      54,       23,
      49,       22,      33,       28,      20,       40,      34,       60,
    4095,     4095,      29,    2263₈,      00,     6351₈,      27,     4095,
      12,     4095,      48,     4095,      61,       39,      14,     4095,
      44,     4095,      26,     4095,      15,     4095,      58,     4095,
      11,     4095,      17,     4095,      32,       31,      45,     4095;
LOAD CONSTANTS:..
```

```
5
STORAGE = 1587, BLOCK NUMBER, BUFFER, CASE FLAG, INPUT SYMBOL,
LAST MAG TAPE INDEX, LINE(10), LIST INDEX, LOWER LIMIT,
MAG TAPE AREA(1320), MAG TAPE INDEX, MAG TAPE INPUT FLAG,
MAG TAPE OUTPUT FLAG, NUMBER OF PAGES, PAGE NUMBER, PRINT BAR(240),
SYMBOL, SYMBOL COUNT, UPPER LIMIT, WORD, WORD COUNT;
LOAD DIMENSIONING:..
```

```
5;
FIND PAGE: |1 = MAG TAPE INDEX(1)MAG TAPE INDEX+659
    |ALL SPACES → MAG TAPE AREA[1]|
E|NTRY: FIND SYMBOL,
    SYMBOL = CARRIAGE RETURN ∪ SYMBOL = STOP CODE: ; FIND LINE,
```

```
        1 = 0(1)9, |MAG TAPE INDEX + 1 → j, LINE[i] → MAG TAPE AREA[j]|;
      SYMBOL ≠ STOP CODE: MAG TAPE INDEX + 10 → MAG TAPE INDEX <
            LAST MAG TAPE INDEX: ENTRY.;;;|
FIND LINE:  |1 = 0(1)9 |ALL SPACES → LINE[i]| 0 → WORD COUNT,
E|NTRY 1: FIND WORD, WORD COUNT + 1 → WORD COUNT < 10:
      WORD → LINE[WORD COUNT],
        SYMBOL = CARRIAGE RETURN ∪ SYMBOL = STOP CODE: ; ENTRY 1.;
        1 = 0(1)8 |LINE[i+1] → LINE[i]| WORD → LINE[i];|
FIND WORD:  |0 → SYMBOL COUNT, ALL SPACES → WORD,
E|NTRY 2: WORD × 2↑6 → WORD, SYMBOL → WORD(0→5), FIND SYMBOL,
      SYMBOL COUNT + 1 → SYMBOL COUNT ≥ 8: ENTRY 3.;
      SYMBOL = CARRIAGE RETURN ∪ SYMBOL = STOP CODE: ; ENTRY 2.
E|NTRY 3: SYMBOL COUNT + 1 → SYMBOL COUNT < 9:
      WORD × 2↑6 → WORD, ENTRY 3.;|..


5;
FIND SYMBOL:  |E|NTRY: WAIT TO READ PAPER TAPE,
      INPUT SYMBOL(0→5) → SYMBOL, 100₈ INPUT SYMBOL[1] → [1],
      741₈ INPUT SYMBOL, SYMBOL = UPPER CASE CODE: 64 → CASE FLAG, ENTRY.;
      SYMBOL = LOWER CASE CODE: 0 → CASE FLAG, ENTRY.;
      SYMBOL + CASE FLAG → SYMBOL,
      SYMBOL TABLE[SYMBOL] → SYMBOL = ILLEGAL CODE: ENTRY.;|
WAIT TO READ PAPER TAPE:  |747₈ 9,| ACTIVATE READER: |740₈ 11200₈,|
CLEAR STORAGE:  |1 = 1(1)STORAGE |0 → STORAGE[1]||
SET TAPE AREA TO SPACES:  |SET PART 1 TO SPACES, SET PART 2 TO SPACES|
SET PART 1 TO SPACES:  |1 = 0(1)659 |ALL SPACES → MAG TAPE AREA[i]||
SET PART 2 TO SPACES:  |1 = 660(1)1319 |ALL SPACES → MAG TAPE AREA[i]||
SET PRINT BARS TO SPACES:  |1 = 0(1)239 |16 → PRINT BAR[i]||
RESTORE PAGE:  | : 740₈ 66000₈, 747₈ 66000₈, 740₈ 66004₈,|..


5;
FIND TAPE AREA:|WAIT TO READ MAG TAPE, REWIND READ TAPE,
      CLEAR STORAGE, WAIT TO READ MAG TAPE, READ PART 1,
      L → BLOCK NUMBER = 0 ∪ BLOCK NUMBER = 1: EXIT.;
E|NTRY: READ MAG TAPE, MAG TAPE AREA[MAG TAPE INDEX] →
      NUMBER OF PAGES = END TAPE FLAG: EXIT.;
      PAGE NUMBER = 1(1)NUMBER OF PAGES |READ MAG TAPE|
      BLOCK NUMBER - 1 → BLOCK NUMBER ≥ 2: ENTRY.;
E|XIT: CLEAR STORAGE, WAIT TO READ MAG TAPE|
FIND TAPE WRITE AREA:  |ACTIVATE READ MAG TAPE 3,
      ACTIVATE WRITE MAG TAPE 3, FIND TAPE AREA, POSITION BACK WRITE|
FIND TAPE READ AREA:  |ACTIVATE READ MAG TAPE 3, FIND TAPE AREA,
      POSITION BACK READ|..


5;
LIST PAGE:  |0 → LIST INDEX, n = MAG TAPE INDEX(10)LAST MAG TAPE INDEX-1
      |1 = n(1)n+9 |MAG TAPE AREA[i] → BUFFER,
      SYMBOL COUNT = 1(1)8 |BUFFER(42→47) → PRINT BAR[LIST INDEX],
      BUFFER × 2↑6 → BUFFER, LIST INDEX + 1 → LIST INDEX||
      WAIT TO LIST, LIST INDEX ≥ 120: 0 → LIST INDEX,
      100₈ PRINT BAR[240] → [6], 746₈ PRINT BAR[120];
      120 → LIST INDEX, 100₈ PRINT BAR[120] → [6], 746₈ PRINT BAR;||
WAIT TO LIST:  |747₈ 61₈, 740₈ 66000₈, 747₈ 66000₈,|
SET INFORMATION LINE:  |1 = LOWER LIMIT(1)UPPER LIMIT |n = 1(1)8
      |FIND SYMBOL, SYMBOL = CARRIAGE RETURN ∪ SYMBOL = STOP CODE: EXIT.;
      MAG TAPE AREA[i] × 2↑6 → MAG TAPE AREA[i],
      SYMBOL → MAG TAPE AREA[i](0→5)||
E|NTRY: FIND SYMBOL,
      SYMBOL = CARRIAGE RETURN ∪ SYMBOL = STOP CODE: ; ENTRY.
```

E|XIT: n = n(1)8 |MAG TAPE AREA[1] × 2↑6 → MAG TAPE AREA[1]||..

5;
READ INFORMATION PAGE: |E|NTRY 1: FIND SYMBOL, 0 < SYMBOL < 11: ; ENTRY 1.
E|NTRY 2: MAG TAPE AREA[342] × 2↑6 → MAG TAPE AREA[342],
    SYMBOL → MAG TAPE AREA[342](12→17), SYMBOL = 10: 0 → SYMBOL;;
    NUMBER OF PAGES × 10 + SYMBOL → NUMBER OF PAGES → MAG TAPE AREA,
    FIND SYMBOL, 0 < SYMBOL < 11: ENTRY 2.;
E|NTRY 3: SYMBOL ≠ CARRIAGE RETURN: FIND SYMBOL, ENTRY 3.;
E|NTRY 4: FIND SYMBOL, 0 < SYMBOL < 11: ; ENTRY 4.
E|NTRY 5: MAG TAPE AREA[302] × 2↑6 → MAG TAPE AREA[302], SYMBOL →
    MAG TAPE AREA[302](12→17), FIND SYMBOL, 0 < SYMBOL < 11: ENTRY 5.;
E|NTRY 6: SYMBOL ≠ CARRIAGE RETURN: FIND SYMBOL, ENTRY 6.;
E|NTRY 7: FIND SYMBOL, SYMBOL = CARRIAGE RETURN: ENTRY 7.;
    0 < SYMBOL < 8 ∪ SYMBOL = 10: ;
    04 12 12 12 12 20 20 20ₛ → MAG TAPE AREA[322], ENTRY 9.
E|NTRY 8: MAG TAPE AREA[322] × 2↑6 → MAG TAPE AREA[322],
    SYMBOL → MAG TAPE AREA[322](12→17), FIND SYMBOL,
    0 < SYMBOL < 8 ∪ SYMBOL = 10: ENTRY 8.;
E|NTRY 9: SYMBOL = STOP CODE: EXIT.;
    SYMBOL ≠ CARRIAGE RETURN: FIND SYMBOL, ENTRY 9.;
E|NTRY 10: FIND SYMBOL, SYMBOL = STOP CODE: EXIT.;
    SYMBOL = CARRIAGE RETURN: ENTRY 10.;
    241 → LOWER LIMIT, 249 → UPPER LIMIT, SET INFORMATION LINE,
E|NTRY 11: SYMBOL = STOP CODE: EXIT.; FIND SYMBOL,
    SYMBOL = STOP CODE ∪ SYMBOL = CARRIAGE RETURN: ENTRY 11.;
    261 → LOWER LIMIT, 269 → UPPER LIMIT, SET INFORMATION LINE,
E|NTRY 12: SYMBOL = STOP CODE: EXIT.; FIND SYMBOL,
    SYMBOL = STOP CODE ∪ SYMBOL = CARRIAGE RETURN: ENTRY 12.;
    281 → LOWER LIMIT, 289 → UPPER LIMIT, SET INFORMATION LINE,
E|XIT: SYMBOL ≠ STOP CODE: FIND SYMBOL, EXIT.;ALPHA PROGRAMS →
    MAG TAPE AREA[303], ALPHA FIRST LOCATION → MAG TAPE AREA[323],
    ALPHA FIRST LOCATION[1] → MAG TAPE AREA[324],
    ALPHA PAGES → MAG TAPE AREA[343]|..

5;
READ MAG TAPE: |MAG TAPE INPUT FLAG ≠ 0: ENTRY 2.;
    1 → MAG TAPE INPUT FLAG, 0 → MAG TAPE INDEX,
    660 → LAST MAG TAPE INDEX,
E|NTRY 1: WAIT TO READ MAG TAPE, L|ENGTH CHECK 1: 747ₛ 32005ₛ READ ERROR 1.
P|ARITY CHECK 1: 747ₛ 32003ₛ READ ERROR 1. READ PART 2, EXIT.
R|EAD ERROR 1: POSITION BACK READ, READ PART 1, ENTRY 1.
R|EAD ERROR 2: POSITION BACK READ, READ PART 2,
E|NTRY 2: 0 → MAG TAPE INPUT FLAG, 660 → MAG TAPE INDEX,
    1320 → LAST MAG TAPE INDEX, WAIT TO READ MAG TAPE,
L|ENGTH CHECK 2: 747ₛ 32005ₛ READ ERROR 2.
P|ARITY CHECK 2: 747ₛ 32003ₛ READ ERROR 2. READ PART 1, E|XIT:|
WAIT TO READ MAG TAPE: |747ₛ 32000ₛ, | POSITION BACK READ: |740ₛ 32006ₛ, |
READ PART 1: |747ₛ 32000ₛ, 100ₛ MAG TAPE AREA[660] → [3],
    743ₛ MAG TAPE AREA, |
READ PART 2: |747ₛ 32000ₛ, 100ₛ MAG TAPE AREA[1320] → [3],
    743ₛ MAG TAPE AREA[660], |
ACTIVATE READ MAG TAPE 3: |740ₛ 32031ₛ, | REWIND READ TAPE: |740ₛ 32005ₛ, |..

5;
WRITE MAG TAPE: |MAG TAPE OUTPUT FLAG ≠ 0: ENTRY 2.;
    1 → MAG TAPE OUTPUT FLAG, 0 → MAG TAPE INDEX,
    660 → LAST MAG TAPE INDEX,
E|NTRY 1: WAIT TO WRITE MAG TAPE, L|ENGTH CHECK 1: 747ₛ42005ₛ WRITE ERROR 1.

P|ARITY CHECK 1: 747_8 42003_8 WRITE ERROR 1.
  WRITE PART 2, SET PART 1 TO SPACES, EXIT.
W|RITE ERROR 1: POSITION BACK WRITE, WRITE PART 1, ENTRY 1.
W|RITE ERROR 2: POSITION BACK WRITE, WRITE PART 2,
E|NTRY 2: 0 → MAG TAPE OUTPUT FLAG, 660 → MAG TAPE INDEX,
  1320 → LAST MAG TAPE INDEX, WAIT TO WRITE MAG TAPE,
L|ENGTH CHECK 2: 747_8 42005_8 WRITE ERROR 2.
P|ARITY CHECK 2: 747_8 42003_8 WRITE ERROR 2.
  WRITE PART 1, SET PART 2 TO SPACES, E|XIT:|
WAIT TO WRITE MAG TAPE: |747_8 42000_8,| POSITION BACK WRITE: |740_8 42006_8,|
WRITE PART 1: |747_8 42000_8, 100_8 MAG TAPE AREA[660] → [4],
  744_8 MAG TAPE AREA,|
WRITE PART 2: |747_8 42000_8, 100_8 MAG TAPE AREA[1320] → [4],
  744_8 MAG TAPE AREA[660],|
ACTIVATE WRITE MAG TAPE 3: |$740_8 42031_8$,| REWIND WRITE TAPE: |$740_8 42005_8$,|..

5
FIRST COMPILER LOCATION = 40 000_8, LAST COMPILER LOCATION = 77 777_8;
NELIAC 1604 MOD 4c: SET UP INITIAL CONDITIONS,
E|NTRY: PROGRAM COUNT + 1 → PROGRAM COUNT = 1:
    TRANSFER → COMPUTER WORD(42÷47), STORE;; PROCESS DECLARATIONS,
  PROGRAM COUNT = 1: RESERVE COMPILER STORAGE;; PRINT PROGRAM TITLE,
  PROCESS LOGIC, CLEAR TEMPORARY NAMES, TRF HALT → FUNCTION CODE,
  FIRST LOCATION → ADDRESS, STORE COMMAND, FILL LOWER HALF WORD,
  STORE LIST UNDEFINED NUMBERS, OBJECT PROGRAM → PROGRAM LOCATION,
  PROGRAM COUNT < NUMBER OF PROGRAMS: ENTRY.;
COMPILER EXIT: PRINT LAST PROGRAM LOCATION, PRINT UNDEFINED NAMES,
  'PRINT DEFINED NAMES, FAULT FLAG = 0: 760_8 40 000_8;; PRINT PROGRAM,..

5
MASTER STORAGE = 6541, BLOCK NUMBER, FIRST LOCATION, LAST LOCATION,
LAST MAG TAPE INDEX, LAST SYMBOL, LOCATION TEMP STORAGE,
MAG TAPE AREA(1320), MAG TAPE INDEX, MAG TAPE INPUT FLAG, NUMBER OF PAGES,
NUMBER OF PROGRAMS, OBJECT PROGRAM, PAGE NUMBER, PROGRAM COUNT,
PROGRAM LOCATION, SAVE SYMBOL, SPACE SYMBOL, SYMBOL, SYMBOL BUFFER,
SYMBOL COUNT, NAME LIST INDEX, NAME LIST(2100), NAME LOCATIONS(700),
UNDEFINED NAME INDEX, UNDEFINED NAMES(1200), UNDEFINED NAME LOCATIONS(400),
NUMBER LIST(200), NUMBER LOCATIONS(200), UNDEFINED NUMBER LIST(200),
UNDEFINED NUMBER LOCATIONS(200); MASTER DIMENSIONING:..

5
FLAG STORAGE = 31, OPERATOR, LAST OPERATOR, PREVIOUS OPERATOR,
OPERAND(4), PRESENT OPERATOR, NEXT OPERAND(4), NEXT OPERATOR,
ALPHA OPERAND FLAG, CLEAR SUBTRACT FLAG, COMPARE FLAG, COMPARE INDEX FLAG,
DOUBLE STORAGE FLAG, END PROGRAM FLAG, FAULT FLAG, HALF WORD FLAG,
INCOMPLETE VALUE FLAG, LOCAL OPERAND FLAG, LOGIC FLAG, LOOP TYPE FLAG,
MINUS FLAG, MULTIPLY DIVIDE FLAG, PARTIAL WORD FLAG, POWER MINUS FLAG,
SKIP ADDRESS FLAG, TEMPORARY NAME FLAG; SPECIAL DIMENSIONING:..

5
SUB STORAGE = 292, ADDRESS, BRACE TABLE(40), BUFFER(4), COMMAND,
COMPARE TABLE(81), COMPARE WORD, COMPUTER WORD, COUNT, DECIMAL BUFFER,
DECIMAL COUNT, DECIMAL DIGIT COUNT, DECIMAL PLACE COUNT, DESIGNATOR,
FAULT BUFFER, FILL, FUNCTION CODE, HI, INCREMENT, INCREMENT SIGN,
NDEX, INTEGER COUNT, LAST LOWER WORD, LAST NAME INDEX, LAST UPPER WORD,
LOAD NUMBER, LOCATIONS, LOOP OPERAND(4), LOW, LOWER WORD LIMIT,
NUMBER'BUFFER, OCTAL DIGIT COUNT, POWER COUNT, POWER NUMBER,
POWER OF 2, PRINT BAR(120), PRINT LOCATION, RESERVE CELL, TEMPORARY ADDRESS,

TEMPORARY DESIGNATOR, TEMPORARY FUNCTION CODE, TEMPORARY HALF WORD,
TEMPORARY INCREMENT, TEMPORARY OBJECT PROGRAM, TEMPORARY OPERAND(4),
UPPER WORD LIMIT; DIMENSIONING TEMPORARY:..

5
ABSOLUTE = 25, ALL SPACES = 20 20 20 20 20 20 20 20₈, ARROW = 15,
BOOLEAN AND = 13, BOOLEAN OR = 14, COLON = 1, COMMA = 6, COMMA 1612 = 33₈,
DIVISION = 18, END TAPE FLAG = 17 17 17 17 17 17 17 17₈, EQUAL = 7,
GREATER = 9, GREATER OR EQUAL = 10, LEFT BRACE = 2, LEFT BRACKET = 22,
LEFT PAREN = 20, LESS OR EQUAL = 12, LESS THAN = 11, MINUS = 17,
MULTIPLICATION = 19, NOT EQUAL = 8, NUMBER FLAG = 15 15 15 15₈,
OCTAL = 26, OCTAL 1612 = 53₈, PERIOD = 4, PERIOD 1612 = 73₈, PLUS = 16,
RIGHT BRACE = 3, RIGHT BRACKET = 23, RIGHT PAREN = 21, SEMI COLON = 5,
SET = 585, SEVEN SPACES = 20 20 20 20 20 20 20₈, SPACE = 16, TEN = 10. × 0,
UP ARROW = 24, UPPER CASE = 39; DIMENSIONING CONSTANTS:..

5
SHFT ART = 01, SHFT QRT = 02, SHFT AQR = 03, SHFT ALF = 05, ENTER A = 10₈,
INCR A = 11₈, CL ADD = 12₈, CL SUBT = 13₈, ADD = 14₈,
SUBTRACT = 15₈, LOAD Q = 16₈, STORE A = 20₈, STORE Q = 21₈,
COMPAR A = 22₈, COMPAR Q = 23₈, MULT INT = 24₈, DIV INT = 25₈,
MULT FRA = 26₈, DIV FRA = 27₈, FL ADD = 30₈, FL SUBT = 31₈,
FL MULT = 32₈, FL DIV = 33₈, SEL REPL = 43₈, LOAD LOG = 44₈,
ADD LOG = 45₈, SUBT LOG = 46₈, ENTR INX = 50₈, ID INXLo = 53₈,
ST INXLo = 57₈, REP ADLo = 61₈, TRANSFER = 75₈, TRF HALT = 76₈;
FUNCTION CODES:..

5
ALGOL DO = 64 46 20₈, ALGOL NOTHING = 45 46 23 70 71 45 67 20₈,
ALGOL FOR = 66 46 51 20₈, ALGOL GO TO = 67 46 20 23 46 20₈,
ALGOL IF = 71 66 20₈, ALGOL IF NOT = 71 66 20 45 46 23 20 20₈,
ALPHA DEFINED TWICE(2) = 64 65 66 71 45 65 64 20₈, 23 26 71 63 65 20 20 20₈,
ALPHA FAULT = 66 61 24 43 23 20 20 20₈, ALPHA L = 43₈,
ALPHA LAST PROGRAM LOCATION(3) = 43 61 22 23 20 47 51 46₈,
67 51 61 44 20 43 46 63₈, 61 23 71 46 45 20 20 20₈,
ALPHA NAME LIST(2) = 45 61 44 65 20 43 71 22₈, 23 20 20 20 20 20 20 20₈,
ALPHA NO TITLE = 45 46 20 23 71 23 43 65₈, ALPHA U = 24₈,
ALPHA UNDEFINED NAMES(2) = 24 45 64 65 66 71 45 65₈, 64 20 45 61 44 65 22 20₈,
INDEX NAMES(6) = 71 20 20 20 20 20 20₈, 41 20 20 20 20 20 20₈,
42 20 20 20 20 20 20 20₈, 43 20 20 20 20 20 20₈, 44 20 20 20 20 20 20 20₈,
45 20 20 20 20 20 20₈, SYMBOL TABLE(64) =

1,			7,	8,	12,	2,	22,
	18,						
		23,	6,	20,	15,	3,	13,
17,							
		14,	26,	19,	24,	27,	9,
16,							
		11,	4,	21,	10,	25,	5,

OPERATOR CODE TABLE(28) =

	0,	16₈,	36₈,	73₈,	77₈,	33₈,	13₈,
14₈,	57₈,	75₈,	72₈,	15₈,	37₈,	52₈,	35₈,
60₈,	40₈,	21₈,	54₈,	34₈,	74₈,	17₈,	32₈,
55₈,	76₈,	53₈,	56₈;	SYMBOLS:..			

5
LAST FAULT NUMBER = 27, FAULT TALLY(27) =

0,	3,	9,	14,	15,	16,	20,	24,
27,	31,	35,	39,	43,	49,	54,	60,

```
   66,      69,      73,        76,      82,      86,      92,      96,
   99,     103,     106,            FAULT TABLE (110) =
```

456 1446520437122₈,	23204625655 16643₈,	462620202020202020₈,
475 14667516144 20₈,	61516561206346 45₈,	664371632322202 6₈,
712370206346444 7₈,	7143655120615 165₈,	6120202020202020 20₈,
63464566437163 23₈,	204020476167652 0₈,	614564204751466 7₈,
516144204524446 2₈,	655120202020202 0₈,	454623202422656 4₈,
45462320242265 64₈,	244564656671456 5₈,	642045614465204 3₈,
7122232046256551₈,	664346262020202 0₈,	244564656671456 5₈,
64204524446265 51₈,	204371222320462 5₈,	655166434626202 0₈,
45244462655120 43₈,	712223204625655 1₈,	664346262020202 0₈,
454620464765516 1₈,	234651206166236 5₈,	512061204524446 2₈,
655120202020202 0₈,	517167702320476 1₈,	516545204471222 2₈,
714567207145206 3₈,	464444654523222 0₈,	464765516145642 0₈,
447122227145672 0₈,	714520634644476 1₈,	517122464522202 0₈,
454620615151462 6₈,	207145204761512 3₈,	716143202646516 4₈,
206346452351464 3₈,	476151237161432 0₈,	264651642063464 5₈,
235146432043462 6₈,	655120437144712 3₈,	204546232061204 5₈,
244462655120202 0₈,	454620517167702 3₈,	204761516545207 1₈,
452047615123716 1₈,	432026446516420 63₈,	464523514643202 0₈,
476151237161432 0₈,	266451642063464 5₈,	235146432024474 7₈,
655120437144712 3₈,	204546232061204 5₈,	244462655120202 0₈,
464765516145642 0₈,	664643434626714 5₈,	672051716770232 0₈,
476151654520714 5₈,	204761512371614 3₈,	202646516420202 0₈,
454620634643464 5₈,	206646434346267 1₈,	456720237123436 5₈,
714343656761432 0₈,	464765516123465 1₈,	207145206471446 5₈,
452271464571456 7₈,	436566232062516 1₈,	636520447122227 1₈,
456720202020202 0₈,	714343656761432 0₈,	464765516123465 1₈,
207145206471446 5₈,	452271464571456 7₈,	204666206346452 2₈,
236145232220202 0₈,	454620517167702 3₈,	206251616342652 3₈,
207145202224622 2₈,	635171472371456 7₈,	222462226351714 7₈,
232051716770232 0₈,	625161634265232 0₈,	664643434626656 4₈,
206230204647655 1₈,	614564202020202 0₈,	714343656761432 0₈,
464765516123465 1₈,	207145204346677 1₈,	632020202020202 0₈,
517167702320625 1₈,	616365204471222 2₈,	714567202020202 0₈,
652747464565452 3₈,	206261226520462 3₈,	706551202370614 5₈,
200220202020202 0₈,	652747464565452 3₈,	614520272046512 0₈,
244462655120202 0₈,	462370655120237 0₈,	FAULT TITLES:..
212026712370202 4₈,	472061515146262 0₈;	

```
5;
ADD INCOMPLETE VALUE: |INCOMPLETE VALUE FLAG = 0: EXIT.; SAVE COMMAND,
    LOCATION TEMP STORAGE → ADDRESS, INCOMPLETE VALUE FLAG ≠ 0:
        FL ADD → FUNCTION CODE; ADD → FUNCTION CODE;
    STORE COMMAND, RESET COMMAND, 0 → INCOMPLETE VALUE FLAG, E|XIT:|
STORE INCOMPLETE VALUE: |ADD INCOMPLETE VALUE, SAVE COMMAND,
    SET → SKIP ADDRESS FLAG, FIND ADDRESS, 0 → SKIP ADDRESS FLAG,
    OPERAND[3](12→14) → INCOMPLETE VALUE FLAG, LOCATION TEMP STORAGE →
    ADDRESS, STORE A → FUNCTION CODE, STORE COMMAND, RESET COMMAND|
SAVE OPERAND: |OPERAND → TEMPORARY OPERAND, OPERAND[1] →
    TEMPORARY OPERAND[1], OPERAND[2] → TEMPORARY OPERAND[2],
    OPERAND[3] → TEMPORARY OPERAND[3]|
RESET OPERAND: |TEMPORARY OPERAND → OPERAND, TEMPORARY OPERAND[1] →
    OPERAND[1], TEMPORARY OPERAND[2] → OPERAND[2],
    TEMPORARY OPERAND[3] → OPERAND[3]|
SAVE COMMAND: |FUNCTION CODE → TEMPORARY FUNCTION CODE,
    DESIGNATOR → TEMPORARY DESIGNATOR,
    ADDRESS → TEMPORARY ADDRESS, INCREMENT → TEMPORARY INCREMENT,
    0 → FUNCTION CODE → DESIGNATOR → ADDRESS → INCREMENT|
```

RESET COMMAND: |TEMPORARY FUNCTION CODE → FUNCTION CODE,
    TEMPORARY DESIGNATOR → DESIGNATOR, TEMPORARY ADDRESS → ADDRESS,
    TEMPORARY INCREMENT → INCREMENT|..

5;
ADDITION: |OPERAND ≠ 0: PRESENT OPERATOR = MULTIPLICATION ∪
    PRESENT OPERATOR = DIVISION: STORE INCOMPLETE VALUE,
        GENERATE CLEAR ADD COMMAND; GENERATE ADD COMMAND;;;|
GENERATE CLEAR ADD COMMAND: |PARTIAL WORD FLAG ≠ 0:
    0 → PARTIAL WORD FLAG, GENERATE LOAD Q COMMAND, LOAD LOG →
    FUNCTION CODE; CL ADD → FUNCTION CODE, FIND ADDRESS; STORE COMMAND|
GENERATE ADD COMMAND: |PARTIAL WORD FLAG ≠ 0: 0 → PARTIAL WORD FLAG,
    GENERATE LOAD Q COMMAND, ADD LOG → FUNCTION CODE;
    FIND ADDRESS, OPERAND[3](12→14) ≠ 0: FL ADD → FUNCTION CODE;
        ADD → FUNCTION CODE;; STORE COMMAND|..

5;
COMPILE SUBROUTINES: |BRACE TABLE + 1 → BRACE TABLE,
    OBJECT PROGRAM → BRACE TABLE[BRACE TABLE], TRANSFER → FUNCTION CODE,
    STORE COMMAND, FIND OPERATOR|
EXIT COMPILE SUBROUTINES: |TRANSFER → FUNCTION CODE,
    BRACE TABLE[BRACE TABLE + 1] → ADDRESS, STORE COMMAND,
E|NTRY: COMPARE TABLE ≥ 1: 3 → COMPARE FLAG, UPGRADE COMPARISONS, ENTRY.;|
COMPUTER LANGUAGE: |OPERAND[1] < 512: OPERAND[1](0→2) → DESIGNATOR,
    OPERAND[1](3→8) → FUNCTION CODE, FIND OPERATOR,
    OPERAND = NUMBER FLAG: OPERAND[1] → ADDRESS; FIND ADDRESS;;
    OPERAND[1](0→14) → ADDRESS, OPERAND[1](15→17) → DESIGNATOR,
    OPERAND[1](18→23) → FUNCTION CODE;
    PRESENT OPERATOR = LEFT BRACKET: SUBSCRIPT;; STORE COMMAND|..

5;
DEFINE LOCATION: |LOGIC FLAG ≠ 0: FILL LOWER HALF WORD;;
    OPERAND = 0: EXIT.; NAME LIST INDEX → m, OPERAND → ,
E|NTRY 1: 645₈ NAME LIST, ENTRY 2.
    OPERAND[1] = NAME LIST[m+700] ∩ OPERAND[2] = NAME LIST[m+1400]:
        PRINT NAMES DEFINED TWICE, EXIT. ENTRY 1.
E|NTRY 2: NAME LIST INDEX = m = 0: ENTRY 4.; 0 → ,
E|NTRY 3: 645₈ NAME LIST, ENTRY 4. ENTRY 5.
E|NTRY 4: NAME LIST INDEX = m + 1 → NAME LIST INDEX ≥ 500:
    1 → FAULT BUFFER, FAULT.;
E|NTRY 5: 575₈ LAST NAME INDEX, OPERAND → NAME LIST[m],
    OPERAND[1] → NAME LIST[m+700], OPERAND[2] → NAME LIST[m+1400],
    OBJECT PROGRAM → NAME LOCATIONS[m],
    OPERAND[3] ≠ 0: SET → NAME LOCATIONS[m](18→20);;
    FILL UNDEFINED ADDRESS, E|XIT:|
FILL LOWER HALF WORD: |HALF WORD FLAG ≠ 0: STORE PASS COMMAND;;|

FILL UPPER HALF WORD: |HALF WORD FLAG = 0: STORE PASS COMMAND;;|
,STORE PASS COMMAND: |SAVE COMMAND, ENTR INX → FUNCTION CODE,
    STORE COMMAND, RESET COMMAND|..

5;
DELETE ALGOL WORDS: |E|NTRY 1: NEXT OPERAND = ALGOL IF NOT:
    0 → NEXT OPERAND → NEXT OPERAND[1] → NEXT OPERAND[2] →
    NEXT OPERAND[3] → TEMPORARY NAME FLAG, EXIT.;
    NEXT OPERAND(30→47) = ALGOL IF: ENTRY 2.;
    NEXT OPERAND(30→47) = ALGOL DO: ENTRY 2.;
    NEXT OPERAND(24→47) = ALGOL FOR: ENTRY 3.;
    NEXT OPERAND(12→47) = ALGOL GO TO: ENTRY 4.;
    NEXT OPER
       X   E

```
NEXT OPERAND = ALGOL NOTHING: NEXT OPERAND[1] → NEXT OPERAND,
    NEXT OPERAND[2] → NEXT OPERAND[1],
    NEXT OPERAND[3] → NEXT OPERAND[2];; EXIT.
E|NTRY 2: NEXT OPERAND(0→29) → NEXT OPERAND(18→47),
    NEXT OPERAND[1](30→47) → NEXT OPERAND(0→17),
    NEXT OPERAND[1](0→29)  → NEXT OPERAND[1](18→47),
    NEXT OPERAND[2](30→47) → NEXT OPERAND[1](0→17),
    NEXT OPERAND[2](0→29)  → NEXT OPERAND[2](18→47),
    NEXT OPERAND[3](30→47) → NEXT OPERAND[2](0→17),
    NEXT OPERAND[3](0→29)  → NEXT OPERAND[3](18→47),
    20 20 20₈ → NEXT OPERAND[3](0→17), ENTRY 1.
E|NTRY 3: NEXT OPERAND(0→23) → NEXT OPERAND(24→47),
    NEXT OPERAND[1](24→47) → NEXT OPERAND(0→23),
    NEXT OPERAND[1](0→23)  → NEXT OPERAND[1](24→47),
    NEXT OPERAND[2](24→47) → NEXT OPERAND[1](0→23),
    NEXT OPERAND[2](0→23)  → NEXT OPERAND[2](24→47),
    NEXT OPERAND[3](24→47) → NEXT OPERAND[2](0→23),
    NEXT OPERAND[3](0→23)  → NEXT OPERAND[3](24→47),
    20 20 20 20₈ → NEXT OPERAND[3](0→23), ENTRY 1.
E|NTRY 4: NEXT OPERAND(0→11) → NEXT OPERAND(36→47),
    NEXT OPERAND[1](12→47) → NEXT OPERAND(0→35),
    NEXT OPERAND[1](0→11)  → NEXT OPERAND[1](36→47),
    NEXT OPERAND[2](12→47) → NEXT OPERAND[1](0→35),
    NEXT OPERAND[2](0→11)  → NEXT OPERAND[2](36→47),
    NEXT OPERAND[3](12→47) → NEXT OPERAND[2](0→35),
    NEXT OPERAND[3](0→11)  → NEXT OPERAND[3](36→47),
    20 20 20 20 20 20₈ → NEXT OPERAND[3](0→35), ENTRY 1. E|XIT:|..
```

```
5;
DIVIDE: |OPERAND ≠ 0: GENERATE DIVIDE COMMAND;;|
GENERATE DIVIDE COMMAND: |PARTIAL WORD FLAG ≠ 0: SAVE COMMAND,
    STORE A → FUNCTION CODE, LOCATION TEMP STORAGE + 1 → ADDRESS,
    STORE COMMAND, RESET COMMAND, GENERATE LOAD Q COMMAND,
    LOAD LOG → FUNCTION CODE, STORE COMMAND, SHFT AQR → FUNCTION CODE, 48 ←
    ADDRESS, STORE COMMAND, CL ADD → FUNCTION CODE,
    LOCATION TEMP STORAGE + 1 → ADDRESS, STORE COMMAND,
    STORE Q → FUNCTION CODE,
    LOCATION TEMP STORAGE + 1 → ADDRESS, STORE COMMAND;;
MULTIPLY DIVIDE FLAG ≠ 0: DIV INT → FUNCTION CODE;
    HALF WORD FLAG → TEMPORARY HALF WORD, OBJECT PROGRAM →
    TEMPORARY OBJECT PROGRAM, SHFT AQR → FUNCTION CODE,
    47 → ADDRESS, STORE COMMAND, DIV FRA → FUNCTION CODE;
PARTIAL WORD FLAG ≠ 0: 0 → PARTIAL WORD FLAG,
    LOCATION TEMP STORAGE + 1 → ADDRESS; FIND ADDRESS;
OPERAND[3](12→14) ≠ 0: FL DIV → FUNCTION CODE, MULTIPLY DIVIDE FLAG = 0:
    TEMPORARY HALF WORD → HALF WORD FLAG, TEMPORARY OBJECT PROGRAM →
    OBJECT PROGRAM;;;; STORE COMMAND, 0 → MULTIPLY DIVIDE FLAG|..
```

```
5;
DOWNGRADE BRACE TABLE: |BRACE TABLE - 1 → BRACE TABLE < 0:
    19 → FAULT BUFFER, FAULT.;
    BRACE TABLE[BRACE TABLE + 1](15→47) ≠ 0: POST LOOP CONTROL;
    EXIT COMPILE SUBROUTINES; PREVIOUS OPERATOR = PERIOD ∩
    NEXT OPERATOR = SEMI COLON: COMMA → NEXT OPERATOR;;|
EXPONENT: |OPERAND ≠ NUMBER FLAG ∪ OPERAND[1] ≠ 2:
    25 → FAULT BUFFER, FAULT.;
    PREVIOUS OPERATOR → PRESENT OPERATOR, FIND OPERATOR,
    OPERAND ≠ NUMBER FLAG: 26 → FAULT BUFFER, FAULT.;
    PREVIOUS OPERATOR = DIVISION: SHFT ART → FUNCTION CODE,
```

```
        0 → MULTIPLY DIVIDE FLAG; PREVIOUS OPERATOR ≠ MULTIPLICATION:
            27 → FAULT BUFFER, FAULT. SHFT ALF → FUNCTION CODE;;
    OPERAND[1] → ADDRESS, STORE COMMAND|..


5;
FAULT: FAULT FLAG + 1 → FAULT FLAG, SET PRINT BARS TO SPACES,
    LOGIC FLAG = 0: PRINT LINE;;
    FAULT BUFFER > LAST FAULT NUMBER: ALPHA FAULT → BUFFER, 4 → LOW,
        SET PRINT BARS, FAULT BUFFER → NUMBER BUFFER,
        12 → LOW, 15 → HI, SET DECIMAL PRINT BARS, 20 → LOW;
        FAULT TALLY[FAULT BUFFER - 1] → LOWER WORD LIMIT,
        FAULT TALLY[FAULT BUFFER] - 1 → UPPER WORD LIMIT, 4 → LOW,
        INDEX = LOWER WORD LIMIT(1)UPPER WORD LIMIT
            |FAULT TABLE[INDEX] → BUFFER, SET PRINT BARS|;
    FAULT BUFFER < 9: PRINT LINE, COMPILER EXIT.; LOW + 3 → LOW,
    OPERATOR CODE TABLE[PREVIOUS OPERATOR] → PRINT BAR[LOW],
    LOW + 2 → LOW, OPERAND → BUFFER ≠ 0:
        BUFFER = NUMBER FLAG: OPERAND[1] → NUMBER BUFFER,
            LOW + 11 → HI, SET DECIMAL PRINT BARS,
            FILL = 16: 10 → PRINT BAR[LOW+6];; LOW + 11 → LOW;
            SET PRINT BARS, OPERAND[1] → BUFFER ≠ 0: SET PRINT BARS,
                OPERAND[2] → BUFFER ≠ 0: SET PRINT BARS;;;;;; LOW + 2 → LOW,
    OPERATOR CODE TABLE[PRESENT OPERATOR] → PRINT BAR[LOW],
    LOW + 2 → LOW, NEXT OPERAND → BUFFER ≠ 0:
        BUFFER = NUMBER FLAG: NEXT OPERAND[1] → NUMBER BUFFER,
            LOW + 11 → HI, SET DECIMAL PRINT BARS,
            FILL = 16: 10 → PRINT BAR[LOW+6];; LOW + 11 → LOW;
            SET PRINT BARS, NEXT OPERAND[1] → BUFFER ≠ 0: SET PRINT BARS,
                NEXT OPERAND[2] → BUFFER ≠ 0: SET PRINT BARS;;;;;;;
    LOW + 2 → LOW, OPERATOR CODE TABLE[NEXT OPERATOR] → PRINT BAR[LOW],
    PRINT LINE, LOGIC FLAG = 0:
    E|NTRY.1: PRESENT OPERATOR = COLON: EXIT PROCESS DECLARATIONS.;
        END PROGRAM FLAG ≠ 0: COLON → PRESENT OPERATOR;
        FIND OPERATOR; ENTRY 1.; 0 → BRACE TABLE,
    E|NTRY 2: END PROGRAM FLAG ≠ 0: EXIT PROCESS LOGIC.;
    PRESENT OPERATOR = COLON ∩ NEXT OPERATOR = LEFT BRACE:
        0 → LOGIC FLAG, ENTRANCE PROCESS LOGIC.;
    FIND OPERATOR, ENTRY 2..


5;
FILL UNDEFINED ADDRESS: |UNDEFINED NAME INDEX → m,
E|NTRY: OPERAND → , : 645₈ UNDEFINED NAMES, EXIT. OPERAND[1] =
    UNDEFINED NAMES[m+400] ∩ OPERAND[2] = UNDEFINED NAMES[m+800]:
        UNDEFINED NAME LOCATIONS[m](45→47) = 6:
            UNDEFINED NAME LOCATIONS[m](24→38) → L,
            UNDEFINED NAME LOCATIONS[m](42→44) ≠ 0:
                FILL LOWER ADDRESS; FILL UPPER ADDRESS;;;
        UNDEFINED NAME LOCATIONS[m](0→14) → L,
        UNDEFINED NAME LOCATIONS[m](18→20) ≠ 0:
            FILL LOWER ADDRESS; FILL UPPER ADDRESS;
        0 → UNDEFINED NAMES[m] → UNDEFINED NAMES[m+400] →
        UNDEFINED NAMES[m+800] → UNDEFINED NAME LOCATIONS[m];; ENTRY. E|XIT:|
FILL UPPER ADDRESS: |[L](24→38) → ENTRY 1(24→38),
E|NTRY 1: 100₈ 0, + OBJECT PROGRAM → [L](24→38)|
FILL LOWER ADDRESS: |[L](0→14) → ENTRY 2(24→38),
E|NTRY 2: 100₈ 0, + OBJECT PROGRAM → [L](0→14)|..
```

```
5;
FIND ADDRESS:
   |0 → ADDRESS → OPERAND[3], OPERAND = 0 ∪ OPERAND = SET: EXIT.;
   OPERAND = NUMBER FLAG: OPERAND[1] → NUMBER BUFFER,
      FIND NUMBER ADDRESS, EXIT.; NAME LIST INDEX → m,
E|NTRY 1: OPERAND → , : 645₈ NAME LIST, ENTRY 2.
   OPERAND[1] = NAME LIST[m+700] ∩ OPERAND[2] = NAME LIST[m+1400]:
      NAME LOCATIONS[m](0→14) → ADDRESS,
      NAME LOCATIONS[m](24→38) → OPERAND[3], EXIT.; ENTRY 1.
E|NTRY 2: SKIP ADDRESS FLAG ≠ 0: EXIT.; UNDEFINED NAME INDEX → m,
E|NTRY 3: OPERAND → , : 645₈ UNDEFINED NAMES, ENTRY 4.
   UNDEFINED NAME LOCATIONS[m](45→47) = 6: ENTRY 3.;
   OPERAND[1] = UNDEFINED NAMES[m+400] ∩ OPERAND[2] = UNDEFINED NAMES[m+800]
      6 → UNDEFINED NAME LOCATIONS[m](45→47),
      HALF WORD FLAG → UNDEFINED NAME LOCATIONS[m](42→44),
      OBJECT PROGRAM → UNDEFINED NAME LOCATIONS[m](24→38), EXIT.; ENTRY 3.
E|NTRY 4: UNDEFINED NAME INDEX → m = 0: ENTRY 5.;
   0 → , : 645₈ UNDEFINED NAMES, ENTRY 5. ENTRY 6.
E|NTRY 5: UNDEFINED NAME INDEX → m + 1 → UNDEFINED NAME INDEX ≥ 400:
      6 → FAULT BUFFER, FAULT.;
E|NTRY 6: OPERAND → UNDEFINED NAMES[m], OPERAND[1] → UNDEFINED NAMES[m+400],
   OPERAND[2] → UNDEFINED NAMES[m+800],
   3 → UNDEFINED NAME LOCATIONS[m](45→47), HALF WORD FLAG →
   UNDEFINED NAME LOCATIONS[m](18→20), OBJECT PROGRAM →
   UNDEFINED NAME LOCATIONS[m](0→14), E|XIT:|..


5;
FIND ALPHA OPERAND:
   | 0 → 1 → LOCAL OPERAND FLAG, SET → ALPHA OPERAND FLAG,
E|NTRY 1: SYMBOL → NEXT OPERAND[1], FIND SYMBOL,
   n = 1(1)7 |NEXT OPERAND[1] × 2↑6 → NEXT OPERAND[1],
E|NTRY 2: OPERATOR ≠ 0: PRESENT OPERATOR ≠ ABSOLUTE ∩ OPERATOR = ABSOLUTE:
      SET → LOCAL OPERAND FLAG, FIND SYMBOL, ENTRY 2.; SPACE →
      NEXT OPERAND[1](0→5); SYMBOL → NEXT OPERAND[1](0→5), FIND SYMBOL;|
E|NTRY 3: OPERATOR = 0: 1 + 1 → 1 < 4: ENTRY 1.; FIND SYMBOL, ENTRY 3.;
   DELETE ALGOL WORDS, LOCAL OPERAND FLAG → NEXT OPERAND[3],
   0 → ALPHA OPERAND FLAG|..


5;
FIND COMPARE WORD: |SET COMPARE INDEX, COMPARE TABLE[m](45→47) = 0:
      COMPARE TABLE[m](0→23) → COMPARE WORD;
      COMPARE TABLE[m](24→47) → COMPARE WORD;|
STORE COMPARE WORD: |SET COMPARE INDEX, COMPARE WORD(21→23) = 0:
      COMPARE WORD → COMPARE TABLE[m](0→23);
      COMPARE WORD → COMPARE TABLE[m](24→47);|
SET COMPARE INDEX:
   |COMPARE TABLE → k, COMPARE TABLE[k](18→20) × 10 + k → m|
INCREASE COMPARE SUB INDEX: |COMPARE WORD(21→23) ≠ 0:
      COMPARE TABLE[k](18→20) + 1 → COMPARE TABLE[k](18→20),
      m + 1 → m, 0 → COMPARE WORD(21→23); 1 → COMPARE WORD(21→23);|
DECREASE COMPARE SUB INDEX: |COMPARE TABLE[k](18→20) < 1:
      COMPARE WORD(21→23) ≠ 0:
         0 → COMPARE TABLE[k](45→47); 0 → COMPARE TABLE[k];;
      COMPARE WORD(21→23) ≠ 0: 0 → COMPARE TABLE[m](45→47);
         COMPARE TABLE[k](18→20) - 1 → COMPARE TABLE[k](18→20);;|..


5;
FIND FLOATING POINT NUMBER:
   |0 → POWER NUMBER → POWER MINUS FLAG, FIND SYMBOL.
```

```
        OPERATOR = MINUS: SET → POWER MINUS FLAG, FIND SYMBOL;
            OPERATOR = PLUS: FIND SYMBOL;;;
E|NTRY 1: OPERATOR = 0 ∩ SYMBOL < 10: POWER NUMBER × 10 + SYMBOL →
        POWER NUMBER, POWER COUNT + 1 → POWER COUNT, FIND SYMBOL, ENTRY 1.;
    NUMBER BUFFER → , 346₈ 2057₈, 576₈ POWER OF 2, 030₈ 11, → NUMBER BUFFER,
    232₈ ENTRY 2, NUMBER BUFFER + 1 → NUMBER BUFFER,
    NUMBER BUFFER(36→36) ≠ 0:
        4000 0000 0000₈ → NUMBER BUFFER, POWER OF 2 + 1 → POWER OF 2;;
E|NTRY 2: POWER OF 2 → NUMBER BUFFER(36→46),
    POWER MINUS FLAG ≠ 0: - POWER NUMBER → POWER NUMBER;;
    POWER NUMBER - DECIMAL PLACE COUNT → POWER NUMBER < 0:
        - POWER NUMBER → POWER NUMBER,
    m = 1(1)POWER NUMBER |NUMBER BUFFER / TEN → NUMBER BUFFER|;
    m = 1(1)POWER NUMBER |NUMBER BUFFER × TEN → NUMBER BUFFER|;|..


5;
FIND NUMBER ADDRESS:
    |m = 1(1)NUMBER LIST |NUMBER LIST[m] = NUMBER BUFFER:
        NUMBER LOCATIONS[m] → ADDRESS, EXIT.;|
    UNDEFINED NUMBER LIST + 1 → UNDEFINED NUMBER LIST → m ≥ 200:
        7 → FAULT BUFFER, FAULT.;
    NUMBER BUFFER → UNDEFINED NUMBER LIST[m], OBJECT PROGRAM →
    UNDEFINED NUMBER LOCATIONS[m], HALF WORD FLAG →
    UNDEFINED NUMBER LOCATIONS[m](18→20), E|XIT:|
STORE LIST UNDEFINED NUMBERS:
    |L = 1(1)UNDEFINED NUMBER LIST |m = 1(1)NUMBER LIST
    |UNDEFINED NUMBER LIST[L] = NUMBER LIST[m]: ENTRY.;|
    NUMBER LIST + 1 → NUMBER LIST → m ≥ 200:
        8 → FAULT BUFFER, FAULT.;
    UNDEFINED NUMBER LIST[L] → NUMBER LIST[m] → [OBJECT PROGRAM],
    OBJECT PROGRAM → NUMBER LOCATIONS[m],
    OBJECT PROGRAM + 1 → OBJECT PROGRAM,
E|NTRY: UNDEFINED NUMBER LOCATIONS[L] → k,
    UNDEFINED NUMBER LOCATIONS[L](18→20) ≠ 0: NUMBER LOCATIONS[m] +
    [k](0→14) → [k](0→14); NUMBER LOCATIONS[m] + [k](24→38) → [k](24→38);
    0 → UNDEFINED NUMBER LIST[L] → UNDEFINED NUMBER LOCATIONS[L]|
    0 → UNDEFINED NUMBER LIST|..


5;
FIND NUMBER OPERAND:
    |0 → DECIMAL BUFFER → DECIMAL PLACE COUNT → OCTAL DIGIT COUNT →
    DECIMAL DIGIT COUNT, SYMBOL → NUMBER BUFFER → DECIMAL BUFFER,
    PRESENT OPERATOR = PERIOD ∩ LOGIC FLAG = 0:
        DECIMAL COUNT + 1 → DECIMAL COUNT, ENTRY 2.;
E|NTRY 1: FIND SYMBOL, INTEGER COUNT + 1 → INTEGER COUNT,
    OPERATOR = 0 ∩ SYMBOL < 10:
        OCTAL DIGIT COUNT + 1 → OCTAL DIGIT COUNT < 16:
            NUMBER BUFFER × 2↑3 + SYMBOL → NUMBER BUFFER;;
        DECIMAL DIGIT COUNT + 1 → DECIMAL DIGIT COUNT < 13:
            DECIMAL BUFFER × 10 + SYMBOL → DECIMAL BUFFER;
            DECIMAL PLACE COUNT + 1 → DECIMAL PLACE COUNT; ENTRY 1.;
    OPERATOR = OCTAL: FIND SYMBOL, EXIT.; DECIMAL BUFFER → NUMBER BUFFER,
    OPERATOR = PERIOD: E|NTRY 2: FIND SYMBOL,
        OPERATOR = 0 ∩ SYMBOL < 10: DECIMAL COUNT + 1 → DECIMAL COUNT,
        DECIMAL DIGIT COUNT + 1 → DECIMAL DIGIT COUNT < 13:
            NUMBER BUFFER × 10 + SYMBOL → NUMBER BUFFER,
            DECIMAL PLACE COUNT + 1 → DECIMAL PLACE COUNT;; ENTRY 2.;;
        LOGIC FLAG ≠ 0: EXIT.;;
    OPERATOR = MULTIPLICATION: FIND FLOATING POINT NUMBER;;
```

E|XIT: NUMBER BUFFER → NEXT OPERAND[1], NUMBER FLAG → NEXT OPERAND,
    OPERATOR = 0: 9' → FAULT BUFFER, FAULT.;|..

5;
FIND OPERATOR:
    |1 = 0(1)5 |PRESENT OPERATOR[1] → PREVIOUS OPERATOR[1]|
E|NTRY 1: FIND NEXT OPERATOR,
    PRESENT OPERATOR = LEFT PAREN ∩ NEXT OPERATOR = COLON:
    E|NTRY 2: FIND SYMBOL, OPERATOR = PERIOD ∩ LAST SYMBOL = PERIOD 1612:
        10 → FAULT BUFFER, FAULT.; OPERATOR ≠ RIGHT PAREN: ENTRY 2.;
    FIND NEXT OPERATOR, NEXT OPERATOR → PRESENT OPERATOR,
    OPERAND = 0: 1 = 0(1)3 |NEXT OPERAND[1] → OPERAND[1]| ENTRY 1.;
    NEXT OPERAND = 0: ENTRY 1.; COMMA → PRESENT OPERATOR;;|
FIND NEXT OPERATOR: |0 → NUMBER BUFFER → INTEGER COUNT → DECIMAL COUNT →
    POWER COUNT, ALL SPACES → NEXT OPERAND → NEXT OPERAND[1] →
    NEXT OPERAND[2] → NEXT OPERAND[3], FIND SYMBOL,
    OPERATOR = 0: SYMBOL < 10: FIND NUMBER OPERAND; FIND ALPHA OPERAND;;;
    NEXT OPERAND ≠ NUMBER FLAG: 1 = 0(1)3 |NEXT OPERAND[1] = ALL SPACES:
        0 → NEXT OPERAND[1];;|; INTEGER COUNT → NEXT OPERAND[2],
    DECIMAL COUNT → NEXT OPERAND[2](6→11), POWER COUNT →
    NEXT OPERAND[2](12→14), 0 → NEXT OPERAND[3];
    OPERATOR → NEXT OPERATOR|..

5;
FIND SYMBOL:
    |OPERATOR = PERIOD ∩ LAST SYMBOL = PERIOD 1612: SET → END PROGRAM FLAG,
        EXIT.; SYMBOL → LAST SYMBOL, OPERATOR → LAST OPERATOR,
    SAVE SYMBOL ≠ 0: SAVE SYMBOL → SYMBOL, 0 → SAVE SYMBOL, ENTRY 2.;
E|NTRY 1: SYMBOL → SPACE SYMBOL, SYMBOL COUNT + 1 → SYMBOL COUNT ≥ 8:
        MAG TAPE INDEX + 1 → MAG TAPE INDEX ≥ LAST MAG TAPE INDEX:
            READ MAG TAPE;; MAG TAPE AREA[MAG TAPE INDEX] →
        SYMBOL BUFFER ≠ ALL SPACES: 0 → SYMBOL COUNT;;;;
    SYMBOL BUFFER(42→47) → SYMBOL, SYMBOL BUFFER × 2↑6 → SYMBOL BUFFER,
E|NTRY 2: SYMBOL TABLE[SYMBOL] → OPERATOR = ABSOLUTE:
        SYMBOL TABLE[SAVE SYMBOL] = ABSOLUTE: 0 → SAVE SYMBOL, SPACE → SYMBOL;
        SYMBOL → SAVE SYMBOL, ENTRY 1.; SAVE SYMBOL ≠ 0:
    SAVE SYMBOL → OPERATOR, SYMBOL + 70000₈ → SAVE SYMBOL,
    OPERATOR → SYMBOL, SYMBOL TABLE[SYMBOL] → OPERATOR;;
    SYMBOL = SPACE ∩ SPACE SYMBOL = SPACE: ENTRY 1.;
    ALPHA OPERAND FLAG ≠ 0: EXIT.; SYMBOL = SPACE: ENTRY 1.;
    OPERATOR ≠ 0: EXIT.; SYMBOL = 10: 0 → SYMBOL;; LAST SYMBOL = OCTAL 1612:
        ENTRY 3.; SYMBOL ≥ 10 ∩ LAST SYMBOL < 10 ∩ LAST OPERATOR ≠ COLON:
    E|NTRY 3: SYMBOL → SAVE SYMBOL, COMMA → OPERATOR, COMMA 1612 →
        SYMBOL;; E|XIT:|..

5;
GENERATE TRANSFER:
    |OPERAND = NUMBER FLAG: COMPUTER LANGUAGE, EXIT.;
    DESIGNATOR ≠ 0: FILL LOWER HALF WORD, ST INXLo → FUNCTION CODE,
        OBJECT PROGRAM + 1 → ADDRESS, STORE COMMAND,
        ENTER A → FUNCTION CODE, STORE COMMAND,
        OPERAND ≠ 0: INCR A → FUNCTION CODE; ENTR INX → FUNCTION CODE;
        FIND ADDRESS, STORE COMMAND, INCR A → FUNCTION CODE,
        STORE COMMAND, REP ADLo → FUNCTION CODE, OBJECT PROGRAM → ADDRESS,
        STORE COMMAND;;
    OPERAND ≠ 0: PRESENT OPERATOR ≠ PERIOD: 4 → DESIGNATOR; 0 → DESIGNATOR;
        TRANSFER → FUNCTION CODE, FIND ADDRESS, STORE COMMAND,
        PRESENT OPERATOR ≠ PERIOD: FILL LOWER HALF WORD;;;; E|XIT:|..

5;

LOAD WORKING REGISTER: |PRESENT OPERATOR = EQUAL ∩
   NEXT OPERATOR = LEFT PAREN ∪ NEXT OPERATOR = PLUS ∪
   NEXT OPERATOR = MINUS: PRE LOOP CONTROL, EXIT.;
   PRESENT OPERATOR = MINUS: SET → CLEAR SUBTRACT FLAG;; OPERAND ≠ 0:
     0 → CLEAR SUBTRACT FLAG, GENERATE CLEAR ADD COMMAND;; E|XIT:|
GENERATE LOAD Q COMMAND: |LOAD Q → FUNCTION CODE, FIND ADDRESS,
   STORE COMMAND, LOWER WORD LIMIT ≠ 0: SHFT QRT → FUNCTION CODE,
     LOWER WORD LIMIT → ADDRESS, STORE COMMAND;;
   FIND MASK, FIND NUMBER ADDRESS|
FIND MASK: |0 → NUMBER BUFFER, UPPER WORD LIMIT – LOWER WORD LIMIT →
   COUNT, m = 0(1)COUNT |NUMBER BUFFER × 2↑1 + 1 → NUMBER BUFFER|]..

5;
MULTIPLE COMPARISON: |OPERAND = 0: 11 → FAULT BUFFER, FAULT.;
   COMPARE INDEX FLAG = 0: SET → COMPARE INDEX FLAG,
     COMPARE TABLE + 1 → COMPARE TABLE;;
   PREVIOUS OPERATOR = BOOLEAN OR ∪ PREVIOUS OPERATOR = BOOLEAN AND:
     GENERATE CLEAR ADD COMMAND; GENERATE SUBTRACT COMMAND,
     PRESENT OPERATOR = BOOLEAN OR:
       SET TRUE COMPARISON; SET FALSE COMPARISON;
     UPGRADE COMPARISONS, PRESENT OPERATOR = BOOLEAN OR ∪
     PRESENT.OPERATOR = BOOLEAN AND: ; GENERATE CLEAR ADD COMMAND;; |
FINISH COMPARISON: |OPERAND = 0: 11 → FAULT BUFFER, FAULT.;
   COMPARE INDEX FLAG ≠ 0:
     0 → COMPARE INDEX FLAG; COMPARE TABLE + 1 → COMPARE TABLE;
   GENERATE SUBTRACT COMMAND, SET FALSE COMPARISON, UPGRADE COMPARISONS,
   NEXT OPERATOR = LEFT BRACE: BRACE TABLE + 1 → BRACE TABLE,
     0 → BRACE TABLE[BRACE TABLE], COMMA → NEXT OPERATOR;; |..

5;
MULTIPLY: |OPERAND ≠ 0: GENERATE MULTIPLY COMMAND;;
   PRESENT OPERATOR = DIVISION: SET → MULTIPLY DIVIDE FLAG;; |
GENERATE MULTIPLY COMMAND: |PARTIAL WORD FLAG ≠ 0:
     0 → PARTIAL WORD FLAG, SAVE COMMAND, STORE A → FUNCTION CODE,
     LOCATION TEMP STORAGE + 1 → ADDRESS, STORE COMMAND, RESET COMMAND,
     GENERATE LOAD Q COMMAND, LOAD LOG → FUNCTION CODE, STORE COMMAND,
     LOCATION TEMP STORAGE + 1 → ADDRESS; FIND ADDRESS,
     OPERAND[3](12→14) ≠ 0: FL MULT → FUNCTION CODE, EXIT.;;
   MULT INT → FUNCTION CODE, E|XIT: STORE COMMAND|..

5;
PARTIAL WORD CONTROL:
   |SAVE OPERAND, PREVIOUS OPERATOR → PRESENT OPERATOR, FIND OPERATOR,
   PRESENT OPERATOR ≠ ARROW: 12 → FAULT BUFFER, FAULT.;
   OPERAND ≠ NUMBER FLAG: 13 → FAULT BUFFER, FAULT.; OPERAND[1] →
   LOWER WORD LIMIT, PREVIOUS OPERATOR → PRESENT OPERATOR, FIND OPERATOR,
   PRESENT OPERATOR ≠ RIGHT PAREN: 14 → FAULT BUFFER, FAULT.;
   OPERAND ≠ NUMBER FLAG: 15 → FAULT BUFFER, FAULT.;
   OPERAND[1] → UPPER WORD LIMIT, SET → PARTIAL WORD FLAG,
   PREVIOUS OPERATOR → PRESENT OPERATOR, FIND OPERATOR,
   OPERAND ≠ 0: 16 → FAULT BUFFER, FAULT.; RESET OPERAND|
POST LOOP CONTROL: |TRANSFER → FUNCTION CODE,
   BRACE TABLE[BRACE TABLE + 1](0→14) → ADDRESS, STORE COMMAND,
   FILL LOWER HALF WORD, BRACE TABLE[BRACE TABLE + 1](24→38) → 1,
   OBJECT PROGRAM → [1](0→14)|..

5;
PRE LOOP CONTROL: |SAVE LOOP OPERAND, FIND OPERATOR, CHECK SUBSCRIPT,
   GENERATE CLEAR ADD COMMAND, ·

```
E|NTRY 1: FIND OPERATOR, CHECK SUBSCRIPT, PREVIOUS OPERATOR ≠ LEFT PAREN:
     PREVIOUS OPERATOR = MINUS: GENERATE SUBTRACT COMMAND;
          GENERATE ADD COMMAND; ENTRY 1.; 0 → LOOP TYPE FLAG,
     FILL UPPER HALF WORD, TRANSFER → FUNCTION CODE, STORE COMMAND,
     BRACE TABLE + 1 → BRACE TABLE,
     OBJECT PROGRAM → BRACE TABLE[BRACE TABLE],
E|NTRY 2: PRESENT OPERATOR ≠ RIGHT PAREN: PRESENT OPERATOR = MINUS:
          SET → LOOP TYPE FLAG;; FIND OPERATOR, ENTRY 2.; SAVE OPERAND,
     RESET LOOP OPERAND, GENERATE CLEAR ADD COMMAND, RESET OPERAND,
     LOOP TYPE FLAG ≠ 0: GENERATE SUBTRACT COMMAND; GENERATE ADD COMMAND;
     RESET LOOP OPERAND, FILL LOWER HALF WORD, BRACE TABLE[BRACE TABLE] -
     1 → n, OBJECT PROGRAM → [n](0→14), GENERATE STORE COMMAND,
E|NTRY 3: FIND OPERATOR, CHECK SUBSCRIPT, PREVIOUS OPERATOR = MINUS:
          GENERATE ADD COMMAND; GENERATE SUBTRACT COMMAND;
     PRESENT OPERATOR = COMMA: FIND OPERATOR;;
     PRESENT OPERATOR ≠ LEFT BRACE: ENTRY 3.; COMPAR A → FUNCTION CODE,
     LOOP TYPE FLAG ≠ 0: SET DECREMENT TRANSFER; SET INCREMENT TRANSFER;
     OBJECT PROGRAM → BRACE TABLE[BRACE TABLE](24→38), STORE COMMAND|
CHECK SUBSCRIPT: |PRESENT OPERATOR = LEFT BRACKET: SUBSCRIPT;;|..


5;
PRINT DEFINED NAMES: |RESTORE PAGE, SET PRINT BARS TO SPACES,
     ALPHA NAME LIST → BUFFER, 10 → LOW, SET PRINT BARS,
     ALPHA NAME LIST[1] → BUFFER, SET PRINT BARS, PRINT LINE,
     m = 0(1)NAME LIST INDEX |NAME LIST[m] → BUFFER ≠ 0:
          SET PRINT BARS TO SPACES, 8 → LOW, SET PRINT BARS,
          NAME LIST[m+700] → BUFFER ≠ 0: SET PRINT BARS,
               NAME LIST[m+1400] → BUFFER ≠ 0: SET PRINT BARS;;;
          NAME LOCATIONS[m](0→14) → NUMBER BUFFER, 40 → LOW, 44 → HI,
          SET NUMBER PRINT BARS, PRINT LINE;;||
PRINT LINE: |747₈ 61₈, 740₈ 66000₈, 747₈ 66000₈, 100₈ PRINT BAR[120] → [6],
     : 746₈ PRINT BAR, 747₈ 61₈,|
SET PRINT BARS: |1 = LOW+7(-1)LOW |BUFFER(0→5) → PRINT BAR[1],
     BUFFER / 2↑6 → BUFFER| LOW + 8 → LOW|
SET NUMBER PRINT BARS: |1 = HI(-1)LOW |NUMBER BUFFER(0→2) → BUFFER = 0:
     10 → BUFFER;; BUFFER → PRINT BAR[1],
     NUMBER BUFFER / 2↑3 → NUMBER BUFFER||
SET PRINT BARS TO SPACES: |1 = 0(1)119 |16 → PRINT BAR[1]||
RESTORE PAGE: |: 740₈ 66000₈, 747₈ 66000₈, 740₈ 66004₈,|..


5;
PRINT PROGRAM TITLE: |PRESENT OPERATOR ≠ COLON: 17 → FAULT BUFFER, FAULT.;
     OPERAND = 0 ∪ OPERAND = NUMBER FLAG: ALPHA NO TITLE → OPERAND,
     ALL SPACES → OPERAND[1] → OPERAND[2];; SET PRINT BARS TO SPACES,
     PROGRAM COUNT → NUMBER BUFFER, 0 → LOW, 4 → HI, SET DECIMAL PRINT BARS,
     OPERAND → BUFFER, 10 → LOW, SET PRINT BARS,
     OPERAND[1] → BUFFER ≠ 0: SET PRINT BARS, OPERAND[2] → BUFFER ≠ 0:
          SET PRINT BARS;;;; PROGRAM LOCATION → NUMBER BUFFER,
     35 → LOW, 39 → HI, SET NUMBER PRINT BARS, PRINT LINE|
SET DECIMAL PRINT BARS: |OCTAL TO DECIMAL,
     1 = 1(1)LOW-HI+11 |NUMBER BUFFER × 2↑4 → NUMBER BUFFER| 16 → FILL,
     1 = LOW(1)HI |NUMBER BUFFER(44→47) → BUFFER = 0: FILL → BUFFER;
          10 → FILL; BUFFER → PRINT BAR[1], NUMBER BUFFER × 2↑4 → NUMBER BUFFER||
PRINT NAMES DEFINED TWICE:
     |SET PRINT BARS TO SPACES, LOGIC FLAG = 0: PRINT LINE;;
     OPERAND → BUFFER, 4 → LOW, SET PRINT BARS, OPERAND[1] → BUFFER ≠ 0:
          SET PRINT BARS, OPERAND[2] → BUFFER ≠ 0: SET PRINT BARS;;;;
     ALPHA DEFINED TWICE → BUFFER, 30 → LOW, SET PRINT BARS,
     ALPHA DEFINED TWICE[1] → BUFFER, SET PRINT BARS, PRINT LINE|..
```

5;
PRINT UNDEFINED NAMES: |m = 0(1)UNDEFINED NAME INDEX
   |UNDEFINED NAMES[m] ≠ 0: ENTRY.;| EXIT.
E|NTRY: RESTORE PAGE, SET PRINT BARS TO SPACES,`
   ALPHA UNDEFINED NAMES → BUFFER, 10 → LOW, SET PRINT BARS,
   ALPHA UNDEFINED NAMES[1] → BUFFER, SET PRINT BARS, PRINT LINE,
   m = 0(1)UNDEFINED NAME INDEX |SET PRINT BARS TO SPACES,
   UNDEFINED NAMES[m] → BUFFER ≠ 0: 8 → LOW, SET PRINT BARS,
      UNDEFINED NAMES[m+400] → BUFFER ≠ 0: SET PRINT BARS,
         UNDEFINED NAMES[m+800] → BUFFER ≠ 0: SET PRINT BARS;;;;
      UNDEFINED NAME LOCATIONS[m] → LOCATIONS,
      LOCATIONS(45→47) = 6: LOCATIONS(24→38) → NUMBER BUFFER, 40 → LOW,
         44 → HI, SET NUMBER PRINT BARS, LOCATIONS(42→44) ≠ 0:
            ALPHA L → PRINT BAR[45]; ALPHA U → PRINT BAR[45];;;
      LOCATIONS(0→14) → NUMBER BUFFER, 50 → LOW, 54 → HI,
      SET NUMBER PRINT BARS, LOCATIONS(18→20) ≠ 0: ALPHA L →
         PRINT BAR[55]; ALPHA U → PRINT BAR[55]; PRINT LINE;;| E|XIT:|..

5;
PROCESS DECLARATIONS:
   |CLEAR SUB STORAGE, COMMA → OPERATOR → NEXT OPERATOR,
   COMMA 1612 → SYMBOL, FIND OPERATOR, FIND OPERATOR,
   OPERAND = NUMBER FLAG: OPERAND[1] → LOAD NUMBER, FIND OPERATOR;;
E|NTRY 1: PREVIOUS OPERATOR = SEMI COLON: EXIT PROCESS DECLARATIONS.;
   OPERAND = 0 ∪ OPERAND = NUMBER FLAG: FIND OPERATOR, ENTRY 1.;
   DEFINE LOCATION, 1 → RESERVE CELL, FIND OPERATOR,
   PREVIOUS OPERATOR = LEFT PAREN ∩ PRESENT OPERATOR = RIGHT PAREN ∩
   OPERAND = NUMBER FLAG:
      OPERAND[1] → RESERVE CELL, FIND OPERATOR, FIND OPERATOR;;
   PREVIOUS OPERATOR = EQUAL: STORE CONSTANTS;; 0 → COMPUTER WORD,
E|NTRY 2: RESERVE CELL ≥ 1: STORE, RESERVE CELL - 1 → RESERVE CELL,
      ENTRY 2.; PREVIOUS OPERATOR = COMMA: ENTRY 1.;
   PREVIOUS OPERATOR ≠ SEMI COLON: 18 → FAULT BUFFER, FAULT.;
EXIT PROCESS DECLARATIONS:|..

5;
PROCESS LOGIC: |ENTRANCE PROCESS LOGIC:
   LOGIC FLAG = 0: SET → LOGIC FLAG, ENTRY 2.;
E|NTRY 1: END PROGRAM FLAG ≠ 0: EXIT PROCESS LOGIC.; FIND OPERATOR,
E|NTRY 2: PREVIOUS OPERATOR < EQUAL: COMMA < PRESENT OPERATOR <
      LEFT PAREN: LOAD WORKING REGISTER, ENTRY 1.; LEFT BRACE <
      PRESENT OPERATOR < EQUAL: GENERATE TRANSFER, ENTRY 3.;
   PRESENT OPERATOR = COLON: DEFINE LOCATION,
      NEXT OPERATOR = LEFT BRACE: COMPILE SUBROUTINES;; ENTRY 1.;
   PRESENT OPERATOR = LEFT BRACE: GENERATE INPUT OUTPUT, ENTRY 1.;;;
   COMMA < PREVIOUS OPERATOR < ARROW:
      PRESENT OPERATOR = COLON: FINISH COMPARISON, ENTRY 1.;
      COMMA < PRESENT OPERATOR < ARROW: MULTIPLE COMPARISON, ENTRY 1.;;;
   PREVIOUS OPERATOR = ARROW ∩ COLON < PRESENT OPERATOR < LEFT PAREN:
      STORE WORKING REGISTER, ENTRY 1.;
   COMMA < PRESENT OPERATOR < LEFT PAREN:
      PREVIOUS OPERATOR = PLUS: ADDITION, ENTRY 1.;
      PREVIOUS OPERATOR = MINUS: SUBTRACTION, ENTRY 1.;
      PREVIOUS OPERATOR = DIVISION: DIVIDE, ENTRY 1.;
      PREVIOUS OPERATOR = MULTIPLICATION: MULTIPLY, ENTRY 1.;;;
   PRESENT OPERATOR = LEFT BRACKET: SUBSCRIPT, ENTRY 2.;
   PRESENT OPERATOR = LEFT PAREN: PARTIAL WORD CONTROL, ENTRY 2.;
   PRESENT OPERATOR = UP ARROW: EXPONENT, ENTRY 1.;
      23 → FAULT BUFFER, FAULT.

E|NTRY 3:
    PRESENT OPERATOR = PERIOD ∪ PRESENT OPERATOR = SEMI COLON:
        COMPARE TABLE ≥ 1: 3 → COMPARE FLAG, UPGRADE COMPARISONS;;;
    PRESENT OPERATOR = RIGHT BRACE: DOWNGRADE BRACE TABLE;;; ENTRY 1.
EXIT PROCESS LOGIC: BRACE TABLE ≠ 0: 24 → FAULT BUFFER, FAULT.;|..

5;
READ MAG TAPE: |PAGE NUMBER > NUMBER OF PAGES: 3 → FAULT BUFFER, FAULT.;
    PAGE NUMBER + 1 → PAGE NUMBER, MAG TAPE INPUT FLAG ≠ 0: ENTRY 2.;
    1 → MAG TAPE INPUT FLAG, 0 → MAG TAPE INDEX, 660 → LAST MAG TAPE INDEX,
E|NTRY 1: WAIT TO READ MAG TAPE, L|ENGTH CHECK 1: 747_8 32005_8 READ ERROR 1.
P|ARITY CHECK 1: 747_8 32003_8 READ ERROR 1. READ PART 2, EXIT.
R|EAD ERROR 1: POSITION BACK READ, READ PART 1, ENTRY 1.
R|EAD ERROR 2: POSITION BACK READ, READ PART 2,
E|NTRY 2: 0 → MAG TAPE INPUT FLAG, 660 → MAG TAPE INDEX,
    1320 → LAST MAG TAPE INDEX, WAIT TO READ MAG TAPE,
L|ENGTH CHECK 2: 747_8 32005_8 READ ERROR 2.
P|ARITY CHECK 2: 747_8 32003_8 READ ERROR 2. READ PART 1, E|XIT:|
WAIT TO READ MAG TAPE: |747_8 32000_8,| POSITION BACK READ: |740_8 32006_8,|
READ PART 1: |747_8 32000_8, 100_8 MAG TAPE AREA[660] → [3],
    743_8 MAG TAPE AREA,|
READ PART 2: |747_8 32000_8, 100_8 MAG TAPE AREA[1320] → [3],
    743_8 MAG TAPE AREA[660],|
ACTIVATE READ MAG TAPE 3: |740_8 32031_8,| REWIND READ TAPE: |740_8 32005_8,|..

5;
RESERVE COMPILER STORAGE: |SAVE OPERAND, CLEAR OPERAND,
    OBJECT PROGRAM → LOCATION TEMP STORAGE, 0 → COMPUTER WORD, STORE, STORE,
    n = 0(1)5 |INDEX NAMES[n] → OPERAND, DEFINE LOCATION, STORE|
    OBJECT PROGRAM → [FIRST LOCATION](24→38),
    n = 0(1)5 |ST INXLo → FUNCTION CODE, n + 1 → DESIGNATOR,
    INDEX NAMES[n] → OPERAND, FIND ADDRESS, STORE COMMAND| RESET OPERAND|
CLEAR TEMPORARY NAMES:
    |m = 0(1)NAME LIST INDEX |NAME LOCATIONS[m](18→20) ≠ 0:
        0 → NAME LIST[m] → NAME LIST[m+700] →
        NAME LIST[m+1400] → NAME LOCATIONS[m];;||
CLEAR ALL STORAGE: |m = 1(1)MASTER STORAGE |0 → MASTER STORAGE[m]|
    CLEAR SUB STORAGE|
CLEAR SUB STORAGE: |m = 1(1)SUB STORAGE |0 → SUB STORAGE[m]|
    m = 1(1)FLAG STORAGE |0 → FLAG STORAGE[m]||
CLEAR OPERAND: |0 → OPERAND → OPERAND[1] → OPERAND[2] → OPERAND[3]|..

5;
SET DECREMENT TRANSFER: |FILL UPPER HALF WORD, 3 → DESIGNATOR|
SET INCREMENT TRANSFER: |FILL LOWER HALF WORD, 0 → DESIGNATOR,
    OBJECT PROGRAM + 1 → ADDRESS, STORE COMMAND, COMPAR A →
    FUNCTION CODE, 2 → DESIGNATOR|
SAVE LOOP OPERAND: |OPERAND → LOOP OPERAND, OPERAND[1] → LOOP OPERAND[1],
OPERAND[2] → LOOP OPERAND[2], OPERAND[3] → LOOP OPERAND[3]|
RESET LOOP OPERAND: |LOOP OPERAND → OPERAND, LOOP OPERAND[1] → OPERAND[1],
LOOP OPERAND[2] → OPERAND[2], LOOP OPERAND[3] → OPERAND[3]|
GENERATE LOAD INDEX: |SAVE COMMAND, LD INXLo → FUNCTION CODE, FIND ADDRESS,
    6 → DESIGNATOR, STORE COMMAND, RESET COMMAND, 6 → DESIGNATOR|..

5;
SET FALSE COMPARISON: |COMPAR A → FUNCTION CODE,
PREVIOUS OPERATOR = EQUAL: 1 → DESIGNATOR, EXIT.; PREVIOUS OPERATOR =
    NOT EQUAL: EXIT.; PREVIOUS OPERATOR = GREATER:
        5 → COMPARE FLAG, 3 → DESIGNATOR, UPGRADE COMPARISONS,

```
            COMPAR A → FUNCTION CODE, 0 → DESIGNATOR, EXIT.;
        PREVIOUS OPERATOR = GREATER OR EQUAL: 3 → DESIGNATOR, EXIT.;
        PREVIOUS OPERATOR = LESS THAN: 2 → DESIGNATOR, EXIT.;
        PREVIOUS OPERATOR = LESS OR EQUAL: FILL LOWER HALF WORD,
            OBJECT PROGRAM + 1 → ADDRESS, STORE COMMAND,
            COMPAR A → FUNCTION CODE, 2 → DESIGNATOR;;
E|XIT: 5 → COMPARE FLAG|..


5;
SET TRUE COMPARISON:
    |COMPAR A → FUNCTION CODE, PREVIOUS OPERATOR = EQUAL: EXIT.;
        PREVIOUS OPERATOR = NOT EQUAL: 1 → DESIGNATOR, EXIT.;
        PREVIOUS OPERATOR = GREATER: FILL LOWER HALF WORD,
            OBJECT PROGRAM + 1 → ADDRESS, STORE COMMAND,
            COMPAR A → FUNCTION CODE, 2 → DESIGNATOR, EXIT.;
        PREVIOUS OPERATOR = GREATER OR EQUAL: 2 → DESIGNATOR, EXIT.;
        PREVIOUS OPERATOR = LESS THAN: 3 → DESIGNATOR, EXIT.;
        PREVIOUS OPERATOR = LESS OR EQUAL: 7 → COMPARE FLAG, 3 → DESIGNATOR,
            UPGRADE COMPARISONS, COMPAR A → FUNCTION CODE, 0 → DESIGNATOR;;
E|XIT: 7 → COMPARE FLAG|..


5;
SET UP INITIAL CONDITIONS: |ACTIVATE READ MAG TAPE 3,
E|NTRY 1: WAIT TO READ MAG TAPE, REWIND READ TAPE, CLEAR ALL STORAGE,
    READ PART 1, L → BLOCK NUMBER = 0 ∪ BLOCK NUMBER = 1: ; 1 → COUNT,
    E|NTRY 2: READ MAG TAPE, MAG TAPE AREA[MAG TAPE INDEX]' →
        NUMBER OF PAGES = END TAPE FLAG: 0 → L, ENTRY 1.;
        0 → PAGE NUMBER, n = 1(1)NUMBER OF PAGES |READ MAG TAPE|
        COUNT + 1 → COUNT < BLOCK NUMBER: ENTRY 2.;
        0 → COUNT → MAG TAPE INPUT FLAG → PAGE NUMBER,
        WAIT TO READ MAG TAPE, POSITION BACK READ, READ PART 1;
    READ MAG TAPE, MAG TAPE AREA → NUMBER OF PAGES, ALL SPACES →
    MAG TAPE AREA, PRINT ID PAGE, n = 1(1)6 |MAG TAPE AREA[302](42→47) →
    SYMBOL = SPACE ∪ SYMBOL = 10: 0 → SYMBOL;;
    NUMBER OF PROGRAMS × 10 + SYMBOL → NUMBER OF PROGRAMS,
    MAG TAPE AREA[302] × 2↑6 → MAG TAPE AREA[302],
    MAG TAPE AREA[322](42→47) → SYMBOL = SPACE ∪ SYMBOL = 10: 0 → SYMBOL;;
    FIRST LOCATION × 2↑3 + SYMBOL → FIRST LOCATION,
    MAG TAPE AREA[322] × 2↑6 → MAG TAPE AREA[322]|
    FIRST LOCATION → OBJECT PROGRAM → PROGRAM LOCATION, RESTORE PAGE,
    READ MAG TAPE, MAG TAPE AREA[MAG TAPE INDEX] → SYMBOL BUFFER|..


5;
STORE COMMAND: |FUNCTION CODE → COMMAND(18→23),
    DESIGNATOR → COMMAND(15→17), ADDRESS + INCREMENT → COMMAND(0→14),
    HALF WORD FLAG = 0:
        1 → HALF WORD FLAG, COMMAND → COMPUTER WORD(24→47);
        0 → HALF WORD FLAG, COMMAND → COMPUTER WORD(0→23), STORE;
    0 → FUNCTION CODE → DESIGNATOR → ADDRESS → INCREMENT|
STORE: |COMPUTER WORD → [OBJECT PROGRAM], OBJECT PROGRAM + 1 →
    OBJECT PROGRAM, FIRST COMPILER LOCATION < OBJECT PROGRAM <
    LAST COMPILER LOCATION: 2 → FAULT BUFFER, FAULT.;|
OCTAL TO DECIMAL: |0 → BUFFER, INDEX = 1(1)12 |BUFFER / 2↑4 → BUFFER,
    NUMBER BUFFER / 10 → DECIMAL BUFFER, - DECIMAL BUFFER × 10 +
    NUMBER BUFFER → BUFFER(44→47), DECIMAL BUFFER → NUMBER BUFFER|
    BUFFER → NUMBER BUFFER|..


5;
STORE CONSTANTS: |PRESENT OPERATOR ≠ LEFT BRACE: ENTRY 2.; FIND OPERATOR,
```

```
        OPERAND = 0 ∪ PRESENT OPERATOR ≠ RIGHT BRACE: 20 → FAULT BUFFER, FAULT.;
        OPERAND ≠ NUMBER FLAG: 1 → HALF WORD FLAG, FIND ADDRESS,
            ADDRESS → COMPUTER WORD, STORE, 0 → HALF WORD FLAG → ADDRESS;
            OPERAND[1] → NAME LOCATIONS[LAST NAME INDEX]; FIND OPERATOR, ENTRY 3.
  E|NTRY 1: FIND OPERATOR, E|NTRY 2: PREVIOUS OPERATOR ≠ SEMI COLON:
        PRESENT OPERATOR = MINUS: SET → MINUS FLAG, ENTRY 1.;
        PRESENT OPERATOR = PLUS ∪ PRESENT OPERATOR = PERIOD: ENTRY 1.;
        OPERAND = NUMBER FLAG ∪ OPERAND = 0: MINUS FLAG ≠ 0:
            0 → MINUS FLAG, -OPERAND[1] → COMPUTER WORD; OPERAND[1] →
            COMPUTER WORD; STORE, OPERAND[2] →
        NAME LOCATIONS[LAST NAME INDEX](24→38),
      E|NTRY 3: RESERVE CELL ≥ 1: RESERVE CELL - 1 → RESERVE CELL;;
        ENTRY 1.;;;|..
```

```
5;
STORE WORKING REGISTER:
   |ADD INCOMPLETE VALUE, OPERAND ≠ 0: GENERATE STORE COMMAND;;|
GENERATE STORE COMMAND: |PARTIAL WORD FLAG = 0: ENTRY.; SAVE COMMAND,
   COMMA < PRESENT OPERATOR < LEFT PAREN ∩ DOUBLE STORAGE FLAG = 0:
        STORE A → FUNCTION CODE, LOCATION TEMP STORAGE + 1 →
        ADDRESS, STORE COMMAND;; DOUBLE STORAGE FLAG ≠ 0 ∩ LOWER WORD LIMIT =
   LAST LOWER WORD ∩ UPPER WORD LIMIT = LAST UPPER WORD: ;.
   LOWER WORD LIMIT ≠ 0: SHFT ALF → FUNCTION CODE, LOWER WORD LIMIT →
        ADDRESS, STORE COMMAND;; FIND MASK,
        m = 1(1)LOWER WORD LIMIT |NUMBER BUFFER × 2↑1 → NUMBER BUFFER|
        - NUMBER BUFFER → NUMBER BUFFER, LOAD Q → FUNCTION CODE,
   FIND NUMBER ADDRESS, STORE COMMAND; RESET COMMAND, SEL REPL →
   FUNCTION CODE, FIND ADDRESS, STORE COMMAND, RESET COMMAND,
E|NTRY: STORE A → FUNCTION CODE, FIND ADDRESS, STORE COMMAND,
   OPERAND(0→41) = SEVEN SPACES: OPERAND(42→47) - 31 → DESIGNATOR = 26:
        1 → DESIGNATOR;; 0 < DESIGNATOR < 6: LD INXLo → FUNCTION CODE,
        FIND ADDRESS, STORE COMMAND; 0 → DESIGNATOR;;;
   PARTIAL WORD FLAG ≠ 0: 0 → PARTIAL WORD FLAG, COLON < PRESENT OPERATOR <
   EQUAL: ; CL ADD → FUNCTION CODE,
        LOCATION TEMP STORAGE + 1 → ADDRESS, STORE COMMAND;;;
   PREVIOUS OPERATOR = ARROW ∩ PRESENT OPERATOR = ARROW:
        SET → DOUBLE STORAGE FLAG, LOWER WORD LIMIT → LAST LOWER WORD,
        UPPER WORD LIMIT → LAST UPPER WORD; 0 → DOUBLE STORAGE FLAG;|..
```

```
5;
SUBSCRIPT: |SAVE OPERAND, 0 → INCREMENT SIGN, PREVIOUS OPERATOR →
   PRESENT OPERATOR, FIND OPERATOR, OPERAND ≠ 0: ENTRY 2.;
E|NTRY 1: PRESENT OPERATOR = MINUS: SET → INCREMENT SIGN;
   PRESENT OPERATOR ≠ PLUS: ENTRY 2.;;
   PREVIOUS OPERATOR → PRESENT OPERATOR, FIND OPERATOR,
E|NTRY 2: OPERAND = NUMBER FLAG: INCREMENT SIGN ≠ 0:
        - OPERAND[1] → INCREMENT; OPERAND[1] → INCREMENT;
        PRESENT OPERATOR ≠ RIGHT BRACKET: 21 → FAULT BUFFER, FAULT.;;
        OPERAND(0→41) = SEVEN SPACES:
            OPERAND(42→47) - 31 → DESIGNATOR; 100 → DESIGNATOR;
        DESIGNATOR = 26: 1 → DESIGNATOR;
        0 < DESIGNATOR < 6: ; GENERATE LOAD INDEX;
        PRESENT OPERATOR ≠ RIGHT BRACKET: ENTRY 1.;;
   PREVIOUS OPERATOR → PRESENT OPERATOR, FIND OPERATOR,
   OPERAND ≠ 0: 22 → FAULT BUFFER, FAULT.; RESET OPERAND,
   OPERAND = 0: SET → OPERAND;;|..
```

```
5;
SUBTRACTION: |OPERAND ≠ 0: CLEAR SUBTRACT FLAG ≠ 0:
```

```
           0 → CLEAR SUBTRACT FLAG, GENERATE CLEAR SUBTRACT COMMAND;
           PRESENT OPERATOR = MULTIPLICATION ∪ PRESENT OPERATOR = DIVISION:
              STORE INCOMPLETE VALUE, GENERATE CLEAR SUBTRACT COMMAND;
           GENERATE SUBTRACT COMMAND;;;;|
GENERATE CLEAR SUBTRACT COMMAND: |PARTIAL WORD FLAG ≠ 0:
        0 → PARTIAL WORD FLAG, ENTER A → FUNCTION CODE, STORE COMMAND,
        GENERATE LOAD Q COMMAND, SUBT LOG → FUNCTION CODE;
        CL SUBT → FUNCTION CODE, FIND ADDRESS; STORE COMMAND|
GENERATE SUBTRACT COMMAND: |PARTIAL WORD FLAG ≠ 0: 0 → PARTIAL WORD FLAG,
        GENERATE LOAD Q COMMAND, SUBT LOG → FUNCTION CODE; FIND ADDRESS,
        OPERAND[3](12→14) ≠ 0: FL SUBT → FUNCTION CODE; SUBTRACT →
           FUNCTION CODE;; STORE COMMAND|..


5;
UPGRADE COMPARISONS: |E|NTRY 1: FIND COMPARE WORD,
    COMPARE WORD(15→17) = 7: ENTRY 3.; COMPARE WORD(15→17) = 5: ENTRY 5.;
    COMPARE WORD(15→17) = 3: ENTRY 7.; 0 → COMPARE WORD(18→23),
E|NTRY 2:
    COMPARE FLAG → COMPARE WORD(15→17), OBJECT PROGRAM → COMPARE WORD(0→14),
    STORE COMPARE WORD, FILL UPPER HALF WORD, STORE COMMAND, EXIT.
E|NTRY 3: COMPARE FLAG = 5: ENTRY 6.;
E|NTRY 4: INCREASE COMPARE SUB INDEX, ENTRY 2.
E|NTRY 5:
    COMPARE FLAG ≠ 3: ENTRY 4.; TRANSFER → FUNCTION CODE, 0 → DESIGNATOR,
E|NTRY 6: COMPARE WORD(0→14) → L, OBJECT PROGRAM + 1 → [L](0→14),
    DECREASE COMPARE SUB INDEX, ENTRY 1.
E|NTRY 7: FILL LOWER HALF WORD, COMPARE WORD(0→14) → L,
    OBJECT PROGRAM → [L](0→14), 0 → COMPARE TABLE[k], COMPARE TABLE - 1 →
    COMPARE TABLE, E|XIT:|..


5;
PRINT PROGRAM: |FIRST LOCATION → LOCATIONS,
E|NTRY 1: 1 = LOCATIONS(1)LOCATIONS+191 |[1] ≠ 0: ENTRY 3.;|
E|NTRY 2:
    LOCATIONS ≥ LAST LOCATION: EXIT.; LOCATIONS + 192 → LOCATIONS, ENTRY 1.
E|NTRY 3: RESTORE PAGE, SET PRINT BARS TO SPACES, PRINT LINE,
    PRINT LOCATION = LOCATIONS(8)LOCATIONS+47 |
    ADDRESS = PRINT LOCATION(1)PRINT LOCATION+7 |0 → j,
    1 = ADDRESS(48)ADDRESS+191 |[1] → BUFFER[j], j + 1 → j|
    ADDRESS → OBJECT PROGRAM, SET PRINT BARS TO SPACES, 0 → j,
    k = 0(1)3 |16 → SYMBOL BUFFER, n = 1(1)2 |n = 1:
        ADDRESS = PRINT LOCATION: OBJECT PROGRAM → NUMBER BUFFER,
            1 = j(1)j+4 |NUMBER BUFFER(12→14) → SYMBOL = 0: 10 → SYMBOL;;
            SYMBOL → PRINT BAR[1], NUMBER BUFFER × 2↑3 → NUMBER BUFFER|;
            OBJECT PROGRAM(0→2) → SYMBOL = 0: 10 → SYMBOL;; SYMBOL →
            PRINT BAR[j+4];;; 1 = j+7(1)j+9 |BUFFER[k](45→47) → SYMBOL = 0:
        SYMBOL BUFFER → SYMBOL; 10 → SYMBOL BUFFER; SYMBOL → PRINT BAR[1],
    BUFFER[k] × 2↑3 → BUFFER[k]| 1 = j+11(1)j+15 |BUFFER[k](45→47) →
    SYMBOL = 0: SYMBOL BUFFER → SYMBOL; 10 → SYMBOL BUFFER;
    SYMBOL → PRINT BAR[1], BUFFER[k] × 2↑3 → BUFFER[k]| j + 11 → j|
    j + 9 → j, OBJECT PROGRAM + 48 → OBJECT PROGRAM| PRINT LINE|
    SET PRINT BARS TO SPACES, PRINT LINE, PRINT LINE| ENTRY 2. e|XIT:|..


5;
PRINT ID PAGE:
    |RESTORE PAGE, SET PRINT BARS TO SPACES, n = 40(10)659 |0 → INDEX,
    1 = n(1)n+9 |MAG TAPE AREA[1] → BUFFER,
    SYMBOL COUNT = 1(1)8 |BUFFER(42→47) → PRINT BAR[INDEX],
    BUFFER × 2↑6 → BUFFER, INDEX + 1 → INDEX|| PRINT LINE||
```

PRINT LAST PROGRAM LOCATION: |SET PRINT BARS TO SPACES, 10 → LOW,
    J = 0(1)2 |ALPHA LAST PROGRAM LOCATION[J] → BUFFER, SET PRINT BARS|
    OBJECT PROGRAM → PROGRAM LOCATION - 1 → NUMBER BUFFER → LAST LOCATION,
    35 → LOW, 39 → HI, SET NUMBER PRINT BARS, PRINT LINE|..

5;
GENERATE INPUT OUTPUT: |FIND OPERATOR, PRESENT OPERATOR = LESS THAN:
        GENERATE OUTPUT; GENERATE INPUT;|
GENERATE INPUT:
    |OPERAND = FLEX 1 ∪ OPERAND = FLEX 8: GENERATE FLEX INPUT;
    OPERAND = CARD: GENERATE CARD INPUT; GENERATE MT INPUT;;|
GENERATE FLEX INPUT: |FIND OPERATOR, FILL UPPER HALF WORD,
    747₈ 11₈, → [OBJECT PROGRAM](0→23), OBJECT PROGRAM + 1 → OBJECT PROGRAM,
    OPERAND = FLEX 8:
        GENERATE FLEX WORD INPUT. GENERATE FLEX FRAME INPUT.
GENERATE FLEX WORD INPUT: OBJECT PROGRAM → 1, INPUT CODE + 1 + 11 → [1],
    1 + 1 → 1, INPUT CODE[1] + 1 + 2 → [1], 1 + 1 → 1,
    INPUT CODE[2] + FACTOR × 1 + FACTOR × 10 → [1], 1 + 1 → 1,
    1 + 8 → LIMIT, For 1 = 1(1)LIMIT |0 → [1]| INPUT CODE[3] + FACTOR ×
    1 - FACTOR → [1], 1 + 1 → 1, INPUT CODE[4] → [1], 1 + 1 → 1,
    INPUT CODE[5] + 1 - 11 → [1], 1 + 1 → 1,
    INPUT CODE[6] + 1 - 1 → [1], 1 + 1 → OBJECT PROGRAM, FIND ADDRESS,
    INPUT CODE[7] + FACTOR × OBJECT PROGRAM - FACTOR × 5 + ADDRESS →
    [OBJECT PROGRAM], OBJECT PROGRAM + 1 → OBJECT PROGRAM,
EXIT FLEX INPUT:
    PRESENT OPERATOR ≠ LESS THAN: 99 1 → FAULT BUFFER, FAULT.; FIND OPERATOR,
    PRESENT OPERATOR ≠ RIGHT BRACE: 99 2 → FAULT BUFFER, FAULT.;
    0 → HALF WORD FLAG, COMMA → PRESENT OPERATOR|..

5
CARD = 51 49 41 52 20 20 20 20₈, FLEX 1 = 66 43 65 27 20 01 20 20₈,
FLEX 8 = 66 43 65 27 20 10 20 20₈,
INPUT CODE(8) = 740 11200   100 00000₈, 200 00001 741 00000₈,
    750 00000   500 00000₈, 571 00000 747 00011₈, 040 00077 501 00000₈,
    050 00006 431 00000₈, 541 00007 750 00000₈, 531 00000   200 00000₈,
FACTOR = 100000000₈, LIMIT;
GENERATE OUTPUT: |99 3 → FAULT BUFFER, FAULT.|
GENERATE MT INPUT: |99 4 → FAULT BUFFER, FAULT.|
GENERATE CARD INPUT: |99 5 → FAULT BUFFER, FAULT.|
GENERATE FLEX FRAME INPUT:
    FIND ADDRESS, INPUT CODE + ADDRESS + 1 → [OBJECT PROGRAM],
    OBJECT PROGRAM + 1 → OBJECT PROGRAM, FIND ADDRESS,
    INPUT CODE[1] + ADDRESS → [OBJECT PROGRAM],
    OBJECT PROGRAM + 1 → OBJECT PROGRAM, EXIT FLEX INPUT..

D-NELIAC C

The Donnelly Decompiler shown in this Appendix has been taken primarily from the Navy Electronics Laboratory *Technical Memorandum No. 427*, Sept., 1960, entitled, "A Decompiler for the Countess Computer," by J. K. Donnelly. It is presented here primarily to demonstrate the approach and the feasibility of the concepts involved, rather than the techniques employed. It serves to "Close the Loop," thereby showing that the Neliac dialect of Algol may perhaps be capable of serving not only as a problem-oriented language, or POL, but perhaps also as a Universal Computer Oriented Language, or UNCOL.

Table XIII contains the complete repertoire of machine instructions for the computer involved, in order that the process followed by the D-Neliac program can be followed.

In the Countess computer, the various parts of an instruction word can be described in the following Neliac noun definition.

Instruction Word: {Function Code(24 → 29), FF(24 → 29),
 Branch Designator(21 → 23), J(21 → 23),
 Operand interpretor(18 → 20), K(18 → 20),
 Index designator(15 → 17), B(15 → 17),
 Operand Address(0 → 14), yyyyy(0 → 14),},

TABLE XIII

MACHINE LANGUAGE INSTRUCTION REPERTOIRE OF THE
UNIVAC M-460 COUNTESS COMPUTER

FF	Function	FF	Function
00	Illegal	40	Enter logical product
01	Shift Q right	41	Add logical product
02	Shift A right	42	Subtract logical product
03	Shift AQ right	43	Mask comparison
04	Compare	44	Replace logical product
05	Shift Q left	45	Replace add logical product
06	Shift A left	46	Replace subtract logical product
07	Shift AQ left	47	Store logical product
10	Enter Q register	50	Selective set
11	Enter accumulator	51	Selective complement
12	Enter B register	52	Selective clear
13	Enter C register	53	Substitute
14	Store Q register	54	Replace selective set ˙
15	Store accumulator	55	Replace selective complement
16	Store B register	56	Replace selective clear
17	Store C register	57	Replace substitute
20	Add	60	Arithmetic jump
21	Subtract	61	Manual jump
22	Multiply	62	Input jump
23	Divide	63	Output jump
24	Add replace	64	Arithmetic return jump
25	Subtract replace	65	Manual return jump
26	Q add	66	Input return jump
27	Q subtract	67	Output return jump
30	Load A add Q	70	Initiate repeat
31	Load A subtract Q	71	Index skip
32	Add Q and store	72	Index jump
33	Subtract Q and store	73	Initiate input transfer
34	Replace add Q	74	Initiate output transfer
35	Replace subtract Q	75	Initiate input buffer
36	Replace add one	76	Initiate output buffer
37	Replace subtract one	77	Illegal.

5
INSTRUCTION: | ff($24 \to 29$), ffj($21 \to 29$), jj($21 \to 23$), kk($18 \to 20$),
bb($15 \to 17$), yy($0 \to 14$), |(750), INSTRUCTION FLAG:
| indicator($24 \to 29$), loop j desig($21 \to 23$), scan flag($15 \to 17$),
loop final value($9 \to 14$), loop index($0 \to 8$), |(750),
symbol string(1500), a store, q store, save index, skip flag, paren index,
next index, end loop index, a flag, q flag, zero flag, upper case flag,
a store used, q store used, paren counter, input ready, output ready,
condition, workspace, storage, store index, ts(10), UNTOUCHABLES:
first address, entrance, exit index, last address, max index,
NAME LIST 1: | first letter($0 \to 5$), second letter($6 \to 11$), |(200),
NAME LIST 2: | name k desig($18 \to 20$), mult name flag($15 \to 17$),
name address($0 \to 14$), |(200), name list index, jump index,
subroutine index, ts index, data index, m store, n store, k store,
sequence number, sub name index, subroutine address(50),
letter(26) = 1, 2, 3, 4, 5, 6, 7, 10_8, 11_8, 12_8, 13_8, 14_8, 15_8, 16_8,
17_8, 20_8, 21_8, 22_8, 23_8, 24_8, 25_8, 26_8, 27_8, 30_8, 31_8, 32_8,
number(10) = 33_8, 34_8, 35_8, 36_8, 37_8, 40_8, 41_8, 42_8, 43_8, 44_8;
DIMN STATEMENT: . .

5
addr sym str = | symbol string |, ds index;
COMMAND EXEC: CE3: name program,
i = entrance(1)exit index| max index < i: 10 $\to$ k, error; ;
test masking, test entry or loop, ff[i] = 10_8: test sub q; ;
test io, translate instruction, test conditional skip, ce4: |,
CE5: subroutine index $\neq$ 0: | generate exit jump,
    return address[2] $\to$ return address[0],
    C|E55: generate subroutine, subroutine index $\neq$ 0: ce55. ;
    generate exit, |; double period, stop code;
CE6: store index + 5 $\to$ store index $\to$ ds index, store dimensioning statement,
start punch, leader, ds index + addr sym str $\to$ j, 0 $\to$ condition,
dump dimensioning statement, addr sym str $\to$ j, set $\to$ condition,
dump flowchart, leader, stop punch, 61400_8dump name list. .

5;
STORE(p): | k $\to$ store($15 \to 29$), m $\to$ ts[9], store index $\to$ k,
0 $\to$ zero flag, p = 0: end store. ;
P|ASS ZERO: p($24 \to 29$) = 0: zero flag + 1 $\to$ zero flag, p × $2\uparrow6 \to$ p,
pass zero. ; 5 - zero flag $\to$ zero flag,
m = 1(1)zero flag| d|ecode: symbol string[k]($24 \to 29$) = 0:
    symbol string[k] × $2\uparrow6 \to$ symbol string[k], p($24 \to 29$) $\to$
    symbol string[k]($0 \to 5$), p × $2\uparrow6 \to$ p, 0 $\to$ p($0 \to 5$); k + 1 $\to$ k, decode.
E|ND STORE: k $\to$ store index, store($15 \to 29$) $\to$ k, ts[9] $\to$ m, |
UPPER CASE: |, | LOWER CASE:|, | CRUTCH CODE: | store(45_8), |
EXPONENT SIGN: | store(77_8), | GREATER SIGN: | store(65_8), |
LESS EQUAL SIGN: | store(64_8), | LEFT BRACE: | store(56_8), |
RIGHT BRACE: | store(57_8), | LEFT BRACKET: | store(54_8), |
RIGHT BRACKET: | store(55_8), | GREATER EQUAL SIGN: | store(62_8), |
LESS SIGN: | store(63_8), | BOOLEAN AND: | store(76_8), |
BOOLEAN OR: | store(75_8), | CARRET: | store(74_8), | STOPCODE: |, | SPACE: |, |
PERIOD: | store(50_8), | DOUBLE PERIOD: | store(5050_8), |
RIGHT PAREN: | store(53_8), | LEFT PAREN: | store(52_8), |
PLUS: | store(67_8), | MINUS: | store(70_8), |
MULTIPLY SIGN: | store(72_8), | DIVIDE SIGN: | store(71_8), |
EQUAL SIGN: | store(60_8), | NOT EQUAL SIGN: | store(61_8), |
ARROW: | store(66_8), | OCTAL SIGN: | store(45_8), |
COMMA: | store(46_8), | SEMICOLON: | store(47_8), | COLON: | store(51_8), |. .

5
word a store(2) = 30042401_8, 031220_8, word q store(2) = 35042401_8, 031220_8,
word name list dump(3) = 0630072004_8, 1114240104_8, 2234075545_8;
PRINT(p): | m → print(15 → 29), m = 1(1)5| p × $2\uparrow6$ → p,
p(0 → 5) ≠ 0: 13130_8p; ;
P|RINT DELAY: 62100_8print delay. |, print(15 → 29) → m, |
PRINT UPPER CASE: | upper case flag ≠ 1:
    print(47_8), 1 → upper case flag, ; |
PRINT LOWER CASE: | upper case flag ≠ 0:
    print(57_8), 0 → upper case flag; ; |
PRINT CARRET: | print(45_8), | PRINT SPACE: | print(04_8), |
PRINT EQUAL SIGN: | print upper case, print(7004_8), |
PRINT OCTAL SIGN: | print lower case, print(76_8), |
PRINT COMMA: | print upper case, print(46_8), |
PRINT SEMICOLON: | print lower case, print(44_8), |
START FLEX: | stop punch, $17040_8$0, $13100_8$0, $17100_8$0, 50000_8163_8,
$13300_8$0, $13070_8$0, 70000_8100_8, 13300_810026_8, $13300_8$0, 70000_810000_8,
13300_81001_8, $13300_8$0, 70000_8100_8, 13300_810012_8, $13300_8$0,
1 → output ready, |
STOP FLEX: | $17040_8$0, 52000_83, 50000_8160_8, $13300_8$0, $13070_8$0, 70000_810000_8,
13300_810014_8, $13300_8$0, 70000_8100_8, 13300_810016_8, $13300_8$0, 0 →
output ready, |
START PUNCH: | stop flex, $17040_8$0, $17100_8$0, 50000_8163_8, $13300_8$0, $13070_8$0,
70000_8100_8, 13300_810016_8, $13300_8$0, 70000_810000_8, 13300_810023_8, $13300_8$0,
70000_8100_8, 13300_810022_8, $13300_8$0, 1 → output ready, |
STOP PUNCH: | $17040_8$0, 52000_83, 50000_8160_8, $13300_8$0, $13070_8$0, 70000_810000_8,
13300_810024_8, $13300_8$0, 70000_8100_8, 13300_810026_8, $13300_8$0,
0 → output ready, |
LEADER: | n = 150(1)0| $13100_8$0, L|EADER DELAY: 62100_8leader delay. |, |. .

5
p|r list = | read 0, read 1, read 2, read 3, read 4, read 5, read 6,
read 7, store 0, store 1, store 2, store 3, store 4, store 5, store 6,
store 7, |;
PROCESS NAME(arith, class): | 0 → ts → save name index,
class = 1: 8_8 → class, ; arith ≠ 0: 10_8 → ts → ts; ;
bb[1] ≠ 0: 4 → ts → ts; ; yy[1] ≠ 0: 2 → ts → ts; ;
scan flag[1] = 4: 1 → ts → ts; ; kk[1] + class → n, 12 → k, pr list[n], |
R|EAD 0: R|EAD 4: ts = 0 ∪ ts = 8: zero;
ts = 1 ∪ ts = 3 ∪ ts = 9 ∪ ts = 11: n2; ts = 2 ∪ ts = 10: n3;
ts = 4 ∪ ts = 12: n4; ts = 5 ∪ ts = 7: n2, plus, n4; ts = 6: n3, plus, n4;
ts = 13 ∪ ts = 15: left paren, n2, plus, n4, right paren;
ts = 14: left paren, n3, plus, n4, right paren; ; ; ; ; ; ; |
R|EAD 1: | read 123, n7, | R|EAD 2: | read 123, n8, |
R|EAD 3: R|EAD 123: | 0 → ts(3 → 3),
ts = 1 ∪ ts = 3: left bracket, n2, right bracket; ;
ts = 5 ∪ ts = 7: left bracket, n2, plus, n4, right bracket; ;
ts = 0 ∪ ts = 2: n5; ts = 4: first address = 0: n5; n6; ;
ts = 6: yy[1] < first address ∩ yy[1] < 10: n9; n5, n6; ; ; ; |
R|EAD 5: | read 1, extend sign, | R|EAD 6: | read 2, extend sign, |
R|EAD 7: | ts ≥ 12: left paren; ; find a operand, |
3 < ts < 8: plus, n4; ; ts ≥ 12: plus, n4, right paren; ; |
S|TORE 0: | rf[1] = 14_8: n10, space, 2 → q flag;
    test a interrupt, ts ≥ 10_8: 6 → q flag; 3 → q flag; ; 77_8 → condition, |
S|TORE 1: | store 123, n7, |. S|TORE 2: | store 123, n8, |.
S|TORE 3: S|TORE 123: | 0 → ts(3 → 3),
ts = 5 ∪ ts = 7: left bracket, n2, plus, n4, right bracket; ;
ts = 0 ∪ ts = 2: n5; ts = 1 ∪ ts = 3: left bracket, n2, right bracket;
ts = 4: first address = 0: n5; n6; ;

```
ts = 6: yy[1] < first address ∩ yy[1] < 10: n9; n5, n6; ; ; ; ; ;  |
S|TORE 4: |  ff[1] = 15ₐ: n10, 2 → a flag;
     test q interrupt, ts ≥ 10ₐ: 6 → a flag; 3 → a flag; ; 77ₐ → condition,  |
S|TORE 5: | n10, n7, arrow, store 1, |
S|TORE 6: | n10, n7, arrow, store 2, |
S|TORE 7: | store(24 23ₐ), comma, minus, store(24 23ₐ), arrow, store 3, |
N|2: | loop final value[1] → k, generate ts, |
N|3: | kk[1] = 4: yy[1](14 → 14) = 1: 77777ₐ → yy, translate yy,
            store(storage); ; ;
yy[1] → yy, translate yy, storage(6 → 29) ≠ 0:
     store( storage ), octal sign; store( storage );  |
N|4: | bb[1] → k, store(letter[k + 7] ),
        save name index → k, 7 → mult name flag[k],  |
N|5: | search for noun name, store ( storage ),  |
N|6: | left bracket, n4, right bracket,  |
N|7: | left paren, zero, arrow, store( 34 37ₐ ), right paren.  |
N|8: | left paren, store (34 40ₐ), arrow, store(3544ₐ), right paren,  |
N|9: | left bracket, n4, plus, n3, right bracket,  |
N|10: | store(24 23ₐ), comma, minus, store(24 23ₐ),  |
E|XTEND SIGN: | multiply sign, store(35ₐ), exponent sign, store( 34 40ₐ ),
divide sign, store(35ₐ), exponent sign, store( 34 40ₐ),  |. .


5;
RESTORE VARIABLES: | 0 → i → j → k → l → m,
n = 0(1)3028| 0 → instruction[n],  |, return address[1] →
return address[0], n = 0(1)199| 0 → mult name flag[n], |,  |
CLEAR NAME LIST: | n = 0(1)450| 0 → name list 1[n],  |,  |
STORE NAME LIST: | start reader,
P|REPARE TO READ:
name list index → k + 1 → name list index, 0 → storage,
R|EAD NAME: read one frame, workspace = 04ₐ: read name. ;
workspace = 44ₐ: read k desig. ;
j = 1(1)35| workspace = flex code letter[j]: storage × 2↑6 → storage,
        workspace → storage(0 → 5), read name. ; |, read name.
R|EAD K DESIG: storage → name list 1[k],
E|NTER A: read one frame, workspace = 04ₐ: enter a. ;
workspace = 37ₐ: 0 → name k desig[k], read address.
        | workspace = 70ₐ: 3 → name k desig[k], read address. enter a.  |;
R|EAD ADDRESS: 0 → storage, read one frame, read five numbers,
storage → name address[k],
R|EAD END ADDRESS: read one frame, workspace = 42ₐ: out. ;
workspace = 46ₐ: prepare to read. read end address.
O|UT: stop reader,  |. .


5;
LOAD SOURCE PROGRAM: | start reader, read five numbers,
storage → first address, exit index - first address → exit index,
entrance - first address → entrance, read 1a.
R|EAD 1: read one frame, workspace = 42ₐ ∪ workspace = 43ₐ:
        stop reader, end read source program. ; read five numbers,
R|EAD 1A: 0 → storage, read five numbers, read five numbers,
storage → instruction[i], i + 1 → i, read 1.
E|ND READ SOURCE PROGRAM: i - 1 → max index,  |
READ FIVE NUMBERS: | n = 0(1)4| r|ead 2:
l = 0(1)7| workspace = flex code number[l] ∩ upper case flag = 0:
        storage × 2↑3 + l → storage, read one frame, step read five. ;  |,
read one frame, read 2. s|tep read five:  |,  |
READ ONE FRAME: | r|ead 4: 17130ₐworkspace, delay read,
workspace = 0 ∪ workspace = 77ₐ: read 4. ;
```

workspace = 47_8: 1 → upper case flag;
    | workspace = 57_8: 0 → upper case flag; ; |; |
D|ELAY READ: | r|ead delay: 63100_8 read delay.
START READER: | $17040_8 0$, $17100_8 0$, $52000_8 2$, $50000_8 161_8$, $13300_8 0$, $13070_8 0$,
$70000_8 10000_8$, $13300_8 10033_8$, $13300_8 0$, $70000_8 100_8$, $13300_8 10031_8$, $13300_8 0$,
W|AIT ONE: 63100_8 wait one, 1 → input ready, |
STOP READER: | $17040_8 0$, $52000_8 3$, $50000_8 160_8$, $13300_8 0$, $13070_8 0$,
$70000_8 10000_8$, $13300_8 10034_8$, $13300_8 0$, $70000_8 100_8$, $13300_8 10036_8$, $13300_8 0$,
0 → input ready, |. .

5
b|ranch point index(50), b|ranch point counter;
INITIAL SCAN: | 1 → save index, 0 → branch point counter,
S|EARCH: 1 = save index(1)exit index| max index < 1: 9 → k, error; ;
scan flag[1] ≠ 0: test end initial scan. ; test instruction,
S|TEP LOOP: 7 → scan flag[1], s|tep: |,
T|EST END INITIAL SCAN: 0 < branch point counter:
        branch point counter → j - 1 → branch point counter,
        branch point index[j] → save index,
        0 ≤ save index ∩ save index ≤ max index: search.
            test end initial scan. ;; |
T|EST INSTRUCTION: | ff[1] = 60_8 ∪ ff[1] = 61_8: process jump; ;
ff[1] = 64_8 ∪ ff[1] = 65_8:
        | ffj[1] = 640_8: step loop. advance sub list, step. |; ;
ff[1] = 71_8: | yy[1 + 1] - first address → n, indicator[n] = 10_8 ∪
    indicator[n] = 17_8: ; indicator[n] + 10_8 → indicator[n];
    jj[1] → loop j desig[n], 1 → loop index[n],
    7 → scan flag[1], 1 + 1 → i, step loop. |; ;
ff[1] = 72_8: | yy[1] - first address → n, indicator[n] = 20_8 ∪
    indicator[n] = 27_8: ; indicator[n] + 20_8 → indicator[n];
    jj[1] → loop j desig[n], step loop. |; ;
test skip, skip flag = 1: | jj[1] ≠ 1:
        branch point counter + 1 → branch point counter → j,
        1 + 1 → branch point index[j];
        7 → scan flag[1], 1 + 2 → save index, search. |; ; |
P|ROCESS JUMP: | ffj[1] = 600_8: step loop. ;
ffj[1] = 601_8 ∪ ffj[1] = 610_8: | subroutine index → m,
    m = m(1)0| yy[1] = subroutine address[m]: 7 → scan flag[1],
        test end initial scan. ; |,
    tag entry point, n → save index, search. |; ; |
ffj[1] = 614_8: tag entry point, test end initial scan. ; tag entry point,
branch point counter + 1 → branch point counter → j,
1 + 1 → branch point index[j], n → save index, search. |
T|AG ENTRY POINT: | name list index - 1 → j < 0:
    | j = j(1)0| yy[1] = name address[j]: | yy[1] - first address → n,
        indicator[n](0 → 2) ≠ 7: indicator[n] + 7 → indicator[n]; ;
        end tag. |; |, |; yy[1] - first address → ts,
max index ≥ ts ∩ ts ≥ 0: 7 → scan flag[1]; 6 → scan flag[1], 1 + 1 → n,
    end tag. name list index → j + 1 → name list index,
jump index → k + 1 → jump index, yy[1] → name address[j] -
first address → n, 0 → name k desig[j], 5 16 24 00 00_8 → name list 1[j],
4 → mult name flag[j], letter[k] → first letter[j],
indicator[n] + 7 → indicator[n], e|nd tag: |
A|DVANCE SUB LIST: | subroutine index → j = 0: ;
    | j = j(1)0| yy[1] = subroutine address[j]: end adv. ; |;
yy[1] - first address → ts, 7 → scan flag[1],
ts ≥ 0 ∩ ts < max index: ; asl.
branch point counter + 1 → branch point counter → l,
subroutine index + 1 → k → subroutine index,

yy[i] → subroutine address[k] + 1 - first address → branch point index[l],
a|s1: name list index - 1 → j < 0: ;
    j = j(1)0| yy[i] = name address[j]: end adv. ; |;
name list index → j + 1 → name list index, yy[i] → name address[j],
0 → name k desig[j], 23 25 02 00 00₈ → name list 1[j],
4 → mult name flag[j], sub name index → k + 1 → sub name index,
letter[k] → first letter[j], e|nd adv: |. .

5;

TEST ENTRY OR LOOP: | indicator[i](0 → 2) = 7: generate entry; ;
indicator[i] = 10₈ ∪ indicator[i] = 17₈: | test interrupt,
    lower case, loop j desig[i] → k + 7 → k, store(letter[k]),
    space, equal sign, lower case, store(letter[k]), left paren,
    lower case, store(number[1]), right paren, 1 → ts[6], loop index[i] → 1,
    process name(0, 0), ts[6] → 1, left brace, space, |; ;
indicator[i] = 20₈ ∪ indicator[i] = 27₈: test interrupt,
    lower case, loop j desig[i] → k + 7 → k, store(letter[k]),
    space, equal sign, lower case, store(letter[k]),
    left paren, lower case, store(number[1]), right paren,
    zero, left brace, space; ; |
GENERATE ENTRY: | test interrupt, name list index - 1 → n,
n = n(1)0| 1 = name address[n] - first address: end ge. ; |,
E|ND GE: carret, upper case, store(name list 1[n]), colon, |. .

5
save name index;
FIND A OPERAND: | a flag = 1: store(a store); a flag = 4: crutch a store;
    a flag = 0 ∪ a flag = 5: crutch a store; ; ; ; |
FIND Q OPERAND: | q flag = 1: store(q store); q flag = 4: crutch q store;
    q flag = 0 ∪ q flag = 5: crutch q store; ; ; ; |

C|RUTCH Q STORE: | left bracket, space, right bracket, left paren,
zero, space, arrow, lower case, store(35 44₈), right paren, |
C|RUTCH A STORE: | left bracket, right bracket, left paren,
store(36 33₈), arrow, lower case, store(40 44₈), right paren, |
SAVE PAREN SPACE: | store index → paren index + 2 → store index, 6 → k, |
TEST A INTERRUPT:
| a flag = 2: comma, 1 → a flag, place parens, save paren space;
    | a flag = 3 ∪ a flag = 6 ∪ a flag = 7: arrow, crutch a store,
    place parens, comma, 4 → a flag, save paren space; ; |; |
TEST Q INTERRUPT:
| q flag = 2: comma, 1 → q flag, place parens, save paren space;
    | q flag = 3 ∪ q flag = 6 ∪ q flag = 7: arrow, crutch q store,
    place parens, comma, 4 → q flag, save paren space; ; |; |
TEST INTERRUPT: | test a interrupt, test q interrupt, |
GENERATE A TS:
| 1 → a store used, n = 0(1)1| store(word a store[n]), |, |
GENERATE Q TS:
| 1 → q store used, n = 0(1)1| store(word q store[n]), |, |
TRANSLATE FLEX YY: | yy = 0: 37₈ → storage, end trans yy. ;
0 → storage → zero flag, k = 0(1)4| zero flag = 0:
    | yy(12 → 14) = 0: yy × 2↑3 → yy, step trans yy. ; |; ;
yy(12 → 14) → n, flex code number[n] → storage(24 → 29),
1 → zero flag, yy × 2↑3 → yy, storage × 2↑6 → storage,
s|tep trans yy: |, e|nd trans yy: lower case, |
TRANSLATE YY: | yy = 0: 33₈ → storage, end ty. ;
0 → storage → zero flag, k = 0(1)4| zero flag = 0:
    | yy(12 → 14) = 0: yy × 2↑3 → yy, step ty. ; |; ;

yy(12 → 14) → n, number[n] → storage(24 → 29),
1 → zero flag, yy × 2↑3 → yy, storage × 2↑6 → storage,
s|tep ty: |, e|nd ty: lower case, |
ASSIGN NAME: | m store → m, n store → n, k store → k + 1 → k store,
name list index → j + 1 → name list index, letter[m] → second letter[j],
k - n → l, letter[l] → first letter[j], k = 25: 1 → m, 26 → n;
   | k = 51: 2 → m, 52 → n; | k = 77: 3 → m, 78 → n; ; |; |;
name list 1[j] → storage, m → m store, n → n store, yy[1] → name address[j],
3 → name k desig[j], 4 → mult name flag[j], j → save name index, |
SEARCH FOR NOUN NAME:
| l = name list index(1)0| name address[l] = yy[1]: name list 1[l] →
   storage, l → save name index, mult name flag[l] = 0:
        4 → mult name flag[l]; ; end search. ; |, assign name, e|nd search:|
place parens:
| paren counter ≠ 0: | store index → ts, paren index → store index,
n = 1(1)paren counter| left paren, |,
0 → paren counter, ts → store index, |; ;
paren index → n, 0 → zero flag → ts, m → ts[2], k → ts[1],
n = 0: end pp. ; symbol string [n] = 0: n → k, pp]. n + 1 → k;
P|P: symbol string[n](24 → 29) = 0: .symbol string[n] × 2↑6 → symbol
   string[n], zero flag + 1 → zero flag, pp. ;
P|P1: n = n(1)store index| symbol string[n + 2] = 0:
   n - 1 → store index, end pp. ; symbol string[n + 2] →
symbol string[k], 0 → symbol string[n + 2], zero flag = 0: step pp. ;
P|P2: 0 → ts, symbol string[k](24 → 29) = 0: symbol string[k] ×
   2↑6 → symbol string[k], pp2.;
m = 1(1)zero flag| symbol string[n + 1] × 2↑6 → symbol string[n + 1],
ts × 2↑6 → ts, symbol string[n + 1](0 → 5) + ts → ts,
0 → symbol string[n + 1](0 → 5), |, symbol string[n] + ts →
symbol string[n], s|tep pp: k + 1 → k, |, e|nd pp: ts[2] → m, ts[1] → k, |..

5
t|ranslate table = | error, shift q right, shift a right,
shift aq right, compare, shift q left, shift a left, shift aq left,
enter q, enter a, enter b, enter c, store q, store a, store b,
store c, add, subtract, multiply, divide, add replace, sub replace,
q add, q subtract, load a add q, load a sub q, add q and store,
sub q and store, replace add q, replace sub q, replace add one,
replace sub one, enter log prod, add log prod, sub log prod, mask comp,
repl log prod, repl add log prod, repl sub log prod, store log prod,
selective set, selective comp, selective clear, substitute,
repl sel set, repl sel comp, repl sel clear, repl substitute,
arithmetic jump, manual jump, input jump, output jump,
arithmetic ret jump, manual ret jump, input ret jump,
output ret jump, repeat, index skip, index jump, input transfer,
output transfer, input buffer, output buffer, error, |;
TRANSLATE INSTRUCTION: | ff[1] → m, 6 → k, translate table[m], |
ERROR: | test interrupt, start flex, print carret, print(47₈),
print(flex code letter[k + 1]), print space, print(20121203₈),
print(120457₈), 1 + first address → yy, translate flex yy,
print(storage), stop flex, return address[0] = return address[1]: ce5.
ce6. |
S|ELECTIVE SET: S|ELECTIVE COMP: S|ELECTIVE CLEAR: S|UBSTITUTE:
R|EPL SEL SET: R|EPL SEL COMP: R|EPL SEL CLEAR: E|NTER C:
S|TORE C: I|NPUT JUMP: O|UTPUT JUMP: I|NPUT RET JUMP: O|UTPUT RET JUMP:
I|NPUT TRANSFER: O|UTPUT TRANSFER: I|NPUT BUFFER: O|UTPUT BUFFER:
M|ASK COMP: CRUTCH INSTRUCTION:
| test interrupt, crutch upper half, process name(0,0), comma, |
CRUTCH UPPER HALF: | instruction[1](15 → 29) → yy, translate yy,
storage(24 → 29) = 0: number → storage(24 → 29); ;
store(storage), crutch code,

```
kk[1] ≠ 0: kk[1] = 4: 0 → kk[1]; 3 → kk[1]; ; ;
0 → bb[1], 0 → jj[1], 5 → scan flag[1],    |
RETURN ADDRESS: ce 4. ce 4. sb. .


5;
SHIFT Q RIGHT: | test a interrupt, 71₈ → ts, q shift,    |
SHIFT A RIGHT: | test q interrupt, 71₈ → ts, a shift,    |
SHIFT AQ RIGHT: | yy[1] ≠ 36₈: test continue masking,
    condition = 1: mask exec. ;
    test interrupt, 71₈ → ts, shift aq, 5 → a flag → q flag;
    a flag → q flag, 5 → a flag, a store → q store, 0 → a store;    |
SHIFT Q LEFT: | test a interrupt, 72₈ → ts, q shift,    |
SHIFT A LEFT: | test q interrupt, 72₈ → ts, a shift,    |
SHIFT AQ LEFT: | yy[1] ≠ 36₈: test continue masking,
    condition = 1: mask exec. ;
    test interrupt, 72₈ → ts, shift aq, 5 → a flag → q flag;
    a flag → ts, q flag → a flag, ts → q flag, q store → ts,
    a store → q store, ts → a store;    |
G|ENERATE SHIFT:
| store(ts), store(number[2]), exponent sign, process name(1,0),    |
A|SHIFT: | find a operand,
a flag = 6: right paren, paren counter + 1 → paren counter; ;
generate shift, 7 → a flag,    |
Q|SHIFT: | find q operand,
q flag = 6: right paren, paren counter + 1 → paren counter; ;
generate shift, 7 → q flag,    |
S|HIFT AQ: | aq register, store(ts), store(35₈), exponent sign,
process name(1, 0), arrow, aq register, comma, carret,    |
A|Q REGISTER: | left bracket, right bracket, left paren, zero,
arrow, store(40 44₈), right paren, |. .


5;
ADD: | test q interrupt, find a operand, space, plus, process name(0,0),
6 → a flag,    |
SUBTRACT: | test q interrupt, find a operand, space, minus,
process name(1,0), 6 → a flag,    |
MULTIPLY: | test a interrupt,
q flag = 6: right paren, paren counter + 1 → paren counter; ;
find q operand, space, multiply sign, process name(1,0), 7 → q flag,    |
DIVIDE: | test a interrupt,
q flag = 6: right paren, paren counter + 1 → paren counter; ;
find q operand, space, divide sign, process name(1,0),
7 → q flag, 5 → a flag,    |
Q ADD: | test a interrupt, find q operand, space, plus, process name(0,0),
6 → q flag,    |
Q SUBTRACT: | test a interrupt, find q operand, space, minus,
process name(1,0), 6 → q flag,    |. .


5
c|ompare table = | no skip, skip, skip 2, skip 3, skip 4, skip 5,
skip 6, skip 7,    |;
COMPARE: | jj[1] → j, j ≥ 2: test interrupt; ; compare table[j],
place parens, 1 + 1 → 1, generate alternatives,    |
N|O SKIP: | return address.    | S|KIP: | 1 + 1 → 1, return address.    |
S|KIP 2:
| find q operand, space, greater equal sign, process name(0,0), colon,    |
S|KIP 3: | find q operand, less sign, process name(0,0), colon,    |
S|KIP 4: | find q operand, greater equal sign, process name(0,0),
boolean and, find a operand, less sign, process name(0,0), colon,    |
```

S|KIP 5: | find q operand, less sign, process name(0,0), boolean or,
find a operand, greater equal sign, process name(0,0), colon, |
S|KIP 6: | find a operand, greater equal sign, process name(0,0), colon, |
S|KIP 7: | find a operand, less sign, process name(0,0), colon, |. .

5;
ENTER Q: | test interrupt, save paren space, process name(0,0),
storage → q store, 3 → q flag, |
ENTER A: | test interrupt, save paren space, process name(0,0),
storage → a store, 3 → a flag, |
ENTER B: | test interrupt, process name(0,0), arrow, jj[i] → j,
store(letter[j + 7]), comma, |
STORE Q: | test a interrupt, find q operand, arrow, test ts needed,
condition ≠ 0: 0 → condition; process name(0,1), storage → q store;
place parens, condition ≠ 77₈: 2 → q flag; 0 → condition; |
STORE A: | test q interrupt, find a operand, arrow, test ts needed,
condition ≠ 0: 0 → condition; process name(0,1), storage → a store;
place parens, condition ≠ 77₈: 2 → a flag; 0 → condition; |
STORE B:
| test interrupt, jj[i] ≠ 0: jj[i] → j, store(letter[j + 7]); zero;
arrow, test ts needed, condition ≠ 0: 0 → condition; process name(0,1);
place parens, comma, |
T|EST TS NEEDED: | 0 → condition,
yy[i] - first address → m, m < 0 ∪ m > max index: ;
kk[i] - 1 ∩ scan flag[m] ≠ 0: bb[i] ≠ 0: 13 → k, error; ;
    7 → condition, scan flag[m] - 4: loop final value[m] → k;
        ts index → k + 1 → ts index; ; ; condition = 7:
    4 → scan flag[m], k → loop final value[m], generate ts; ; |
GENERATE TS: | lower case, store(24 23 00₈), store(letter[k]), |. .

5;
ADD REPLACE:
| test q interrupt, find a operand, space, plus, process name(0,0),
space, arrow, storage → a store, process name(0,1), place parens,
2 → a flag, |
SUB REPLACE:
| test q interrupt, find a operand, space, minus, process name(1,0),
space, arrow, storage → a store, process name(0,1), place parens,
2 → a flag, |
ENTER LOG PROD: | test interrupt, save paren space, process name(0,0),
storage → a store, generate bit limits, 3 → a flag, |
ADD LOG PROD:
| space, plus, process name(0,0), generate bit limits, 6 → a flag, |
SUB LOG PROD:
| space, minus, process name(1,0), generate bit limits, 6 → a flag, |
REPL LOG PROD: | test a interrupt, process name(0,0), storage → a store,
generate bit limits, space, arrow, process name(0,1), 2 → a flag, |

REPL ADD LOG PROD: | space, plus, process name(0,0), storage → a store,
generate bit limits, space, arrow, process name(0,1), 2 → a flag, |
REPL SUB LOG PROD: | space, minus, process name(1,0), storage → a store, gen
bit limits, space, arrow, process name(0,1), 2 → a flag, |
STORE LOG PROD: | test a interrupt, process name(0,0), generate
bit limits, space, arrow, process name(0,1), comma, carret, 1 → a flag, |
REPL SUBSTITUTE: | space, arrow, process name(0,1), storage → a store,
generate bit limits, comma, carret, 1 → a flag, |
G|ENERATE BIT LIMITS: | left paren, lower bit limit → storage,

store decimal conversion, space, arrow, upper bit limit → storage,
store decimal conversion, right paren, |
S|TORE DECIMAL CONVERSION:
  | storage < 10: storage → n, lower case, store(number[n]);
    | storage < 20: storage - 10 → n, lower case, number[n] → ts,
        number[1] → ts(6 → 11), store(ts); storage - 20 → n, lower case,
  number[n] → ts, number[2] → ts(6 → 11), store(ts); |; |. .

5;
LOAD A ADD Q: | test a interrupt, find q operand, space, plus,
process name(0,0), 6 → a flag, |
LOAD A SUB Q: | test interrupt, save paren space, process name(0,0),
space, minus, ff[1 - 1] = 10_8: 1 - 1 → 1, process name(0,0), 1 + 1 → 1;
    find q operand; 6 → a flag, |
ADD Q AND STORE: | test q interrupt, find a operand, space, plus,
ff[1 - 1] = 10_8: 1 - 1 → 1, process name(0,0), 1 + 1 → 1; find q operand;
space, arrow, process name(0, 1), storage → a store, place parens,
2 → a flag, |
SUB Q AND STORE: | test q interrupt, find a operand, space, minus,
ff[1 - 1] = 10_8: 1 - 1 → 1, process name(0,0), 1 + 1 → 1; find q operand;
space, arrow, process name(0, 1), storage → a store, place parens,
2 → a flag, |
TEST SUB Q: | ff[1 + 1] → ts, 30_8 < ts < 36_8: return address. ; |. .

5;
REPLACE ADD Q: | test interrupt, process name(0,0), space, plus,
ff[1 - 1] = 10_8: 1 - 1 → 1, process name(0,0), 1 + 1 → 1; find q operand;
space, arrow, storage → a store, process name(0, 1), place parens,
2 → a flag, |
REPLACE SUB Q: | test interrupt, process name(0,0), space, minus,
ff[1 - 1] = 10_8: 1 - 1 → 1, process name(0,0), 1 + 1 → 1; find q operand;
space, arrow, storage → a store, process name(0, 1), place parens,
2 → a flag, |
REPLACE ADD ONE: | test interrupt, process name(0,0), space, plus,
lower case, store(number[1]), space, arrow, storage → a store,
process name(0, 1), place parens, 2 → a flag, |
REPLACE SUB ONE: | test interrupt, process name(0,0), space, minus,
lower case, store(number[1]), space, arrow, storage → a store,
process name(0, 1), place parens, 2 → a flag, |. .

5;
ARITHMETIC JUMP: | test interrupt,
1 < jj[1]: jj[1] → m, comparison table[m], generate jump,
    semicolon, carret;. jj[1] = 1:
        yy[1] = sub entrance: finish subroutine. ;
        generate jump, carret, find next instruction; ; ; |
MANUAL JUMP: | test interrupt, jj[1] = 0:
    yy[1] = sub entrance: finish subroutine. ;
    generate jump, find next instruction;
    jj[1] = 4: 1 ≠ exit index: generate exit jump; ; |
        crutch upper half, generate jump, carret; ; |
GENERATE JUMP: | name list index - 1 → l,
l = l(1)0| yy[1] = name address[l]: lower case, store(name list l[l]),
    4 → mult name flag[l], period, end gen jump. ; |, e|nd gen jump: |
F|IND NEXT INSTRUCTION: | scan flag[1 - 1] = 5: return address. ;
1 + 1 → j, j = j(1)max index| indicator[j](0 ÷ 2) = 7: j - 1 → 1,
    return address. ; |, return address. |. .

5;
ARITHMETIC RET JUMP: | test interrupt,

1 < jj[1]: jj[1] → m, comparison table[m], generate ret jump,
   semicolon, semicolon, carret;
      jj[1] - 1: generate ret jump, comma, carret; ; ; |
MANUAL RET JUMP: | test interrupt, jj[1] - 0: generate ret jump,
   comma, carret; crutch upper half, generate ret jump, comma, carret; |
generate ret jump: | name list index - 1 → l,
l - l(1)0| yy[1] - name address[l]: lower case, store(name list 1[l]),
   4 → mult name flag[l], end gen ret jump. ; |,
e|nd gen ret jump: 5 → a flag → q flag, |. .

5
comparison table - | comparison 1, comparison 2, comparison 3,
comparison 4, comparison 5, comparison 6, comparison 7, |,
q comp table - | comparison 1, comparison 6, comparison 7,
comparison 8, comparison 9, comparison 2, comparison 3, |,
resume index, s|ave a flag, s|ave q flag;
TEST CONDITIONAL SKIP: | test skip,
skip flag - 1: | jj[1] ≥ 2: test interrupt; ; jj[1] - 1 → m,
   ff[1] - 26$_a$ ∪ ff[1] - 27$_a$: q comp table[m]; comparison table[m];
   place parens, i + 1 → i, generate alternatives, |; ; |
GENERATE ALTERNATIVES:
| a flag → save a flag, q flag → save q flag, test skip,
skip flag - 1: 1 → save index + 1 → i, generate alt, 1 + 1 → resume index; r$^?$
   semicolon, carret, 1 → save index + 1 → resume index;
save a flag → a flag, save q flag → q flag, space, space, space,
save index → i, generate alt, resume index - 1 → 1, 5 → a flag → q flag, |
TEST SKIP: | ff[1] - 12$_a$ ∪ ff[1] - 16$_a$: 0 → skip flag, end test skip.
   | n - 60$_a$(1)76$_a$| ff[1] - n: 0 → skip flag, end test skip. ; |, |;
jj[1] ≠ 0: 1 → skip flag; 0 → skip flag; e|nd test skip: |
G|ENERATE ALT: | g|en alt:
ffj[1] - 601$_a$ ∪ ffj[1] - 610$_a$: generate jump, carret, end gen alt. ;
translate instruction, test skip, skip flag - 1: | 1 + 1 → i, test skip,
   skip flag - 1: 1 + 1 → i, gen alt. test interrupt, semicolon; |;
   test interrupt, semicolon; e|nd gen alt: |
ZERO: | lower case, store(number), |
C|OMPARISON 1: | i + 1 → i, return address. |
C|OMPARISON 2: | find q operand, space, greater equal sign,
zero, colon, 5 → q flag, |
C|OMPARISON 3:
| find q operand, space, less sign, zero, colon, 5 → q flag, |
C|OMPARISON 4:
| find a operand, space, equal sign, zero, colon, 5 → a flag, |
C|OMPARISON 5:
| find a operand, space, not equal sign, zero, colon, 5 → a flag, |
C|OMPARISON 6:
| find a operand, space, greater equal sign, zero, colon, 5 → a flag, |
C|OMPARISON 7:
| find a operand, space, less sign, zero, colon, 5 → a flag, |
C|OMPARISON 8:
| find q operand, space, equal sign, zero, colon, 5 → q flag, |
C|OMPARISON 9:
| find q operand, space, not equal sign, zero, colon, 5 → q flag, |. .

5;
REPEAT: | test interrupt, crutch upper half, yy[1] → yy, translate yy,
lower case, store(storage), storage(6 → 29) - 0: ; octal sign;
comma, space, i + 1 → i, crutch instruction, |
INDEX SKIP: | test interrupt, right brace, comma, i + 1 → i, |
INDEX JUMP: | test interrupt, right brace, comma, |. .

```
5
sub entrance;
GENERATE SUBROUTINE: | 0 → a flag → q flag, subroutine index → j - 1 →
subroutine index, subroutine address[j] → sub entrance, name subroutine,
sub entrance + 1 - first address → 1,
1 = 1(1)maxindex| max index < 1: 1| → k, error; ;
test masking, test entry or loop, ff[i] = 10₈: test sub q; ;
test io, translate instruction, test conditional skip, sb: |,
F|INISH SUBROUTINE: right brace,     |
N|AME SUBROUTINE: | name list index - 1 → ts,
n = ts(1)0| name address[n] = sub entrance: end ns. ;   |,
E|ND NS: store(name list 1[n]), colon, left brace, space,     |
SUBROUTINE EXEC: return address[2] → return address[0], subroutine index +
1 → k → subroutine index, name list index → j + 1 → name list index,
entrance + first address → name address[j] → subroutine address[k],
23 25 02 22 00₈ → name list 1[j], sequence number + 1 → sequence number → k,
letter[k-1] → first letter[j], 4 → mult name flag[j],
S|E1: generate subroutine, subroutine index ≠ 0: se1. ;
double period, stop code, ce6.
GENERATE EXIT JUMP: | store(10 01 14 24₈), period, carret,    |
GENERATE EXIT: | store(10 01 14 24₈), colon, double period, stopcode,   |. .


5;
DUMP NAME LIST:
name list index = 0: 61400₈ manual load. ; 0 → upper case flag, start punch,
65100₈ start flex, 61100₈ dnl1. leader, dnl1: print carret,
n = 0(1)1| print(word name list dump[n]),   |,
print carret, print(11 14 07₈), print(14 01 24₈), type limits,
print carret, name list index - 1 → 1,
j = 0(1)1| mult name flag[j] = 0: step nl dump. ;
print lower case, print flex(name list 1[j]), storage → ts,
n = 0(1)4| ts(24 → 29) = 0: print space; ; ts × 2↑6 → ts,   |,
print space, print lower case, name k desig[j] → k,
print(flex code number[k]), print space, name address[j] → yy,
translate flex yy, print(storage), name address[j] < first address ∪
max index + first address < name address[j]:
print space, print(34 06 22 20 26₈), print(14 06 20 22₈); ;
print carret, s|tep nl dump:  |, e|nd dump: 61100₈ dnl2. leader,
dnl2: stop punch, 65100₈ stop flex, 61400₈ manual load.
STORE DIMENSIONING STATEMENT: | rearrange name list,
test ts used, name list index = 0: end dds. ; name list index - 1 →
a store, j = 0(1)a store| name address[j] - first address → m,
name k desig[j] = 3 ∩ m ≥ 0 ∩ m ≤ max index ∩ mult name flag[j] ≠ 0:
mult name flag[j] = 7: ; step multiple name; ; step dump.
scan flag[m] ≠ 0: step dump. ; store ( name list 1[j]),
instruction[m] ≠ 0: equal sign, translate constants, store( ts[3]),
store( ts[4] ), instruction[m](3 → 29) ≠ 0: octal sign; ; ; ;
comma, step dump: |, e|nd dds: semicolon,     |
TEST TS USED:
| a store used = 1: n = 0(1)1| store(word a store[n]),   |, comma; ;
q store used = 1: n = 0(1)1| store(word q store[n]),   |, comma; ;
ts index ≠ 0:
    n = 1(1)ts index| store(24 23 00₈), store(letter[n - 1]), comma,   |; ;   |
NAME PROGRAM: | sequence number + 1 → sequence number → k,
entrance + first address → ts, entrance → n, indicator[n](0 → 2) = 7:
    end np. ; name list index → n + 1 → name list index,
23 24 22 24 00₈ → name list 1[n], letter[k - 1] → first letter[n],
4 → mult name flag[n], ts → name address[n],
entrance → n, indicator[n] + 7 → indicator[n], e|nd np:  |
```

TRANSLATE CONSTANTS: | 0 → ts[3] → ts[4] → zero flag, instruction[m] → ts,
l = 3(1)4| k = 0(1)4| zero flag ≠ 0: tran con 1. ;
ts(27 → 29) = 0: ts × 2↑3 → ts, step tran con. ;
T|RAN CON 1: ts(27 → 29) → n, number[n] → ts[l](24 → 29), 1 → zero flag,
ts × 2↑3 → ts, ts[l] × 2↑6 → ts[l], s|tep tran con: |, |, |
REARRANGE NAME LIST:
| name list index ≥ 2: name list index - 1 → ts - 1 → ts[3],
    j = 0(1)ts[3]| name k desig[j] = 3: name address[j] → ts[2],
        l = j + 1(1)ts| name address[l] < ts[2] ∩ name k desig[l] = 3:
            name list 1[l] → ts[1], name list 1[j] → name list 1[l],
            ts[1] → name list 1[j], name list 2[l] → ts[1],
            name list 2[j] → name list 2[l], ts[1] → name list 2[j],
            name address[j] → ts[2]; ; |; ; |; ; |
PRINT FLEX(p): | p = 0: end pfn. ;
0 → storage → zero flag, m → ts[1], n → ts[2],
m = 0(1)4| p(24 → 29) → n, storage × 2↑6 → storage, n = 0 ∩ zero flag = 0: ;
    set → zero flag, storage + flexcode[n] → storage; p × 2↑6 → p, |,
print(storage), ts[1] → m, ts[2] → n, e|nd pfn: |. .

5
S|HIFT INSTR: | s|hift ff(24 → 29), s|hift yy(0 → 14), |,
E|NTER MASK INSTR: | e|nter kk(18 → 20), e|nter yy(0 → 14), |,
C|OMMAND: | c|om ff(24 → 29), c|om index(0 → 14), |,
E|XTRA COMMAND: | e|x com ff(24 → 29), |,
lower bit limit, upper bit limit, s|tart mask flag, o|ld mask,
m|ask, e|nd mask flag;
TEST MASKING: | ff[i] = 10₈: jj[1] = 0: 1 + 1 → n; 1 + 2 → n;
    test mask instr, condition = 1: mask exec. ; ; ; |
TEST CONTINUE MASKING: | n = 1(1)1 + 3| test mask instr,
condition = 1: end tcm. ; |, e|nd tcm: |
T|EST MASK INSTR:
| 37₈ < ff[n] < 50₈ ∪ ff[n] = 57₈: 1 → condition; 0 → condition; |
MASK EXEC: mask → old mask, n = 0(1)4| 0 → shift instr[n], |,
test entry or loop, store mask sequence, process mask, com index + 1,
translate instruction, resume index + 1, test continue masking,
condition = 1: mask exec. ; ff[1] = 7: a flag → q flag, 5 → a flag;
    1 - 1 → 1; return address.
S|TORE MASK SEQUENCE:
| ff[1] = 7 ∪ ff[1] = 3: instruction[1] → shift instr, 1 + 1 → 1; ;
ff[1] = 10₈: instruction[1] → enter mask instr,
    jj[1] = 1: instruction[1 + 1] → mask, 1 + 2 → 1; 1 + 1 → 1; ; ;
    1 → n, test mask instr, condition = 1: instruction[1] → command,
        1 → com index, 1 + 1 → 1; ff[1] = 53₈:
            instruction[1] → extra command, 1 + 1 → 1; ; 1 → resume index, |
P|ROCESS MASK: | enter kk = 0 ∩ enter mask instr ≠ 0: enter yy → mask;
enter kk = 3 ∩ mask = 0: enter yy - first address → m,
    m < 0 ∪ m > max index: 1 → mask; instruction[m] → mask; ;
    enter kk = 4: enter yy → mask,
        enter kk(12 → 14) > 3: 77777₈ → mask(15 → 29); ; ; ; ; ;
        mask = 0 ∩ shift ff ≠ 0: find bits from shift;
        mask = 0 ∩ shift ff = 0: ·old mask → mask; ; ;
    com ff = 57₈: - mask → mask; ;
    find bit limits, e|nd process mask: |
F|IND BIT LIMITS: | 0 → lower bit limit → start mask flag → end mask flag,
mask → ts, m = 0(1)29| start mask flag = 0:
    ts(0 → 0) = 1: m → lower bit limit, 1 → start mask flag; ; ;
    end mask flag = 0: ts(0 → 0) = 0: m - 1 → upper bit limit,
        1 → end mask flag; ; ts(0 → 0) = 1: 3 → k, mask error. ; ; ;
    ts / 2↑1 → ts, |, |

F|IND BITS FROM SHIFT: | shift ff = 3: shift yy → ts ≥ 30: ts - 60 → ts; ;
    lower bit limit - ts → lower bit limit, upper bit limit - ts →
    upper bit limit; shift ff = 7:
        shift yy → ts ≥ 30: ts - 60 → ts; ; lower bit limit + ts →
        lower bit limit, upper bit limit + ts → upper bit limit; ; ; |
M|ASK ERROR: error, . .

5;
TEST MULTIPLE NAME:
| mult name flag[j] = 0: step dump. ; name address[j] < first address
    ∪ max index + first address < name address[j]: step dump. ;
mult name flag[j] ≠ 7: end test mult name. ;
name address[j] + 1 → ts - 1 - first address → save index,
0 → end loop index,
T|EST MULT NAME: m = name list index(1)0| ts = name address[m]:
    finish mult name. ; |, ts - first address → m,
scan flag[m] ≠ 0: finish mult name. ;
end loop index + 1 → end loop index, ts + 1 → ts, test mult name.
F|INISH MULT NAME:
end loop index = 0: end test mult name. ; store(name list 1[j]),
left paren, end loop index + 1 → yy, translate flex yy, store(storage),
right paren, save index → m + end loop index → end loop index,
scan flag[m] ≠ 7: m = save index(1)end loop index| instruction[m] ≠ 0:
    dump cells. ; |; ; comma, step dump.
D|UMP CELLS: equal sign, m = save index(1)end loop index
| instruction[m] ≠ 0: translate constants, store(ts[3]), store(ts[4]),
    instruction[m](3 → 29) = 0: ; octal sign; ; ; comma, |,
    step dump. e|nd test mult name: |. .

5
a|reg, f|un code, e|quip flag;
TEST IO:
| ff[1] → ts, ts = 13₈ ∪ ts = 17₈: io exec. ; 72₈ < ts < 77₈: io exec. ;
61₈ < ts < 64₈: io exec. ; 65₈ < ts < 70₈: io exec. ; |.
I|O EXEC: ff[1] = 17₈ ∩ ff[1 + 1] = 62₈: generate output. ;
ff[1] = 17₈ ∩ ff[1 + 1] = 63₈: generate input. ;
I|O 1: instruction[1](15 → 29) = 50000₈: yy[1] → a reg, 1 + 1 → 1;
    1 + 1 → 1, io 1. a reg = 160₈: turn off. ; a reg = 161₈: turn on input.;
J = 0(1)2| 1|o 2: ffj[1] = 133₈ ∩ yy[1] ≠ 0: yy[1] → fun code, 1 + 1 → 1;
    1 + 1 → 1, io 2. |, fun code(3 → 5) = 1: 1 → equip flag;
    3 → equip flag; 1 + 1 → 1, gen equip wds.
T|URN OFF: j = 0(1)1| 1|o 3: ffj[1] = 133₈ ∩ yy[1] ≠ 0: yy[1] → fun code,
1 + 1 → 1; 1 + 1 → 1, io 3. |, fun code(3 → 5) = 1: 11₈ → equip flag;
    fun code(3 → 5) = 2: 13₈ → equip flag; 12₈ → equip flag; ;
    1 + 1 → 1, gen equip wds.
    T|URN ON INPUT: I|O 4:
ffj[1] = 631₈: 1 + 1 → 1; 1 + 1 → 1, io 4. 2 → equip flag,
G|EN EQUIP WDS: test interrupt, space, upper case,
equip flag(3 → 5) = 0: store(24013012₈); store(24010355₈); space,
equip flag(0 → 2) = 1: store(26112027₈);
equip flag(0 → 2) = 2: store(552012₈); store(52455₈); ;
comma, carret, 1 - 1 → 1, return address.
G|ENERATE OUTPUT: test interrupt, space, upper case, store(22340755₈), jump.
G|ENERATE INPUT: test interrupt, space, upper case, store(26141111₈),
J|UMP: left paren, space, process name(0, 0), right paren,
comma, carret, 1 + 1 → 1, return address. .

5;
MANUAL LOAD: j → exit index, k → entrance, restore variables, 0 → 1,

load source program, start flex, type limits, stop flex,
61400₈ manual clear names.
TYPE LIMITS: | print carret, yy → ts[7], first address → yy,
translate flex yy, 1 → upper case flag, print lower case, print(storage),
print space, first address + max index → yy, translate flex yy,
print (storage), print carret, entrance + first address → yy,
translate flex yy, print (storage), print space, exit index + first address →
yy, translate flex yy, print(storage), print carret, ts[7] → yy, |. .

5;
MANUAL CLEAR NAMES: clear name list, 61400₈ manual decompile. .

5;
MANUAL DECOMPILE: entrance → i, initial scan, command exec. .

5;
MANUAL DCMPL SUBR: entrance → i, 7 → scan flag[i], i + 1 → i,
initial scan, subroutine exec..

5;
MANUAL STORE NAMES: store name list; 61400₈ manual decompile. .

5
t|emp;
MANUAL SET PARAMETERS: max index → temp, j - first address → exit index,
k - first address → entrance, return address[1] → return address[0],
n = 750(1)3028| 0 → instruction[n], |,
n = 0(1)199| 0 → mult name flag[n], |, temp → max index, start flex,
type limits, stop flex, 61400₈ manual clear names. .

5
set = 7,
FLEX CODE: flex code letter(27) = 4, 30₈, 23₈, 16₈, 22₈, 20₈, 26₈, 13₈,
5, 14₈, 32₈, 36₈, 11₈, 07, 6, 3, 15₈, 35₈, 12₈, 24₈, 1, 34₈, 17₈, 31₈,
27₈, 25₈, 21₈,
flexcode number(10) = 37₈, 52₈, 74₈, 70₈, 64₈, 62₈, 66₈, 72₈, 60₈, 33₈,
F|LEX CODE OPERATORS(27) = 76₈, 47465704₈, 4404₈, 4204₈, 47445704₈,
473357₈, 473757₈, 476457₈, 476257₈, 47565704₈, 456₈, 447705704₈,
447505704₈, 447545704₈, 447665704₈, 45404₈, 44604₈, 447425704₈,
447525704₈, 447745704₈, 447725704₈, 447605704₈, 2, 50₈, 47504₈,
447755704₈, 477657₈,
   |c|c comma(15 → 29), c|c semicolon(0 → 14) | = 4600047₈,
   c|c period(15 → 29), c|c colon(0 → 14) | = 5000051₈,
   c|c left paren(15 → 29), c|c right paren(0 → 14) | = 5200053₈,
   c|c left brace(15 → 29), c|c right brace(0 → 14) | = 5600057₈,
   c|c left bracket(15 → 29), c|c right bracket(0 → 14) | = 5400055₈,
   c|c equal sign(15 → 29), c|c less than(0 → 14) | = 6000063₈,
   c|c not equal sign(15 → 29), c|c greater than(0 → 14) | = 6100065₈,
   c|c right arrow(15 → 29), c|c plus(0 → 14) | = 6600067₈,
   c|c minus(15 → 29), c|c divide(0 → 14) | = 7000071₈,
   c|c multiply(15 → 29), c|c color shift(0 → 14) | = 7200073₈,
   t|emp name sign(15 → 29), c|c absolute(15 → 29),
c|c crutch(15 → 29), c|c crutch code(15 → 29), c|c or(0 → 14) | = 7400075₈,
   c|c and(15 → 29), c|c octal sign(0 → 14) | = 7600045₈,
   c|c exponent sign(15 → 29), a|n operator(0 → 14) | = 7700046₈,
   p|unct area minus 1(15 → 29), p|unct area plus 1(0 → 14) | = 4500052₈,
   a|number(15 → 29), a|letter(0 → 14) | = 3300032₈,
D|UMP BUFFER: | f|irst frame dump buffer(0 → 5),
l|ast frame dump buffer(24 → 29), |, function flag,

```
FLOWCHART BUFFER: | f|irst frame flowchart buffer(0 → 5),  |,
| c|urrent operator(0 → 14), p|resent character(15 → 29),  |,
temp fb storage, temp fc storage, temp pc storage, flochrt addr storage,
| f|rame counter(0 → 14), c|haracter counter(15 → 29),  |,
| c|arriage return counter(0 → 14), u|pper loop limit(15 → 29),  |,
| c|omparison counter(0 → 14), c|omparison type(15 → 29),  |,
| n|ame found flag(0 → 14), c|ase flag(15 → 29),  |,
| c|onstant flag(0 → 14), o|ptional end of line(15 → 29),  |,
| p|unctuation counter(0 → 14), c|olon counter(15 → 29),  |,
| p|rint flag(0 → 14), e|nd of line count(15 → 29),  |,
t|emporary storage(10);

DUMP FLOWCHART: DUMP DIMENSIONING STATEMENT:
| l = 18(1)0| 0 → dump buffer[l],  |, read next character,
store flowchart parameters, 1 → upper case flag, carriage return
lowercase, condition ≠ 0: dds enter. ; 50₈ → last frame dump buffer[l],
dump one number, d|ds enter: carriage return lower case,
0 → upper loop limit, set → name found flag,
E|NTER: character counter + 1 → character counter ≥ end of line count ∩
print flag ≠ 0: return carriage, indent, 1 → character counter,
    56 → end of line count, 0 → print flag → punctuation counter →
    case flag → optional end of line, store flowchart parameters; ;
S|TART: print flag ≠ 0: print character. ;
cc right brace < present character < cc right arrow: 0→name found flag; ;
present character = cc right arrow ∩ current operator = cc left paren ∩
punctuation counter ≠ 0 ∩ skip flag = 0: reset. ;
current operator ≠ cc left bracket ∩ cc right arrow < present character <
cc exponent sign: character counter → optional end of line; ;
present character = cc right arrow ∩ current operator ≠ cc left paren:
    character counter → optional end of line; ;
current operator = cc colon ∩ present character ≠ cc right brace ∩
present character ≠ cc period ∩ present character ≠ cc comma:
    colon counter + 1 → colon counter, reset. ;
constant flag = 0: | temporary storage[4] ≥ an operator ∩ a letter <
    present character < cc octal sign: set → constant flag; ;  |;
    | present character = cc period:
        cc octal sign → present character; ;  |;
punct area minus 1 < present character < cc colon ∩ function flag = 0:
    | current operator = cc left paren: set → function flag;
        set → name found flag, character counter → punctuation counter; |;;
present character = cc right paren ∩ current operator ≠ cc left paren ∩
current operator ≠ cc right arrow: 0 → function flag; ;
present character = cc right brace: character counter → punctuation counter;;
present character = cc right brace ∪
present character = cc left brace: | set → name found flag,
    punctuation counter ≠ 0: set → skip flag; ;  |; ;
present character < cc octal sign ∪ present character = temp name sign:
    | character counter + upper loop limit ≥ 56 ∩
    current operator ≠ cc left paren: | punctuation counter = 0:
        | optional end of line = 0: character counter →
            punctuation counter; optional end of line →
            punctuation counter;  |; ; reset.  |;
    | skip flag ≠ 0: | punct area minus 1 < current operator <
        cc colon ∪ current operator = cc left brace ∪
        current operator = cc left bracket: reset. ;  |; ;  |;  |;
current operator → temporary storage[1],
0 → constant flag, present character → current operator;
print flag = 0: margin control. ;
P|RINT CHARACTER: present character = temp name sign ∩ case flag ≠ 0:
```

```
print(575047₈), look ahead. ;  present character → l ≥ cc octal sign:
| present character → current operator = cc colon:
    cc comma → current operator; ;  |;
| l ≥ a number ∩ case flag ≠ 0: print lower case, decode and print,
    print uppercase, look ahead. ;  |;
decode and print, [j - 1] = 0: exit. ;  look ahead.
M|ARGIN CONTROL: comparison type ≠ 0: | present character = cc period ∪
    present character = cc semicolon: | character counter →
    punctuation counter, comparison counter < 2:
        1 + comparison counter → comparison counter; ;
        comparison counter = 2: set → skip flag; ;  |; ;
    present character = cc right brace ∪ present character = cc colon ∪
    present character = cc left brace: comparison type -
        comparison counter → comparison type, 0 → comparison counter; ;
    comparison type = comparison counter:
        0 → comparison type → comparison counter; ; |; ;
L|OOK AHEAD: present character → temporary storage[4],
read any character, enter.
R|ESET: colon counter < 2 ∩ punctuation counter ≠ 0:
    punctuation counter → end of line count; | 0 → colon counter,
    name found flag ≠ 0 | temporary storage[1] = cc left brace: go on. ;
        set → case flag, return carriage, uppercase,
        carriage return counter = 28: return carriage; ; indent,  |;
    2 + comparison type → comparison type,
G|O ON: cc comma → current operator, character counter - 1 →
    punctuation counter, margin control. character counter - 1 →
    end of line count,  |; set → print flag, 0 → character counter →
skip flag, restore flowchart parameters, start.
I|NDENT: | comparison type - comparison counter → upper loop limit,
upper loop limit(0 → 0) ≠ 0: 1 + upper loop limit → upper loop limit; ;
upper loop limit × 2 → upper loop limit ≥ 1:
    L = 1(1)upper loop limit| fd space,  |; ;  |,
R|ETURN CARRIAGE: | print carret, carriage return counter ≥ 29:
    L = 3(1)0| print carret,  |, 0 → carriage return counter; ;  |,
E|XIT:
R|EAD NEXT CHARACTER: | e|xtract next frame:
frame counter - 1 → frame counter < 0: [j] → flowchart buffer,
    j + 1 → j, 4 → frame counter; ; flowchart buffer × 2↑6 →
flowchart buffer, flowchart buffer(0 → 5) → present character = 0:
    extract next frame. ;  |
R|EAD ANY CHARACTER: | frame counter - 1 → frame counter < 0:
    [j] → flowchart buffer, j + 1 → j, 4 → frame counter; ;
flowchart buffer × 2↑6 → flowchart buffer,
flowchart buffer(0 → 5) → present character,  |
D|UMP ONE NUMBER: | L → dump one number(15 → 29), dump buffer[1] × 2↑3 →
dump buffer[1], dump buffer[1](0 → 2) + 27 → L, decode and print,
dump one number(15 → 29) → L,  |
D|ECODE AND PRINT: | print(flexcode[L]),  |
C|ARRIAGE RETURN: | print(45₈), 1 + carriage return counter →
carriage return counter,  |
C|ARRIAGE RETURN LOWER CASE: | carriage return, print lower case,  |
C|ARRIAGE RETURN UPPER CASE: | carriage return, print upper case,  |
S|TORE FLOWCHART PARAMETERS:
| flowchart buffer → temp fb storage, frame counter → temp fc storage,
present character → temp pc storage, j → flochrt addr storage,  |
R|ESTORE FLOWCHART PARAMETERS:
| temp fb storage → flowchart buffer, temp fc storage → frame counter,
temp pc storage → present character, flochrt addr storage → j,  |
F|D SPACE: | print(4),  |..
```

```
5;
MANUAL BIO LOAD: j → exit index, k → entrance, restore variables,
0 → 1, start reader,
B|L: read bio frame, workspace = 0: bl. ;
read five frames, ts(15 → 29) → first address, ts(0 → 14) -
first address → max index → j,
i = 1(1)j| read five frames, ts → instruction[i],  |, stop reader,
exit index - first address → exit index, entrance - first address →
entrance, start flex, type limits, stop flex, 61400₈manual clear names.
READ FIVE FRAMES: | 0 → ts,
n = 0(1)4| read bio frame, ts × 2↑6 + workspace → ts,  |,  |
READ BIO FRAME: | 17130₈workspace, rbfd|elay: 63100₈rbfdelay,  |. .
```

INDEX

CONTENTS

www.ingramcontent.com/pod-product-compliance
Lightning Source LLC
La Vergne TN
LVHW012204040326
832903LV00003B/121

* 9 7 8 1 0 1 3 6 2 4 0 3 2 *